A Modern History of Hong Kong

D1239422

To Rhiannon

A Modern History

of

Hong Kong

Steve Tsang

I.B. TAURIS
LONDON · NEW YORK

Paperback edition published in 2007 by I.B. Tauris & Co Ltd
6 Salem Road, London W2 4BU
175 Fifth Avenue, New York NY 10010
www.ibtauris.com

In the United States of America and in Canada distributed by
Palgrave Macmillan, a division of St Martin's Press
175 Fifth Avenue, New York NY 10010

First published in hardback in 2004 by I.B. Tauris & Co Ltd
Copyright © Steve Tsang, 2004

ISBN 978 1 84511 419 0

A full CIP record for this book is available from the British Library
A full CIP record for this book is available from the Library of Congress

Library of Congress catalog card: available

Typeset in Garamond by Steve Tribe, Andover
Printed and bound in India by Replika Press Pvt. Ltd

Contents

Preface and
Acknowledgements

The history of Hong Kong is a fascinating one. It is not so much because it transformed itself from 'a barren island with hardly a house upon it' into a great metropolis of seven million in a century and a half, though this is itself a great story. It is, in my view, the British colonial administration's creation of a government that met the expectation of as good a government as possible in the Chinese political tradition that has made it so special. The real measure of Hong Kong's extraordinary achievement was confirmed as the Communist and highly nationalistic government of the People's Republic of China committed itself to maintain the system and way of life in Hong Kong for 50 years when it negotiated an end to British imperial rule.

British rule also left its mark on Hong Kong in a more important and sustainable way. It led to the rise of a people that remains quintessentially Chinese and yet share a way of life, core values and an outlook that resemble at least as much, if not more, that of the average New Yorker or Londoner, rather than that of their compatriots in China. A modern history of Hong Kong must therefore address how the residents of Hong Kong came of age as a people with a common identity and shared worldview. The people of Hong Kong is also by all conventional measures in political science a population which, though ready for democracy, has not vigorously pushed for and built one. This is just one of the various paradoxes or ironies that marked Hong Kong under British rule and deserves an impassioned examination and explanation.

With the question of its future hanging in the balance for much of its history, as Hong Kong transformed itself from an outpost of the British Empire into a leading trading and financial centre of the world, a modern history must also account for how this problem came about and how it was eventually resolved. The issue of Hong Kong's future under British rule is consequently a major sub-theme that receives considerable treatment.

Writing a history of Hong Kong shortly after the end of British imperial rule raises serious questions of perspective and balance. It has been usual, not least in the former British Empire itself, for post-colonial historians to err on the side of political correctness and nationalism. They tend to underplay the role of the British colonists and overstress the contributions made by the local or indigenous people. To do so produces a history as inadequate as one that sets out to blow the imperial trumpet for Hong Kong's time as a Crown Colony. A native son of Hong Kong who has lived roughly as long in Hong Kong as outside it, and having been trained in British imperial history and having spent two decades working on the history and politics of China, my intention is to ignore political correctness and present a modern history that does justice to all who were or have been part of this shared history. In this book I set out to explain and analyse clearly, simply and as objectively as possible the forces which made Hong Kong into what it was when British imperial rule ended in 1997. Whether I have succeeded or not is for you to judge.

A Modern History of Hong Kong is meant as much for general readers as for specialists. General readers should ignore the fairly large number of notes. As I aim to disperse a number of widely popularised misconceptions and myths about Hong Kong's history, I have decided against dispensing with references. General readers may not wish to get into the academic debates but specialists may like to check on the authenticity and reliability of the sources or use them to further their own scholarly pursuits.

Readers are advised that, in China, the surname precedes the given name. In Hong Kong, most ethnic Chinese follow the same rule – but not everyone does so. In the case of those who give their names in the English way, their preference is respected. In the transliteration of names and Chinese terms, the *pinyin* system adopted in the People's Republic has been followed. Exceptions have been made for personal or place names in Hong Kong or for Chinese personalities and cities well known to English readers. In these cases their usual form is used.

Acknowledgements

This volume is the result of research carried out over two decades, though it was largely written in 2001 and 2002. Some of the basic work was done in conjunction with other projects. The relentless but invariably gentle and good-humoured prodding from Dr Lester Crook of I.B.Tauris has played a key part in making sure this longstanding ambition of mine was turned into reality. He has also kindly arranged for some copyright material published in an earlier work, *Hong Kong: An Appointment With China*, to be used in this volume. My wife, Rhiannon, ensures that I have the best possible environment to write in. It was not just her love and tender care but also her understanding and the many discussions I had with her about elements of this book that made this venture a joy. To her this volume is dedicated with love and affection.

In undertaking the research which directly helped the preparation of this volume I would like to thank Carmen Tsang for her assistance with various sources in Hong Kong over the years. I am grateful to Lieutenant-General Fu Ying-chuan for special access to the Ministry of National Defence archives of the Republic of China, to the Foreign Ministry for access to its papers in Taipei, and to the Tung Wah Group of Hospitals for access to its archives. I am also obliged to the keepers of the Public Record Office (Kew), Rhodes House Library (Oxford), the Hung On-to Memorial Library (Hong Kong University), the Hong Kong Public Records Office, the Butler Library (Columbia University), the Eisenhower Library (Abilene, Kansas), and the Truman Library (Independence, Missouri) for access to and permission to cite from archival material under their care. The staff at St Antony's College Library and the Institute for Chinese Studies Library, both at Oxford, at the University of Hong Kong Library and at the Institute for Modern History Library (Academia Sinica, Taipei) have also provided kind assistance and congenial environments for my work over the years. I am also grateful to colleagues at the Centre of Asian Studies and Robert Black College at the University of Hong Kong, which provided a home to me when I conducted some of my research in Hong Kong.

In the course of the last two decades I benefited greatly from in-depth interviews conducted with more than 40 former members of the Hong Kong government, the British diplomatic service, the Executive and Legislative Councils of Hong Kong and the Basic Law Drafting Committee. Most though not all of these interviews were conducted when I was director of the Oxford University Hong Kong Project. The Hong Kong Project interviews were conducted on a confidential basis. The oral records and the tens of thousands of pages of transcripts are kept at the Rhodes House Library and are mostly still closed to public access. Because of the need to honour the pledge of confidence, I have made no use of any interview record still subject to a time-ban. However, I cannot unlearn what I have learnt. The perspective which I have taken in this volume has been affected by the many intensive hours of historical discourse. To all the contributors to the Project – whom I shall not name but you know who you are – I owe a debt of gratitude.

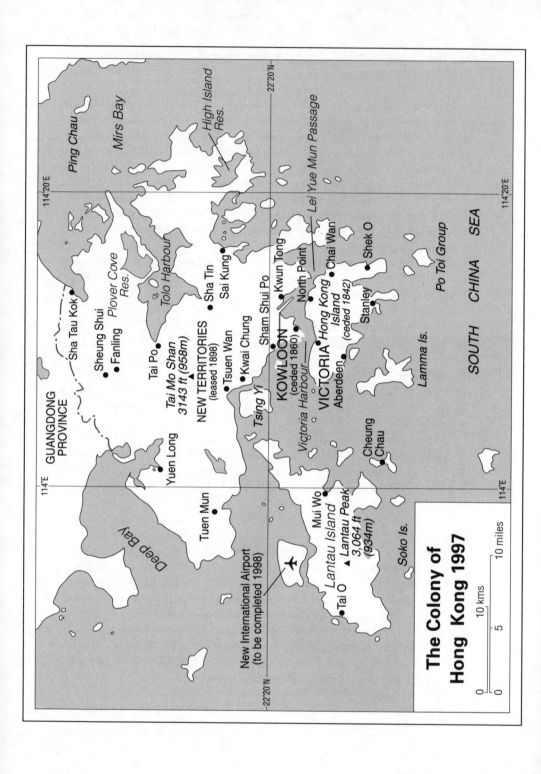

The Colony of
Hong Kong 1997

GUANGDONG
PROVINCE

SOUTH CHINA SEA

Ping Chau

Mirs Bay

High Island Res.

Lei Yue Mun Passage

Po Toi Group

Sha Tau Kok

Sheung Shui
Fanling

Plover Cove Res.

Tai Po

Tolo Harbour

Sha Tin

Sai Kung

Sham Shui Po

Kwun Tong

North Point

Chai Wan

Shek O

Stanley

Tai Mo Shan
3143 ft (958m)

NEW TERRITORIES
(leased 1898)

Tsuen Wan

Kwai Chung

KOWLOON
(ceded 1860)

VICTORIA
Aberdeen

Hong Kong
Island
(ceded 1842)

Tsing Yi

Victoria Harbour

Yuen Long

Tuen Mun

Lamma Is.

Cheung
Chau

Deep Bay

Mui Wo

Lantau Island

▲ Lantau Peak
3,064 ft
(934m)

Tai O

Soko Is.

New International Airport
(to be completed 1998)

22°20'N

114°20'E

114°E

114°20'E

114°E

22°20'N

10 kms

10 miles

0   5

0   10

Part I

The Foundations of Modern Hong Kong

Chapter 1

War and Peace

The Crown Colony of Hong Kong was a product of the First Anglo-Chinese War (1839–42), popularly known as the 'Opium War'. This was, in fact, much more than a war over the opium trade, though the economic benefit of the trade for the British and the costs to the Chinese were certainly important considerations for policymakers on both sides. Basic changes in the modern world were in any event pushing Britain and China to a major confrontation as the 1830s drew to a close. Two forces stood out in this regard.

The most fundamental change, which brought confrontation closer than ever, was the Industrial Revolution. Great advancements in communication and other technologies as well as in organisational capacities in Europe had enabled the leading industrial nation, Britain, to project power in a substantial way across more than 10,000 miles of ocean. This was greatly assisted by the availability to the British of India and other imperial outposts as key staging posts for economic and imperial activities in the East. The continued process of the Industrial Revolution in Britain was also fuelled by capturing overseas markets, which meant Britain had, since the start of the Industrial Revolution, adopted an aggressive foreign policy backed by war and imperial expansion.[1]

These changes gave rise to the second factor. For the first time in human history, Britain – the premier power in Europe after the defeat of Napoleon, master of the oceans, workshop of the world and an expansionist imperial power – came face to face with the Celestial Chinese Empire.[2]

Although China would soon be revealed to be a 'paper tiger' in its confrontation with Britain, it deemed itself the greatest empire on earth. It saw itself as the centre of the universe with its emperor enjoying the mandate of heaven. This apparently extravagant claim of grandeur is not without basis.

China was clearly the world leader in scientific developments, communication, production technologies and administrative organisation until around the sixteenth century. At the height of its power in the early fifteenth century, China was the only country that had the capability to deploy a naval taskforce of an estimated 317 ships and 27,000 men across great distances, as its navy sailed as far as Malindi on the east coast of Africa, just north of Mombasa.[3] To put this in perspective, Vasco de Gama did not make the first successful sea journey from Europe to India and back until 1498, over half a century later. Likewise, the Spanish Armada that sailed for England in 1588 – the destruction of which marked the rise of British naval supremacy – boasted a fleet of a mere 132 vessels. Similarly, the vast Chinese empire on land was held together by superior organisation and logistics in the pre-modern world. This enabled the Emperor to supervise urgent and important matters through a chain of relay riders that could deliver a despatch to a distance of 357 miles in 24 hours.[4]

The great advantage that China had over Europe was subsequently lost partly because of the dramatic advancements in Europe following the Industrial Revolution. It was also because the Chinese had fallen into the 'high-level equilibrium trap'. By the time of late imperial China, 'both in technological and investment terms, agricultural productivity per acre had nearly reached the limits of what was possible without industrial-scientific inputs, and the increase of population had therefore steadily reduced the surplus product above what was needed for subsistence'.[5] Nevertheless, the Chinese economy continued to expand as its population rose exponentially. From the time when China first took a population count in 2AD to the end of the fourteenth century or the beginning of the Ming dynasty, its population fluctuated between 37 and 60 million.[6] It reached an estimated 100 million in the 1650s, just after the Manchu or Qing dynasty superseded the Ming, rising to between 400 and 450 million in the 1850s. This dramatic increase demonstrated how efficient the Chinese economy had become in the pre-modern mode of production and management but it also had a negative effect on technological advancement.

Achieving this 'high-level equilibrium' allowed China to enjoy a degree of unity and stability over a vast empire unmatched for centuries in the pre-modern world but it also removed the incentive to innovate.[7] Consequently, when the modernity unleashed by the Enlightenment and the Industrial Revolution enabled Europe to overcome great distance and knock on the gate of the Chinese Empire, the latter responded mostly by basking in its old glory and failing to recognise the real significance of this new development. Late imperial China had continued to operate without a central treasury, or reliable vital statistics, or civil laws that linked government operations with the rising economic trends, and had remained a gigantic 'conglomeration of village communities'.[8] It was the greatest and most advanced empire, to use a Western analogy, essentially still of the late medieval or at least pre-industrial kind when it found itself forced to deal with Queen Victoria's emerging modern and rapidly industrialising British Empire.

Sharing little in outlook or core values in the handling of international relations, and increasingly tangled in expanding commercial and other relations that gave rise to conflicts and misunderstandings, the British and the Chinese empires behaved like all empires had previously done. They sized each other up, with the more powerful one moving towards a contest for supremacy when the furtherance of its perceived interests made this desirable. The scene for a major confrontation was set.

Tea, Opium and Trade

Late imperial China exercised strict controls over its external trade. It was in part because the vast expanse of the empire across various climatic zones had given it a very high degree of self-sufficiency. This condition underlined the arrogant claim that Emperor Qianlong made to King George III of Britain during Lord Macartney's first embassy to China (1792–4). According to Qianlong, 'our Celestial Empire possesses all things in prolific abundance and lacks no product within its own borders' and 'there was therefore no need to import the manufactures of outside barbarians in exchange of our own produce'.[9] This attitude towards foreign imports and trade was further reinforced by the central government's determination to avoid stability in the empire being disturbed by foreign influences, particularly the spread of religious beliefs. This Chinese attitude notwithstanding, trade between the two countries expanded, but from the middle of the eighteenth century it was mainly confined to the southern city of Canton (Guangzhou), far away from the imperial capital of Beijing (Peking). In the conduct of trade, the Chinese government relied on merchants, known as *cohongs*, as agents to deal with the British, who were required to send communications to senior officials through their Chinese merchant contacts and were subjected to numerous restrictions.[10]

On the British side, prior to 1834 the China trade was handled by the East India Company (EIC) under a monopoly. The EIC was founded in 1600 by a royal charter granted by Queen Elizabeth I, which gave it great scope to take any measures necessary to support trade in the perilous waters and often hostile environment in the East in order to compete against its bigger European rivals, particularly its Dutch counterpart. This included the privilege of raising armed forces and taking over the administration of territories deemed essential for trade under the charter. The costs of administration, maintaining order and security in the Company's dominion in India were so high that by the late eighteenth century the EIC was almost constantly under great financial pressure. In order to augment its revenue and to counter the smuggling or illegal private trade that was going on between India and China, the EIC granted licences to private traders who engaged themselves in this increasingly lucrative country trade.[11]

In spite of the distance and the insular attitude of the Chinese Empire, the China trade was a significant one for Britain and the EIC. For much of the middle of the nineteenth century, China was the fourth most important source of imports for Britain and enjoyed a very favourable balance of direct bilateral trade.[12] The most important British import from China was tea, followed by raw silk. The tea trade was important not only because tea had become practically a daily necessity in Britain by the 1830s, but also because the import duty London extracted from it was so high that it had also become a significant source of government income. It amounted to about 16 per cent of customs revenue in Britain in the five years preceding the First Anglo-Chinese War, and was sufficient to pay for about 83 per cent of the costs for maintaining the Royal Navy.[13]

The unfavourable balance of trade for Britain was redressed by a triangular trade involving British India, which at that time produced the only highly sought-after commodity in the otherwise largely self-sufficient China. This was opium, prohibited in China but imported through normal channels to Britain where it was openly available. Mainly taken orally for medicinal purposes and not (as was widely done in China) smoked, using opium was not at that time illegal or considered dangerous and immoral in Britain.[14]

The combined British and Indian trade with China produced a picture opposite to that of direct British trade with China. Once the export of opium from British India to China is included in the trade, the British side enjoyed a healthy balance of payments. In other words, the British export of opium from India would more than pay for the British import of tea and silk from China.[15]

For India or the EIC, revenue from the opium trade accounted for over 8 per cent of the overall revenue of British India for the five years preceding the First Anglo-Chinese War.[16] By the end of the eighteenth century, the profits that the EIC generated from India were absorbed by the huge costs of governing India, and its profit came mainly from the China trade.[17] Much was therefore at stake in the China trade for Britain and British India, for which important economic interests required the continuation of the lucrative opium trade.

This triangular trade was significant to the Chinese in a very different and almost opposite way. The long-established view that the Chinese economy suffered from the net physical outflow of silver – the key monetary medium in this period – as a result of the unfavourable balance of this trade has now been challenged.[18] The actual flow of silver in and out of China was in fact distorted by the use of remittance by draft for settlement of international trade, for which London served as the financial hub.[19] Whatever the reality, with the flow of silver there was a shortage in China.[20] As a result, opinions within the Chinese officialdom increasingly depicted an exaggerated outflow of silver, which by 1837 had seriously alarmed Emperor Daoguang.[21]

Key policymakers and leaders of powerful cliques in the bureaucracy and the literati, such as Viceroy Lin Zexu, also believed the shortage of silver was a result of the opium trade.[22] Furthermore, they were worried that opium smoking had become so widespread and entrenched that it had sapped the strength of the country. When military debilitation became evident in 1832 following the inability of the garrison to suppress a rebellion by the Yao minority in the Guangdong-Hunan border, even Emperor Daoguang became seriously concerned.[23] Thus, this triangular trade had also become a matter of major significance for the Chinese Empire.

The 1830s therefore saw major debates among Chinese policymakers on the subjects of opium suppression and the control of this undesirable trade. Different options, ranging from cutting off the import by a trade embargo, to suppression to legalisation, were explored, examined and debated. Such policy deliberations and wider discussions were conducted in the context of the bureaucratic constraints imposed by the structure and vested interests of the empire, official jostling for imperial favour, a limited understanding of the military strength of the British and therefore the potential costs of a trade embargo.[24] Suppression of the trade did not become policy until the eve of the First Anglo-Chinese War.

Diplomacy and Conflicts

If Sino-British trade caused friction in bilateral ties, the conduct of formal relations between the two empires was even more problematic and acrimonious. The great tension over ceremonial and protocol matters, particularly over the performance of the kowtow that wrecked Macartney's first British embassy to China at the end of the eighteenth century, grew more problematic in the 1830s.[25] The Chinese Empire did not see or treat Britain as an equal.

Until the end of its monopoly, the EIC almost exclusively handled what the British saw as the indignities involved in dealing with Chinese officials. They were deemed unpleasant and offensive but were tolerated by what was, above all, a profit-driven commercial organisation.

The taking over of the EIC's roles in dealing with the Chinese authorities by a representative of the British government implied a basic change. The prestige, dignity and honour of the British Empire were now at stake, but this important development received no recognition from the Chinese.[26] The basic differences in the correct manner of conducting relations between the two empires caused regular disputes. Since no compromise solution could be devised to satisfy both sides, in the long term either the British Empire – a rising power in the world scene – would have to continue to defer to the condescending Chinese approach, or the Chinese would be forced to accept the European norm in diplomatic relations.[27]

Until 1860, when the Chinese finally accepted a resident Minister Plenipotentiary to represent Britain, relations between the two countries were in fact conducted without diplomatic relations in the modern sense. Indeed, China did not send a resident diplomatic representative to Britain, its first to any Western power, until as late as 1877.[28]

Differences over the proper way to conduct bilateral relations came up as soon as Lord Napier set about discharging his responsibilities as the first ever British Chief Superintendent of the China trade in 1834, following the end of the EIC's monopoly.[29] In addition to taking over the management of British trade that the EIC used to supervise, Napier was also instructed by the British government to explore the possibility of extending trade beyond Canton and establishing diplomatic relations. The Chinese form for contacting the Viceroy in Canton was that communications should be styled as 'petitions' and conveyed through the cohongs. Acting to defend the 'dignity' of the British Empire, Napier broke with the Chinese rule and sailed up to Canton in a naval ship; he then insisted on announcing his arrival formally by presenting a letter to the Viceroy. This, from the Chinese point of view, unconventional approach caused considerable resentment and was firmly rejected by Viceroy Lu Kun. An impasse ensured for two months. It ended only when illness left Napier with no choice but to beat a less than dignified retreat to the Portuguese enclave of Macao where he soon died.

Napier was replaced as Chief Superintendent by two former EIC men in rapid succession, and both reverted to avoiding confrontation with the Chinese authorities.[30] Even Napier's third successor, Captain Charles Elliot, a Royal Navy rather than a Company man, at first attempted to take a conciliatory approach after he took up office in 1836. His preparedness to use the 'undignified' form of contacting the Viceroy or the provincial governor did not gain him much headway. His tolerance of this indignity was not endorsed by Lord Palmerston, the British Foreign Secretary, who instructed him to stop this practice.[31] Not much happened in fact, since London did not as yet have a coherent policy towards China, and Palmerston generally 'made do with no opinion with China beyond the vague feeling that... China was like any other power and should be treated as such'.[32] This did not mean London was not concerned with the issue of national dignity; there was simply at this stage insufficient cause to focus attention on it.

The differences between the two empires in their attitudes towards the conduct of international relations had a parallel in their approaches to the administration of law and justice. By the nineteenth century, the British had already developed and adopted, however imperfectly, the concept of the rule of law based on the due process, the presumption of innocence, trial by jury and the testing of evidences through adversarial discourse in a court of law. Justice, in the British view, was deemed to have been done when the law had been allowed to run its course, and the punishment to be meted out was to be directed against the convicted personally and to be proportionate to the severity of the crime.

The Chinese, in contrast, had a rather different approach. Although the Chinese legal system was not simply primitive, arbitrary and barbaric, as it was generally seen by the British at the time, but was in fact highly developed and rationally based, it worked on principles fundamentally different from the British system.

To the Chinese, justice was deemed to have been done not when the law had run its course but when the right decision was reached and implemented, whether this was achieved by strict adherence to the law or not. For the magistrate, to do the right thing did not mean to be arbitrary or simply to enforce the law; it was supposed to be based on careful deliberation of the results of his investigations, including, where appropriate, the use of torture to secure a confession from the suspect. The degree of punishment was usually linked to the social norm and prevailing morality so that, for example, the killing of a father by an unfilial son would attract an extremely severe punishment, while the killing of an unfilial son by a father would receive a much lighter sentence. It was also meant to uphold public morality and through its demonstrative effect maintain social order.[33] Collective responsibility, in contrast to individual responsibility in British law, was the norm. While the Chinese legal system was sophisticated in its own way, the actual administration of justice was greatly influenced or undermined by endemic corruption and the non-separation of judicial from other powers.

In light of the basic differences between the Chinese and the British approaches to law and justice, it was not surprising that cases involving Britons or Westerners – who were seen as barbarians by the Chinese – almost invariably proved thorny for both sides and were often causes of dispute. There is no need to rehearse here various incidents of the early nineteenth century in which the British and the Chinese were engaged in disputes over the administration of law and justice on British subjects who might have broken Chinese laws.[34] Suffice it to say that, although they were important irritants in bilateral relations, they were not sufficiently serious to provoke the two sides to go to war. However, the mutual resentment over this issue was longstanding, and it provided added incentive on the part of the British to seek redress to what they saw as an unsatisfactory basis for the conduct of bilateral relations, particularly when this infringed seriously upon British economic interests.

The First Anglo-Chinese War

When Elliot took office as Chief Superintendent of Trade in 1836, the Chinese government was engaged in a major policy review of the opium trade and control of the apparent outflow of silver. Emperor Daoguang was initially more inclined towards legalisation that would provide better control over the trade and the flow of silver. However, he was persuaded by one of the influential and ambitious groupings of officials and literati, known as the Spring Purificationists (*zhanchunji*), which produced damning allegations against the pro-legalisation clique to reverse his decision.[35] He now favoured the suppression of opium.

Further deliberations on how to achieve this objective without provoking a war went on for some time and led to an important official and ally of the Spring Purificationists, the Viceroy of Hunan and Jiangxi Lin Zexu, volunteering to take on this difficult task. The Spring Purificationists and Lin picked Guangdong to start the anti-opium campaign as they realised that a countrywide one could not be implemented. They reckoned the most effective way was to cut off the supply where it entered the country. To do so, they planned to cause a temporary collapse of trade in Canton in order to produce a commercial panic among the British so that the latter would sacrifice the opium trade for the profits of other commerce.[36] Lin volunteered, as he hoped a spectacular success would enable him to gain sufficient credibility and stature to introduce a crucial and yet sensitive reform, that of the tribute-grain system.[37]

In March 1839, Lin took up office as Special Imperial Commissioner in Canton and set about his anti-opium crusade. Although generally seen as a progressive and broadminded mandarin for his time, Lin did not have a real understanding of his British opponents or the great gap that the Industrial Revolution had produced between the might of the modern British Empire and the essentially still medieval Chinese Empire. While neither he nor the Spring Purificationists expected a war they, for domestic considerations, were unwittingly steering the Chinese Empire on a collision course with the British Empire by an attempt to cut off the most profitable element of Britain and British India's China trade.

Eight days after he had arrived in Canton, Lin ordered the foreigners to surrender all opium in their possession and to undertake to bring in no more. The British merchants were at first hesitant not least because they thought Lin could be bribed or was probably not really serious. However, Lin was as determined as he was incorruptible. He put great pressure on the British in Canton, confining them to the factory or warehouse compound and cutting off their supplies.

On his return to Canton, Elliot, who was in Macao as Lin issued his demand, decided that Lin's demand would be met in order to secure safe passage for Britons out of Canton, with the costs involved and other injuries the Chinese inflicted on them to be resolved between the two governments. With Elliot promising that the British government would in due course pay for their opium stock, the merchants surrendered their entire stock of 20,283 chests. The opium became technically the property of the British government, before Elliot handed it over to the Chinese. Once he had received the opium, Lin destroyed it in public.

With the value of the opium estimated at £2 million, it caught the attention of the British and the Indian governments when the news finally reached them (in August in the case of London). Although not a formidable sum, neither the British government under Prime Minister Lord Melbourne, which already had a budgetary deficit of £1 million for the year, nor the EIC, which had just fought an expensive campaign in the First Afghan War, found it politically tolerable. When the issue was discussed in the British Cabinet in September 1839, it was quickly agreed that the Chinese should be made to pay for this destruction of British property by the threat or actual use of force if required.[38]

The British and Indian governments then proceeded to put together an expeditionary force. It was to be entrusted to Elliot and his cousin, Rear Admiral Sir George Elliot, until then Commander-in-Chief of the Cape Station of the Royal Navy, as joint plenipotentiaries at the beginning of 1840. The expedition was to be a 'punitive exercise... to bring an obtuse Peking government to the conference table'.[39] Britain had decided on war, not to impose British manufactures on China, nor to bring the Chinese to salvation by spreading the gospel, though there were groups in Britain who desired one or the other and used the results of this war for their purposes. To Foreign Secretary Palmerston, it was not even to force opium on the Chinese, despite the fact that British opium traders seized on the war to further their trade and profits. As he emphatically stressed to the Chinese government, the British government did not question China's right to prohibit the imports, it merely objected to the way this was handled.[40] From Palmerston's point of view, since the prohibition order had not been imposed for years, its sudden strict enforcement amounted to laying a trap for the foreign traders, and the confinement of British traders in Canton with supplies cut off was tantamount to an attempt to starve them to death or into submission.[41]

What the war was meant to do was to 'efface an unjust and humiliating act, to recover the value of certain property plus expenses... and almost by and by to put England's relations with the Middle Kingdom on a new and proper footing'.[42] To achieve these purposes, Palmerston gave the Elliot cousins fairly clear instructions: to occupy one of the Zhoushan islands off Zhejiang province in East China, to present a letter from himself to a senior Chinese official for transmission to the Emperor, then to proceed to the Gulf of Bohai in the north to sign a treaty with the Chinese, and should the Chinese prove intransigent, blockade the key ports and both the Yangtze (Yangzi) and Yellow rivers to force the Chinese hand.[43] Palmerston was so clear in what he wanted that he sent to Charles Elliot a draft treaty for peace, stressing all its provisions were to be met. The resources put at the disposal of the plenipotentiaries were 4,000 troops, supported by a fleet of 16 warships and 28 transports. These included three third-rate, 74-gun ships of the line and four newly designed armed steamers or gunboats, with a total of 540 guns on board the ships.[44]

The Chinese, including Lin, were caught by surprise, as they had expected the British to seek to resolve the matter in Canton. When the British demonstrated their naval prowess in Bohai, which was just over a hundred miles from the imperial capital of Beijing, the Court was shocked and a senior official, Qi Shan (or Keshen as he was known to the British), was tasked to persuade the British to retire to the southern city of Canton and negotiate there. With Qi replacing Lin as Special Commissioner in Canton, negotiations dragged on through the autumn of 1840. The British again forced Qi to come to an agreement after a further display of naval superiority. Qi had no choice and reached a tentative agreement with Charles Elliot, known as the Chuenpi Convention. By this agreement, the island of Hong Kong was to be ceded to the British; an indemnity of six million silver dollars was to be paid over six years; official relations between the two empires was to be direct and on equal footing and trade was to be reopened immediately.[45] As a result, the British took possession of Hong Kong and British rule began on 26 January 1841.

Elliot had chosen Hong Kong rather than Zhoushan as instructed by Palmerston, because he had reservations about opening more ports in China. In his judgement, more ports would only create more opportunities for the scattered British communities to be taken hostage, whereas the excellent harbour of Hong Kong had proved itself a valuable base to support the British trading community in Canton.[46]

The Chuenpi Convention proved unacceptable to both the Chinese and the British governments, and the two protagonists were replaced by their respective governments. Qi's biggest problem was the territorial cession, which angered not only the Emperor but also officialdom in general. As far as the British were concerned, they were unhappy with Elliot's performance and his failure to implement Palmerston's specific instructions.[47] London thus appointed Sir Henry Pottinger, a Major General of the EIC's Bombay army known for his toughness and daring in the recent Afghan war, to take over as Chief Superintendent and Pleni-potentiary. Pottinger was given reinforcements that enlarged the fleet to 25 men-of-war (including ten steamers) and the expeditionary force to about 12,000 men.[48]

London was determined to get what it wanted by war. The thinking was that if British forces could occupy strategic points that would allow them 'to control the internal commerce of the Chinese empire' they could exert 'pressure upon the Court of Pekin irresistible'.[49] Once the forces were in place and ready in Hong Kong in September 1841, Pottinger started a series of campaigns in the lower Yangtze region, eventually fighting their way up this mighty river to threaten the city of Nanjing (Nanking) almost a year later. By then the British had already taken control of the key points in the lower reaches of the Yangtze, the most important waterway for commerce and communications in the richest part of China. They had also cut off the Grand Canal, historically the designated channel for the transport of tribute-grain from the south and the east to the imperial capital.

With repeated demonstrations of British naval and military superiority, as well as great mobility, the Court in Beijing had to take into account the implied threat that the British forces could swiftly redeploy to threaten the Beijing-Tianjin area once they had stormed Nanjing. This left the Chinese with little choice but to make peace, a task that fell on Yilibu (Elepoo to the British) and Qi Ying, two new Special Commissioners. The result of the negotiations was the Treaty of Nanking, which was signed by the plenipotentiaries of both sides on board the 72-gun HMS *Cornwallis* in Nanjing on 29 August 1842. Ratification was exchanged in Hong Kong on 26 June 1843, an act that formally allowed Hong Kong to be created a Crown Colony.

The real priorities for the British were reflected in the way the war was handled. The advancement of British economic interests, which meant maximising trade and seeking Chinese compensation for costs incurred, was clearly paramount. Although Canton was, for example, on more than one occasion threatened and could have been taken, no such attempt was made in order not to disrupt trade, particularly the tea trade which was also highly profitable.[50] The right for Britain to export Indian opium to China was not itself a matter of major concern to the British in this period, but the opportunity for British traders to continue to profit from it was. Hence, neither in the draft peace treaty Palmerston gave Elliot in February 1840 nor in the Treaty of Nanking itself did the British demand the legalisation of the opium trade.

The main British concern was to secure the right to trade in China and make as much profit as possible. In general, the British government did not see the opium trade in moral terms and merely treated it as a most profitable commerce that would continue as long as the Chinese general public desired it and the Chinese officialdom remained too corrupt to enforce its own prohibition order on a sustainable basis.[51] The distinction between securing by force the right to trade for which opium was a major commodity and to wage a war to impose opium on China might seem spurious but it was not, at least not to the British government.[52] The difference was between waging an imperialist war for economic benefits and doing so to impose a contraband drug that the imperial power itself deemed immoral.[53] The war was not so much a case of a state using its superior power to impose an illicit drug trade on a weaker state as a classic case of the flag following and protecting trade in an era when imperialism carried a positive connotation in Europe.

The inability of the vast Chinese Empire to defend itself against a relatively small British expeditionary force requires explanation. A couple of the individual engagements, particularly the battle of Zhenjiang (July 1842), demonstrated that when led effectively the regular Chinese army, a Banner garrison in this case, could put up a valiant and stubborn fight against vastly superior numbers and overwhelming odds.[54] Where the Chinese Empire fell short lay as much in its near medieval defence, logistical organisation and communication systems as in its antiquated military and naval technologies. It is true that Chinese military and naval technologies were such that the British did not lose a single warship to the Chinese in combat. However, it is not true that the British forces always won against much larger Chinese forces on land or at sea. In many of the land battles, the British either fought against a comparably sized opponent or enjoyed a numeric superiority thanks to superior logistics, organisation and mobility provided by the fleet.

The inherent weakness of the Chinese defence lay in the military system. The Chinese national army, to use a modern term, consisted of the Banner force, comprising Manchurian, Mongolian and Han Chinese Banners. It was entrusted with the task of protecting national security by defending the imperial capital and garrisoning the main strategic points. The mobilisation, concentration and deployment of this main field force, which totalled less than a quarter of a million, required time and efficient transportation. Neither was available to the Chinese since the seaborne British expeditionary force enjoyed elusive mobility. In addition to the Banner force, there was the territorial army, known as the Green Standard Army, consisting of fewer than half a million Han Chinese soldiers. The two armies came under completely separate command and control systems, with the Banner force being strategically deployed to provide a check against the loyalty of the Green Standard Army.[55] The latter was, in any event, more a gendarmerie than an army, since its main responsibility was internal security. It was neither trained, equipped, organised nor deployed for effective defence against an external enemy, least of all against a modern European army that had already consigned most of the weapons used by the Chinese to museum display. In short, the Chinese army did not have an integrated command and control system and Chinese commanders did not have the means to gather intelligence to assess the intention of the seaborne invader, nor to deploy troops for the effective defence of vulnerable points susceptible to an invasion.

Likewise, the Chinese navy had no headquarters or central command structure and was basically subdivided and commanded by 15 admirals stationed in key ports along the coast. The fleets were trained and equipped mainly as parallel anti-piracy coastguard units rather than as elements of a modern navy.[56]

Furthermore, the Board of War in Beijing served neither as a modern ministry of defence nor as a chiefs of staff committee. The Chinese defence failed because its essentially medieval character could not meet the challenges of a modern army backed up by the most advanced navy and industrial country of the time.

The Treaty of Nanking

Strictly speaking, the grievances of the British Empire that Palmerston outlined in his February 1840 letter to the Chinese Emperor at the beginning of the war, including the perceived insult and harm done to the British, were redressed by the Treaty of Nanking. Palmerston's original demands were met, with only one significant exception. This involved the territorial cession. Instead of securing one of the islands in the Zhoushan group, the British accepted Hong Kong, Elliot's choice, which was initially dismissed by Palmerston as 'a barren island with hardly a house upon it'.[57] This was partly because since British occupation Hong Kong had proved its worth. It was also because Palmerston had by then been replaced as Foreign Secretary by Lord Aberdeen, after Melbourne's Whig government was succeeded by Robert Peel's Tory ministry in 1841. The other main provisions of the treaty settled the war by Britain extracting from a reluctant China an indemnity of 21 million silver dollars to cover the value of the destroyed merchandise as well as all British expenses; the opening of five seaports including Canton to foreign trade with official British trade and consular representation sanctioned; the ending of the old cohong system for trade; and equality between British and Chinese officials.[58]

The treaty did not in fact go far enough to create the conditions for bilateral relations to be conducted in a mutually satisfactory manner, as the basic problems that had led to the war were not removed. This was partly because the inherent problems of two pompous and distant empires becoming involved with each other as a result of changing technologies were not addressed. To the British, the treaty was meant to open up China to further trade, to the economic advantage of British citizens. Hong Kong was taken primarily for these purposes. The British expected the treaty to enable trade to be expanded and profits to be enhanced though no serious thought had gone into how these would be achieved. To the Chinese, the treaty was but a necessary evil to get the belligerent British barbarians to end the war. They had no intention of expanding economic or any other ties with the British.

Indeed, the treaty did not even deal with the issue, which provided the impetus for the Chinese actions that became the immediate cause for the war, namely the export of opium to China by British traders being barred under Chinese law. Since opium was not even mentioned in the treaty, it continued to be imported into China by British smugglers working with the cooperation of their Chinese partners and corrupt Chinese officials.[59] Its illicit nature meant that it remained a source of tension.

More fundamentally, nothing was done to deal with the thorny question of establishing diplomatic representation, and even the treaty's provision for Britain to send consular and trade representatives to the five designated Chinese ports was not fully respected by the Chinese. After the ratification of the treaty, there remained no effective channel with which Britain could settle fresh disputes directly with the government in Beijing. The British Plenipotentiary, by then based in Hong Kong where he was also Governor, had to continue to deal with the Viceroy in Canton.

The First Anglo-Chinese War and the Treaty of Nanking did not cause a fundamental change in the way the Chinese looked at the British, beyond a limited recognition of the latter's military and naval superiority and of the inadvisability of attempting strict enforcement of the opium trade prohibition lest it should provoke a renewal of hostilities. Once the war ended, the Chinese Empire merely tried to restore normality as it had prevailed previously. Neither the war nor the peace treaty shocked China into seeking a basic reform as American Commodore Matthew Perry's squadron of 'black ships' did in Japan a decade later. Senior officials in China, even someone like Viceroy Qi Ying – who was known for his ability to understand the British and who managed to maintain relatively good relations with them in the aftermath of the war – merely tried to update and improve upon the old method of managing the barbarians by attempting to understand the British customs and practices and avoiding confrontations.[60] Among ordinary people, the Cantonese were the most directly exposed to the British. It was in Canton that the ordinary people, inspired and led by the local gentry, proved most hostile to the British and threatened the security of the British if the Viceroy were to fulfil the terms of the Nanking Treaty and open Canton city proper to the British.[61]

Although the Treaty of Nanking did not put Anglo-Chinese relations on a satisfactory footing or remove the underlying conflicts, leading to a new war within two decades, it did mark the beginning of a new era in China's relations with the West. It also gave rise to the British colony of Hong Kong.

Chapter 2

The Foundation of
a Crown Colony

British Occupation

Although the British had on occasion used Hong Kong as a base for operations in the early stages of the First Anglo-Chinese War, they did not lay any claim to the island until after the Convention of Chuenpi. By order of Plenipotentiary Charles Elliot, Commodore Sir Gordon Bremer of the Royal Navy duly took possession in the morning of 26 January 1841. Accompanied by officers of the naval squadron, a few army officers and a party of Royal Marines, Bremer landed at the north-west shore of the island, toasted Queen Victoria and claimed Hong Kong in her name after a royal salute from the men-of-war in the harbour.[1] The scene of this high drama came to be known as Possession Point. It was kept an open space and generally used as a place for recreation and entertainment by the local Chinese under a different name, Tai Tat Tei. It was developed in the 1980s and incorporated into a hotel and commercial complex, which is also part of the new Hong Kong-Macao Ferry Terminal. This beautiful subtropical island whose spectacular landscape reminded generations of Scots of their home has a great deep-water natural harbour by its north shore and good quality fresh water supplies, and was at that time home to fewer than 7,500 Chinese residents, mostly fishermen and farmers.[2] The British occupation met with no resistance.

Since the Chuenpi Convention and the policies followed by both Elliot and his Chinese counterpart over Hong Kong were subsequently disallowed by the sovereigns of the two empires, the status of Hong Kong in fact remained unsettled until after the Treaty of Nanking was signed and ratified. However, Elliot did not learn of this rebuke and his recall until August 1841.

After he joined Bremer in this new British possession, for which his affection grew steadily, Elliot proceeded to proclaim and assert, pending royal pleasure, the full right of the British Crown to administer the island as a British dominion and to offer protection to its residents. He also declared that 'the natives of the island... and all natives of China thereto resorting, shall be governed according to the laws and customs of China, every description of torture excepted'.[3] Despite his preoccupation with relations with the Chinese authorities, Elliot laid down the foundations for a new colony before his departure.[4] He declared Hong Kong a free port, appointed his Deputy Superintendent of Trade, A.R. Johnston, to take charge of day-to-day affairs and held the first sale of land by auction in June.[5] The small beginnings of an administration were formed.[6]

In the meantime, entrepreneurial British traders, led by Jardine Matheson, for their part took advantage of the protection of the British flag in the enclave to promote their China trade, including particularly the storage and shipping of opium.[7] After the first sale of land, for 34 lots, construction of buildings, roads and other infrastructure followed – so much so that the 'elements of a regular establishment were soon formed, and the nucleus of a powerful European community soon planted'.[8] Chinese nationals were also attracted to Hong Kong as labour was required for the building of a new town, which would become the city of Victoria, a name that has long since been eclipsed by Central District in popular usage. The birth of a modern city in Hong Kong thus started to happen after British possession, despite uncertainty over its future following the recall of Elliot. Indeed, so much had been done that within a year of his arrival, Pottinger reported to London, that 'whatever may be the result of the war... and whatever may be hereafter decided upon with respect to other insular positions, this settlement had already advanced too far to admit of its ever being restored to the authority of the Emperor consistent with the Honour and Advantage of Her Majesty's Crown and Subjects'.[9] The logic of imperial expansion led by trade and the initiatives of the colonists was gathering momentum of its own.

At the beginning there was a difference of views between London and its men on the spot in estimating the value of Hong Kong. Foreign Secretary Palmerston thought it would 'not be the Mart of Trade any more than Macao' when he first learned of Elliot's insubordination.[10] Even his successor, Aberdeen, had doubts over its acquisition since it would incur expenses in its administration, and complicate relations with the Chinese Empire and other nations.[11]

In contrast, Elliot believed Hong Kong was both easily defensible and of 'first rate importance for our own trade and interests', as it had proved itself 'the chief basis of our operations in China, Militarily, Commercially, and Politically'.[12] Even his successor, Pottinger, quickly became a devotee. He saw it as 'an asset both as a naval base and a mart' that 'should not be abandoned'.[13] In taking this decision as the man on the spot, Pottinger did not act in accordance with his instructions from Aberdeen, but what he did was in line with previous directives from Palmerston when the latter was still Foreign Secretary. As Pottinger set off for China, he was told by Palmerston that he should 'examine with care the natural capacities of Hong Kong, and you will not agree to give up that Island unless you should find that you can exchange it for another in the neighbourhood of Canton, better adapted for the purposes in view; equally defensible; and affording sufficient shelter for Ships of War and Commerce'.[14]

Whether Pottinger was right or wrong in not following the instructions of Aberdeen, geography and history have proved that he did right by British interests. Hong Kong offered an excellent harbour and location for the purposes that the British had in mind, indeed, it could not have been surpassed within several hundred miles either side of Canton along the Chinese coast.

Crown Colony

By Article III of the Treaty of Nanking, under which the Chinese Emperor ceded to Queen Victoria 'the Island of Hong Kong, to be possessed in perpetuity by Her Britannick Majesty, her Heirs and Successors, and to be governed by such laws and regulations as Her Majesty the Queen... shall see fit to direct', the future of Hong Kong was settled and secured.[15] Following the exchange of ratification in June 1843, the Colony of Hong Kong formally came into existence, with Pottinger, who had taken over the administration from Johnston in February 1842, as its first Governor. The necessary authorisation and instructions for the founding of this new colony were sent from London ahead of time.[16] The most important documents forming its constitution were the Letters Patent and the Royal Instructions from Queen Victoria.[17] With these two documents, the constitutional structure of a Crown colony was prescribed, which was a form of government then shared by most other British overseas territories.

Under the Letters Patent of 5 April 1843, which is also known as the Hong Kong Charter, this new imperial outpost was to be governed by a Governor appointed at royal pleasure and assisted by both an Executive Council and a Legislative Council. As the representative of the Crown and chief executive of the colony, the Governor was given 'full power and authority', subject only to review and disallowance from London. Although the Letters Patent were amended and on occasions reissued during the 153 years of British sovereignty to accommodate changes of the time, the basic structure of Hong Kong's political system remained essentially as it was defined by the Hong Kong Charter until it was handed back to the contemporary successor to the Chinese Empire, the People's Republic of China, on 1 July 1997.

In light of the high mortality rate in those days, particularly of Europeans in the tropical world including Hong Kong where the scorching sun, poorly understood tropical diseases, and inadequate sanitary and hygienic provisions kept life expectancy low, a clear line of succession to the tremendous authority of the Governor was defined. In the event of the Governor dying in office or being absent from the colony – the latter a real possibility since he continued to hold concurrently the offices of the British Plenipotentiary and Chief Superintendent of Trade in China – his authority would be vested in a duly appointed Lieutenant-Governor or, next in line, the Colonial Secretary. In Hong Kong no Governor in fact died in office until Sir Edward Youde in 1987. Although the office of Lieutenant-Governor was almost immediately filled in 1843 by the appointment of the General Officer in command of the land forces, George D'Aguilar, as an office it did not establish itself firmly in the colonial government and had been allowed to lapse by the early 1870s, though it had on special occasions been revived temporarily.[18]

While the Letters Patent defined the basic constitutional structure, it was the Royal Instructions that provided the details laying down how Hong Kong should be organised and governed. Although an Executive Council and a Legislative Council were provided for to advise the Governor in the exercise of his authority and in legislation, and they both consisted of official and non-official members, they were meant to be strictly advisory in nature. Parliamentary supremacy, which was already the constitutional norm in Westminster in the nineteenth century, did not apply to Hong Kong. Nor did it, for that matter, apply in any other Crown colony. In practice, no sensible governor would consistently and continuously act against the views of his Councils or the citizens of the colony, as they had access to the democratically elected government in London and the failure of a governor to maintain stability, good order and prosperity would provoke inquiries from London and could lead to his own removal. Nevertheless, the power and authority of the Governor provided for in the Royal Instructions were such that the definition of the government could in its narrowest sense be taken to mean the Governor, or the Governor working in consultation with his Executive Council, generally described as the Governor-in-Council.

The executive-led nature of the colonial government was fully reflected in the Royal Instructions to the Governor that 'no Law or Ordinance shall be made or enacted by the said [Legislative] Council unless the same shall have been previously proposed by yourself, and that no question shall be debated at the said Council unless the same shall first have been proposed for that purpose by you', though the right of Councillors to express their views fully in debates was enshrined. Indeed, the Legislative Council was given the authority to pass local ordinances enforceable in the colony but they must not prove repugnant to English law, and none of them could sanction the grant of money or land to the Governor, in order to pre-empt corruption.[19]

As to the judiciary, the Governor was empowered by the Letters Patent 'to constitute and appoint Judges, and in cases requisite, Commissioners of Oyer and Terminer, Justices of the Peace, and other necessary Officers and Ministers in our said Colony, for the due and impartial administration of justice'. As the Crown's representative, the Governor was also charged with exercising certain royal prerogatives including that of pardon and of suspending 'from the exercise of his Office, within our said Colony, any person exercising any office or Warrant granted, or which may be granted by us'.[20]

In strictly constitutional terms the Crown Colony system as practised in Hong Kong did not provide for a clear separation of powers or constitutional checks and balances. The weakest of the three branches of government was the legislature, which did not enjoy full parliamentary power or standing. However, it ought to be recognised that the Crown Colony system was never meant to be a democratic system. As would become general practice in the British Empire by the twentieth century, democratisation in such a system would involve gradual expansion of representation in the Legislative Council leading to it being given full parliamentary power, at which point the system would give way to a responsible government in the Westminster tradition. The independence of the judiciary was in practice generally respected, since the theoretical autocratic power of the governor was checked by the British government in London, which was in turn democratically supervised by the elected parliamentarians of the United Kingdom. Furthermore, the colony's court of final appeal was constituted by the law lords of the Privy Council.

Although Crown Colonies shared much in common in their political systems, Hong Kong stood out from its earliest days. In the words of Lord Stanley, the Secretary of State for the Colonies, at its foundation, it was 'a small island, geographically and until now practically an insignificant appendage to the vast empire of which the polity and the institutions have no counterpart amongst those of the other nations of the world' and it was 'governed by an officer who is, at once, to negotiate with the Emperor of China or his officers, to superintend the trade of the Queen's subjects in the seas, rivers and coasts of his empire, and to regulate all the internal economy of the settlement itself'.[21] It was with such considerations in mind that Stanley agreed that 'proceedings unknown in other British colonies must be followed' in Hong Kong making the Governor responsible to both his office and to that of the Foreign Secretary concurrently.[22]

The anomalous position of the Governor was finally removed in 1859 towards the end of the Second Anglo-Chinese War (1856–60), as Britain finally appointed a resident Minister in Beijing as Envoy Plenipotentiary to take care of diplomatic, consular and trading relations with the Chinese Empire. This did not alter the reality that the colony was so closely tied to Anglo-Chinese relations that, as a more recent Governor aptly observed, 'practically every major issue that arose in Hong Kong, and on which London had to be consulted, was a matter of foreign policy'.[23] Existing as it did in the shadow of China, major policy departures in Hong Kong were often taken only after consideration of their implications for Anglo-Chinese relations or of the likely reactions from China.

Raison d'être

Hong Kong was not picked for a colony by the government in London, and was 'occupied not with a view to colonisation, but for diplomatic, commercial and military purposes'.[24] It was in an important sense the unintended result of the British Empire pursuing its economic interests in East Asia. From the very moment the British government put at Elliot's disposal an expeditionary force, it had sought a territorial base along the coast of China to support the trading relations it wished to establish with the Chinese Empire.

As Palmerston explained to the Chinese government, Hong Kong was seized 'in order that British Merchants trading to China may not be subject to the arbitrary caprice either of the Government in Peking, or its local Authorities at the Sea-Ports of the Empire'.[25] In the instructions he gave his men on the spot, Palmerston spelt out the criteria for choosing the territorial bases. It 'ought to be conveniently situated for commercial intercourse; not merely with Canton but other trading places on the Coast of China' and must 'have good harbours, and to afford natural facilities for Military defence, and should also be capable of being easily provisioned'.[26] The British objective was clear from the very beginning: Hong Kong was taken 'not at all because of any natural advantages which it possesses, but simply as subsidiary to the intercourse between the British and the Chinese empires' for which the most important was trade.[27]

Palmerston's favoured location for a British trading station was in fact one of the islands in the Zhoushan group off the coast of Zhejiang province, close to the rich Yangtze basin. Hong Kong was the choice of Elliot and was subsequently embraced by Pottinger. Elliot explained his preference for Hong Kong rather than somewhere else in East China:

> Reflection and experience have satisfied me against all my pre-conceptions and personal wishes, firstly, that Settlement at this point of the Empire is *necessary*; and secondly that Settlement to the Eastward, will only be productive of an indefinite protraction of hostilities in China, at an enormous expence, and thus defeat or most seriously retard the very purposes for which it is undertaken – purposes assuredly susceptible of accomplishment through a quiet possession of that Settlement to the Southward with which we cannot dispense.[28]

The main difference between Elliot and Palmerston was only over the choice of Hong Kong as an imperial outpost, not over the acquisition of one, since both deemed it highly desirable for British trade to secure a territorial base along the Chinese coast free from the whims of Chinese jurisdiction. In short, the British Empire acquired Hong Kong first and foremost to promote its economic interests in China, and only secondarily to support diplomatic contacts for which naval and military backup was often required.[29]

It was indeed because of the primacy of commercial considerations that Elliot proclaimed Hong Kong a free port as soon as he took possession in January 1841. He declared that 'her majesty's government has sought for no privilege in China exclusively for the advantage of British ships and merchants'.[30] This generous offer to open Hong Kong to traders of all nations including China was made in light of the ascending might and rising economic power of early Victorian Britain. These were such that free trade posed little if any threat to British commercial supremacy in Chinese waters. Instead, free trade worked to British advantage, allowing Britain to hold the lion's share of trade and supporting economic and financial activities in China for the rest of the nineteenth century. Elliot's initiative to make Hong Kong a free port was subsequently endorsed by the British government.[31]

Hong Kong's value for diplomatic purposes was significant but limited. In its first decade as a Crown colony, it was highly treasured as the base for the head of the British representation to the Chinese Empire. However, that was mainly because the entire mode for the conduct of relations between the two empires remained unsatisfactory. This made the convenience and protection provided by the British flag valuable. Hong Kong's importance, as predicted by Elliot, underlined the need for the state of relations between the two empires to be altered in a fundamental way. When that happened after the Second Anglo-Chinese War, Hong Kong's place in support of British diplomacy dropped dramatically, as the consular, commercial and negotiating roles of the Governor were transferred to the British Minister resident in Beijing, an office that became separate from the Governorship of Hong Kong. After 1860, Hong Kong became more an issue for Anglo-Chinese diplomacy than a base that advanced British diplomatic interests in China, though it remained the forward base for the projection of power in support of British diplomacy.

As an imperial outpost, Hong Kong was intended to be a significant naval station rather than a military base for further territorial expansion. The British Empire in East Asia was primarily interested in trade and economic benefits rather than territorial acquisition. Indeed, Aberdeen's initial reservation over the retention of Hong Kong was predicated on the costs likely to be incurred for its administration and defence.[32] One of Hong Kong's main attractions for Elliot was the relative ease and low costs of its security.

With Britannia ruling the waves, the defence of Hong Kong in the nineteenth century relied heavily on the Royal Navy, leading to a situation in its early years in which it was unassailable while the fleet was in harbour but once it 'left to do its job, Hong Kong was completely defenceless'.[33] It was for this reason that a small volunteer defence force was raised in 1854 when the British Empire went to war with Russia in the Crimea and China was embroiled in the turmoil of the Taiping Rebellion, as the local garrison had less than 500 soldiers fit for duty.[34]

Throughout its history, Hong Kong seldom maintained a large garrison except in time of exigency. It was its long historical links with the China Station (reduced to a mere Hong Kong Squadron towards the end of empire) and the Royal Marines that evoked a strong bond between Hong Kong and the Royal Navy.[35] Much as Hong Kong was a valued naval base, its military and strategic values to the British Empire were mostly limited to acting as the support base for operations in East Asia. The most important occasion when Hong Kong proved invaluable in military terms was during the Second Anglo-Chinese War when it served as the staging ground for the expeditionary forces.[36] Even as a naval station, the commander was required from the very beginning 'to impress upon the officers of his Squadron the necessity of cultivating as much as possible the friendly feelings which it may be hoped that the Chinese Authorities and People will be disposed to entertain towards them' in order to enhance the colony's utility in promoting British trade.[37]

As an outpost of empire, Hong Kong was certainly not founded with any 'civilising' mission in mind on the part of the British government. Unlike some other nations defeated by the British Empire, China was recognised by the British as a major civilisation in its own right – it merely did not follow Christian ethics and European standards in law and the norm in the conduct of external relations. All that the British had planned to do once they acquired Hong Kong was to ensure that the Christian faith would be upheld and certain undesirable conducts proscribed.

The clearest indication of the lack of a civilising mission on the part of the British government was the instructions sent to Pottinger for the administration of justice. London was not prepared to go as far as Elliot, who proclaimed in 1841 that 'the natives of Hong Kong and all natives of China thereto resorting, shall be governed according to the laws and customs of China, every description of torture excepted'.[38] This was disallowed. London decided that English law should in general prevail in Hong Kong but considerations should be given particularly by the local legislature to ensure that they would be applicable to the local circumstances.[39]

London's concern was to uphold the integrity of British jurisdiction and maintain the basic Christian nature of this imperial outpost, not to create an enclave to train Chinese Celestials to become yellow Englishmen. The eventual creation in Hong Kong of a community that happily married the Confucian culture to Western capitalism and way of life, as well as embracing the Anglo-Saxon concept of the rule of law, was certainly not part of the British *raison d'etre* when it was founded as a colony.

Governance

Until Hong Kong was made a Crown Colony its administration was provided by a small cadre of assistants at the British Plenipotentiary's office. Since it was a product of the war, the initial costs of its governance were charged against the expedition and thus eventually covered by the Chinese through the reparation paid under the Treaty of Nanking.[40] Once a British possession it became the responsibility of the Colonial Office and thus a charge against British taxpayers since it could not generate sufficient income to cover its administrative costs in its formative years. As a result, Hong Kong was subjected to Treasury control. This meant its government had to submit its annual estimates to London every year before they could take effect or be put to the Legislative Council. This requirement was rigorously enforced until 1858, several years after Hong Kong ceased to receive a Treasury subvention.[41] In its early days, the Treasury was keen to hold its financial burden to the lowest level and thus required the colonial government to keep its expenses to a bare minimum.[42]

As a result, Hong Kong was used to having as small a government as possible, from its foundation. To put this in perspective, just prior to the

Second World War, a century after its foundation, the colonial government was still basically run, in addition to a few specialist officers in charge of medical services, public works and policing, by an establishment of merely 33 administrative officers filling 23 offices, with the balance being either on leave, under training or on secondment elsewhere.[43]

Being a small colony with a mixed population also affected the nature of the administration that was created in Hong Kong. The colony was scarcely more than a township in its first decade and the government would have little to do if it had handed over municipal responsibilities to a separate body. The Governor was therefore also its de facto mayor, though he was answerable to London rather than to an elected municipal council or to the local ratepayers.[44] Given the great gap that separated the Chinese from the European residents and the reluctance on the part of the colonial government to get involved in administering the Chinese community, the Hong Kong government at first focused its resources and attention on the much smaller European expatriate community. In its earliest days, governance was largely a matter of administering justice and the municipal services, as well as providing security and order for the small expatriate civilian residents who never exceeded a couple of percentage points of the total population.

The provision of civil administration to the majority of the people, the indigenous and fast-expanding immigrant Chinese residents, was not a matter of priority for the colonial government. In the early years, the primary concern of the British over the Chinese population, apart from whether they should be subjected to Chinese or British law, was to ensure they did not pose a major problem for security or public order.[45] It was not until 1845 that the government appointed a senior official, the Registrar General, to take responsibility for the Chinese community. The relative insignificance of this new office was reflected by its exclusion from membership of the Executive Council until 1883, four decades later.[46] As an office the Registrar General was renamed Secretary for Chinese Affairs in 1913, more accurately reflecting the nature of its responsibilities. It only acquired the modern-sounding new title of Secretary for Home Affairs in 1969, when it was finally accepted that it would no longer be appropriate to distinguish the expatriate from the local Chinese communities.[47]

What gradually developed into a pattern in the middle of the nineteenth century was that while the bulk of mundane government activities, such as the provision of sanitary facilities, policing and licensing, registration of births and deaths, as well as the collection of rates, taxes and other dues, in fact affected first and foremost the Chinese community, which constituted over 95% of the population, the colonial government focused disproportionately upon the views and interests of the expatriate community when it worked out its policies. Until a Chinese person, Sir Shouson Chow, was finally appointed as an unofficial member of the Executive Council in 1926, the Registrar General was the only member of the government whose responsibility it was to speak for and defend the interests of the Chinese community.

However disproportionately the colonial government might have devoted its attention and resources to the expatriate community, it also prevented the British expatriates from establishing themselves as any kind of elected oligarchy of ratepayers at the expense of the Chinese community by asserting their right to municipal self-government. Shortly after Hong Kong's foundation, the expatriates petitioned the British government for 'the formation of a Municipal Body, vested with the usual power of deciding on the appropriation of the monies raised for Local purposes'.[48] This was rejected, as London believed Hong Kong was 'different from any state of Society existing in this country or any British Colony'.[49]

Two basic problems applied to Hong Kong. First, 'it would be almost impossible to draw the line between Colonial and Municipal matters' where the colony and the municipality were practically co-extensive.[50] Furthermore, the colonial government was equally unwilling to allow the Chinese residents, who formed the overwhelming majority of ratepayers by the latter part of the nineteenth century, to dominate an elected municipal council as it was unprepared to let the expatriate community function as an oligarchy over the Chinese.[51]

The colonial government took it upon itself to provide what it believed to be a fair and equitable administration for both communities, though it did most of the time act on the unspoken but prevalent bias of the time.[52] What this meant in practice was that it responded first and foremost to the welfare and views of the expatriate community for the entire first century of British rule and continued to do so to a lesser extent even in the earlier part of the post-war period, though it also looked after the Chinese community paternalistically.

The somewhat haphazard start of the civil service in Hong Kong entered a new stage in 1861, when Governor Sir Hercules Robinson successfully introduced the Hong Kong Cadetship. This was intended to redress the clear anomaly where most senior colonial officials could not communicate with the overwhelming majority of the local population. This scheme was to 'supply the Civil Service in Hong Kong with an efficient staff of Interpreters', by recruiting young graduates from Britain to receive intensive training in Cantonese and written Chinese for two years, before deploying them on a fast track in the civil service.[53] It followed the introduction of a Civil Service Commission in Britain itself six years earlier for the recruitment of government officials on merit rather than by patronage, and a painful inquiry into the misconduct of Registrar General Daniel Caldwell, upon whom the colonial government had previously depended heavily in dealing with the local Chinese community.[54] It was not a scheme unique to Hong Kong, as it was introduced in parallel to a similar one for Ceylon and for the China Consular Service. In Hong Kong the experiment proved so successful that the cadets soon became the elite.

Cadet officers gradually and increasingly formed the backbone of the civil administration. Some rose not only to head the civil service as colonial secretaries, but a few also advanced further to take up gubernatorial offices in Hong Kong and in other colonies. Although administrative officers from other colonies, counterparts to the cadets, had also been transferred to Hong Kong, the bulk of the administrative service was always made up of Hong Kong cadets after 1861. The rise of the cadets gave the colonial bureaucracy its own character. It included a significant enhancement of the ability of senior policymakers to understand the views of the Chinese population, the predominance of the generalists, and a generally paternalistic though benevolent attitude in dealing with the local Chinese.

A major change that happened after the Second World War was the recruitment of ethnic Chinese into this small elitist service, which had previously been reserved for men of pure European descent. This relaxation of the colour bar was introduced slowly and was followed by the recruitment of women officers. They did not change the character, function or standing of the service. Cadets were eventually renamed Administrative Officers in the 1950s but they remained the elite of the civil service until the end of British rule.[55]

The Question of Representation

Endowed with a Crown Colony system, Hong Kong was not founded as a democracy but as an autocracy to serve British interests. Be that as it may, this was not on its own sufficient to prevent Hong Kong from following the example of other British dependencies in developing a representative government and eventually graduating into a self-governing and democratic dominion or nation within the framework of the British Commonwealth. Hong Kong did not make any significant progress in this direction during the first century of British rule, mainly because the question of representation proved intractable. The basic problem was rooted in Hong Kong's position as an imperial outpost at the edge of the Chinese Empire and the reality that it was populated overwhelmingly by hardworking and enterprising Chinese, who already constituted over 80 per cent of ratepayers as early as the mid-1850s, a decade after it became a British colony.[56]

There were two dimensions to the question of representation in the nineteenth century. The first concerns the representation of the Chinese community in the Legislative Council. The second involves the right of British taxpayers or ratepayers to be represented in a local council for the management of their own affairs. They were both separate issues and at the same time closely intertwined as a growing number of the Chinese population of Hong Kong were also British subjects by birth and were ratepayers, even though it was highly questionable whether all of them could or should be distinguished from other immigrant Chinese residents in their way of life, general attitude and focus of loyalty.

Although unofficial members were appointed to the Legislative Council as early as 1850, the issue of elected representation did not arise as an issue until it was raised by Governor Sir John Bowring in 1856. In an effort to strengthen the Council, he proposed to enfranchise 2,000 ratepayers, including among them ethnic Chinese, out of a population of 75,000, though membership of the Council was to be restricted to British subjects.[57] This was rejected by London. On the one hand, it did not believe the Chinese community would use the franchise responsibly. On the other hand, it deemed it invidious to restrict the franchise to transient expatriates and exclude the Chinese population since this would 'give power over the permanent population to temporary settlers, differing from them in race, language and religion, and not influenced by their opinions'.[58]

The actual selection of a Chinese person to the Legislative Council only came up in 1880, under the initiative of Governor Sir John Pope-Hennessy, who was seen by the expatriates as particularly pro-Chinese. Even on this occasion, when Pope-Hennessy picked Ng Choy (alias Wu Tingfang), a Chinese born in British Singapore, educated in England where he was called to the bar, and deemed by Chief Justice Sir John Smale as the most 'honourable and straightforward' gentleman in Hong Kong, it was met with some scepticism in the Colonial Office.[59] The main reservation voiced was simply that an ethnic Chinese member could not be trusted to keep a British secret from the Chinese authorities in the event of a breakdown in Anglo-Chinese relations.[60] In the end, the sceptics within the Colonial Office were overruled by the top official and ministers, who did not feel it right to reject the principle that the Queen's Chinese subjects should have a voice in the Council, and Ng appeared to be a particularly good candidate.[61] Consequently, London sanctioned Ng's temporary appointment but only as a reversible experiment.[62] Ng's service proved valuable and the appointment of an ethnic Chinese to the Legislative Council to represent the Chinese community thus became a general practice.[63]

The demand for elected representation in the Legislative Council finally came up in the 1890s, when the expatriate British community tried to assert control over government policy, particularly as related to expenditure. It culminated in a petition being made by 362 merchants, bankers and ratepayers to the House of Commons in 1894, in which they demanded 'the common right of Englishmen to manage their local affairs and control the Expenditure of the Colony, where Imperial considerations are not involved', mainly through the introduction of elected unofficial members to the Legislative Council.[64] This petition was dismissed by the British government since its apparent demand for representation was little more than a thinly veiled attempt to 'place the power in the hands of a select few, and to constitute a small oligarchy, restricted by the lines of race'.[65] This was indeed so: the petitioners in effect asked for no more than 800 white British male expatriates to be enfranchised out of a total population of 221,400, of whom 211,000 were ethnic Chinese.[66] As the Secretary of State, Lord Ripon, stated, this was objectionable since 'the well-being of the large majority of the inhabitants is more likely to be safeguarded by the Crown Colony system – under which, as far as possible no distinction is made of rank or race'.[67] Ripon's successor, Joseph Chamberlain, went further, observing that 'the Chinese community is the element which is least represented while it is also far the most numerous'. He expressed a desire 'to attach them more closely to the British connection, and to increase their practical interest in public affairs'.[68] Following Chamberlain's ruling, the colonial government increased the number of Chinese unofficial members in the Legislative Council by one, giving two of the six unofficial seats to this numerically largest community.

Appointing Chinese unofficial members of the Legislative Council was a fundamentally different issue from having elected ones. The former was acceptable to the British government, as the appointment system allowed for the selection of trusted and sound British subjects, an outcome that could not be guaranteed under popular elections. In other words, even had the Chinese British subjects of Hong Kong who were ratepayers pressed strongly for the election of one or more of their members to the Legislative Council in the nineteenth century, it would have been extremely unlikely that the governments of Hong Kong or of Britain would have accepted it.

The negative reactions of both the colonial and the imperial governments to the British expatriates' petition of 1894 set the tone for handling similar demands from the same community in the earlier part of the twentieth century.[69] They reflected two important strands of thinking. To begin with, once the Crown Colony system of government had settled in, both the colonial and the imperial governments gradually developed a sense of responsibility for the Chinese people of Hong Kong. Much as racial prejudice was inherent in the spirit of the time, British policymakers often found it awkward or unacceptable to defend or uphold in public a blatantly racist policy. Closely related was the acute recognition that the British expatriate community of Hong Kong was much more concerned with advancing their narrow and transient interests than that of either the colony as a whole or of British interests generally.[70]

This commitment on the part of the colonial and imperial government to protect the local Chinese from the narrow self-interest of the expatriate community did not mean the latter was in any way disadvantaged. Hong Kong was a British outpost to serve British interests and British voices carried greater weight in official circles. The colonial government merely resisted being turned into an instrument of local partisan interest in the way it handled the demands of the expatriate community for representation.

Chapter 3

Imperial Expansion

The British Empire went to war with China between 1839 and 1843 to secure economic benefits from trade and to redress what it saw as an unsatisfactory mode for the conduct of relations. The Treaty of Nanking (1843) was meant to fulfil these objectives for the British. Instead, the only truly concrete achievement the British obtained was to add Hong Kong to their Empire. The opening up of four coastal ports in addition to Canton did not, as the British had hoped, lead to a major expansion of trade and profit. The conduct of bilateral relations remained problematic as the British did not gain the right to station a diplomatic representative in the Chinese capital. The British Plenipotentiary and Superintendent of Trade did not even enjoy free and ready access to the Chinese Viceroy and Imperial Commissioner in Canton. Indeed, despite the provision in the English text of the Treaty, the British were denied entry to the city of Canton itself, though they were, in accordance with the Chinese text, allowed access to its port.[1] The opium trade, which was the immediate cause for the war, also remained contraband under Chinese law, though enforcement against it was deliberately lax. The state of economic and diplomatic affairs between the two empires left much to be desired from the British viewpoint, since their real objectives essentially remained unfulfilled.[2]

Another war was consequently fought between 1856 and 1860, which put trade and diplomatic relations between the two empires on a stable and sustainable basis. As had been the case in the original seizure of Hong Kong, this new war resulted in new territorial acquisition for the British. Hong Kong was expanded in 1860 to include a small area of the peninsula of Kowloon on the north shore of its harbour. This was not envisaged when hostilities started but occurred as a by-product.

The Second Anglo-Chinese War and the Acquisition of Kowloon

The failure of the Treaty of Nanking to deliver to the British Empire what it wanted resulted in increasing pressure for a revision of the terms of the treaty.[3] This proved problematic as the treaty itself had no provision for revision and the Chinese government saw no need for it.

Although the British did not have legal grounds to press for treaty revision, they raised the issue formally in 1854.[4] Specifically, they sought to open selected parts of the interior of China to trade; obtain the right to navigate the Yangtze River up to Nanjing; legalise the opium trade; avoid taxation on the transit of foreign goods imported to China or local products in transit between the point of purchase and the port for export; secure the right to diplomatic representation in Beijing and ready access to provincial governors where Britain had a consul; ensure cooperation in the suppression of piracy; and gain acceptance that the English text of the revised treaty would take precedence in the event of disputes.[5]

In its desire to open China, the British Empire enjoyed the support of other leading Western powers, particularly the French and the Americans. To the French, who trailed far behind the British in the China trade but were much more supportive of the evangelical efforts of their countrymen, higher priority was put on establishing proper diplomatic relations.[6] The United States of America, which alone among the Western powers was entitled under the Treaty of Wanghia (1844) to have its terms revised, by July 1856 felt the two most important issues were to secure diplomatic representation in Beijing and to extend American trade as far as possible all over China.[7] The Americans in fact went beyond the British demands in desiring 'a universal grant of freedom of opinion' and the opening of all China – not just specified ports – to trade.[8]

Whether Britain (or, for that matter, France or any European power) could have claimed, under the most favoured nation clause, the American right to treaty revision or not is legally dubious. When the law officers in the British government were consulted after hostilities started in 1857, they took the view that Britain was not legally entitled to do so.[9] However, the uncertain legality did not prevent Britain from continuing its policy to revise the terms of or replace the Treaty of Nanking with French and American backing.

After the Crimean War ended in 1856 and British resources and attention were no longer absorbed by it, senior British officials in the China region favoured a forward policy. The British Plenipotentiary and Governor of Hong Kong, Sir John Bowring, advocated a forceful display of naval might in order 'to extend and improve our relations with China'.[10] Less than two months prior to the *Arrow* incident that provided the occasion for a new war (see p.32), Bowring took the view that 'non-action is by far the most perilous policy, and that its perils will increase with time'.[11] His preference to do something was shared by the young and tempestuous Consul in Canton, Harry Parkes.[12] London, for its part, was actively consulting the French and the Americans to enlist them to support an attempt to persuade the Chinese to respond positively to the revision of the Treaty of Nanking.[13]

Closely linked to the issue of treaty revision was that of the right for the British to enter the city of Canton. The admission of the British to the city proved a particularly thorny problem as the local people had become strongly anti-British. This was the combined result of the British assaults on Canton in the First Anglo-Chinese War and, above all, the creation of the Sanyuanli myth by which the militia led by the local gentry, in contrast to the regular army, was supposed to have made such a gallant stand against the British that the latter became afraid of the militia. The growing myth of Sanyuanli encouraged the local Cantonese to be intransigent towards the British.[14] Since the Chinese officials in Guangdong 'realised that their continuation in office depended entirely on their ability to maintain good will of the leaders of local public opinion' they used every means available to deny the British entry to the city.[15]

The Chinese tactic of procrastination worked for over a decade mainly because the British government decided entry to the walled city itself was not worth a new war as trade continued at the port of Canton. Entry to the city nevertheless remained a major irritant in Anglo-Chinese relations, particularly during Bowring's tenure as he was keen to resolve this problem.[16]

In addition to the problem of British access to Canton city, personalities and differences over protocol for contact between British and Chinese officials continued to make relations between them tense, difficult, distrustful and unfriendly. In spite of the Treaty of Nanking, not all successive British Plenipotentiaries and Consuls in Canton established good working relations with the Chinese Viceroy and other senior Chinese officials in Canton.

The situation reached a low point in the mid 1850s after Bowring was promoted from Consul in Canton to be Plenipotentiary and Governor of Hong Kong, and was succeeded by Parkes. When he first took up his office in Canton in 1849, Bowring had a bad start. Having had a parliamentary career and an audience with Queen Victoria before departing for China, he considered himself a man of some standing despite his modest rank as a Consul. He also had a rather poor understanding of the Chinese bureaucracy, although he thought he understood it. Upon arrival in Canton, Bowring asked to be greeted by an official senior to the provincial Treasurer who had received his predecessor, though he also mistakenly nominated officials junior to the Treasurer for this purpose. Since the next senior Chinese official to the Treasurer was the provincial Governor, his request was declined. An official junior to the ones Bowring nominated was appointed to play host to him, which he regarded as a deliberate insult, happening as it did at the time when the Chinese successfully made a strong stand against the British demand for access to the city.[17] Bowring thus developed a strong dislike of Chinese officialdom and an obsession over the issue of access to the city, which deeply affected his judgement after his promotion to Hong Kong.[18] Parkes, Bowring's successor in Canton, was only 28 in 1856. He was disposed to take an aggressive approach, believing that 'the only way of avoiding trouble with the Chinese was to stand firm from the start on every part of one's rights, significant or insignificant'.[19]

On the Chinese side, Bowring's opposite number in Canton, Viceroy and Imperial Commissioner Ye Mingchen had, for his part, 'imbibed a thorough distrust of foreigners from his initial contacts with them in 1847'.[20] His negotiating style was that of defending firmly all matters he deemed to be of basic importance, such as not allowing the British to gain access to the city, behind a veneer of politeness.[21] To the restless British, his approach reinforced the stereotypical image of the inscrutable Chinese mandarin. Thus, in the middle of the 1850s, senior British and Chinese officials in the Canton region did not have the mutual understanding, trust and good working relationship needed to defuse a major crisis even if either or both sides wished to do so.

Against this background, in early October 1856, the detention by the Chinese authorities in the harbour of Canton of a *lorcha*, the *Arrow*, quickly escalated into a major incident and the immediate cause for a new war. This Chinese-built lorcha – a ship with a European shape hull and Chinese rig – was owned by a Chinese, who had registered it in Hong Kong in order to enjoy the protection of the British flag but was not legally entitled to such protection at the time as its registration had already expired, albeit for only 11 days. There is much controversy over what exactly happened. Parkes claimed at the time that the British flag was flying aboard but was hauled down by Chinese officers while the ship's Chinese crew of 12 was arrested 'regardless of the remonstrance of' the British master, and thus constituted 'an insult of very grave character'.[22] This assertion has been challenged by recent research, which suggests no British flag could have been flying on board and therefore no insult to it could have happened.[23]

Whatever actually happened at the *Arrow* and the original intention of the Chinese authorities, the incident was seized on by Parkes and Bowring to pursue a forward policy which they were already contemplating. In their efforts to seek redress, neither was prepared to give the Chinese authorities much scope to work out an amicable settlement.[24] Indeed, a week after the incident started, Bowring told Parkes that 'we have now a stepping stone from which with good management we may move on to important sequences', the first of which was British access to the walled city.[25]

For his part, Ye failed to grasp the real significance of the aggressive British overtures.[26] He thus left Bowring and Parkes with great scope to incite feelings on the British side, persuade the British government to sanction and support the hostile actions they had already taken against the Chinese, including the bombardment of Canton, and turn a minor incident into the immediate cause of a new war.

Although the prospect of war with China was highly controversial in London, the British government under Palmerston endorsed Bowring's actions. It was partly because Palmerston believed the British flag was insulted, which required redress for the prestige of the Empire, and partly because he wished to use this incident to seek a full revision of the Treaty of Nanking.[27] This did not mean he accepted Bowring's case and gave the latter carte blanche; rather, Palmerston was aware of Bowring's shortcomings. He appointed the Eighth Earl of Elgin Plenipotentiary in March 1857 to take over from Bowring responsibilities for the military and diplomatic operations in China with a view to securing a new and satisfactory treaty.[28] Elgin was given additional forces of some 2,500 troops and was instructed to cooperate with his French and American colleagues in China to pursue various objectives.

France was at that time an empire under Napoleon III, aggressively pursuing imperial glory. The French agreed to join the British, and ordered an expeditionary force to Hong Kong under their own Plenipotentiary, Baron Gros. The French pretext was to avenge the execution by the Chinese of a French missionary, Père Chapdelaine, in Guangxi province earlier in the year. Although the Americans also desired treaty revision they were not prepared to join the British in the use of force.[29]

Elgin was given the task of seeking from the Chinese government reparations for injuries to and compensation for losses incurred by British subjects in the hostilities that followed the *Arrow* incident, full implementation of treaties signed, full diplomatic representation at the Emperor's court in Beijing, and a revision of existing treaties to expand trade to other Chinese ports and cities, both coastal and along inland waterways.[30] In order to secure these terms, London did not share Bowring's focus upon Canton and instructed Elgin to threaten Beijing, stressing the occupation of part of Canton should be the last resort. The British government was interested not in settling scores with Ye and the Canton authorities, although Bowring was keen, but in furthering British diplomatic and above all commercial interests.

Although Elgin arrived in Hong Kong in July 1857, he was not in a position to force China's hand, as the Indian Mutiny had broken out in the meantime and he had ordered most of his army units to India to meet the military exigency.[31] Indeed it was this Chinese expeditionary army that relieved the beleaguered British garrisons and communities in Lucknow and Cawnpore.[32] This redeployment of the army and slow deployment of the French forces meant only local naval operations were conducted from Hong Kong for much of the rest of the year.[33] It was not until December, when it was clear that the Indian Mutiny would continue to tie down most army units and he would not have the forces required to impose his demands on the Chinese government near Beijing, that Elgin decided to attack Canton. This was duly achieved before the end of the year by the combined Anglo-French force of just over 5,000 marines and armed sailors. Canton was occupied and the old issue of entry forcefully resolved. The city came to be administered by an Allied Commission that superimposed itself upon the Chinese bureaucracy for three years.

It was April 1858 when Elgin found himself in a position to launch an expedition north to force Emperor Xianfeng's hand. Still without an army, the Anglo-French fleet bombarded the Dagu Forts outside Tianjin and forced the Chinese government to negotiate. Under the Treaty of Tientsin (1858), the Chinese agreed to all the major British demands, including the opening of more ports, navigation up the Yangtze, legalisation of the opium trade and diplomatic representation in Beijing. However, despite the terms of the treaty, the Emperor had no intention of accepting either a resident British Minister or the exchange of ratification in the imperial capital with a British delegation protected by more than ten armed guards.[34]

When the time for ratification came in 1859, Elgin had returned for England and handed over his responsibilities to his younger brother, Frederick Bruce, who had served as his deputy. It was upon Bruce's appointment as Minister to China that the diplomatic office previously combined with the Governorship of Hong Kong was separated for good. Once Bowring realised that half of his responsibilities would be taken from him on a permanent basis he preferred retirement. From this point onward, the Governor of Hong Kong no longer had responsibilities for Britain's relations with China. Although Bruce sailed north with a modest fleet intending to display Western naval superiority, he did not expect armed resistance.

As it turned out, Emperor Xianfeng had ordered the Mongolian General Senggelinqin, who had built up a considerable reputation in suppressing the Taiping rebels, to take charge of the defence of the Beijing-Tianjin region, and required the Western envoys to travel to Beijing not on board their warships but on land and without their instruments of war.[35] Bruce, his French colleague, and his naval commander chose to force their way up the Beihe River to Beijing and met with fierce resistance at the re-fortified Dagu Forts. On this occasion the troops under Senggelinqin's command used their artillery effectively against the small landing force and the 11 gunboats that could navigate the shallow estuary, sinking, destroying or otherwise disabling half the steamships and causing almost 1,000 British and French casualties.[36]

The British reaction to this unexpected defeat, which was seen to have undesirable implications for the prestige of its empire, was strong and forceful. With the Indian Mutiny now suppressed, a land force of 16,500 and some 70 warships, supported by 7,600 French and other support ships were put at the disposal of Elgin who had again been appointed Plenipotentiary to take charge.[37]

In the summer of 1860, Elgin returned to north China with the greatest force Britain and France ever assembled in this part of the world. He outflanked the Dagu defenders and captured the forts without a costly frontal naval assault, occupied Beijing and razed the magnificent Yuanmingyuan Palace to the ground until the Treaty of Tientsin was ratified and an additional peace treaty, the Convention of Peking, was signed. The French also signed parallel peace treaties with the Chinese.

In imposing these peace treaties, which would form the basis of what came to be known as the treaty system in China, the British Empire was determined to get what it wanted and at the lowest cost. Now that the Chinese Empire had been shocked to its foundation, it became possible for the British to feel confident that the treaty system would be enforced.[38] This was to be achieved by the stationing in Beijing of a resident Minister by Britain (and other Western powers) and the creation by the Chinese of an office for foreign affairs, known as the Zongli Yamen.

Britain intended to maintain itself as the dominant power in China, maximise its trading and economic advantages in the whole country, and thus guarded carefully against the prospect of a partition. The unity of China under its central government was therefore highly valued. As a result the British sought to secure the authority of the Chinese Emperor against any untoward ambitions of other Western powers, particularly France, and subsequently against the Taiping and other rebels within China.[39] The British had no intention of turning China into a second India in light of the enormous costs involved in its administration. The British policy was a classic manifestation of what has since been described as the imperialism of free trade.[40]

It was in the course of this conflict – and as a sideshow – that the British Empire took over the tip of the mainland opposite the island of Hong Kong known as Kowloon. After the British occupied Canton at the end of 1857, Sir Charles van Straubenzee, Major-General in command of the land forces there, took the lead to advocate its annexation. The main consideration was to enhance the security of the colony, though the Chinese garrison in Kowloon posed no threat. The objective was to pre-empt the taking of Kowloon, on the northern side of Hong Kong's magnificent Victoria Harbour, by another Western power which could fortify the place and pose a threat to the British colony and shipping.[41]

Van Straubenzee's recommendation was supported by Governor Bowring and endorsed by London. However, when London finally gave its approval, the Treaty of Tientsin had already been concluded. Up to this stage the annexation was merely a desirable additional objective but had little real significance for British interests. Once the Dagu debacle led to the massive deployment of forces to Hong Kong in preparation for a major assault on China, the flat land of Kowloon proved valuable training and resting ground for the reinforcements. The tip of this peninsula was thus occupied by the British. Thereupon, in March 1860, Consul Parkes secured from the Acting Viceroy in Canton, while the city was still under Allied occupation, a lease for Kowloon in return for an annual rent of 500 silver dollars.

This lease was converted into permanent cession and incorporated into Article VI of the Convention of Peking (1860), and the extension of British jurisdiction formally came into effect by the issue of a Royal Order in Council on 4 February 1861.[42] The area concerned included the land south of what today are Boundary Street and Stonecutter's Island and amounted to about 4.3 square miles.

In sanctioning this expansion, Foreign Secretary Lord Russell made it clear to Elgin that while the annexation 'would undoubtedly be a great convenience as far as the interests of Her Majesty's Colony of Hongkong are concerned... if it were to form a precedent for a demand of a corresponding concession on the part of any other Powers in some other quarter, the convenience would be too dearly purchased'.[43] While the British behaved in a classic imperialist manner, their priority was not territorial expansion. What they were really after was to secure the wider economic interests to be derived from trading with China as a whole. This small piece of land was taken because it was desirable from the point of view of the British colonists and the local commander and it could be acquired at minimal cost.

What was truly remarkable was not the opportunistic British expansion but the readiness of the Chinese government to accept this further territorial cession. Unlike in the 1840s, on this occasion the Chief Chinese negotiator, Prince Gong, meekly accepted Elgin's demand, added as it were at the last moment when the Convention of Peking was being finalised.[44] Gong and Emperor Xianfeng, who had himself fled from the capital, had little choice. In October 1860, the survival of Manchurian rule in China was hanging in the balance, with Elgin in a stronger position to tip the balance than the Emperor himself.[45] The old arrogance of the Celestial Empire had to give way to a more sober assessment of the political reality. The enlargement of Hong Kong was an incidental issue in this wider scheme of war and peace settlement.

The New Territories

Over the remainder of the nineteenth century, the power of the British Empire reached its zenith. It was powerful, serene and self-confident. Although the British government had no further territorial ambition, local agitation for further expansion quickly followed. In 1863, some people advised building a battery on land that still belonged to China on the northern shore of the harbour's eastern approach.[46] In the 1880s and 1890s, successive commanders of the local garrison urged the War Office to acquire the entire peninsula of Kowloon for military purposes. Sir Paul Chater, a leading local advocate for expansion, summed up the thinking behind this:

> The same arguments that prevailed in 1860 must prevail now. We want now only what we wanted then: what is essential to the safety of the Colony. What was enough then, has become from the changes in weapons and the alterations in modes of warfare wholly insufficient now, and we must have more.[47]

They enjoyed the support of Sir William Robinson, who was Governor from 1891 to 1898.[48] Although China was clearly in no position to pose a military threat, local advocates for expansion nevertheless laid heavy emphasis on hypothetical defensive requirements.

There were other grounds for local agitation for expansion. Most were utterly trivial, such as a need for more land and open space on which to exercise troops, or for cemeteries and barracks. A real driving force was the land speculators' urge to make profits. The British Minister to China, Sir Claude MacDonald, observed in 1898 that '[m]any of the Colonists have been for years past buying up ground on the Kowloon promontory and adjacent islands as a speculation on the chance of our getting what we are now more or less on the point of getting'.[49] It was not a coincidence that the most vocal advocates of expansion, Chater and several of the local Navy League's prominent members, were leading land developers or speculators. They had vested interests in extension.

Until the beginning of 1898, London resisted expansion on the grounds that it worked against Britain's basic interests in China, which was economic. Although only 1.5 per cent of its exports that year went to China, Britain's share of China's trade was larger than that of the rest of the world combined.[50] Almost 62 per cent of China's external trade was with Britain. It was therefore in Britain's interests to keep China as a whole open to free trade. This would prevent European powers dividing it into imperial possessions, as had happened in Africa. This explains why, as late as January 1898, the British government stressed that the 'integrity and independence of China... may be considered to be the cardinal base of our policy... We are opposed to the alienation of any portion of Chinese territory, or the sacrifice of any part of Chinese independence'.[51] Britain also generally carried great weight with the Chinese government, so keeping an 'open door' in China best served its interests.

The change in British policy in 1898 resulted from developments the British were powerless to stop. The chain of events started with the exposure of the full extent of the Chinese Empire's weakness when Japan defeated it in a war over Korea, a Chinese vassal, between 1894 and 1895. Unlike Europe's great powers, Japan was an oriental country. It was forced open to the West by the US Navy only in 1853. Many were therefore surprised by China's inability to hold its own against Japan. It tempted various European powers with imperialist pretensions to turn their attentions to China. The aggressiveness of the Japanese demand for large territorial cessions under the Treaty of Simonoseki (1895), including Taiwan, the Pescadores islands and the Liaodong peninsula in southern Manchuria, prompted Russia, Germany and France to interfere. They forced the Japanese to return Liaodong (with its ice-free ports that Russia coveted) to China in exchange for vastly increased reparations paid by the Chinese. Behind their protestations of friendship and support, these powers were seeking to establish territorial bases in China at its time of weakness.[52] Their actions set an example to other powers. From 1898 to 1899, various countries joined in the scramble for concessions from China. They were afraid of being excluded in the event of the Chinese Empire facing the same fate as Africa.

The British government initially responded by declaring that Britain did 'not regard China as a place for conquest or acquisition by any European Power' but 'the most hopeful place' for the commerce of Britain and the world at large.[53] Despite several attempts, including the offer of an alliance, Britain failed to persuade Germany to abandon its territorial ambition.[54] Instead, the Kaiser's government used the killing of two German missionaries in November 1897 as a pretext to occupy Jiaozhou (now part of Qingdao) on the southern side of the Shandong promontory in north China. By March 1898, the Germans had imposed a treaty on the hapless Chinese and had leased Jiaozhou for 99 years.

Britain was equally unsuccessful in preventing Russia from taking over the ice-free ports of Lushun (Port Arthur) and Dalien in the Liaodong peninsula. Russia followed the German example and occupied the ports in December 1897. In March 1898, the Russians forced the Chinese to lease the two ports for 25 years.

British diplomacy's attempt to maintain the 'open door' in China achieved only two tangible results. These were to guarantee equal trading rights for everyone in all foreign-controlled Chinese ports and to substitute outright annexation for long leases.

Unable to prevent Russia and Germany from pursuing their territorial ambitions, Britain tried to counter them by leasing the port of Weihaiwei from China for as long as Russia occupied Lushun.[55] Britain chose Weihaiwei because it was the only port of any significance remaining on the coast of north China whose occupation could be seen as a counterpoise to restore British prestige and pre-eminence.[56] It is on the north side of the Shandong promontory, directly opposite Lushun and Dalien across the Gulf of Bohai and to the north-east of Jiaozhou.

This turn of events marked a major adaptation of the policy to uphold China's territorial integrity. The British government still insisted that it 'desired neither territorial acquisition in China nor even the extension of British influence in the Chinese government beyond such extensions and such influences as may be necessary for the protection and maintenance of [its] commercial position in China'. Nonetheless, it accepted the existence in China of foreign, including British, 'spheres of interest'.[57] This change was to 'preserve in an age of competition' what Britain 'had gained in an age of monopoly'.[58] It also marked the end of London's resistance to the colonists' demands to extend Hong Kong.

The French acquisition, again by a 99-year lease, of Canton Bay (now Zhanjiang), 210 miles south-west of Hong Kong, provided an immediate reason to expand.[59] The French also tried to get the Chinese to agree not to alienate certain provinces to other powers, including that of Guangdong, of which Hong Kong was originally a part. This alarmed the British.[60] The old hypothetical arguments about defence suddenly seemed relevant, for the French could turn out to be an enemy of a completely different sort from the Chinese. Britain's response was to seek to extend Hong Kong.

The area concerned was the rest of the Kowloon peninsula south of the Shenzhen River and 230 surrounding islands, a total area of about 370 square miles. This was ten times the size of the colony at the time and came to be known as the New Territories once it came under British rule.

Though defence was the only argument the British put forward for the extension, the defensive requirements remained more hypothetical than real. The long-established enmity towards and imperial competition with France helped the expansionists' cause. However, at the turn of the century, neither France nor any other power posed a military threat to Hong Kong. Indeed, after the British secured the New Territories lease, they failed to take possession for ten months. Also, British forces built no significant fortifications in the New Territories for decades. The acquisition was naked imperial expansion.

An Appointment with China

The Minister in Beijing, Sir Claude MacDonald, represented Britain at the negotiations. Veteran diplomat and reformer Li Hongzhang led the Chinese team. MacDonald was anxious not to hasten the dismemberment of China and saw it in Britain's interest to ask for only enough to cover the defence of Hong Kong.[61] Once the negotiations opened in early April 1898, the parties quickly reached an agreement in principle. The whole process took two months. The Chinese were in no position to resist. For them it was a matter of minimising the losses. They formally signed the second Convention of Peking on 9 June and it came into effect on 1 July.

Negotiators from both sides shared an important common ground. They wanted to prevent other powers seizing on the extension of Hong Kong to demand further territorial concessions from China. Thus, while the negotiations were tough, given the circumstances, they took place in a remarkable atmosphere of cooperation. Both sides proceeded expeditiously.

Although the Chinese fought their corner hard against all major British demands, they yielded almost immediately to the basic principle of Hong Kong's extension. What they tried to secure were above all the non-permanent cession of any territory and the retention of the symbol of Chinese sovereignty.[62] The Chinese negotiators were influenced by the emergence of nationalism as a political force, which, in turn, was a response to the imperialist encroachments on Chinese sovereignty in the preceding decades. A significant component of this new nationalist approach was 'a willingness to make heavy financial sacrifices in order to curtail even theoretical infringements on Chinese sovereignty'.[63] The Chinese manifested this by insisting on the New Territories being leased for a specific period only. They also insisted that China retain the fort of Kowloon near its southern tip and that Chinese officials keep their right of free access to the fort. Though the question of paying rent arose, the negotiators later dropped it because the Chinese wanted to avoid being accused of selling off their country's sacred territories.[64] The Chinese also wanted to protect their customs revenues, but did not insist on retaining customs collection houses in the New Territories. Mistakenly, they relied instead on a British promise not to use the territory to the detriment of Chinese interests.[65] As it turned out, the Hong Kong government subsequently prevented the Chinese maritime customs from operating within the New Territories. However, the Chinese negotiators' main endeavours were basically successful.

The Chinese managed to minimise their losses partly because the British were keen to wrap up the negotiations quickly. It was also because MacDonald and, to a lesser extent, his government were so confident of British supremacy that they signed the agreement before tying up all the loose ends. In an important sense, the British saw the preservation of various Chinese rights merely as a matter of detail.

The British fairly readily accepted the Chinese position that the instrument for transferring the New Territories should be a 99-year lease.

MacDonald merely deemed it a permanent cession in disguise.[66] From London's point of view, it accepted a lease 'so as to follow the example of Germany and Russia, and to avoid accusations of going one better and beginning the break up of China'.[67] The negotiations did not properly consider the long-term future status of the colony and the implications for British jurisdiction. Indeed, when the question of jurisdiction came up later, the Secretary of State for the Colonies, Joseph Chamberlain, simply pronounced that the New Territories should 'be treated as an integral part of the colony'.[68] He did not take seriously the prospect that China might reform itself sufficiently to build up the necessary strength to enforce the lease and recover the territory in due course. This was nevertheless the observation that Chater, the leading local expansionist, made in 1894. He warned that in a few decades China might turn itself into 'a powerful nation fully armed and with the skill and knowledge that [would] enable her to make use of her vast strength' to pose a threat to British Hong Kong.[69] In the era of Rule Britannia, Britain dismissed the idea that China could ever pose a challenge to the might of the British Empire – too readily in retrospect.

Other important provisions the Chinese insisted on including in the agreement concerned the fort of Kowloon and the right of access by Chinese officials. The fort had a population of 744, of whom 544 were serving military personnel under the command of a colonel. The remaining civilians were either in the employ of the Chinese government or were dependent on the military.[70] It was not a city in any real sense. However, as a result of poor translation, it has since generally become known as the 'walled city of Kowloon'. The 1898 Convention states that 'the Chinese officials now stationed there shall continue to exercise jurisdiction except so far as may be inconsistent with the military requirements for the defence of Hong Kong'. It also states that 'Chinese officials and people shall be allowed as heretofore to use the road from Kowloon to Hsinan [Xinan]'.[71] It was absurd that Britain should extend the colony to improve its defence but permit the Chinese to maintain a fort in the New Territories. The Chinese had built the fort in 1846–7 specifically to counter the British presence in Hong Kong.[72] It was equally ridiculous for the Convention to provide 'that the existing landing-place near Kowloon city shall be reserved for the convenience of Chinese men-of-war, merchant and passenger vessels, which may come and go and lie there at their pleasure'. It also stated that 'Chinese vessels of war, whether neutral or otherwise, shall retain the right to use' Deep Bay and Mirs Bay, which the Chinese also leased to the British.[73]

At that time, the British obviously did not regard these Chinese reservations as major problems. Hong Kong's colonial secretary, James Stewart Lockhart, who conducted a survey of the territory prior to the British takeover, considered the fort an issue that would resolve itself. He believed that the functions of the fort lay primarily in keeping public order in its vicinity and expected the garrison to be 'disbanded or transferred elsewhere'.[74] In a similar vein, MacDonald thought it was 'not to be supposed that the city of Kowloon will remain outside British jurisdiction with the surrounding district subject to it'.[75] MacDonald also took an offhand view about the Chinese navy's right of access to the jetties adjacent to the fort, to Deep Bay and to Mirs Bay.[76] With regard to the exact boundary of the New Territories, MacDonald and the British government were content that they be 'fixed when proper surveys have been made'.[77] The British were so confident of their own dominance that they were certain such an arrangement could not harm their interests.

Although the Convention forms the basis of the leasehold, the authority for the extension of British jurisdiction comes from a different instrument, the Royal Order in Council of 20 October 1898. By this order, the New Territories were made 'part and parcel of Her Majesty's Colony of Hong Kong in like manner and for all intents and purposes as if they had originally formed part of the said Colony'.[78] The duration of this extension of jurisdiction was, however, limited to the period 'during the continuance of the said lease'.[79] Under British law, British jurisdiction would expire by midnight on 30 June 1997, unless this stipulation were superseded. The British formally took possession of and exercised jurisdiction in the New Territories on 16 April 1899. This was the last territorial extension of Hong Kong under British rule.

In the short term, the Convention was a diplomatic triumph. It gave Britain what it wanted at no cost and did not damage its relations with China or the other powers. MacDonald negotiated it with a cavalier attitude. He initiated the negotiations without an up-to-date map and was happy to proceed with only a general idea of the extent of the territory he demanded for his government.[80] Arrogance characterised Britain's handling of the negotiations. In the long term and in retrospect, the Convention must be seen as a major blunder for British diplomacy. As a treaty, it had left far too many important issues with significant implications unresolved. In time, they would haunt the British and raise questions about the long-term future of even the original colony of Hong Kong.

Whatever assumptions MacDonald and his colleagues in London and Hong Kong might have made about the 99-year lease, by signing the Convention they had made an appointment with China. Like other appointments, it could be overtaken by events, nullified, ignored, cancelled, altered, forgotten or kept. Unique among the several leases of territories which the Chinese Empire was forced to concede in the 1890s, the lease for the New Territories ran its full course. This appointment Britain made with China would be kept at midnight on 30 June 1997 with consequences deemed unthinkable by MacDonald and his colleagues.

Part II

The Heyday of Imperial Rule

Chapter 4

Law and Justice

The eventual creation in Hong Kong of a model of British justice in Asia, admired for its rule of law and independent judiciary, does not mean the colony had always justifiably enjoyed such a high reputation. In fact in the early days of British rule the administration of justice was problematic, and the introduction of the rule of law was not without its deficiencies.

Hong Kong was founded at a time when disorder and social upheaval prevailed in China. When it was taken over by the British, the island was merely a peripheral part of the Xinan county.[1] Although it fell into an area nominally supervised by the Assistant Magistrate of Guanfu, who could call upon the service of two archers when needed, it really did not have in place a formal local government.[2] What the British had to do was to create from scratch a legal and judicial system in a society constituted by British and other Western adventurers as well as poor and mostly uneducated labourers from the fringe of Chinese society.

Not a settlement colony, Hong Kong started with merely a few hundred civilian British persons of whom only a few had legal qualifications or any strong sense of civic responsibility to this transient community. It was not surprising, therefore, that the quality of justice that the British expatriates, whether as law officers or as jurors, could deliver in the 1840s left much to be desired.

Equally, having inherited a local population of several thousand, mostly farmers and fishermen, in a remote part of the Chinese Empire, the island communities of Hong Kong boasted few, if any, scholars or retired officials who might constitute the local gentry and an established elite, as was the prevailing pattern in much of China proper.[3] Such local leadership as existed in the scattered villages on the island did not provide a ready pool of collaborators for the British, who established their right to rule by conquest and in any event focused their attention on building a new town on the north shore rather than at the main villages.

The original Chinese residents of Hong Kong became British subjects under British law once the Treaty of Nanking was ratified. However, in reality neither they nor the British administration took this seriously. With a steady and growing influx of Chinese immigrants, the distinction between the original Queen's Chinese subjects and new Chinese settlers became blurred.[4] The failure to maintain a clear distinction between these two groups was not due to lack of political will alone; practical considerations also contributed. Given the small indigenous population base, the need for cheap labour for the building of the new city of Victoria, and the desire to attract Chinese traders, Hong Kong had to open its doors widely to Chinese workers and businessmen. Since few Chinese intended to settle in this British enclave and merely went there for work, to make profit or seek temporary asylum from disorders at home, the bulk of the Chinese population was inevitably transient in nature. They quickly and increasingly swamped the original residents, and their migratory habits made them ineligible for consideration as British subjects.

With a highly limited ability to distinguish one Chinese from another, the colonial government made no attempt to treat the two groups of Chinese differently. To the original Queen's Chinese subjects, who spoke no English and had nothing to do with the British expatriates unless they started to work for the latter as servants or had a brush with the law, the technical change in their nationality was largely irrelevant even if they had been duly informed of it. In the administration of justice in early Hong Kong they hardly enjoyed any advantage in comparison to other Chinese immigrant workers. It did not take long for the original Queen's Chinese subjects as a distinctive group to fade out in usage; for all practical purposes they quickly merged with the rest of the Chinese community.

In Hong Kong's formative years there were two particularly pressing issues for the British authorities to address. The first was to decide on whether the local Chinese inhabitants should be subjected to the full force of British law or be allowed to be governed under Chinese law and customs. The second was to build up a machinery for the administration of law and justice. The rule of law was a concept taken for granted by the British but its implementation was affected by local conditions. They included the prevalence of racism, bigotry based on a sense of racial and cultural superiority among the British expatriates, as well as conflict of interest and other inadequacies inherent in a small transient trading community being required to furnish the resources required, such as sufficient number of jurors and interpreters, for the British judicial system to function in a colony overwhelmingly inhabited by people of a different heritage.

Native Laws and Customs

The existence of a long gap between Hong Kong coming under British occupation in 1841 and its formal foundation as a Crown Colony meant that, for a period of about two years, Hong Kong was under British rule before important issues like the appropriate form of government and the judicial system were settled. The British government's disallowance of the initial proclamation by Elliot that the local Chinese should be 'governed according to the laws and customs of China, every description of torture excepted' did not put an end to this issue.[5] The unsettled nature of the future of Hong Kong and the continuation of hostilities between the two empires until the Treaty of Nanking was signed meant much debate continued on this matter.

In the end, the British decided that the local Chinese should be permitted to be governed by local customs and law in so far as possible, provided this would not infringe upon Hong Kong's status as a British colony, with no distinction being given to visitors and the original Queen's Chinese subjects. In setting up British jurisdiction, Pottinger was finally instructed that while English law should in general prevail, following the model applied in British India, and no English law 'shall be in force which may be inapplicable to the local circumstances of the Colony or of its inhabitants'.[6] This sanction for the application of Chinese law and customs to Chinese inhabitants was clearly limited, however. It must not in any way 'derogate the Queen's sovereignty' or be applied over 'the right of succession to immovable property'. Furthermore, 'if there be any Chinese law repugnant to those immutable principles of morality which the Christians must regard as binding on themselves at all times and in all places, the enforcement of any such law even against the Chinese must not be permitted within the Queen's dominions'.[7]

In practice a limited application of Chinese law and customs was allowed in recognition of the great cultural differences between the Chinese and British people.[8] Although this was originally a well-intentioned concession, it often resulted in much harsher punishments being meted out to Chinese than to European residents. In those days, there was a widespread belief that the Chinese were not deterred from crimes by 'lenient' British criminal justice. There also existed a sense of racial and cultural superiority among the British expatriates. As a result few questions were asked when Chinese were routinely punished in manners that would have caused an uproar if applied to Caucasians.[9]

Administration of Justice

In the nineteenth century, there was arbitrariness and serious deficiencies in the administration of justice in Hong Kong.[10] Indeed, a body of 'anti-Chinese legislation' existed and was enforced.[11] In general terms, Chinese residents were singled out and subjected to laws, regulations and punishments that were not imposed on Caucasian residents. They were discriminated against with regard to personal movement. They also suffered more from the low standard of justice administered, particularly in the magistracy, than the expatriates who generally could afford to appeal against any unfair ruling.

Among the most popular punishments summarily imposed on Chinese men only was having their queues (the then mandatory hairstyle imposed by imperial edict of the Manchu Emperor) cut off and then expelled for no greater offence than loitering or failing to carry a ticket of registration. This may appear a trivial matter in the twenty-first century, but it was a serious punishment for Chinese men in the 1840s, as it exposed them to further punishment.[12] As they were routinely handed back to the Chinese authorities, which the British considered corrupt, abusive and brutal, those punished were further put under the tender mercy of the latter. In addition, only Chinese offenders in Hong Kong could be required to wear a *cangue*, 'a large square wooden frame fastened around the neck to prevent the wearer from resting'.[13]

Equally discriminatory was the public flogging of Chinese for petty offences. Floggings were regularly meted out on the basis of the mostly summary and sometimes arbitrary process administered by a police magistrate or justice of the peace. In the mid 1840s, flogging was so widespread that it happened almost daily and it was not unknown for 54 men to be caned in one day.[14] In contrast, corporal punishment would not normally be imposed on a European without the due process having run its course in the Supreme Court. Even then its actual administration was not assured as the public flogging of one of their number in the presence of Chinese was, for example, deemed to undermine the prestige of the white race.[15] Equality in the face of the law across ethnic lines was not always upheld in nineteenth-century Hong Kong.

Various local ordinances also discriminated against the Chinese by imposing regulations and restrictions on them that were not required of non-Chinese residents. Although many of them were also class based, as the Chinese generally occupied the lower strata of the society and worked in menial occupations that no European would take, the racial overtone was unmistakable. Many of these requirements were petty, such as subjecting chair bearers and rickshaw pullers to regulation, since only Chinese persons would be engaged in such work.[16] However, a few restrictions were much more serious. In 1844, Chinese inhabitants were subjected to registration and obliged to carry a registration ticket following the start of the Second Anglo-Chinese War.[17] In 1857, they were further required to carry night passes. Should one be caught between eight in the evening and sunrise the following day without such a pass 'elsewhere than in his own Habitation', he could be 'summarily punished' by fine, imprisonment, public flogging or exposure in the stock.[18] This was subsequently augmented by a requirement for Chinese persons to carry a lighted lantern after dark. The night pass requirement was not repealed until 1897.

In addition to restrictions being put on their movements, the Chinese came to be excluded from living wherever they chose. By the European District Preservation Ordinance of 1888, 'a certain portion of the Town' was reserved officially 'not for exclusively European occupation, but for houses built according to European models and occupied in much more limited numbers than is usual with Chinese'.[19] Despite the official disclaimer, the intention was clearly to exclude the Chinese from what were deemed European parts of Hong Kong, even though the two communities had, hitherto in any event, largely chosen to live in separate areas. The racially exclusive overtone became clear with the passing of the Peak Preservation Ordinance in 1904, which specifically reserved the Peak, often compared to the Caucasian retreat of Simla in India, as a residential area for expatriates.[20] Before the Pacific War, the only Chinese family that was given the privilege to live at the Peak was that of Sir

Robert Hotung. Hotung was in fact Eurasian, though he 'adopted the manners, deportment, and costume of a Chinese gentleman and did not seek to pass as a European'.[21] He was reputedly the wealthiest man in Hong Kong in the first half of the twentieth century, and was sufficiently well regarded to be among the first Chinese to be knighted.[22] Making an exception for him and his family hardly amounted to a breach of the colour bar. The existence of restrictions against the Chinese from living at the Peak, which was later augmented by a section of the island of Cheung Chau, was only removed in 1946 after the Second World War.[23]

The Chinese community also suffered a disproportionate share of the poor quality of justice administered because they were subjected to the jurisdiction of the magistracy much more than the non-Chinese. As a matter of fact, the overwhelming majority of criminal cases were tried by the magistracy, which made it the most important instrument for the administration of justice. It was at the magistracy that miscarriage of justice happened most often. This was partly a result of its tremendous caseload, which could amount to 'more than 18,000 in the mid-1890s' to be handled by two magistrates a year.[24]

More importantly, the early magistrates 'had no legal qualifications and little formal education'.[25] The first Chief Magistrate, Captain William Caine, for example, could claim prior training merely on the basis of service in the army in India and as a magistrate in Zhoushan when it came under British military occupation in the course of the First Anglo-Chinese War.[26] They justified themselves 'by claiming that years of "experience in the subtleties of Chinese character" were worth much more than legal qualifications', and worked on 'the assumption that Chinese offenders had to be handled in a special way'.[27] It meant they did not always follow all the procedures in English law. The rules of evidence were at times applied so laxly that charges of gross carelessness were laid. In 1856, for example, Caine's successor as Chief Magistrate, Charles Hillier, remarked that 'my duty is to take down positive and relevant evidence in support of the charge' when he was questioned by the Attorney-General over whether he thought it 'necessary to take evidence in favour of, as well as against, the prisoner'.[28] The situation improved later after Governor Bowring insisted on recruiting a barrister to replace Hillier upon his departure, and the introduction in the 1860s of the practice to appoint a cadet officer to fill one of the two magistrate posts.[29] This was a positive step forward, as cadets were graduates who were also trained in the Cantonese language and in general terms required to acquire a knowledge of the law, and a number of them actually earned a legal qualification.

The quality of justice administered by the magistracy also suffered because it was the main instrument by which the 'early colonial government sought to deter crime by extensive use of exemplary corporal punishment and through the imposition of crime prevention measures that, by necessity, relied more on penal sanctions than on appeals to cooperation'.[30] The magistracy was not a part of the independent judiciary but a department of the government, which found itself confronted with a serious problem of crime in much of the nineteenth century.[31]

Most of those responsible for crime were Chinese, not least because of the ethnic composition of the population. It was also due to the simple reality that the destitute and outlaws of China were attracted to this foreign enclave because it offered work, easy plunder on the island and in its surrounding waters and relatively light punishments if caught.[32] However, the view among most expatriates that the Chinese were more prone to commit crime than the Europeans was grossly exaggerated. Many Chinese found themselves in front of a magistrate because their usual activities had been criminalised by various local laws and regulations, such as the requirements for registration or carrying a lighted lantern at night.

For better or worse, the colonial government tended to define its relations 'with the Chinese population in terms of crime, or the suspicion of it' in early Hong Kong.[33] As a result, and endowed with an incompetent police, a desire to deter crime and an essentially racist view, the magistracy functioned with a general presumption of guilt when dealing with Chinese defendants. This provided the context for the far too many cases of miscarriage of justice in the magistracy.[34]

Even in the higher courts there were numerous obstacles to justice that worked against the local Chinese. To begin with the Chinese relied critically on the generally low standard of interpretation. With the Chinese having come from different parts of China and speaking mutually unintelligible dialects, being hauled in front of an English-speaking court, as sometimes happened, the inadequacy in provisions for interpretation at the courts of law was blatant. This basic problem was compounded by the fact that there were very few competent interpreters. Daniel Caldwell was in the first decade 'the only reliable interpreter the Colony possessed'.[35] However, in addition to working as an interpreter at the Supreme Court and the magistracy, Caldwell was for a long time the chief detective in the police, and was therefore often required to interpret for the defendant and give evidence for the Crown in the same case in court. Thus, even a Chinese defendant who had the good fortune to have the service of the best court interpreter might still have to live with the reality that this same officer had a vested interest, when wearing another official hat, in securing his conviction. The inadequacies in the provision of interpretation were made worse by the fact that in the first few decades of Hong Kong's colonial history, only expatriates could serve as members of the jury.[36] They were also drawn from a very small pool of Caucasians, some of whom did not understand the English language well.[37]

Since most Chinese defendants were also completely ignorant of the legal procedures and English law, they were at an added disadvantage. Whether it was due to ignorance of the law or not, Chinese defendants and witnesses gained a reputation as prone to make false accusations, malicious counter-charges and inconsistent statements in court.[38] As a result, their testimonies either in defence of their cases or as witnesses were generally given less credence by judges, particularly if they contradicted the testimony of a European. Furthermore, most Chinese defendants had come from the lower social strata. By and large, they could not afford to engage a barrister, whose average basic charge of $50 in the 1840s was roughly a year's income for a Chinese worker, even if they knew enough of the legal system to realise the importance of having a counsel at court.[39] This meant Chinese defendants were much more exposed to the intimidating atmosphere inherent in the adversarial nature of the British judicial process. This was made worse by the frequent 'adoption of bullying' tactics by the prosecutors, the 'racial and class prejudice' of the jury and some judges' inclination to set exemplary sentences to the non-European accused, particularly if property and personal security of expatriates were involved.[40]

The quality of justice was also low because Hong Kong did not have an efficient, effective, well-managed and honest police force. To raise a police force from scratch in a multi-ethnic and multilingual society, where its fast-expanding population was largely transient, was a daunting task for any new settlement. Having found the early attempts to employ the local Chinese policemen 'futile', Governor Pottinger was keen to raise 'an efficient European Police' which he deemed 'absolutely indispensable to the welfare and good order' of Hong Kong.[41] However, Hong Kong proved unattractive to the right kind of Europeans, and it had to settle for a mixed force of Europeans, Indians and Chinese. Those Europeans who joined were mostly discharged soldiers or seamen with the average length of service being three months until as late as the early 1860s.[42] As a result, Hong Kong turned to recruiting from seamen, *sepoys* and then trained policemen from India, though it 'did not solve many of the other problems, including particularly corruption' and the linguistic barrier between the police and the majority of the population.[43] Indeed, the police force was of such poor standing that Governor MacDonnell felt the government must try to replace it entirely 'with the exception of those men who have proved themselves worth retaining' and do so 'as far as the means at its disposal will admit'.[44]

Although MacDonnell sought to contain and reduce the endemic corruption in the police, he laid the heaviest blame on the Chinese for allowing 'themselves to be either terrified or cajoled into paying a sort of black mail to any person clothed with official authority, who chooses to demand it'.[45] Whether MacDonnell was justified or not, the reality was that most Chinese residents of Hong Kong had little choice when faced with a demand from an abusive colonial policeman. Justice was often perverted when few policemen were honest, efficient or even properly trained, a state of affairs which did not begin to change for the better until after the police were put under the charge of a cadet officer and trained police officers recruited from Britain in 1867.

The celebrated case of Daniel Caldwell illustrates how several obstacles to justice could act together to the disadvantage of the Chinese community. Caldwell was born in St Helena, raised in Singapore, married to a Chinese, spoke excellent Chinese, and settled in Hong Kong in the course of the First Anglo-Chinese War.[46] He worked as an interpreter in courts and served in the police, rising to become the Registrar General before being dismissed in 1862 after an inquiry. For almost 20 years, he was the most important channel of communication between the government and the Chinese community. He was much depended upon by governors, the courts, the police and the Royal Navy for interpretation and, above all, for advice in the handling of affairs involving the Chinese.[47] It was therefore understandable that he established himself as a powerful figure in the assessment of the Chinese community. Caldwell was also 'the partner and accomplice of a notorious violator of the laws', Machow Wong, 'over whom he, on occasions, threw the shield of his influence, and whose nefarious designs he assisted in carrying out, by the unscrupulous exercise of power which he derived from his official position'.[48]

Although eventually dismissed, Caldwell was in a position to pervert the course of justice regularly at the expense of the Chinese community. This was achieved 'by influencing proceedings in the Magistrate's Court, and to have used his powers to silence his enemies'[49] or by selective enforcement of the law. With Caldwell being their most 'sympathetic' friend in the colonial government and seen to be tremendously powerful over matters affecting their affairs even before he formally took office as Registrar General and Protector of the Chinese, the majesty of British justice was often denied to members of the local Chinese community, unless they happened to be in his good books.

Rule of Law

The serious deficiencies in the administration of justice should not be taken to mean the rule of law did not exist in nineteenth-century Hong Kong. It did, though it was a poor comparison to what was in place at the end of British rule at the end of the twentieth century. The tremendous changes that happened in between affected the upholding of the rule of law. Courts, judges, lawyers and juries are all products of the time and the environment. What are taboos today, such as enforcing a piece of legislation that goes against basic human rights in an English court, was not unacceptable in Hong Kong or indeed in England itself during the reign of Queen Victoria. British women were not, for example, recognised in their own right in law, and could not own properties in their own names until the Married Women's Property Act was passed in 1882.[50] Likewise, working-class people or domestic servants were, by today's standards, routinely treated abominably by their employers and masters.

In colonial Hong Kong, racial bigotry and prejudice added to the social injustice inherent in the strong class division in Victorian Britain, and they were reflected in the working of the courts. In general terms, the Chinese suffered much more than the expatriates from the low standard in the administration of justice. The colonial establishment, to which judges, government prosecutors and in a sense even lawyers and many members of the jury belonged, did not set out to discriminate against the Chinese in the courts of law. They did so because they shared the bias of the time. It was so prevalent that few questioned it. Whether the rule of law existed or not should not be judged by the standard of justice administered but by whether the law, as it was, prevailed when it was put to the test.

Although appeals and judicial review of any kind over cases involving Chinese defendants were rare in the nineteenth century, there were occasions when the existence of the rule of law itself was tested. The most spectacular case involved an attempt to poison the entire expatriate community in the course of the Second Anglo-Chinese War.[51] On 15 January 1857, the bread produced in the main local bakery by the name of Esing was heavily laced with arsenic and supplied to the expatriate community for breakfast as usual, while its proprietor, Cheong Ahlum, took his entire family to Macao earlier the same morning. As an excessive amount of arsenic was used, it caused stomach upset and was quickly detected by the consumers. No fatality resulted, though the Governor's wife, Lady Bowring, was among the most affected. Nevertheless, this incident, happening as it did after Imperial Commissioner Ye Mingchen had asked the Chinese in Hong Kong to help destroy the British community in the midst of the war, 'inflamed the foreign community'.[52] Cheong was apprehended in Macao and handed back to the Hong Kong police by the Portuguese authority. Governor Bowring insisted that Cheong and his co-defendants be tried by jury, rather than be 'dealt with summarily' in a 'drumhead court-martial' as preferred by the Attorney-General, Chisholm Anstey.[53]

What was in fact put on trial in February 1857 was not only Cheong and his staff, but also the integrity of British justice. The Chief Justice who presided over the case, the Attorney General who prosecuted, the defence counsel, and the seven European members of the jury were all personally victims of this alleged attempt to wipe out the entire expatriate community. Despite the vehemence of the 'panic-stricken Attorney-General' and the anger of the expatriate community, the evidence presented by the Attorney-General proved inconclusive.[54] Guided by Chief Justice J.W. Hulme, who insisted that 'hanging the wrong man will not further the ends of justice', the jury acquitted them.[55] Although Cheong and his co-defendants were promptly rearrested upon leaving the court, detained and eventually expelled under the instruction of the Governor-in-Council, partly to pacify the expatriate community and partly to ensure creditors of Cheong could exact their payments, including the defence counsel's fees from him, there was no doubt that the accused had had a fair trial.[56]

This court case was a magnificent demonstration of British justice at its best and the existence of the rule of law. The fact that other restrictions and regulations against the Chinese, such as the imposition of a curfew on the Chinese inhabitants, were also introduced in this period of war and tension merely highlighted the nature of British justice in Hong Kong. It was that the rule of law existed in parallel to the discriminations against the Chinese in the administration of justice. The latter was regrettably a fact of life in a colonial society which did not accept the equality of the races or the social classes. However, when the Supreme Court was put to the test it did what all properly constituted British courts of law were supposed to do.

In the modern history of British courts, what unfolded in the Supreme Court of Hong Kong in February 1857 was an ordinary case, despite the high drama. Nevertheless, happening as it did in the context of a Chinese community under British rule in the midst of a war between the two countries, it was an extraordinary outcome to those Chinese who observed this incident critically. In this sense the Esing case was one of those landmark events that helped to establish the good reputation of British justice in Hong Kong.

The overall performance of British justice in Hong Kong also needs to be set against the wider context of justice that prevailed in Guangdong province, the general region of which Hong Kong was a part and from where most of its population had come and intended to return for retirement. Although the Qing legal system worked effectively and was in general terms neither unpredictable nor arbitrary,[57] in the middle of the nineteenth century public order and social stability had broken down and the judicial norm no longer functioned in south China.[58] Instead, the provincial government in Canton routinely resorted to extreme measures in order to restore order and deter a complete collapse of imperial authority, particularly when peasant rebellions of various descriptions were raging. The usual careful review and reference to Beijing in capital cases were suspended.[59] One visitor's account suggests that during three months in the summer of 1855, when Imperial Commissioner Ye Mingchen was in charge and a year before the Second Anglo-Chinese War, 75,000 people were beheaded in Guangzhou city.[60] As with many of the executions that were summarily carried out in this period, it was estimated that 'more than half... were declared to be innocent of the charge of rebellion, but that the accusation was made as a pretext to exact money from them'.[61] The same general pattern of summary execution prevailed elsewhere in the province. In one of its eight magisterial jurisdictions, over a period of 15 months in the relatively less turbulent time of the late 1840s and early 1850s, before the Taiping Uprising started, the local magistrate 'captured 10,744 rebels: of these, he had executed 8,757, sent 631 to Canton, released 386 and detained, pending trial, 211; 468 had died of natural causes in custody'.[62] The low standard in the administration of justice in British Hong Kong happened in juxtaposition to the extremely harsh judicial regime in southern China.

However well they compared to the situation in Guangdong, British law could not have a greater appeal to the average (meaning poor) Chinese working men in Hong Kong than any law or regulation they ever encountered, as they were mostly at the receiving end of the punitive effects. Less harsh punishments were still abusive and repugnant if imposed on offences they did not understand or commit. The rule of law was not something the average Chinese labourer would have understood but the relatively benign British legal system that came with it was undoubtedly one of the reasons that made Hong Kong attractive to Chinese immigrant workers.

To the small but growing body of intellectuals who received some Western education, and the better-off Chinese who were building up their businesses, the British legal system and the independent judiciary steadily and increasingly proved attractive. The rhetoric of the expatriate community emphasising the superiority of British Law was either accepted or seized upon by the local Chinese elite when it petitioned against Governor MacDonnell's racially discriminatory policy in licensing gambling in 1871.[63] By the time of Queen Victoria's golden jubilee at the turn of the century, the local Chinese community made 'a striking recognition of British justice' in its 'splendidly embroidered address' to the Queen.[64]

However imperfect it was in nineteenth-century Hong Kong, the rule of law determined the structure and procedures of the legal system, restrained some governors from pursuing certain policies harmful to the local community and helped to secure the acquittal of many wrongly accused. It might have been a little precarious at first but the rule of law did prevail. It was partly because of the courage and the independence of the judges, and partly because of the existence of an authority higher than the local government, which provided a redress to any serious executive encroachment on its integrity. It was due also to the gradual acceptance by the residents of Hong Kong, of all ethnic backgrounds, of its immense value. It took a long time but the rule of law did eventually have its roots planted in nineteenth-century Hong Kong.

Chapter 5
Economy and Society

From the very beginning, in the early 1840s, the British intended to build in Hong Kong not a settlement colony but an imperial outpost for the promotion of trade and economic exchanges with the Chinese Empire, and they expected to enjoy the lion's share of the benefits by virtue of their unrivalled economic and commercial might. The structure of its economy and society consequently bore the imprimatur of this basic policy. Although British links proved highly valuable to its economy, Hong Kong was not turned into an appendage of the British economy, nor was its society modelled on Victorian England. While the British expatriates kept largely to themselves, and in effect turned themselves into the 'upper class' in colonial Hong Kong, and the Anglican Church became the established church, there was no serious attempt to 'civilise the natives'.[1] Restricted by the limited resources at its disposal, the colonial government generally allowed both economy and society to develop freely, as long as the basic liberal principles – as well as the prejudices – held dear in nineteenth-century Britain were not breached. Through the colonial government, the British upheld their interests and kept a benign eye on socio-economic developments in the local community but the very small colonial government preferred not to get actively involved unless British jurisdiction, interests or values were at stake.

Forces for Economic Development

With the British flag planted firmly in Hong Kong following in the footsteps of the traders, commerce was its bloodline in its formative years. Led by what would come to be known as the 'princely *hong*', Jardine Matheson, British traders, most of them involved directly or indirectly in the export of opium to China, rapidly settled in and started to build Hong Kong into a base to support their trading operations, even before its future was decided.[2] After its foundation as a colony, Jardine Matheson relocated its head office from Macao in early 1844. This lead was followed by other major hongs, including Jardine's principal competitor, Dent and Company, and turned this nascent colony into the main location for the headquarters of major British and other companies trading in East Asia.

The British efforts to expand trade with China thus provided an important impetus for economic development.

British jurisdiction provided stability, security and the predictability of British law and government, enabling Hong Kong to flourish as a centre for international trade. Shanghai might have had a considerable advantage over Hong Kong in terms of its location in East China and access to the Yangtze waterway as well as its vast and wealthier hinterland, but it did not enjoy the benefits, in the eyes of the Western traders, of undisputed British jurisdiction.[3] In this early stage of establishing formal relations between Britain and China, having one's headquarters where the senior British representative in China resided and where the Royal Navy based its China Station had advantages.[4] It gave the traders ready access to key British policymakers that could not be enjoyed in Shanghai, and reduced the substantial costs of protecting the opium trade, which was still illegal in China until 1858 and vulnerable to marauding pirates.

Indeed, the opium trade was the most important economic activity in the first decade of British Hong Kong and revenues derived from it were a key source of government funds.[5] Although other trade and economic activities gradually reduced the importance of the opium trade for Hong Kong as a whole, the colonial government continued to be dependent on revenues from its opium monopoly until this was ended with the fall of Hong Kong to the Japanese in the Second World War.[6]

Consequently, Hong Kong became the location of choice for head offices or regional headquarters for British and other major trading firms engaged in the China trade, even though Shanghai surpassed Hong Kong as a metropolis in much of the nineteenth and the first half of the twentieth century. The rising and well-connected firms like Jardine Matheson, and at a later stage the Hong Kong and Shanghai Bank, based in the colony soon built up a social and financial network to leading international cities in Europe, America and elsewhere in Asia. The links to London were particularly important, as it was the global pivot of trade and capital. The construction of such a network provided 'a relatively non-redundant set of contacts across the channels of trade and finance, providing these firms with extraordinary access to commercial and political intelligence'.[7]

The international network so important to Western traders also benefited Chinese traders in providing financial and other services in support of their international trade. With access to this network and the protection of British jurisdiction, Chinese merchants who set up operations in Hong Kong were able to bypass Chinese regulations and restrictions over foreign trade and 'join international intermediaries as full partners in trade with China and the rest of Asia'.[8] Chinese merchants made good use of Hong Kong, whether they were middlemen in the China trade of the Westerners or were themselves engaged in trading with Southeast Asia. Hong Kong therefore 'became the premier meeting-place of the foreign and Chinese social networks of capital in Asia'.[9] Even Chinese traders who focused on trading with Southeast Asia or supplying the rapidly expanding overseas Chinese communities fully utilised Hong Kong's facilities as a free port.[10]

The intermediaries between Western traders and the Chinese were the compradors, who not only acted as agents for their Western employers but also usually set up parallel trading operations of their own.[11] These trading activities often allowed the more astute compradors to amass considerable wealth or capital to finance their own businesses. By 1876, for example, one of the better known, Kwok Acheong who worked for the shipping company Peninsula and Oriental (P&O), had himself become a significant steamship operator and the third-largest ratepayer in Hong Kong.[12] The rise of the compradors continued. By the early half of the twentieth century, the most wealthy man in Hong Kong was generally believed to be Robert Hotung, who worked as a comprador for Jardine's before building up his immense personal fortune.

Although the biggest companies and the leading trading houses in early colonial Hong Kong were all owned and operated by British, American and other expatriates, economic development was made possible and supported by Chinese workers who provided the bulk of the manpower to build a new port city. Chinese labourers not only built houses, roads and other infrastructure, provided many different kinds of menial services to the expatriates and made items of daily use, but also manned ships, loaded and unloaded goods and carried out other tasks essential to sustaining trade and economic expansion. In about a decade, particularly after the start of the Taiping Uprising in China in 1850, the contribution of the Chinese community took on a new and increasingly important dimension as Chinese merchants who had fled from great social upheavals in China began to relocate or set up businesses in Hong Kong.[13]

This coincided with the development of Hong Kong into the key staging post for Chinese emigration. The first major wave occurred after the discovery of gold at Coloma near Sacramento in California in 1848 and the subsequent gold rush. This trend of emigration was enhanced after gold was also discovered in New South Wales three years later, triggering another gold rush which was sustained by further discovery of gold in Victoria, Australia. This coincided with the collapse of social order in south China as a result of the Taiping Uprising. With the lure of a new prospect elsewhere propagated by those engaged in profiteering from this movement of people, other Chinese left in increasing numbers for Southeast Asia, Peru, Cuba and other destinations. To give an indication of the scale of the movement of people through Hong Kong, 30,000 Chinese labourers sailed from Hong Kong to San Francisco alone in 1852 at a time when its long-term population was less than 39,000.[14] Their reliance on Hong Kong as a transhipment centre provided strong impetus for the building of hostels and other supporting services locally. Much of this movement of people in fact involved the trafficking of human beings, with many Chinese going overseas as indenture labourers in appalling conditions.[15] Whatever one may feel about the morality of this traffic, it was an important economic activity in the formative years of Hong Kong as a colony.

The increasing emigration of the Chinese also generated a major re-export trade of Chinese goods to support the rapidly expanding overseas Chinese communities. Those firms concentrating on supplying North America, for which San Francisco was a key centre, came to be called 'Jinshan Zhuang', whereas those trading with Southeast Asia were known as 'Nanyang Zhuang'.[16] Hong Kong also developed a thriving entrepôt trade between China and Southeast Asia (particularly Thailand, the Malay Peninsula, Indochina and the Dutch East Indies or present-day Indonesia) in the 1850s. This came to be known as the Nam Pak Hong (*Nanbeihang*) trade. It involved the import to China in the north of goods from the south in Southeast Asia, consisting mainly of rice, spices, seafood, jewels, timber and coconut oil, and the export of Chinese products such as silk, herbal medicines, peanuts, cooking oil and other traditional produces to Southeast Asia.[17] The growth of this trade really took off at the end of the decade, as the number of Chinese trading houses more than doubled within two years from 35 in 1858. This rapid growth was sustained and the number of traders rose to 315 in 1876 and to 395 by 1881.[18] With such a beginning, in addition to the servicing of the China trade of the Westerners, Hong Kong laid the foundation for its entrepôt trade, which remained the mainstay of its economy until 1950.

With the Chinese community growing fast – rising from 7,500 in 1841 to 22,800 in 1847 and to 85,300 in 1859 – a meaningful domestic market emerged and grew, generating secondary economic activities and growth.[19] By 1859, there were already 2,000 shops or enterprises owned or operated by the Chinese, including 278 traditional grocery stores, 49 stores for Western goods, 51 rice shops, 53 shipbuilders, 92 carpenters, 116 metal workshops and others.[20] In comparison, the size of the non-Chinese community rose to only 1,600 in 1859, and much of this expansion happened after a period of slow growth in the China trade conducted by Western merchants in the first decade of British rule.[21]

Although trade and financial services run by the expatriates also expanded much more quickly after the Second Anglo-Chinese War and the expatriates continued to dominate the economic scene, the balance of economic importance between the two communities had started to shift. Forming the overwhelming majority of the population, the Chinese began to outnumber the expatriates as traders and owners of properties in a little over a decade, though the value of their houses and investments remained generally smaller than that of the expatriates. Nevertheless, as an indication of how much change had taken place, by 1855 there were already more Chinese than expatriates paying rates, which together with income from land leases formed the main sources of government revenue. In that year, among those who paid rates of £10 and above, 1,637 out of 1,999 were Chinese, while of those who paid £40 and above, 410 out of 772 were Chinese.[22] The growing wealth and economic contribution of the Chinese did not alter the reality that real economic power rested in the hands of the expatriate community that formed the colonial establishment. This remained the situation even after the Chinese community as a whole surpassed the expatriates in terms of either total wealth or contribution to the economy towards the end of the nineteenth century.

The centrality of trade in Hong Kong's economic life also led to the development of servicing industries to support trade, both international and regional. The international financial network, of which large British and American firms such as Jardine Matheson and Russell and Company were themselves a part, gradually gave way to the development of modern banks. In addition to the major British and foreign banks which set up operations in Hong Kong, such as the Chartered Mercantile Bank, the Chartered Bank of India, Australia and China, and the Comptoir d'Escompte, Hong Kong became home to a new British overseas bank, the Hong Kong and Shanghai Banking Corporation in 1865. It was founded 'to finance intra-regional trade among the open ports of China, Japan, and the Philippines' for which it would engage in 'financing trading facilities, for example, local steamship lines, docks, tug boats, and small industrial enterprises'.[23] However, it quickly took on the role of an exchange bank, forged a London connection with Westminster Bank and then set up an office in this pivot of world capital. The bank flourished both as a bridge between the financial world dominated by silver in China and sterling in London, and as a regional banking operation based in the colony. By establishing a sound banking sector, exemplified by the success of the Hong Kong Bank, Hong Kong developed itself into a growing financial centre to service trade in East Asia and indeed, to a lesser extent, even the modernisation of China particularly through the provision of loans either individually or by syndicates.

In parallel, the development and expansion of traditional native Chinese banks (or *yinhao*) helped to finance economic expansion among the Chinese community. They served as moneychangers, bullion dealers, moneylenders and remittance houses to the local Chinese businessmen, facilitating their trade with China, Southeast Asia, Japan, North America and elsewhere. As most Chinese businessmen in Hong Kong did not have a sufficient command of the English language or the contacts and knowledge to approach the modern Western banks, and some of the bigger native banks used 'the facilities of modern banks – loans, foreign currency, remittances, and so on – to strengthen their own operations', they also 'acted as intermediaries between foreign banks and certain levels of the local Chinese market'.[24] The early native banks numbered 20 by 1886, and over 30 by 1890, and they were usually operated by Cantonese.[25] They were joined by the formation of modern Chinese banks in the early twentieth century. Despite fierce competition from the modern banks, the native ones continued to flourish and help finance numerous small business operations and remittances until Hong Kong fell under Japanese occupation in 1941. As far as general economic development in Hong Kong was concerned, their competition was a positive and complementary factor.

In addition to stimulating the growth of other financial services, such as insurance, rapidly expanding trade after a slow start in the first decade of British rule also led to the establishment of shipping businesses and a shipbuilding and maintenance industry. This applied as much to the rise of shipping by junks as to the expansion of great British shipping companies. For an indication of the growth of the junk trade, the tonnage carried by junks from China to Hong Kong rose from 80,000 tons in 1847 to 1.35 million tons in 1867, a sixteen-fold increase in two decades.[26] Such expansion also provided the impetus for the building and maintenance of junks, which already existed on a small scale in pre-colonial Hong Kong. By the end of the 1850s, there were already 53 junk yards of various size.

In terms of modern shipping, the British dominated. Leading British hongs like Jardine Matheson or Dent and Company were themselves major players in the shipping business, even before the colony was founded. Other great shipping companies not initially involved with the opium trade, such as P&O, which received its Royal Charter in 1840 and was to become the world's largest shipping company, also inaugurated a shipping and mail service between Britain and Hong Kong in 1845.[27] Butterfield and Swire, a relative latecomer that eventually emerged as one of the greatest of British hongs, for its part opened a branch in Hong Kong in 1870 and soon saw its operation there surpass its original regional headquarters in Shanghai.[28] Although a few Chinese merchants, most notably Kwok Acheong, did operate a dozen steam ships by the 1870s, they paled in comparison with the major British shipping firms.[29]

This steady expansion of shipping also gave rise to establishment of a modern shipbuilding and maintenance industry. The first Western-style shipyard, the Lamont Dock, was built in Aberdeen in 1857. It was intended primarily to support the Royal Navy after the main British-operated yard in Canton was destroyed by the Chinese in the course of the Second Anglo-Chinese War.[30] This was followed by the construction of a handful of shipyards, culminating in the establishment of the Hong Kong Whampoa Dock Company in July 1863, which emerged as the premier dock company in Hong Kong in the nineteenth century. Although the shipbuilding and maintenance industry was given major support from the Navy at first, its survival and subsequent prospering depended on commercial work.[31]

The emergence of this modern shipbuilding and repair industry in the 1860s also marked the beginning of modern industries. Indeed, it was only after the Hong Kong Whampoa Dock Company was founded that Hong Kong passed its first ever Companies Ordinance. The first limited liability company to be incorporated under this law in 1865 was also a shipbuilder. Other major industrial enterprises were later founded by expatriate investors, including most notably a sugar refinery in the 1870s; two ice factories, a ropemaker, a steelmaker, and a cement factory in the 1880s; and another sugar refinery in the 1890s.

While the expatriate investors set up all the major industrial enterprises, the Chinese community also went beyond handicraft industries and started building factories in the 1870s. The most important industries built by Chinese investors included a couple of factories for preserved ginger and other processed food, including traditional Chinese products like soy sauce and preserved fruits, a tannery, a few machine-makers, a paper factory and a match manufacturer.[32] On a smaller scale, numerous other workshops run by the Chinese existed by the early 1880s. These included workshops for making cigars, tobacco, clothing, glass, oars, rifles, ropes, umbrellas, spectacles, tooth-powder and soap, as well as small factories for producing goods in bamboo and rattan.[33]

The industrial developments that took place in the nineteenth century occurred by and large without much support from or impediments imposed by the government.[34] While the beginning of modern industry was a milestone in Hong Kong's history, it was trade, of which opium remained a significant part throughout the nineteenth century, and not industry that formed the mainstay of the economy.[35]

A 'Colonial Society'

Since it was an imperial outpost rather than a settlement colony, Hong Kong developed a 'colonial society' that reflected this reality. This was not the result of a deliberate policy but a product of the time and the prejudice that prevailed while British imperialism asserted itself on the basis of superior organisation, logistics and military might. It resulted in the creation in Hong Kong, as elsewhere in the non-settlement colonies of the British Empire, of a colonial hierarchy in which Britons, by virtue of little more than accident of birth, formed the colonial establishment or, for the less successful, at least an adjunct to it. This was the product of self-confidence and racial arrogance that came with the power of empire.

The government in Hong Kong, like colonial governments elsewhere in the British Empire, generally did not bother to legislate to discriminate against the colonial subjects because it was unnecessary.[36] The vitality and strength of the British economy, politics, armed forces, science, technology and, in their own eyes, their way of life governed by liberal democracy and the Christian faith gave the Victorians venturing to Asia or, for that matter, Africa a sense of superiority over the so-called natives.[37] At the same time, although imperial possessions were seized by force they were mostly maintained by the implied might of British arms to reassert and extend British control if any of them were attacked by the 'natives'. For the highly self-confident and class-conscious Britons managing a far-flung empire, aloofness and segregation from the 'natives' came easily. Exercising authority over the 'natives' through local collaborators under some form of indirect rule was also both cost-effective and sufficiently secure in the era of *pax Britannica*.[38] Hong Kong was not an exception in having a clear and segregating colonial hierarchy.

The existence of a clear distinction between the communities of the Chinese and the expatriate Britons, with the former generally occupying the lower social strata and the latter the upper ones, did not mean social classes were divided simply on ethnic lines. The segregation between the races meant social classes existed both in parallel within the two communities and at the same time across ethnic lines. If the average

Chinese labourers in nineteenth-century Hong Kong had some faint ideas of class distinction in modern usage they would probably see the senior expatriate officials and businessmen as members of the upper class, with expatriates in supervisory roles and Chinese merchants as a kind of middle class in two largely separate communities, while they themselves constituted the lower class. While such a view is far too simplistic as it focuses upon nothing but the local social distinctions, it nevertheless provides a useful rough sketch for outlining the complexity of the colonial society in the first century of British Hong Kong.

As an expatriate community of Britons, Hong Kong had, strictly speaking, few members of the aristocracy or the landed gentry who would normally be deemed members of the British upper class. The overwhelming majority of Hong Kong's officials and senior business leaders had come from the middle class in the UK.[39] Together they constituted the ruling elite in Hong Kong. Their relatively humble backgrounds did not make them any less status conscious than real upper-crust Englishmen. The reverse was true, as they insisted on rigidly following precedence and protocols in society events.[40] Whatever motivated them to do so, their 'preoccupation with status and position, with the establishment of a colonial pecking order, unified colonial society in the way that opposing thrusts help to sustain a stone-work bridge: the strains help to maintain the structure'.[41] With heads of trading houses behaving like merchant princes and colonial officials like senior mandarins, it would be understandable that they would appear 'upper class' if seen only within the confines of the colony. In such a context, professional people and juniors in government or the business world constituted the 'middle class', while those performing supervisory roles in government agencies and factories formed the 'lower or working class' among the expatriates.

A working class in the sense that it was used in the UK did not or was not permitted to exist among Britons in Hong Kong, however. Practically any Caucasian (not just an Englishman), whatever his background, skill or ability, would be employed as an overseer or supervisor rather than a mere labourer as long as he was willing to work.[42] A genuine working class did not exist among the expatriates partly because of strong competition from Chinese artisans, craftsmen and labourers but mainly because 'working class Europeans were seen as lowering the prestige of the white man'.[43] Indeed, the poor whites, usually beachcombers or prostitutes, were treated not as lower class but as outcasts in their own community. In general, they were avoided by other Caucasians in the day, dealt with harshly by the police and were reduced to become creatures of the night, as the expatriate community had a vested interest in not allowing them to, from their perspective, let the side down.[44]

Even though the several thousand original inhabitants of the island of Hong Kong vastly outnumbered the early expatriates, they were quickly swamped by new immigrants from China. Neither the original residents nor the newcomers included any number of nobility, scholar

officials or members of the Chinese gentry, who would be counted as
'upper class' in English usage.[45] As a result, class distinction within the
Chinese community shared one key element in common with that in
the expatriate community. Neither had any number of people from a
genuine upper-class background from their home country. However, a
kind of local 'upper class' among the Chinese gradually emerged, as
merchants, compradors and others who had made fortunes sought to
better their social standing by purchasing official ranks from the Chinese
government, or engaging in much needed and appreciated charitable
work in the local community. A very few even earned British honours
towards the end of the nineteenth century and became peripheral
members of the colonial establishment.

The lower class among the Chinese was easy to identify. Immigrant
labourers, most of the original inhabitants who worked the land or
fished for a living, most of their descendants and the destitute in general
terms constituted members of the lower class. They formed the
overwhelming majority of the Chinese community and indeed of the
population as a whole.

What is much more difficult to define and identify is the middle class
among the Chinese. There was certainly a small but significant number
of Chinese who occupied the middle ground between the wealthy upper
class and the labouring lower class. They consisted mainly of
schoolteachers, clerks and assistants in the bigger firms and in government
services, as well as keepers of small enterprises, be they shops, eating
houses, workshops or similar establishments. Set entirely in the context
of the local Chinese community, they could be seen as belonging to the
'middle class'. However, such a description should be qualified by a
comparison with the 'middle' and 'working' classes of the expatriate
community. In general terms, members of the local Chinese 'middle class'
enjoyed substantially lower social standing and poorer living conditions
than members of the expatriate 'middle class' and generally even those
of the expatriate 'lower class'.

In between the expatriates and the local Chinese were Hong Kong's
Eurasians, most of them born to an expatriate father and a Chinese
mother. Given the racial and other prejudices of the time it was in the
interest of Eurasians to identify and become members of either the
expatriate or the local Chinese community rather than assert themselves
as a distinct community. Since they were not accepted as full members
of the expatriate community and were, for example, barred from becoming
cadet officers, most chose to identify and integrate with the Chinese
community.[46] Although the Chinese community also had its prejudices
against the mixing of ethnicity, it was on the whole more receptive to
Eurasians than was the expatriate community. This was partly because
Eurasians often had English language ability and a modern education
that enabled them to be members of the middle level in the Chinese
social and economic hierarchy. Indeed, some Eurasians were able to
become so successful that they joined the elite of the colonial society, at

least at its periphery, but usually as representatives of the Chinese community. The rise of Robert Hotung and his extended family in Hong Kong society provided the most spectacular example.[47] Most Eurasians ended up working at the junior level in government, public organisations or in the hongs and tried to integrate into the 'middle class' among the Chinese.

In addition, there were three other significant ethnic groups in Hong Kong: the Parsees, the Portuguese and the Indians.[48] The Parsee community originated from Persia and came to Hong Kong after first settling in India. It was small but influential because it was made up mostly of wealthy traders who also engaged in philanthropic and civic affairs. However, Parsees were never fully accepted by the Britons and were only at the fringes of the colonial establishment.

The Portuguese, who numbered second only after Britons among the Westerners, had mostly come from the Portuguese enclave of Macao, which put them in a grey area between the local Chinese and the expatriate communities. With education in the English language provided mainly by Catholic mission schools, many Portuguese worked as clerks, account clerks and interpreters in the colonial government and in Western firms, and generally belonged to the middle class in the context of the colony. Many also married Chinese, spoke Cantonese and practised Catholicism. As a community they tended to inter-marry and maintain a distinctive identity.

The creation of an Indian community was largely the result of the deployment of Indian regiments to Hong Kong and the recruitment of Sikh, Punjabi, Muslim and other policemen from India. In class terms, they generally belonged to the local working class. They became a community of Indians as they were neither accepted nor adopted by any of the other communities.

Segregation

When Hong Kong was founded, the expatriate and the local Chinese communities largely chose to segregate without this requiring government intervention or legislation. The experiences of their sojourn in Canton was fresh in the minds of the expatriates and the original inhabitants of Hong Kong island were treated like their Cantonese countrymen. For their part, the local Chinese had no more wish to live in mixed quarters than the Westerners desired to be their next-door neighbours.[49]

In the earliest days of British occupation, the main concern of Elliot with regard to land policy was to encourage British merchants to commit themselves to Hong Kong by taking out leases but to do so under regulation of his authority pending a settlement of the future of Hong Kong.[50] When this issue came up under the first Governor, Pottinger, the government was again interested mainly in working out a policy that on the one hand reserved the land for the Crown and on the other allocated sufficient land for the mercantile community and the armed services to carry out their functions.[51] The one notable occasion when the government was actually involved in encouraging segregation was to relocate the Chinese settlers in the Upper Bazaar to the Taipingshan area

shortly after the Colony was founded, though this was also motivated by
a desire to regain the land for more profitable developments.[52]

Segregation of the two communities was on the whole not an issue
about which the government had to devise or strictly enforce a clear
policy during the first four decades of colonial rule. It came into existence
largely without legislation. Peaceful and parallel coexistence of various
ethnic communities suited everyone.

As the colony developed and prospered, the preferences of the two
communities in their choices of location for settlement or housing
entrenched residential segregation. Although it started mainly on ethic
lines, segregation was also reinforced by class distinctions. In the areas
where the majority of the Chinese congregated, they lived in conditions
that the expatriates would deem congested and unhygienic. The
differences in the standard of housing, and indeed of living, between
the expatriate community and the Chinese lower and middle classes were
stark, and reinforced segregation.

Although segregation was not backed by any legislation it was 'accepted
in the social life of the colony'.[53] However, as more Chinese had amassed
wealth by the latter 1870s, they preferred to live in housing of a much
higher standard. They not only built better housing eastward from the
central district but also started to purchase and take over properties owned
by expatriates. This provoked a strong reaction within the government
when the liberal-minded Governor, Sir John Pope Hennessy, supported
such a development against strong resistance within the colonial
establishment.[54] Hennessy was overruled by London and 'the image of
the Chinese encroaching upon areas where Westerners had built their
houses led to the legal provision for residential segregation'.[55]

The first legislation to give legality to segregation was the introduction
of the European District Preservation Ordinance in 1888, five years after
Hennessy had retired as governor. This was followed and enhanced by
the Peak Preservation Ordinance (1904), and further restrictions passed
in 1919 to reserve part of the island of Cheung Chau for members of
the expatriate middle class.[56] Although such laws were undoubtedly
introduced to give legal sanction to racial segregation, a formal regime
of apartheid was never introduced. Such a formal arrangement was out
of tone with the liberal façade of Victorian imperialism and was in any
event unnecessary. Segregation was not strongly resented by the local
Chinese community and sufficient flexibility was in any event exercised
to allow the most successful members of the Chinese community, for
example, the Hotung family and the wife of the Chinese leader Chiang
Kai-shek, to reside in the Caucasian citadel of the Peak.

Most Chinese residents never paid any attention to the existence of
such exclusive legislation, let alone took political actions to remove it.[57]
The end of the legal basis for segregation came in 1946 as a result not of
local agitation but of a government initiative, after the Japanese
occupation of Hong Kong caused the officials who re-established the
colonial administration to take on a new outlook.[58]

Governance of the Local Chinese

Given the primarily commercial *raison d'être* behind the founding of Hong Kong, the British had little interest in governing the local Chinese beyond maintaining the stability and good order deemed conducive – even essential – to trade and prosperity. Thus, in the early years local Chinese inhabitants were largely left to their own devices, as long as they did not break the law or otherwise disturb the peace.

In so doing, the colonial government resorted to reviving a Chinese arrangement for maintaining peace and order at the local level, the *baojia* system, which had been formally in place but not in operation in Hong Kong previously.[59] Chinese peace officers with 'the same authorities, privileges and immunities as any constable' were appointed in 1844.[60] They were subjected to the general oversight of the police magistrate. The rationale was that since the mainly non-Chinese police could not dampen criminal activities among the Chinese population, 'Chinese in towns and villages would be best locally governed by their own system consisting precisely of tithings and hundreds superintendents [sic]'.[61] They also served as mediators and arbitrators of minor disputes. How effective they were is difficult to ascertain as there are few records of their work, but the fact that they were all abolished by 1861 suggests that they were not deemed particularly valuable by the government.[62]

Parallel to the Chinese peace officers was the emergence of respected local notables to whom the Chinese increasingly turned for mediation and arbitration of disputes. The most important of such local leaders in the early days, such as Loo Aqui and Tam Achoy, had generally come from those who had profited from working for the British in the founding of Hong Kong, or made fortunes as compradors or in the entrepôt trade. They differed from the more traditional leaders in a Chinese community mainly by their very humble and non-gentry background. Loo was, for example, a Tanka (a kind of outcast boat-people), which would normally have prevented him from establishing himself as a local leader among the Cantonese. However, Hong Kong did not have an established scholar-gentry class, and the wealth Loo gathered provisioning the British enabled him to rise above his lowly origins.[63]

People like Loo and Tam came to be accepted as community leaders after they used their personal wealth to support local good causes, of which a landmark event was the building of the Man Mo Temple on Hollywood Road in the heart of the Chinese community in 1847. As a temple, it was dedicated to the deities for the fortune of men seeking advancement through the Chinese Imperial Examinations, and for loyalty and righteousness particularly among warriors. In addition to being a centre for worship the Temple quickly 'became the main social centre for Hong Kong's Chinese population, regardless of their regional or occupational affiliation'.[64]

By the beginning of the 1850s, those administering the Temple had evolved into a de facto local governing board among the Chinese. They 'secretly controlled native affairs, acted as commercial arbitrators, arranged for the due reception of mandarins passing through the Colony, negotiated the sale of [Chinese] official titles, and formed an unofficial link between the Chinese residents of Hong Kong and the Canton Authorities'.[65] With the colonial government not keen to get deeply involved in governing the local Chinese, the local leadership that sprung up around the Temple filled an important gap and formed the basis for de facto self-government among the Chinese in most everyday affairs.

The roles which the Man Mo Temple Committee played came to be eclipsed, though not entirely replaced, by the governing body of the Tung Wah Hospital after the latter's creation, with the Temple dealing with matters more at the local level and the Hospital at the colony-wide level.[66] The Hospital was founded primarily as a result of a public scandal in 1869. This was over the practice in the Chinese community of leaving terminally ill and destitute individuals in a final resting place to die without any medical or sanitary care, often laid next to those who had already died. It prompted the government to act after Acting Registrar General Alfred Lister accidentally gained knowledge of this practice and reported it in graphic detail.[67] As a result, the government worked with leaders of the Chinese community to build a Chinese hospital for the Chinese residents with government subvention and regular contributions from the prominent Chinese residents.[68] Leaders of various trades and successful compradors were elected on an annual basis to become directors and to run and supervise and financially support its operation.

When an ordinance was passed to found the Hospital the following year, the government finally gave formal recognition to the leadership role played by the local notables and philanthropists among the Chinese.[69] Directorships of Tung Wah became highly regarded positions, which, in turn, reinforced the importance of the Hospital Board in the minds of other Chinese residents. They helped to transform 'a small class of rich Chinese businessmen into a group of Hong Kong notables, recognised as such by their own compatriots and by the British and Chinese Governments'.[70] Recognition from the Chinese came partly because the Tung Wah Directors proved themselves a valuable conduit for the Chinese government to bypass the British authorities in communicating with the Chinese in Hong Kong, and partly because Tung Wah Directors routinely purchased official rank or title from the Chinese government.

The Board of Tung Wah thus became the main core around which the local elite among the Chinese emerged. Below it, the Man Mo Temple Committee and other similar though less prominent bodies carried on working for the community. Included in this category were the *kaifong* associations, which were groupings of civic-minded, status-seeking, paternalistic and usually better-off residents of their neighbourhoods who organised practical affairs and helped the poor in their localities.[71] In the more remote areas where both the government and the Tung Wah's reach was limited, they did good work such as 'repairing bridges, mending roads, promoting educational facilities, providing free medical aid for the poor, and providing free coffins for the indigent dead' until the early post-war period.[72] These lower-level organisations generally served the local Chinese in parallel to the Hospital, which looked after the Chinese community colony-wide. Membership of its board meant high social position, to which the most successful and wealthy merchants or kaifong leaders aspired to gain admission.

After its creation in 1872, the Tung Wah Hospital functioned not only as a hospital but also as the main informal governing body for the Chinese community, implicitly sanctioned by the colonial government. Its non-medical activities should in modern terms be classified as social services. It helped to repatriate destitute people and women kidnapped into prostitution to their home villages in China, bury unclaimed dead bodies, fund and organise relief for victims of disasters and house lunatics of Chinese origins. More importantly, its board of directors came to be seen and used by the local Chinese as a medium between themselves and the government.[73] The subjects about which the local Chinese community sought their advice and help were very wide ranging. They included, for example, issues involving adultery or the authenticity of Chinese marriages, registration of companies or shops, application of night passes, the state of public security, disputes among both individuals and even between companies in the Chinese community.

The Tung Wah Hospital Board was able to perform so many functions because the colonial government was not prepared to commit enough of its own meagre resources for these services. Allowing the Chinese elite to look after their less well-off compatriots was a cost-effective and desirable measure from the point of view of the government.

Putting the matter in a comparative framework, it was obvious that in terms of governance the focus of the government was the much smaller expatriate community. In contrast, only one senior official, the Registrar General and Protector of the Chinese, was tasked specifically to deal with the overwhelmingly larger Chinese community. To a lesser extent, the same was true of the allocation of government resources. Even though in terms of physical infrastructures built by the government both the expatriate and the Chinese communities benefited, most of the infrastructures were nonetheless geared primarily to meet the requirements of the expatriates with the Chinese benefiting from them almost incidentally. Indeed, beyond the most basic physical infra-structures, such as roads and bridges, most Chinese residents did not use many of the other facilities provided by the government, including even government schools and hospitals in the early decades of British rule.[74]

Any retrospective criticism of the government's failure to provide a level of governance and public service to the Chinese similar to those for the expatriates in the nineteenth century should be put in context. To begin with, the Chinese preferred to minimise dealings with the colonial government as far as possible. Furthermore, the government did not have enough officers with sufficient command of the Chinese language to administer the Chinese community effectively even if it had wished to do so. With little effective communication between the colonial government and the Chinese community, which were separated not only by cultural and linguistic barriers but an entire way of life and attitude towards governance, it was understandable that the government did not pay much attention to the Chinese residents who were in any event not making demands for improvements in government services.

The Registrar General and his small department were responsible for liaising with and overseeing the non-medical work of Tung Wah and similar organisations such as the Po Leung Kuk, a society for the protection of women and children, in the Chinese community.[75] Before a Chinese person, Ng Choy, was appointed to membership of the Legislative Council in 1880, the Registrar General was the only senior figure in the colonial establishment in a position to speak for and look after the welfare of the Chinese community. On the whole, the Registrar General and its twentieth-century replacement office, the Secretary for Chinese Affairs, and Tung Wah's Board of Directors maintained a symbiotic relationship in looking after the welfare of the Chinese community.

In addition to being there for members of the Chinese community to approach, the Registrar General relied on the District Watch Force as its main instrument for dealing with the local Chinese on a daily basis. This Force came into existence in 1866, after local Chinese leaders proposed to the government that they should organise a local force of Cantonese-speaking Chinese constables, recruited, controlled and paid for by themselves for the protection of their businesses, properties and persons.[76] When the government agreed to its formation, this force was put under the control of the Registrar General and a District Watch Committee constituted of prominent Chinese. Until its dissolution in the early post-war period it existed as a kind of a Chinese police force for the Chinese community in parallel to the multi-ethnic police. In the nineteenth and early twentieth centuries, the District Watch Force served as runners for the Registrar General generally, police guards, detectives and census enumerators. They also traced runaway girls and intercepted young women brought into Hong Kong for prostitution, while its senior officers mediated local disputes within the Chinese community.[77]

In the early 1890s, the District Watch Committee was significantly reformed and strengthened after close consultation between Registrar General James Stewart Lockhart and various local Chinese leaders. The result was to turn it into the highest advisory body of the Chinese community to the colonial government, though it continued to supervise the District Watch Force. Membership of the Committee became a further progression in social standing than Directorships of Tung Wah among the local Chinese.

In its handling of the Chinese community, which had become increasingly important economically by the latter part of the nineteenth century, the government also started to co-opt some of the Western-educated Chinese to join the colonial establishment. Before 1900, sixteen Chinese were made Justices of the Peace, of whom three were elevated to become unofficial members of the Legislative Council.[78] As such, these Chinese became representatives of the community in the colonial establishment. While their prominence came from colonial patronage, their standing in the Chinese community depended critically on the work they did for the community, often by serving on bodies like Tung Wah or the District Watch Committee and by other philanthropic work.

Their admission to the colonial establishment, usually as members of the legislature, did not alter the fact that they were merely peripheral members who could not, in the nineteenth century, block general policies designed for colony-wide application. However, they were in a position to voice the concerns of their community and promote effectively issues deemed to be of particular importance to their most powerful Chinese constituencies, the merchants and property owners. They proved successful, for example, in resisting the government's wish to improve sanitary conditions in houses for the Chinese in the late 1880s, as it would have significantly increased costs for property owners.[79] Governance of the Chinese community outside of the realm of law and justice continued to be left largely in the hands of the local Chinese elite in the late nineteenth century.

The basic hands-off attitude of the colonial government towards the governance of the Chinese community met its most severe test in 1894, when Hong Kong suffered from the bubonic plague. After the government realised the plague had spread from Canton, it faced the choice between taking swift and strong actions itself or rely on the Chinese elite, particularly the Tung Wah Directors, to deal with it. Although the plague was at first raging only among the Chinese, the risk of infection to the rest of the population could not be ignored. The expatriates took a strong view that even if the Chinese should have the right to 'kill themselves' they should not be allowed to 'kill us' in the process.[80]

The government, for its part, was determined to improve the sanitary conditions in the Chinese community and thus reduce the danger of the plague spreading. This was a sensitive issue as the Chinese community still harboured a great distrust of Western medicine, particularly of surgery, and regarded the sending of sanitary inspectors into their homes to check and disinfect them as grave intrusions. Instead of following the advice of the Tung Wah Board to allow the Hospital to deal with it as a problem within the Chinese community, the government took matters into its own hands. It deployed a hospital ship to deal with plague victims, though few Chinese were willing to go on board for treatment, and employed soldiers as sanitary inspectors to disinfect the Chinese quarters under protection of police guards when resistance proved strong.[81]

The way the government handled the plague illustrates the limits within which it was prepared to allow the local Chinese elite to run the affairs of the Chinese community. For matters that it deemed to affect the Chinese community only with no wider implications, and provided these matters did not violate some principles held dear by the Victorians, the government was prepared to let Chinese community leaders handle them freely, subject to oversight usually exercised loosely through the Registrar General. It did not hesitate to overrule any initiative that went beyond this unspoken understanding.

Chapter 6
Agent for Change in China

However much Hong Kong seemed like a Chinese town to visitors from the West, as a British colony it was the nearest place for most progressive-minded Chinese to gain firsthand knowledge of a functioning Western government.[1] Hong Kong was not founded as a means to change China and bring it to modernity as defined by the West but it did play a key part in promoting the modernisation of China. Its government, legal system and free marketplace for Western ideas provided a living demonstration of an alternative way of life and government. The benefits of this Western model, albeit only in a colonial format, were clearly exhibited in its stability, order and prosperity. Hong Kong's transformation from a 'barren island with hardly a house upon it' into a thriving, peaceful and well-organised trading community under the control of a few dozen British officials inspired the critically minded Chinese intellectuals to explore the secrets of this successful formula.

Furthermore, being under British jurisdiction at the southern edge of the Chinese Empire meant that Hong Kong was a particularly well-suited staging ground for those Chinese dedicated to changing the status quo in China. It provided a safe haven to those whose attempts at revolution or major reform in China failed. By saving the life of many key revolutionaries or reformers, its very existence as an emergency exit greatly enhanced the morale of everyone who sought to change a regime known for its merciless brutality against dissidents and rebels. This function as a safe haven also benefited the people of China. It served as a safety valve in the vicious power politics by providing a way out for those Chinese leaders or senior officials who lost out in a contest for power.

Inspiration for Chinese Reformers

Although the Chinese Empire's humiliating defeat in the First Anglo-Chinese War was, in retrospect, a turning point in the history of China as it exposed the gap that had developed between rapidly industrialising Europe and pre-industrial China, it failed to force the Empire to recognise this momentous change. The Chinese Empire had to wait for another two decades, after it was engulfed in the upheavals of the Taiping and a few other major rebellions as well as suffering from the traumatic fall of the imperial capital to the Anglo-French expeditionary force in the Second Anglo-Chinese War, to accept the need for reform.[2] However, even then the realisation of the changes that took place and the need to reform in order to confront them was limited. Between 1861 and 1900, only 43 individuals commented on record on the significance of the changes underway.[3] The reforms introduced in China, as part of the self-strengthening movement, were therefore understandably limited both in their conception and in their scope. The senior officials who supported reform, from Prince Kong to Li Hongzhang and other relatively progressive-minded regional leaders, mainly came to accept the need for reform after having to deal with the Westerners in their official duties. They confined their efforts in the 1860s and 1870s to learning from the most obvious strength of the West, such as modern weapons, steamships and the management of trade, in order to counter this Western challenge.[4] Without firsthand experience of what a Western society was like or how the Westerners ran a government their mental horizons were restricted. This problem existed in addition to the basic attitude that guided most Chinese reformers until at least the 1890s, which was to rely on Chinese learning for substance and Western learning for applications.

By the time part of the Chinese elite began to realise that China should look beyond acquiring Western technologies and armaments and raised questions of what other important lessons they could learn from the West, British Hong Kong had left behind the agonies of its own birth pains. By the 1860s, Hong Kong was a stable and thriving community and its economy was expanding fast. The colonial administration had also started to tackle more effectively some of its earlier problems of inefficiency and corruption. After the 1860s, Hong Kong increasingly proved itself a positive example of what a reasonably well-administered British territory, inhabited mainly by Chinese people was like to those Chinese intellectuals who had the interest and the critical faculty to take on board this contrast with the situation prevailing in China.

It is therefore not surprising that some of the most perceptive and progressive-minded Chinese supporters for more far-reaching reforms at the time of the self-strengthening movement had lived in Hong Kong. Notable examples include Wang Tao, Cheng Guanying, Hu Liyuan, Ho Kai and Sun Yat-sen.

Wang Tao was often seen as the father of Chinese journalism, as he was the founder of the first independent Chinese-language newspaper, the *Xunhuan Ribao*, published in Hong Kong.[5] He was among the first Chinese intellectuals to observe as early as 1870 or so that the self-strengthening movement did not go far enough. It amounted to, in his words, 'merely copying the superficialities of the Western methods, getting only the name but very little substance'.[6] Wang thought 'the urgent task of our nation today lies primarily in the governance of the people' and that 'superficial imitation in concrete things is not so good as arousing intellectual curiosity'.[7]

Cheng Guanying was a comprador who lived in Hong Kong and become one of the more important Chinese advocates for reforms as he also served as an adviser to Li Hongzhang. He was particularly known for stressing the need for China to change in order to compete against the West in commerce and wealth creation.[8]

Hu Liyuan and Ho Kai were both partly educated in Hong Kong and spent most of their careers there, where they gained real insight into the strength of the West by being able to observe British 'liberal political philosophy in action'.[9] They used Hong Kong 'to promote the Chinese reform movement' by writing essays that 'exposed the corruption, inefficiency, and oppression of China's gentry-dominated ruling bureaucracy' and 'advocated a thorough reorganisation of China's government, with a ministry of commerce taking the leading position'.[10]

Sun Yat-sen was also educated partly in Hong Kong and was a pupil of Ho Kai at the School of Medicine, predecessor of the Medical Faculty at the University of Hong Kong. Despite his reputation as a revolutionary he started his political life advocating wide-ranging reforms to Li Hongzhang, and only turned to revolution after his approach to Li proved fruitless.[11]

Although advocates for reform based in Hong Kong were essentially outsiders whose impact on Chinese policies was peripheral, key leaders of the 1898 reform movement such as Kang Youwei and Liang Qichao were themselves also inspired by this British colony. An accomplished classical scholar, Kang became deeply interested in Western learning after 'visits to Hongkong and Shanghai impressed him with orderliness and prosperity of Western civilisation'.[12] Liang, likewise, only realised that Westerners should not be dismissed as barbarians in 1881 after he first visited Hong Kong, where he admired the orderliness, cleanliness and legal basis of British rule.[13]

Kang and Liang went beyond the generation of leaders of the self-strengthening movement and pushed for constitutional, educational and other reforms that could have far-reaching implications if implemented.[14] As it turned out, their gallant attempt failed and they barely escaped after the Empress Dowager Cixi staged a palace coup against Emperor Guangxu, who supported them. Hong Kong not only inspired Kang, Liang and some of their comrades to push the ill-fated reforms of 1898 but also served as sanctuary for them when they had to flee for their lives.

Even in exile Kang, Liang and their followers continued to use Hong Kong as one of their main bases to advocate a constitutional monarchy for China in fierce competition with the revolutionaries headed by Sun Yat-sen. Hong Kong and its Chinese-language newspapers provided a convenient, safe and free venue for conducting the important debates on the direction China should follow towards the end of the imperial era. In Hong Kong, they were conducted between two local Chinese newspapers, the *Zhongguo Ribao* of Sun's revolutionaries and the *Shang Bao* of Kang-Liang's constitutional reformers.[15] What the two groups were engaged in was not just about winning over the local Chinese community in Hong Kong. The real issue was to win the hearts and minds of as many Chinese intellectuals as possible and material backing from the overseas Chinese communities to support one or the other cause, particularly after an attempted conciliation between Liang and Sun failed in 1899.[16]

Hong Kong's Role in the Chinese Republican Revolution

Hong Kong was in an important sense the cradle of the republican revolution in China. Even though the success of the revolutionary uprising in 1911 was mainly a result of events in China, the idea for a revolution was conceived in Hong Kong, where the original organisation dedicated to revolution also put the idea into action for the first time. This British colony nurtured and helped to shape the basic ideas of the most important leader and ideologist for the revolution, Sun Yat-sen. As he himself admitted, Sun started to think about reform and revolution after he studied in Hong Kong and saw how well it was administered compared with China. Although he attributed his 'ideas for the revolution as having come entirely from Hong Kong' what in fact happened was that he was inspired by his Hong Kong experiences to pursue reform and then revolution in China.[17]

The ideology for the republican movement, the 'Three Principles of the People', was formulated and publicised after Sun embarked on his revolutionary career. In the meantime he had already been banned from Hong Kong for a decade, received wider exposure to various Western ideas and got help from some of his much better educated comrades in working out the framework and the details of this ideology.[18] Be that as it may, without Hong Kong's impact Sun might not have devoted himself to the revolution or conceived the basic ideas for the Three Principles, which came to be adopted as the official ideology of the revolution and its product, the Republic of China.

Hong Kong also produced the first generation of revolutionists who joined Sun in the first uprising of the revolution in 1895. Although the original organisation to promote a revolution, the Xingzhonghui or Revive China Society, was first founded by Sun and his friends in Hawaii a year earlier, it did not really take off until Sun established a Hong Kong branch. There it quickly merged with the Furen Wenshe (or the study society to make sure the right thing is done) under Yang Quyun and started to work for a revolution.

In its attempts to stage revolutionary uprisings, the Xingzhonghui was very much a Hong Kong operation. Its most active leaders were mainly young people from a similar background to Sun based in Hong Kong. As for the first armed uprising, which took place in Canton in 1895, its funds were raised, arms purchased, foot soldiers recruited, the plot hatched and the attempt launched from Hong Kong.[19] The second uprising, which was also staged by the Xingzhonghui, took place in Huizhou in Guangdong province in 1900. It, too, was conducted with Hong Kong as its principal support base, though Sun had also obtained backing from various secret societies and the Japanese.[20] In the first five years of the republican revolution, when the Xingzhonghui was the standard bearer of the revolutionary cause, Hong Kong was its most important operating, coordinating and support base.

In its contribution to the final success of the republican movement that overthrew the imperial government in China in 1912, Hong Kong's contributions must, however, be set in a wider context. To begin with, while a republic was created to take over from the imperial Manchu monarchy, it is arguable whether the events that led to this result constituted a revolution in the way that the American or French Revolutions did. With few fundamental changes following the collapse of the monarchy, Hong Kong could not claim much credit for making republicanism work, even if it had played a pivotal role in bringing it about in China. Furthermore, the success of the uprising in Wuchang in central China in October 1911, which set off a chain of events leading to the collapse of the Chinese Empire, was not expected by any of the top leaders of the revolutionary movement. It was certainly not organised, coordinated, provisioned or directed from Hong Kong.

The success of the revolutionaries in 1911–12 had much more to do with the weakness of the Manchu government, the general disaffection that was by then prevailing in the country and the successful recruitment by the revolutionaries of members of the modern new army units to support them than with the monarchy. Much of this recruitment of a critical mass happened in Japan in the first decade of the twentieth century. What really gave the revolutionaries the critical means to challenge and bring down the Chinese imperial government was the opportunity to infiltrate the new armies and the bureaucracy of the Empire. In this regard it was Japan, not Hong Kong, that provided the biggest scope for the revolutionaries to capture, outside of China proper, the hearts and mind of the young Chinese students and military cadets who proved vital to the success of the revolution. Indeed, the revolutionary movement was 'more disorganised in 1911 than at any time' and 'the Manchu rulers themselves were to blame for the revolution', since they 'gravely disappointed many reformers and generated widespread opposition' by ill-conceived policies over the course of the year.[21] The role that Hong Kong actually played in bringing down the Chinese Empire was therefore limited.

What Hong Kong did offer the revolutionary movement remained important. In general terms it played four roles other than being the cradle of the revolution.

To begin with, it served as the most important forward base for staging uprisings. In spite of its pedigree and devotion, the Xingzhonghui was increasingly eclipsed by other newer revolutionary groups that sprang up after 1900. This happened because China started to send students to Japan after it was defeated in the Sino-Japanese War in 1895. This process accelerated quickly as the Boxer Rebellion of 1900 'placed the weakness of the Qing dynasty on full view and energised the forces of both reform and revolution'.[22] It resulted in new revolutionary organisations being formed by intellectuals in various provinces. The most important of these were the Huaxinghui of Hunan and Hubei under Huang Xing and Song Jiaoren, and the Guangfuhui of Zhejiang and Anhui under Zhang Binglin and Tao Chengzhang. Together with the other groups, they formed a revolutionary alliance for China, the Tongmenghui, in Japan in 1905. Sun was elected its head, as he was the best-known revolutionary. A sensational attempt by the Chinese Embassy in London to abduct him in 1896 had failed spectacularly and turned his name into an internationally recognisable one.[23] With the largest concentration of Chinese students and military cadets outside of China, Japan had by then emerged as the largest base for the revolutionary movement. However, Japan was too far from China to serve as a forward base, and Hong Kong continued to play that role. It housed the most active branch of the Tongmenghui and served as the key centre for coordinating revolutionary activities in four southern Chinese provinces and for staging armed uprisings there. All together, the revolutionaries launched from Hong Kong eight out of a total of 32 uprisings between 1895 and 1911.[24]

The last major uprising staged from Hong Kong was the much celebrated one in Canton in April 1911, the last to fail before the successful Wuchang Uprising of the following October. Publicity of its failure and the subsequent execution of 86 revolutionaries, including many returned students, became a legend that symbolised the dedication and sacrifice of the revolutionaries.[25] They were known as the martyrs of Huanghuagang where they were executed. The creation of this legend gave the Tongmenghui and its successor, the Kuomintang, much value in seizing the moral high ground for promoting the republican cause.[26]

As a forward base, Hong Kong also functioned as a major recruiting and training-ground for the revolutionaries. Until they could recruit from new army units in any number, most of the armed uprisings had to be carried out by paid soldiers or by secret society or triad members. Many of the foot soldiers of the revolution for operations in south China were recruited and given basic military training in Hong Kong. Some extremists also trained themselves in terrorist tactics, particularly in assassination. It was the second most important means used by the revolutionaries after armed uprising. Between 1895 and 1911, they made 11 attempts at assassination, of which three were organised and staged from Hong Kong.[27] The best known was the attempt by Wang Jingwei to assassinate the Prince Regent in early 1910.[28]

In its role as a propaganda centre for the revolution, Hong Kong was the most important base until the publication in Tokyo in 1905 of the *Min Bao*, which replaced the *Zhongguo Ribao* of Hong Kong as the flagship of the revolutionary movement's propaganda machine.[29] While the *Min Bao* was the organ in which the most important ideas for the revolution were set out, expounded and debated, the first major newspaper of the revolutionaries, the *Zhongguo Ribao*, continued to play an important role in promoting the cause. Although it was published in Hong Kong, the *Zhongguo Ribao* targeted its readership in China and the overseas Chinese communities. Among the many journals and newspapers published by the revolutionaries, it was one of the most important, both through its own circulation beyond Hong Kong and in providing support in setting up other newspapers among various overseas Chinese communities.[30] In addition to the *Zhongguo Ribao*, a number of other newspapers advocating the revolutionary cause were also published in Hong Kong, though they were less influential. Furthermore, Hong Kong was used by the Tongmenghui as the key centre to produce dramatic performances to spread the revolutionary cause among the illiterate general public in southern China.[31]

The third major role Hong Kong played was to give financial support to the revolutionary movement. Its Chinese community gave generously. Some of the wealthy merchants also joined the revolution and provided premises and safe houses for all kinds of overt activities and covert operations. The exact amount of the financial contribution Hong Kong or, for that matter, any overseas Chinese community provided cannot be ascertained precisely as 'available records are only partial and fragmentary' given the clandestine nature of the revolution.[32] What is known is that the early uprisings staged by the Xingzhonghui in south China as well as the publication of the *Zhongguo Ribao* were largely financed by supporters in Hong Kong. Among them the biggest contributor was probably Li Jitang, who inherited a million dollars and used his wealth to support the revolution.[33] In addition, Hong Kong's international financial network was used to allow it to function as the main centre for receiving funds raised by Sun and other leaders from overseas Chinese communities all over the world. It further managed the finances as well as organised the purchase of weapons, ammunition, and other essentials for the revolution.[34] Immediately after the success of the Wuchang Uprising and when the military government of Guangdong in the young republic was seriously short of funds, Hong Kong contributed between two and three million Hong Kong dollars in 1912 to sustain its pro-republic activities in Canton.[35]

Finally, Hong Kong served as a safe haven for the revolutionaries to retreat after unsuccessful armed uprisings. Sun Yat-sen himself escaped to Hong Kong after the first uprising of 1895 failed. Once they had crossed the border into this British colony, the long arm of the Chinese security by and large could not reach them. Even in the few cases where the Chinese authorities did seek to retaliate against known leaders of failed uprisings, of which the best-known case was the successful murder in Hong Kong of Sun's associate, Yang Quyun, after the Huizhou Uprising of 1900, they backfired to serve the revolutionary cause. Yang's murder provoked the Hong Kong government to provide police protection and a revolver for self-defence to another well-known revolutionary leader, Chen Shaobai, when established British policy was not to give the revolutionaries any help.[36] It also did not deter Yang's comrades from planning another armed uprising shortly afterwards.[37] On the whole, the availability of Hong Kong as a safe haven helped the revolutionaries to conserve their precious human resources and maintain morale in an endeavour that did not look promising until the Wuchang Uprising succeeded unexpectedly.

The real sentiments of the Chinese population of Hong Kong towards the revolutionary movement were revealed after the revolutionaries seized power in Wuchang in central China. It caught everyone by surprise. The revolutionaries based in Hong Kong and Guangdong were so unprepared for this that they were unable to seize the opportunity and take any meaningful action to support their comrades in Wuchang for two weeks.[38] However, the Chinese people in Hong Kong had already demonstrated their true feelings in the annual celebration of Confucius' birthday a week after the Wuchang Uprising by the deliberate non-display of the Chinese imperial flag and by a mass attack on the premises of the royalists to remove the imperial flags displayed by them.[39] Some also jeered at the newly appointed Manchu Tartar-General of Canton, Feng Shan, when he passed through Hong Kong to take office. He was assassinated within hours of his arrival in Canton by a team from Hong Kong.[40] When the news, which turned out to be false, that Beijing had fallen to the revolutionaries and the Manchus had fled was reported in Hong Kong on 6 November, jubilation reigned among the local Chinese. Governor Sir Frederick Lugard captured their mood: 'The entire Chinese populace appeared to become temporarily demented with joy. The din of crackers... was deafening and accompanied by perpetual cheering and flag-waving – a method of madness most unusual to the Chinese.'[41]

Once the unravelling of the Manchu Dynasty had started, Canton became an important prize for the revolutionaries, as the support of Guangdong province was at stake. The province was at that time under the control of the royalist Viceroy, Zhang Mingqi. He recognised that the central authority of the Empire was faltering but preferred to see the province develop autonomy within a federal arrangement than to support the revolution.[42] Zhang had to flee Canton in the early hours of 9 November when it became clear to him that the revolutionaries had finally got their acts together and the loyalty of his sizeable garrison could no longer be guaranteed. Hong Kong helped to create this condition in Guangdong over a period of 16 years. More immediately, it was the base from which the revolutionary leader Hu Hanmin went on to take over the military governorship in Canton, and the safe haven where Viceroy Zhang sought protection, rather than test the loyalty of his garrison and try to suppress the revolutionaries.

A Safe Haven for Dissidents and Political Refugees

By serving as a safe haven for dissidents, political refugees and officials who had lost power, Hong Kong contributed to political stability and change in China and so acted as a safety valve in the turbulent politics of twentieth century China. The Hong Kong government had a clear policy, which was summarised by an official in the Colonial Office in the following terms:

Hong Kong's policy towards China is one of strict impartiality and non-intervention in Chinese internal affairs. The Colony is concerned to maintain friendly relations with the Chinese government... But the desire to maintain friendly relations with neighbouring Chinese authorities does not, of course, mean that Hong Kong takes side with them in any internal Chinese disputes.[43]

The implication of this policy was that Chinese dissidents and others were permitted to live and get on with their legitimate affairs in Hong Kong, provided no local laws were broken and their presence was not injurious to British interests. The availability of Hong Kong for those who failed in power struggles of one kind or another in China was valuable in reducing political instability in China, since the losers, be they reformers, revolutionaries, royalists, warlords, Kuomintang or Communist leaders, could leave the political arena without having to lose everything and thus be tempted to fight to the bitter end.

Although the basic thinking behind this policy was in place as soon as the issue arose in the 1890s, its implementation was haphazard and not always consistent. Much depended on the judgement of the senior officials in charge. They were influenced by their assessment of what constituted British interests, the state of relations with China at the time and their personal bias.

The issue came up after the first revolutionary uprising of 1895. Sun Yat-sen was banished from Hong Kong for five years, officially on the grounds that his presence would be 'dangerous to the peace and good order of the Colony'.[44] More specifically, it was because Governor Sir William Robinson had 'no intention of allowing... Hong Kong to be used as an Asylum for persons engaged in plots and dangerous conspiracies against a friendly neighbouring Empire'.[45] If the government had been consistent it would also have expelled Sun's comrades, who were also not British subjects, and suppressed the Xingzhonghui, neither of which it did. The decision to banish Sun was in fact made not because of a request from the Chinese government but because the Hong Kong government believed the Chinese government would be pleased with it.[46] This was an arbitrary action calculated to curry favour with the Chinese authorities. When the Colonial Office reviewed the matter as a result of a parliamentary question being tabled, it admitted in private that the ordinance 'under which this man was banished is of a most arbitrary character, which might rouse much criticism, if its contents were known'.[47]

The banishment of Sun should be contrasted with the helpful manner in which the colonial government dealt with constitutional reformer Kang Youwei when his 1898 attempt failed. With Governor Robinson gone, the Officer Administering the Government, Major General Wilsone Black, promptly offered Kang 'accommodation in the Police barracks until suitable arrangements could be made in a Chinese friend's house to receive him' in order to give him a protective welcome.[48] Black did so because he considered some of Kang's reforms 'wise and reasonable'.[49] Black's sympathy for the reformers ensured a different implementation of the same policy of non-involvement in Chinese politics and good neighbourliness. Hong Kong's welcome to Kang did not last, however. Once Kang's presence was deemed to work against British interests several years later, a different Officer Administering the Government, Francis May, banished him. Although not allowing the colony to be used as a base against the Chinese government was again mentioned, the critical factor that worked against Kang was that he and his supporters were arousing 'strong anti-foreign' sentiments in their propaganda against the Chinese government.[50] The British patience for Chinese reformers or revolutionaries ran out quickly if they came to be seen as harmful to British interests.[51]

The willingness of the British not to allow the colony to be used as a base for subverting the government of China was always limited in the first half of the twentieth century. First and foremost, the colonial government reigned over rather than ruled its Chinese population. It did not try – and in any event did not have enough resources – to monitor the activities of the Chinese revolutionaries or reformers. It meant they had tremendous scope for their activities as long as they were not seen to have broken any Hong Kong law. Second, the British were much more concerned with maintaining law and order in the colony than with appeasing the Chinese authorities. As the murders of Yang Quyun and several others indicated, it was not beyond the Chinese authorities to take matters into their own hands in striking against revolutionary leaders based in Hong Kong. Political murder involved the commission of a serious crime, and the colonial government generally reacted firmly. Its basic attitude was that while it would:

> perform its duty in preventing the Colony from being made the base of operations against Canton, the result of which would be injurious to our trade which must suffer from any serious disturbance, the assassination of persons in Hong Kong who may be obnoxious to the Chinese government is intolerable.[52]

After all, the might of the British Empire in the late nineteenth and early twentieth centuries was such that it did not need to concede much to the Chinese government, but for the Hong Kong government it was advantageous and sensible to keep on good terms with the neighbouring Guangdong authorities. This provides the context within which succeeding governors judged the best way to implement the policy of non-intervention in domestic Chinese affairs.

All in all, even though this policy of neutrality was only haphazardly and inconsistently implemented, as a general policy it was followed by the Hong Kong government. It certainly worked to the benefit of the Chinese people as it provided a safe exit and easy option out for those Chinese officials and leaders who lost out in very intense and vicious power struggles, a function that came to be much more valuable in the republican than in the late imperial period. The first real tangible benefit of this policy was enjoyed when the machination of Guangdong politics revealed the precarious position of Viceroy Zhang Mingqi in 1911. The established record of Hong Kong as a sanctuary no doubt helped to persuade Zhang to abandon any idea of using force against the revolutionaries and thus avoided bloodshed and disorder in Canton and possibly much of the rest of the province.

This highly valuable function of Hong Kong for China did not come about because the British had the welfare of the Chinese people in mind. Similar to many other benefits modern Hong Kong brought to the Chinese people, this policy was devised with British, not Chinese, interests in mind. Located at the edge of China, with promoting trade and economic exchanges with China as its *raison d'être,* the interests of the British, which were overwhelmingly economic, could not be advanced by Hong Kong being embroiled in Chinese politics.

Chapter 7

The Great War and
Chinese Nationalism

Even though its fortune was much more closely tied to events in East Asia, as part of the British Empire Hong Kong found itself at war with Germany when the assassination by a Serb of the heir apparent of the Austro-Hungarian Empire in the Bosnian city of Sarajevo in June 1914 provoked a general war in Europe. While Hong Kong did play its part in supporting the British war efforts, the Great War was largely a European affair with only limited impact on life in this East Asian imperial outpost. Geography, as well as strong economic, social and other ties with China, meant even in the course of the war, Hong Kong was more immediately affected by developments in China than by the fortune of the Allied Powers.

The Great War coincided with a period of important changes in China, where the stability and cohesion of the young republic reached breaking point despite the steady rise of Chinese nationalism. The initial unity that followed the end of the Manchu Dynasty was achieved at the cost of a deal between leaders of the revolutionary movement and Yuan Shikai, the most powerful figure in the service of the last Emperor. Indeed, Provisional President Sun Yat-sen of the Republic of China handed over this supreme office to Yuan as a price for securing the latter's allegiance and ensuring the abdication of the Emperor. The republican experiment was derailed a year later when Yuan attempted to build a dictatorship by assassinating the leading advocate for parliamentary politics, Song Jiaoren.[1] Song was the parliamentary leader of the Kuomintang, which was formed by veterans of the Tongmenghui and had just won a landslide in the first parliamentary elections.[2] His murder provoked Sun to organise the so-called 'Second Revolution', which was quickly suppressed by Yuan. Whatever his personal intentions, Yuan made an attempt to restore a monarchy with himself as Emperor in 1915. Seizing the opportunity of the Western powers' preoccupation with the War, Japan tried to impose upon China the infamous 'Twenty-one Demands' that would have reduced China to a protectorate of Japan.[3] Although Yuan managed to resist the most damaging of the Japanese demands, his monarchical attempt discredited him.[4] The collapse of his monarchy in 1916 destroyed the authority of the central government and allowed regional military leaders to seize control of their own domains.[5] This marked the beginning of the warlord era, a state of affairs that was not nominally brought to a close until 1928, when the successful Northern Expedition from Canton led by General Chiang Kai-shek, a follower of Sun, re-established a credible national government.

The failure of the republican experiment, the imperialist ambitions of the Japanese and the sense of helplessness and anger among the intellectuals, students and labour activists converged to produce a powerful outburst of nationalism in China. This exploded spectacularly in the form of the May Fourth Movement, which was a response to what Chinese intellectuals and students saw as the unfair treatment of China at the Versailles Peace Conference and the incompetence of the Chinese government in negotiating the peace treaty in 1919.[6] China had joined the Great War on the side of the Allied Powers in 1917 and contributed nearly 200,000 labourers to serve as non-combat auxiliaries in the battlefields of Europe, suffering no less than 2,000 fatal casualties.[7] This notwithstanding, at Versailles China was treated not as a fellow victor and ally but an inferior country. Its legitimate claim to restore its sovereign rights over the former German Concession and naval base at Jiaozhou in Shandong province was ignored. Instead, the Allied Powers gave the old German privileges in Jiaozhou to the Japanese as spoils of war, in line with secret agreements they had reached with Japan during the war. The public display of indignation and protest among the urban elite of China that followed dramatically accelerated the rise of nationalism in the country, and led to a few major incidents in the 1920s with significant implications for Hong Kong.

The behaviour of the Allied Powers also compared badly with the apparent generosity of the Communist regime that seized control of Russia towards the end of the Great War. In July 1919, the Soviet government announced that it unilaterally gave up the privileges in China inherited from the old Tsarist regime, though this news did not reach China until the following March.[8] This grand gesture 'invoked immediate enthusiasm in China and provoked a dramatic interest' in the Communist ideology.[9] It also encouraged some political leaders, particularly Sun Yat-sen – whose attempts to secure support from the Western countries had repeatedly met with rebuff – to explore seriously the prospect of help from the Soviet Union.[10]

The province of Guangdong was caught up in much of the main drama that unfolded in China. It was one of the most important territorial bases that the Kuomintang had. A Cantonese himself, Sun relied heavily on the province to continue his struggle to entrench republicanism in China. The control of Canton, the provincial capital, changed hands several times in the 1910s and 1920s. It reflected the rise and fall of various warlords and Sun, who sometimes cooperated with and sometimes intrigued against each other. In the middle of the 1920s it also became a major centre for the Chinese Communist Party or CCP (which had joined Sun's Kuomintang in a united front) to recruit, train and organise their supporters.[11] Canton was therefore a hotbed for activists of all kinds. Whatever their individual political persuasion, most of them were also deeply nationalistic, which made them not particularly well disposed to the British colonial regime south of the border.

Hong Kong found itself sucked into the whirlpool of politics in China, and Guangdong in particular, in this period. Sometimes this was the result of involvement in Guangdong affairs by certain sectors of Hong Kong's Chinese community. More often it was caught up in the rapid rise and spread of Chinese nationalism that swept across China but did not stop at the Sino-British border. This was partly because the border was a porous one and the Chinese population of Hong Kong identified themselves and their future more with China than with the British colony. It was also partly because Hong Kong was one of China's main gateways to the West, the port through which numerous Chinese sailed to the West. Those who acquired Western ideas about the rights of individuals, labour unions and other modern concepts did not merely bring them to China but to the working people of Hong Kong too.

The Impact of the Great War

When the Great War started, the British community in Hong Kong greeted it with the same patriotic fervour that prevailed across the British Empire. Few expected the long drawn out, painful, horrific and unprecedented scale of slaughter that the War turned out to entail. Hong Kong called up the locally raised Hong Kong Volunteer Corps to take over most of the garrison duties so that the regular forces could be freed for service in Europe.[12]

With Germany now the enemy, the colonial government needed to deal with the existence of the sizeable German community. It numbered 342 out of the Western civilian population of 5,248 by the 1911 census, and was the second-largest Western community after the British themselves. On the outbreak of war, women and children of German nationality were made to leave while men of military age were interned. They were joined by other German nationals sent from Jiaozhou after it fell into Allied hands. The internment camp was guarded in such a relaxed manner that internees were given tools to build an earthen stage for a theatre hut, but they promptly dug a 180 feet tunnel for a mass escape.[13] The attempt failed, and the three men who got away were arrested before they could cross into China.

Any concern of a German attack disappeared once the China squadron of the German Navy left its base in Jiaozhou to rejoin the main fleet and was subsequently destroyed in the First Battle of the Falklands. By November 1914, what remained of German military power in China was eliminated when an Anglo-Japanese force, including HMS *Triumph* which sailed from Hong Kong, captured Jiaozhou.[14] The security of Hong Kong never came under any threat in the course of the War.

Hong Kong's main contributions to the war efforts lay in the support it gave to Britain. Patriotism among the expatriate British population led to 579 out of a total of 2,157 men volunteering for military service outside the colony.[15] In addition, Hong Kong not only paid the normal military contribution but also made a further financial contribution of $HK10 million, roughly equivalent to the total government revenue for the year 1914.[16] Included in this contribution was $2 million raised from a seven per cent special charge on rates paid by property owners, most of whom were Chinese. Individual Chinese also made donations, of which the best known was Robert Hotung's gift of two Vickers fighter aircraft.[17] Although the Chinese community's support of the war effort should not be confused with the patriotic response of the expatriate Britons, it was nevertheless a reflection of the appreciation the better-off Chinese had for the British administration.

The economy of Hong Kong did not suffer directly from the war. Even though its non-Chinese population fell from 20,710 to 13,600, its population as a whole increased steadily and rapidly, rising from 501,304 in 1914 to 598,100 in 1919.[18] In terms of economic growth, Hong Kong benefited rather than suffered, not least because of expansion in business and other economic activities among the local Chinese. The redirection of British shipping from Hong Kong and China to support the war gave the local Chinese greater scope to expand into modern shipping, particularly in light of the growth of traffic between Hong Kong and Canton.[19] The rapid development of a modern Chinese banking sector also roughly coincided with the war. Although the first modern Chinese bank, the Bank of Canton, was founded in 1912, three others came into existence between 1914 and 1919, including the largest of them all, the Bank of East Asia.[20]

The continued expansion of the economy did not mean Hong Kong was insulated from some of the economic disruptions that came to a head when war finally ended. Severe inflation had occurred as a result of the shortages caused by wartime disruptions and the rapid increase in population, which pushed up rent and the price of various commodities while wages remained static.[21] This rise in the cost of living without a compensatory increase in wages put a serious strain on the working people, with the low-paid labourers being hit the hardest. A manifestation of this problem was the rice riots of 1919. They broke out as prices shot up following the failure of the rice crop in Thailand, restriction of exports in Indo-China and India, as well as an unexpected upsurge in demand in Japan.[22] The fall in living standards among the Chinese working class created serious social tension and laid the ground for a period of labour unrest and social changes after the end of the Great War.

Labour Unrest

The first wave of labour unrest was a 19-day strike organised by the Hong Kong Chinese Engineers' Institute in March 1920, which had been established only six months earlier. Since members of this union were in fact skilled workers who worked mainly as mechanics in dockyards, public utilities and manufacturing industries, they could not easily be replaced.

They were among the best paid of Chinese workers and occupied a relatively strong bargaining position in demanding a pay rise to offset the effect of inflation.[23] After their repeated requests for a 40 per cent wage increase were rejected, they staged a strike and 9,000 left Hong Kong for Canton, where the cost of living was lower and the government under Sun Yat-sen helped them by providing lodging and food for the duration of the strike.[24] Within three weeks their employers, mostly expatriate-owned enterprises and the colonial government itself, agreed to meet most of their demands. It meant a pay rise of 32.5 per cent for those who earned less than $HK100 per month and a 20 per cent rise for those earning more, and the strike ended.[25]

It was the first large-scale strike organised by a modern labour union in Hong Kong. It had the effect of inspiring others to follow. Consequently, carpenters, bricklayers, cabinet-makers, and other skilled workers organised strikes the following year.[26] According to one account, between 1920 and 1922 a total of 42 strikes for better wages occurred.[27]

This wave of labour unrest reached a high point with the seamen's strike of 1922, which has been described as 'the most successful labor movement ever organized by Chinese workers against unfairness and exploitation'.[28] Despite the implied political overtone of this assessment, like most of the strikes of this period, it was driven primarily by economic motives. Organised by the General Union of Chinese Seamen, it was launched to demand wage increases of between 10 and 40 per cent and to reform the system for recruiting seamen. The seamen felt justified in the first demand because their wages had remained static while the cost of living had gone up significantly. In 1922, a Chinese seaman on average wage was paid a monthly income lower than the basic expenditures required to support himself and his family while his Caucasian colleagues were paid several times more and were given a wage increase of 15 per cent.[29] Their second demand was essentially to seek redress for a system of recruitment that allowed the middlemen, the recruiting agencies, to charge exorbitant fees for arranging for them to work on ships.[30]

The strike started with 1,500 seamen on 13 January 1922 after the Union's requests for pay rises were rebuffed for a third time. It escalated as mediation efforts by the government failed. By the end of the month over 10,000 seamen had left Hong Kong for Canton where they received a sympathetic reception. The situation got more serious as sympathy strikes by transport workers also started, and striking seamen in Guangdong were sent by their union to stop fresh food from being shipped to Hong Kong. Further attempts at mediation by the established leaders of the Chinese community, like the Board of Directors of the Tung Wah Hospital, failed.[31]

The government, under Sir Reginald Stubbs (Governor, 1919–25), reacted in a heavy-handed manner. Stubbs completely misread the situation and misunderstood the nature of the strike. Even after it ended, he continued to think it was politically inspired and 'organised from Canton with the sympathy of Sun'.[32] He proscribed the Seamen's Union.

This provoked the union to call for a general strike in Hong Kong, backing it up with intimidation.[33] As a result, before February ended a total of 120,000 workers, more than one-fifth of the total population, had joined the strike and turned the usually bustling and noisy harbour into a remarkably quiet port full of stranded ships.[34] In order to pre-empt an exodus to Canton, whose support enabled the strikers to continue their struggle, the colonial government suspended train services to Canton. This backfired. Striking workers left on foot, leading to a dramatic escalation. The police opened fire and killed five strikers in the town of Shatin on 3 March when they tried to stop the exodus. Outraged by the perceived brutality of the police, sympathy strikes spread very quickly and practically paralysed Hong Kong. This left the government and the shipping companies with little choice but to back down.[35] A compromise was reached two days later and the seamen returned to work on 6 March, ending eight weeks of strike.

The seamen secured pay rises of between 15 and 30 per cent, in contrast to their original demands for 17 to 35 per cent, and a lift of the ban on the Seamen's Union, though the recruitment system was not changed. Although strikes by other unions continued for a short time, they generally ended with a round of wage increases averaging about 30 per cent.[36] By any standard, this was a major achievement, both for the union and for organised labour in Hong Kong. Indeed, it taught the local working men that 'unity among themselves was the most powerful bulwark for the protection of their interests'.[37] This lesson proved to be of great significance three years later when organised labour confronted the colonial authority head on for the first time and as part of a general political and nationalist movement in Guangdong.

The failure of the Chinese elite, drawn mainly from the merchants, to mediate also revealed the gulf between them and the workers. This incident showed that the government's nineteenth-century practice of leaving the local Chinese elite to keep stability and order within the Chinese community had failed. Hong Kong society had changed so much that the government had to deal directly with its working-class Chinese population. It sought to prepare for such disruption of social order and prosperity by increasing the size of the garrison and compiling a register of expatriate citizens who could be called up to perform essential services if required. It also kept the Emergency Regulations Ordinance (1922), which was rushed through the Legislative Council in one day, when the strike was deteriorating fast in February, to arm the Governor in Council with sweeping powers to 'make any regulations whatsoever which he may consider desirable in the public interest'.[38] The strike prompted the colonial government to keep a more watchful eye over its Chinese population.

The strike 'was essentially an economic struggle for better wages', though Chinese Communist writers claim it carried 'political meaning in struggling against imperialism'.[39] The reality that the strike was about improving wages was reflected in the settlement. Governor Stubbs was wrong to consider it politically motivated and led by the Communists.[40]

The actual role played by the CCP was a negligible one. Although a couple of key leaders of the strike, notably Su Zhaozheng and Lin Weimin, were more hardline than were the leaders of the earlier mechanics' strike and would join the CCP later, they did not have close contact with it in 1922. In any event, the CCP was only formed in Shanghai in 1921 and the 'Communist movement in Guangdong was still in its infancy and had certainly not yet extended to Hong Kong'.[41]

In comparison, the Kuomintang authorities in Canton under Sun played a more active role. They provided as much as $100,000 to support the strikers, and made available temples and other public buildings to house them.[42] Vital as these were in enabling the striking workers to sustain their struggle, neither the Kuomintang nor the government in Canton was involved in directing the strike. It was not linked to the rise of nationalism in urban China that followed the May Fourth Movement of 1919. With this strike being the largest and most successful one organised by a modern Chinese labour union, it is more accurate to say the seamen's strike inspired both the Kuomintang and the CCP than the other way round.

The Rise of Chinese Nationalism

In China, modern nationalism emerged forcefully in the latter half of the 1890s after the first Sino-Japanese War (1894–5). The shock of China's defeat by what it had hitherto regarded as an inferior, and the scramble for concessions that followed, had an impact on Chinese intellectuals and the politically aware residents of coastal regions that surpassed any humiliation China had suffered from previous Western imperialist encroachments. This defined the context in which Western-educated individuals like Sun Yat-sen started the revolutionary movement. Its real appeal up to 1911 was based on nationalism, though democracy and advancing people's livelihood were formally the other two main components of the revolution's ideology.[43] At the popular level, the xenophobic Boxer Rebellion of 1900 also showed 'unmistakable signs of an emerging Chinese nationalism'.[44] However, the place where a kind of proto-nationalism of the Chinese people first found expression was Hong Kong, where the Chinese had earlier and greater exposure to Western ideas.[45]

The Chinese working men of Hong Kong appeared to show what Governor Sir George Bowen described as 'popular nationalism' in a strike against working on visiting French warships that culminated in three days of riots in the course of the Sino-French War (1884–5). This war was fought as the Chinese Empire attempted to defend its suzerainty over Indo-China, which was being colonised by the French. What led Bowen to make his assessment was the perceived contrast in the reaction of the local Chinese population compared with that during the Second Anglo-Chinese War (1856–60), when the British and the French apparently had no difficulty recruiting porters and collaborators in Hong Kong.[46] In 1884, according to Bowen, as news of the Sino-French conflict spread, 'Chinese artisans, coolies, and boatmen refused all offers of pay to do any work whatsoever for the French ships'.[47] Be that as it may, it is too simplistic to portray this incident as a straightforward outburst of nationalism among the Chinese working people of Hong Kong.

The anti-French riots that broke out in October 1884 at the end of a month-long boycott were the result of several factors working together. To begin with, the Chinese community in Hong Kong had become much better informed thanks to the introduction of a Chinese-language press. As the press reported news of the Sino-French war, it 'helped to rouse national awareness among the populace'.[48] The Chinese authorities in Canton also promised awards to those who sabotaged the French war efforts and enlisted members of the secret societies or the Triads to help organise this campaign and intimidate the non-strikers. Consequently, a significant number of workers refused to work on the French naval ships that came to Hong Kong for repair. Riots broke out, because the colonial government was heavyhanded in dealing with the strikers. It imposed a fine of five dollars, about a month's income for the average labourer, on the first ten boatmen who refused to work for the French, and thus raised the fear among others that their livelihood might be harmed in the same way too.[49] What finally provoked the riots was that the police fired on striking workers when the latter threw stones at them.[50] Although the riots were not simply an expression of nationalism, there were sufficient nationalistic elements to suggest that an incipient Chinese nationalism of some kind was beginning to come into existence.

At the turn of the century, the Chinese in Hong Kong had genuinely subscribed to the nascent Chinese nationalism. When various groups in Guangdong organised boycotts against the Americans (1905–6) and then the Japanese (1908), they by and large responded to the appeal of their compatriots and took sympathetic and supportive action.[51] In the case of the anti-American boycott, it was over US discrimination against Chinese immigrants, manifested in periodic acts to exclude Chinese immigration and the abuse of Chinese immigrants by American officials. The anti-Japanese boycott arose as the Chinese authorities, which intercepted a Japanese freighter, *Tatsu Maru II*, for smuggling contraband arms and munitions into Guangdong, capitulated to unreasonable Japanese demands to apologise and to compensate for the costs of the cargo intercepted.[52] The support that various sectors of the Chinese community of Hong Kong gave to their Chinese compatriots demonstrated that they too shared the sense of nationalism, which was rising rapidly as a key political force in China. This was spectacularly demonstrated and reaffirmed by the jubilation with which the Chinese community of Hong Kong greeted the collapse of Manchu power and the rise of the Chinese Republic.

Hong Kong's Chinese community generally responded in a similar way when external events again provoked major outbursts of nationalism in China, as it did on the occasion of Japan's imposition of the Twenty-One Demands in 1915 and the Versailles Peace Conference in 1919. In 1915, after the severity of the Japanese demands was leaked by President Yuan Shihkai's government, Chinese students and dockworkers in Hong Kong responded to a campaign to boycott Japanese goods in coastal Chinese cities. They staged sympathetic protests and some even threw stones at Japanese shops.[53] In 1919, Chinese merchants in Hong Kong led a boycott of Japanese goods and a promotion of Chinese products. Chinese-language schools also helped to spread the message by using the boycott as an essay topic for students.[54] On the whole, Hong Kong followed Canton in supporting the anti-Japanese movement, though the intensity of feeling and actions taken were weaker. While Chinese merchants, particularly those involved in the modern retail sector, seized the moment to combine patriotism and their business interests, the more established leaders of the local Chinese community were less actively involved. Those at the top, like the two Chinese unofficial members of the Legislative Council, were closely associated with the colonial regime and had vested interests in maintaining the stability and order of the colony. The entrenchment of Chinese nationalism among the local Chinese would prove to be a major force that the colonial government had to face when another incident in China provoked another massive outburst.

The Canton-Hong Kong Strike and Boycott

In 1925, Hong Kong was caught up in the first major confrontation between Chinese nationalism and British imperialism, and found itself engulfed in a general strike followed by a boycott of 16 months, organised and supported by the Kuomintang-dominated government in Canton, which had admitted into its ranks members of the CCP in a united front the previous year. Although leaders of the seamen's strike like Su Zhaozheng and Li Weimin again played an active role in starting this new general strike, its nature was fundamentally different from the previous strikes. In 1925, Su and Li acted more as members of the CCP, which they had joined after the seamen's strike, than as union leaders.[55] The new general strike was driven not by economic but by political forces.

The origin of the strike-cum-boycott was labour unrest at a Japanese-owned cotton mill in Shanghai, where a violent confrontation between labour and management led to the death of a Chinese worker, Gu Zhenghong.[56] On the day of the memorial service for Gu, 30 May, his colleagues were joined by other protestors, including a large number of students. They marched inside the International Settlement, which was under the jurisdiction not of the Chinese authorities but of the British-dominated Municipal Council in Shanghai. Political demonstrations were illegal there. After some serious confrontation between the police and the demonstrators outside the Louza police station, a small detachment of policemen under the command of a British Inspector fired on the demonstrators when it appeared that the crowd would storm the station.[57] The shootings not only killed nine and injured dozens more, but also provoked the greatest outburst of Chinese nationalism directed against the British. The Japanese were spared partly because many of the leading Chinese felt their country could not take on more than one imperial power at a time, and partly because the labour unrest that led to Gu's death had also resulted earlier in the death of a Japanese.[58]

On the day after the shootings, strong reactions among the unionists, students and the general public in Shanghai were adroitly steered by Li Lisan and his comrades in the CCP into forming a General Trade Union to lead a general strike.[59] When the strike started the following day, there was further bloodshed, as individual or small groups of police officers found themselves in situations where they felt justified to open fire for their personal safety, causing more fatalities. A crisis quickly developed: 74,000 industrial workers in the International Settlement had gone on strike by 4 June, and naval personnel from 22 foreign warships had to be deployed for security duties two days later.[60] The number of strikers rose to between 100,000 and 150,000 later in the month.[61]

Indignation over the shootings reverberated in other major Chinese cities. Massive demonstrations against imperialism, focusing on the British, were organised elsewhere. Before the end of the month, one of these demonstrations turned into another major shooting incident in Canton and took the protest movement to a new level with direct consequences for Hong Kong.

In Shanghai itself, where the Chinese part of the city was under the control of warlord Zhang Zuolin, who was keen to end the confrontation with Britain and the foreign powers, tension was slowly eased and compromises eventually reached among various involved parties. The general strike ended in Shanghai in late September after the General Trade Union was disbanded, and most strikes were called off, except by seamen involved in supporting a parallel boycott against Hong Kong.[62]

What happened in Shanghai turned out to be merely the prelude to a long-drawn and bigger movement. This was the transformation of an outpouring of Chinese nationalism into a general strike in Hong Kong and a boycott against this British colony imposed by and directed from Canton. The Kuomintang authorities in Canton officially sponsored this combined operation, while its Communist partner actively orchestrated and directed it. In an important sense, the Communists worked as the hand inside the glove of the left wing of the Kuomintang, headed by Liao Zhongkai. Liao was the key architect of the united front, director of the Kuomintang's workers' department, head of the finance department of the government in Canton and, until his assassination that August, the most important patron of the Communists within the Kuomintang.[63] Whatever successes the Communists achieved in the 16 months of strike and boycott against Hong Kong, as one of the Communist leaders of the event, Deng Zhongxia, rightly admitted, 'without the financial support of the Kuomintang the strike would have collapsed within a week'.[64] In the first full year of the strike and boycott, the total fund administered by the Strike Committee was about five million Chinese silver dollars, of which 2.8 million came directly from the Kuomintang government in Canton, which also provided further support by putting many properties at the disposal of the committee and the strikers.[65]

Although it had fewer than ten party members and only thirty Youth League members in Hong Kong in May 1925, the CCP was highly successful in exploiting the strong anti-imperialist nationalism that Chinese workers in Hong Kong shared with their colleagues in major Chinese cities.[66] This was partly because in this period Britain 'stood as the chief representative of the Treaty Powers', which made it 'inevitably the main object of attack'.[67] Hong Kong was targeted because it was the ultimate symbol of British imperialism in China. The CCP did not at first realise the intensity of the public reaction and only called for a one-day strike in Guangdong and Hong Kong.[68] However, it adroitly moved to make the most of the strong anti-imperialist and nationalist sentiments of the Chinese working men in Hong Kong after the scale of public support became known. It was only after the party's original modest goal was surpassed by the outbreak of a massive strike that it saw 'a golden opportunity to expand their following' and turned to 'strikers from Hong Kong as the greatest potential source of new members'.[69]

On 19 June, under the influence of the Communists, seamen, tramway workers and printers started what quickly became a general strike in Hong Kong. Over the following three weeks, the strike spread to its height and involved some 250,000 workers, out of a total population of 725,000.[70] Although most chose to strike, some were intimidated into doing so, and most strikers left Hong Kong for Canton where they received an enthusiastic reception.[71] The seven demands which the strikers made were: support for the 17 demands made by the strikers in Shanghai; political freedom; equality before the law; introduction of popular elections; enactment of labour legislation; reduction of rent; and freedom of residence.[72] Except for the reduction of rent, which was arguably an economically motivated demand, the rest were all politically driven. The time lag in Hong Kong's reaction to the original incident in Shanghai was due to the existence of a war between the Kuomintang authorities and two local warlords, which prevented both the left wing of the Kuomintang and the Communists from taking effective action to instigate the general strike.[73]

What really caught the imagination of the ordinary working men in Hong Kong and Guangdong was another major shooting incident that occurred in the foreign concession of Shamian in Canton on 23 June, three days after the Canton sympathetic protest started. Marching in Shamian that day were not only workers, students, military academy cadets, Kuomintang members, Communist leaders like Zhou Enlai and others from Canton, but also the striking workers from Hong Kong. While the precise sequence of events and who fired the first shot cannot be established beyond doubt, shots were fired by both British and French sentries as well as by Chinese demonstrators. They left scores of Chinese and one Frenchman dead and many others, including eight Europeans and one Japanese, injured.[74] This new incident pushed anti-imperialist and anti-British sentiments to 'fever pitch'. Inspired also by the experiences of the seamen's strike of 1922, striking workers from Hong Kong were organised into pickets to stop food and other essentials from being shipped to the British colony.[75] A formal trade boycott against Hong

Kong was introduced on 6 July by order of the Strike Committee, headed
by one of Hong Kong's first members of the CCP, Su Zhaozheng.

Hong Kong was quickly paralysed, though its expatriate community
and the still quite sizeable Chinese population who stayed behind showed
indomitable spirit which enabled them to endure much economic and
other forms of hardship. Two days after the strike first started, the
government called out the Volunteer Defence Corps and then invoked
emergency powers. Troops were posted at key points, naval ratings were
deployed to man the cross-harbour ferries and civilian volunteers were
recruited to maintain essential services and serve as special constables.[76]
They did not stop the strike, which picked up even greater momentum
after the Shamian Incident. By early July, Hong Kong was 'like a ghost
town', where upper-class expatriates used to domestic servants had to do
their own housework, including disposing of their own nightsoil, either
'by burying it in their garden at a depth of no less than two feet' or at
sewer manholes 'opened between 5.30 and 7.30 each morning at
convenient points throughout the colony'.[77] The comfort and luxury of
old colonial Hong Kong that its expatriate and Chinese upper classes
were used to were largely replaced by volunteer work by almost everyone
concerned and an unprecedented degree of cooperation between some
better-off Chinese and the British authorities. The ultimate demonstration
of the willingness of some local Chinese to support the government was
their joining of not only essential services like the ambulance service
but also the Volunteer Defence Corps.[78]

Once the boycott was institutionalised in July, Hong Kong's economic
lifeline was severely restricted. Its previously flourishing entrepôt trade
with Guangdong collapsed, land value tumbled, government revenue fell
drastically, food prices rose six fold, share values dropped 40 per cent in
just over three months and the bankruptcy court was handling 20 cases
every day by September.[79] The scale of losses in trade was reflected by
the drop in import and export in the first calendar year of the strike. The
value of imports into Hong Kong had fallen from £11.67 million in 1924
to £5.84 million in 1925, while its exports dropped from £8.82 million
to £4.71 million in the same period.[80] As for shipping, Hong Kong on
average cleared 210 ships carrying 156,000 tons a day in 1924, but for
the year starting on 1 July 1925, the daily average fell to 34 ships and
56,000 tons.[81] The local economy was 'devastated' as it suffered 'total
economic losses at either $HK2million per day or even £5 million a week',
while 'British exports to China and Hong Kong' for 1925 dropped 'one-
third from 1924's total value of £29 million'.[82] Although the figures quoted
above cannot be relied on absolutely, as Governor Stubbs ordered
statistics not to be kept during the strike, they provide an indication of
how severe the economic costs were.

In confronting this first ever and, by any measure, serious challenge
to their imperial position in Hong Kong, the British and the colony were
unfortunate in having Stubbs as Governor. His ability to understand the
political situation in Guangdong and the politics of Chinese nationalism

was demonstrated in the way he handled the strike. When the Shanghai shootings first happened, he thought they would have little effect on the overwhelmingly Cantonese workers in Hong Kong. Even after the Hong Kong strike started, he still dismissed it as the work of the Communists and did not see the rising tide of Chinese nationalism at work.[83] He thus resorted to heavy-handed measures when faced with an inherently very difficult and highly delicate situation. By invoking emergency powers, Stubbs introduced censorship, gave police officers wide powers to search and detain suspects and attempted to intimidate the strike organisers in Canton by trying to cut off the food shipped there from Hong Kong.[84] These measures backfired. The last in particular was at least partly if not largely responsible for provoking the Strike Committee to institutionalise a boycott against Hong Kong, putting the crisis on a longer-term footing than originally envisaged by its instigators.

All the schemes that Stubbs devised to end the strike-boycott by unseating the Kuomintang government in Canton failed.[85] These included an operation, never authorised by London, to give $HK100,000 to help warlord Chen Jiongming stage a *coup d'état* in Guangdong to set up a government friendly to Hong Kong. This ended up as a costly mis-adventure. Other proposals Stubbs had, such as a naval blockade of the Pearl River, bombardment of the Boca Tigris forts at its estuary or joint military actions against Canton in collaboration with anti-Kuomintang northern Chinese forces, were all overruled by the British government.[86]

The replacement in November of Stubbs with Sir Cecil Clementi (Governor, 1925–30), a Cantonese-speaking former cadet with a good understanding of the Chinese people and their politics, was an improvement. However, there was little that Clementi could do to end the confrontation, which had by then already entered its fifth month and outlived the Shanghai strike. A general pattern had set in and an attempt by Hong Kong's Chinese merchants to broker an amicable solution was already a failure.

Clementi at first took a more accommodating approach and managed to engage in useful dialogue with senior leaders in the Kuomintang government.[87] However, the rising current of nationalism and the complexity of the political situation in Canton frustrated his démarche. After all, it was a time when the Kuomintang government was preparing itself to launch the Northern Expedition to unify the country and leaders of the Kuomintang were still working out a succession to Sun Yat-sen, who had died earlier in March.[88] These preoccupations restricted the scope for anyone in Guangdong to reach a compromise with the British. As one of the Kuomintang's top leaders, Wang Jingwei told Clementi in December that anyone in government in Canton who sought to end the strike-cum-boycott without first securing a large ransom payment from the British to pacify the strikers would be committing political suicide.[89]

Clementi then tried to combine conciliation with toughness when dealing with Canton in 1926. On the one hand, he tried to maintain a dialogue with members of the Kuomintang government, either directly or through the British Consul General in Canton. On the other hand, he was adamant in protecting the dignity and prestige of the colonial government. He was prepared to use gunboats to back up his policy and underline the strength of his position.[90] Although he was much more skilful and diplomatic than his predecessor, he was not able to end the strike-cum-boycott until the political situation in Canton changed sufficiently for the Kuomintang authority there to end its support for the Strike Committee.

Clementi was also much more astute and effective in waging the political and propaganda campaign against the strikers than his predecessor. In countering the propaganda and intimidation used by the Strike Committee to ensure the support of the ordinary Chinese in Hong Kong, he did not merely rely on the heavy-handed tactics of Stubbs. Press censorship, sponsorship of a new anti-strike and anti-Communist newspaper, the *Gongshang Ribao*, employment of dubious characters to counter intimidation and other emergency measures introduced by Stubbs continued. However, Clementi also sought to win the hearts and minds of the wealthy merchants and the Chinese population at large by taking concrete measures to cultivate loyalty.

When the Board of the Tung Wah Hospital got into serious financial trouble as a result of their acting on Stubbs's request to finance Chen Jiongming's ill-conceived coup, Clementi used public funds to bail them out and save them from a major predicament.[91] This was a bold step, as Clementi must have guessed the Colonial Office would consider the Tung Wah venture 'scandalous' though it would have no choice but back him up and 'hush up' the matter.[92]

Above all, he demonstrated to the Chinese population his confidence in them by appointing for the first time an ethnic Chinese person, Sir Shouson Chow, to be one of the two unofficial members of the Executive Council.[93] It was a bold step in the midst of a crisis caused by Chinese nationalism challenging British imperialism. The Executive Council was roughly equivalent to the Cabinet, to which two unofficial members of British origins had been introduced only in 1896.[94] Clementi's rationale was that showing 'confidence is one obvious way of encouraging loyalty' and Chow's appointment was meant to 'afford clear proof of the intention of this Government to frame its policy in close co-operation with leading Chinese of Hong Kong'.[95]

Chinese merchants and capitalists large and small in Hong Kong generally supported the government because they had vested interests to protect, and they were financially the most exposed to the harmful effects of the strike-cum-boycott. They were the most heavily involved in the entrepôt trade with Guangdong and were most vulnerable to the trade boycott. Chinese shops in Hong Kong also suffered badly from the departure of workers in large numbers and the dramatic fall in business that resulted. Chinese-owned banks, which generally had smaller capital than British banks and were overwhelmingly dependent on their Chinese clientele, were substantially more exposed to withdrawals by their Chinese depositors and were thus hit hard by bank runs. As an indication of how suddenly Chinese-owned banks faced a cash flow problem, in the first three days of the strike in June 1925, $16 million were withdrawn from these institutions and taken out of Hong Kong before this was stopped by the government's emergency measures.[96] Chinese banks suffered two bank runs, had to close for business for a week and could reopen only after receiving $6 million dollars in loans from the Hong Kong and Shanghai Bank and the Standard Chartered Bank.[97] Their financial situation was alleviated only after it became known that the British government had provided a £3 million trade loan to Hong Kong.[98]

The fact that the strike-cum-boycott was mainly directed by the Communists also reduced its appeal to the merchants, particularly after the initial furore surrounding the shootings in Shanghai and Canton had subsided. Unlike their counterparts in Guangdong, who in fact greatly benefited from the boycott after suffering some initial losses because much of China's former trade with Hong Kong was diverted to Canton, Hong Kong's Chinese businessmen were the biggest losers.[99]

It was therefore unsurprising that leading merchants who were also leaders of the Chinese community supported the Board of Tung Wah in trying to play a constructive role in seeking a settlement.[100] Chairman Ma Zuichao explained the rationale by saying that 'the Tung Wah was a charitable organisation in Hong Kong which had hitherto avoided involvement in national or political affairs' but the strike 'has already lasted two months, and has had a grave impact on all trades and businesses' and the Board would 'like to save the community from this awful fate'.[101] The Tung Wah's efforts, like similar attempts by other leading Chinese, to broker a settlement failed. The Chinese merchant community of Hong Kong was also prepared to pay what was in effect a ransom to end the boycott, but even this would not satisfy the Strike Committee, which wanted to humiliate the colonial government.[102] Given the political nature of the strike and the boycott, a solution could not be found until the political situation in Canton changed.

There was political jockeying in the government in Canton, where the delicate balance of power between the right and left wings of the Kuomintang after Sun Yat-sen's death in March 1925 shifted in the course of the year and eventually led to the rise of Chiang Kai-shek. Although Chiang was made Commander-in-Chief of the National Revolutionary Army when the Kuomintang proclaimed a national government in Canton in July, he still only ranked fourth in the Kuomintang hierarchy.[103] His status rose quickly when his senior leftwing colleague Liao Zhongkai was murdered in August, and another, Hu Hanmin, leader of the right wing, was implicated and had to leave Canton. In March 1926, Chiang exiled his other senior colleague, Wang Chingwei, to Siberia after implicating Wang in a plot to kidnap him using a gunboat – the *Zhongshan* – which was under the command of a Communist officer.[104] By launching a pre-emptive strike, Chiang not only ousted Wang and thus everyone senior to him in the party leadership, but also disarmed the pickets of the

Communist-dominated Strike Committee.[105] However, he still needed Soviet military aid and the support of the Communists to play a balancing game of power politics in order to consolidate his position in Canton.[106] He therefore returned the arms confiscated from the Strike Committee's pickets, though he did manage to curb the power of the Communists within the united front.

It was only after Chiang launched the Northern Expedition in July and the army under his command successfully reached the Yangtze River in early September that he could afford to lose the support of the Communists. Even then he was not in a position to purge the Communists, a move he could not made until after his forces took Shanghai five months later. Once his forces reached Wuhan, where there were considerable foreign interests, Chiang showed that he was keen to avoid provoking foreign intervention and assured the foreign powers that his forces were under strict orders not to provoke any incident.[107]

Once Chiang had made his position in the Kuomintang almost indispensable, as his army headed towards Shanghai at the beginning of September 1926, the political situation within the Kuomintang government changed. It was by then politically desirable to ensure the Kuomintang government would not get entangled in further confrontations with the British by the Communist-dominated Strike Committee. To Chiang and most of his colleagues in the Kuomintang, Chinese nationalism had a new priority – the reunification of the country rather than anti-imperialism.[108] The CCP, for its part, functioned in this period as the China branch of the Comintern or Communist International.[109] It was under orders from Joseph Stalin to continue cooperation with the Kuomintang and not sustain the boycott against Hong Kong lest it should provide an excuse for the British to intervene against the Northern Expedition.[110] The time had finally come for the boycott to be ended.

In the meantime, for much of 1926, Governor Clementi continued to seek an end to the boycott by negotiations, which were at times backed up by the threat or actual use of force to put pressure on the Canton authorities. The negotiations proved tortuous. In early September, just as the Kuomintang forces were engaged in the bloody siege for Wuchang, the last round of negotiations appeared to have reached a dead end and Clementi made a show of force. Royal Navy gunboats were deployed on 4 September to clear strike pickets from the steamer wharves in Canton, which was achieved without one shot being fired as the picket boats dispersed upon arrival of the British ships.[111] Followed one day later by a separate and unrelated incident in Wanxian on the Yangtze, in which British gunboats bombarded the town in an operation to rescue two British merchant ships seized earlier by the local warlord, the show of force in Canton appeared like a warning shot for more vigorous British military intervention.[112] Negotiations soon resumed between the British and the authorities in Canton, which led to a compromise, namely that Canton would impose an additional 2.5 per cent surcharge on the import tax, which the British tacitly agreed not to challenge. The boycott was formally lifted on 10 October 1926 by order of the government in Canton, the same day that Wuchang fell to the Kuomintang.

The strike and boycott were essentially a politically inspired and externally directed movement against British imperialism. Hong Kong suffered badly mainly because it was the bastion of British imperialism in Chinese eyes. It was also partly because Governor Stubbs's ineptitude removed any possibility of a relatively quick settlement. The event was a landmark in the modern history of Hong Kong, as it represented the highpoint of Chinese nationalism as a force in the British colony. Although the CCP was clearly responsible for instigating and bringing about the strike at first and in instituting the boycott, they managed to do so only because they were championing the cause of Chinese nation-alism.[113] Workers in Hong Kong responded to the initial appeal and reacted strongly to the Shamian shootings not because they found Communism appealing but because they were at least as affected by the rising tide of nationalism as their compatriots were elsewhere in major coastal Chinese cities. Once Chinese nationalism was redirected from anti-British imperialism to reunification under the Kuomintang in China after the launch of the Northern Expedition, the original anti-British nationalism in the Hong Kong region lost its momentum, if not its *raison d'être*.

The tremendous importance of the strike-cum-boycott to the rise of the Communist movement in China should not be taken to mean the Communist cause was particularly appealing to Hong Kong's working class. It was true that the party numbered only 1,000 across China in May 1925, but that expanded to 30,000 at the peak of the boycott in July 1926.[114] It was also true that the Hong Kong strikers who went to Guangdong provided fertile ground for the party to expand. However, the party did not manage to build up an effective network of Hong Kong cadres for organising labour, still less a revolution in the colony. Although Hong Kong became an important base for the CCP for coordinating its activities in southern China after Chiang Kai-shek's purge of Communists from within the Kuomintang in the spring of 1927, the primary value of Hong Kong to the CCP was its relative safety as a base for operations on the Chinese mainland.[115]

What the strike-cum-boycott did for Hong Kong was to complete two processes already started by the labour unrest of the early 1920s. The first was to reinforce the transformation of the Chinese population of Hong Kong from sharing a basically docile and inward-looking attitude preferring to avoid any dealing with government to a more outward-looking approach that made demands on government and society more generally. The second process was the corresponding change in the attitude of the colonial government towards its Chinese population. The demonstration of support to the government by some better-off Chinese, in contrast to those who took part in the general strike, highlighted the diversities in the Chinese community. Instead of taking its Chinese population for granted, as had happened in the nineteenth century, Clementi accepted the need to deal with them directly on a daily basis.[116]

Once the idea that Chinese working men were able to organise themselves to defend or even assert their rights sank in, those in government and also in the judiciary acted on this recognition and gradually changed the arbitrary way that many working-class Chinese had routinely been treated in the previous century.

The government of Hong Kong also learned the importance of maintaining good relations with the government in Canton, not least to avoid having to deal with similar challenges in the future. Although Clementi was prepared to use force to back up his policy towards Canton in the course of the boycott, he preferred to pre-empt the need for such eventualities by keeping on good terms with Canton. This mirrored the general shift in British policy towards China, itself the product of a policy review, the need for which was highlighted by the crises in Shanghai and Hong Kong, and reinforced by the Northern Expedition. The British objective in this exercise was to find a way to protect British nationals and properties in China without appearing weak, and thus they devised a new policy to divert the focus of Chinese nationalism away from the British Empire.[117] The spirit of this new policy was encapsulated in a memorandum issued in December 1926, by which Britain undertook 'to consider in a sympathetic spirit any reasonable proposals that the Chinese authorities, wherever situated, may make' on matters that affect Chinese national rights, and to promote this among the great powers.[118]

Chapter 8

Imperial Grandeur

The Great War ended with not only the dismemberment of the German Empire and the Ottoman Empire but also the transfer of nearly a million square miles and 13 million people in some of their imperial possessions to the jurisdiction of the British Empire as mandated territories. As a result, in terms of its territorial span, the British Empire reached its zenith in the inter-war years. However, the War exhausted it – if not in resources then at least in aggressive spirit.[1] The serenity and security of the British Empire in this period rested as much on its longstanding prestige as on the Empire's capabilities and willingness to use them to keep its place in the premier league of world powers. The fact that, in retrospect, the Empire had already reached and passed its peak did not reduce its imposing presence. Policymakers or nationalists in Asia did not have the benefit of hindsight and the grandeur of the British Empire ensured no effective challenge was made against it until its weakness and fragility came to be exposed by the Japanese at the beginning of the Pacific War.[2]

Although Chinese nationalists confronted British imperialism in the middle of the 1920s, they backed off once their more immediate goal of reunification appeared achievable. They were not prepared to incur the wrath of the British Empire, which they still believed could have intervened sufficiently in Chinese affairs to frustrate their hopes of national unity. While Hong Kong symbolised British imperialism in China and Chinese nationalists began to feel they would like to reclaim it eventually, they were not prepared to challenge the British until they were strong enough to do so successfully. In the 1930s, their focus also increasingly turned towards Japan as it emerged as the most aggressive imperial power in the region.[3] Basking in the splendour of the British Empire, Hong Kong continued to grow, notwithstanding the effect of the Great Depression that followed the collapse of the New York stock market in 1929.

The Politics of Stability

The end of the strike-cum-boycott in October 1926 allowed Hong Kong to rehabilitate its economy and rebuild the conditions that had produced social and political stability. The focus was on suppressing what the government saw as the main source of instability, to be complemented by improving governance for the Chinese in order to pre-empt a repeat of similar confrontations in the future.

The government under Clementi and his successor kept all the emergency powers after the crisis and steadily moved against the main unions and other bodies that played a pivotal role in the general strike and boycott. Organisations like the General Trade Union and the Hong Kong branch of the Chinese Seamen's Union, the most active and prominent sponsors of the general strike known for their close links with the CCP, were proscribed.[4] Politically inspired strikes were outlawed. The police monitored the activities of the Communists, raided their premises, arrested them and deported them to China if sufficient grounds could be established to suggest their presence would be detrimental to the colony's stability, good order and general interest. Sustained efforts by the police eventually 'reduced the Communist existence in Hong Kong to a bare skeleton' in 1932.[5] By the autumn of 1934, 'the entire Communist machinery had disintegrated or disappeared'.[6] Since the Communists were the instigators and main organisers of the strike-cum-boycott, breaking up their organisation in Hong Kong removed a major source of instability from the government's point of view.

The government's suppression of the Chinese Communists, particularly its agreement 'to extradite political criminals under cover as ordinary criminals to Canton', has mistakenly been portrayed as 'completely contrary to the tradition of the British Hong Kong government to offer asylum to political fugitives'.[7] Such an assessment is based on a misunderstanding of the British tradition of offering political asylum and the British policy towards CCP operations in Hong Kong.

The British policy towards Chinese political fugitives was to allow them to use the colony as a gateway to safety or seek refuge locally but not to use it as a base for subverting the government of China or to embroil Hong Kong in confrontations with the Chinese authorities. In the 1930s, Chinese Communists did not go to Hong Kong to escape political prosecution at home. Instead, they used Hong Kong as their regional headquarters for south China to launch armed attacks to overthrow the authorities in Canton and the government of China.[8] Their first major attempt was the Canton Uprising of late 1927. In this period, the Communists in Hong Kong were not political fugitives but members of a foreign political party dedicated to making the most of the relative safety they enjoyed under British jurisdiction to subvert a friendly government recognised by Britain.

More important to the Hong Kong government was that the CCP tried to destabilise the colony. This made it fundamentally different from Sun Yat-sen's revolutionary party a few decades earlier. When it was based in Hong Kong, part of the CCP's 'Central Southern Bureau's mission was to make preparations for an uprising to take place in Hong Kong itself'.[9] Although it failed to stage any uprising, it did try 'to create an atmosphere of "red terror"', usually by murdering Hong Kong police officers.[10] Even those Communists not involved in the physical act of murder broke the law if they stored firearms for their comrades or otherwise acted as co-conspirators. The colonial government had reasonable grounds to treat the CCP as a criminal organisation.

This is not to say that the Hong Kong police were not sometimes, even often, arbitrary in dealing with members of the CCP who were arrested. In this period, the police suffered badly from inefficiency and corruption.[11] It was still often arbitrary when dealing with members of the Chinese community, though abuses had been reduced steadily after the middle part of the nineteenth century. These shortcomings meant some Communist members arrested were badly treated. However, the deficiencies of the police also worked to the advantage of the Communists, as entrenched corruption meant they were sometimes able to get out of trouble through bribery. The inefficiency of the police also meant more time and scope existed for the CCP to operate before its network was destroyed in Hong Kong than if an efficient and effective police had existed.

As a matter of policy, the Hong Kong government did hand over detained Communists to the authorities in China from whence they had come. This was unquestionably followed by a number of them being tortured or even executed by the Chinese authorities once they came under Chinese jurisdiction. This does not, however, constitute 'clear evidence that the Hong Kong government in fact played a pivotal role in the final elimination of a considerable number of Communists in Canton'.[12]

While the colonial government showed no humanitarian concern for the fate of Communists it repatriated to China, there is no evidence to show that it had a policy of sending them to China in order to effect their physical elimination. The government had had a long-established policy since the 1840s of deporting undesirable Chinese back to China with little humanitarian regard for whatever fate might await them. Whatever else they might be, the deported Communists were members of an organisation involved in organised crime. They were, in general, treated no better or worse than, say, other suspected criminals or pirates of Chinese origins against whom there was insufficient evidence to secure conviction in a British court of law. The colonial government chose the easy option, as it routinely did with many other suspected criminals. It deported the Communists to where they came from if they did not have the right of abode and it deemed their presence harmful to the good order of the colony.

In fact, those Chinese Communists arrested by the Hong Kong police did enjoy the protection of British law if they had the means or were important enough to the CCP for it to invest in legal counsel. This again put them on a par with others charged for criminal offences. The arrest and release of Deng Zhongxia, Li Lisan's temporary replacement as head of the CCP in Hong Kong in 1928, shows how senior Communists did benefit from the British legal system. In light of his importance, a 'prominent

British attorney' was engaged by the CCP to represent him. He secured Deng's release 'on the grounds of insufficient evidence'.[13] Other CCP members were deported and faced their fate in China because they were not valuable enough to the party for it to invest in their legal representation.

The existence of the rule of law also ensured that Communist members who could prove they were born in Hong Kong, and thus enjoyed the right of abode, would not be deported.[14] Arbitrary treatment of Communists arrested in Hong Kong occurred mainly when they were under police custody, not in front of a court of law.

After the strike-cum-boycott, the Hong Kong government also paid more attention to its Chinese population, recognising the need to secure the loyalty of the Chinese community. The first major step was taken during the strike-cum-boycott, when Sir Shouson Chow was appointed to the Executive Council. Clementi reinforced this with changes to significantly strengthen the office of the Secretary for Chinese Affairs. Not only did the Secretary receive more resources, including the allocation of more Cadet officers to support his work, he was also made an *ex-officio* member of the Executive Council, and his bureaucratic rank was elevated to that behind the Colonial Secretary in 1929.[15] Such changes strengthened his hand and demonstrated the government's acceptance of the rising importance of the Chinese community. They were also meant to complement the suppression of Communist activities as part of the government's efforts to secure social and political stability.

These changes had the desired result. They succeeded in countering the CCP's attempts to win over the working men of Hong Kong, even during the economic slowdown caused by the Great Depression.[16]

As a result of having to deal with the strike-cum-boycott and the force of Chinese nationalism, Clementi also felt it necessary to tackle the question of Hong Kong's long-term security, particularly with respect to the New Territories' lease. He raised the issue both during and after the strike-cum-boycott but London overruled him.[17] He urged London to review the New Territories' lease and turn the region into 'a permanent part of the colony'.[18]

Clementi was not the first British policymaker to raise the issue. Governor Frederick Lugard (1907–12), had earlier suggested making the permanent cession of the New Territories a condition for Weihaiwei's return to China.[19] His successor, Sir Francis May (1912–19), also recommended 'seizing the first opportunity to convert the 99-year lease… into a cession in perpetuity'.[20] The British government in London considered the matter prior to the Versailles Peace Conference of 1919 and again before the Washington Conference of 1922. On both occasions the possibility of surrendering the New Territories was raised during discussions about the German lease of Shandong and, on both occasions, it was dismissed as out of the question.[21] Although, like his predecessors, Clementi failed to secure London's support, he put down a strong marker.

Clementi's differences with London arose because the colony and Britain had different interests and concerns, and assessed Chinese reactions differently. With his deep knowledge of the Chinese and his experience of handling the strike-cum-boycott, Clementi was alive to the forces and trends of Chinese nationalism. He persisted in his recommendation, because he believed that the 'handing back of the New Territories would be fatal' to Hong Kong.[22] Unless Britain took action while China was divided or weak, China's rising nationalism and military power would eventually rule out such an option. The urgency that was self-evident to the person on the spot was not so apparent to a government half a globe away.

By adopting a new China policy, outlined in the December memorandum of 1926, the British government had already shown a willingness to deal sympathetically with the rising tide of Chinese nationalism. It based this on realism, not altruism, but it was a realism that did not conform to Clementi's assessment. Essentially, London did not consider 'any responsible Chinese authority could be induced in present circumstances to enter into any agreement which provided for a cession of territory to a foreign Power'.[23] Raising the issue would merely indicate British anxiety over the lease. It would also 'expose a weakness, which they would not be slow to exploit, and might well lead to [a] campaign for the rendition'.[24] There was no meeting of minds on this issue between Hong Kong and London.

In the 1930s, all the successive governors of Hong Kong raised the issue at least once during their terms of office, but none did so as forcefully as Clementi. In London, the Foreign Office responded to Clementi's persistence with internal deliberations that went on for so long that they outlasted him. The Foreign Office gradually moved to a position of expecting the Chinese to raise the question of the lease well before the expiry date. It also surmised that Britain should prepare itself to lose exclusive control over Hong Kong.[25]

As far as the governments of Britain and Hong Kong were concerned, prior to the Pacific war, there was no 'Hong Kong question' – whether based on the New Territories' lease or not. Nevertheless, the idea that Hong Kong and the New Territories stood or fell together came to be accepted.[26] By implication, Britain realised that the long-term future of Hong Kong would be tied to the lease for the New Territories. The efforts Clementi made over this issue were aimed at removing the uncertainty over the future of the New Territories and thus a long-term source of instability. With the onset of a world war at the end of the 1930s, the security of Hong Kong, dependent upon the apparent grandeur of the British Empire, came to be dangerously exposed as Britain found itself engaged in a life and death struggle in Europe. By then Clementi's attempt to direct local politics to ensure stability and good order had come to be a hostage to external forces.

Economic and Social Developments

Some major technological developments that started in the nineteenth century matured to become everyday necessities of modern life in the twentieth, and they brought about rapid and important changes to both social and economic life. The technological leaps that impacted upon people's everyday life most at the turn of the century were the harnessing of electricity for everyday use and the motorcar. Some of the new technologies took time for people to embrace.

Electricity was at first met with 'innate distrust', even for lighting, by the local Chinese.[27] However, once electricity came to be accepted, economic developments and social life developed by leaps and bounds. The availability of relatively cheap and fast transportation also made a major impact. Greater mobility and acceptance of modern technological progress led to the gradual but steady incorporation of what were previously deemed as Western ways into everyday life by an increasing number of local Chinese.[28]

As a result of these technological changes, the number of mechanics and industrial workers among the Chinese expanded rapidly as new jobs were created in the power generating industry, with the introduction of trams, motor transportation and other production or servicing industries. The level of skill, and therefore exposure to all aspects of things modern, rose steadily among the Chinese working population. The advent of modern labour unions in the 1920s and the close links they maintained with their supporters in Canton, so critical to the success of the labour movements, were in an important sense a by-product of these changes. Even if Chinese nationalism had not emerged, technological advancements were having a major impact upon the economic and social lives of the Chinese in Hong Kong.

In terms of the economy, while trade remained its mainstay, considerable industrial development also took place. Since reliable statistics on different sectors of the economy are not available for this period, the exact extent and scope of industrial development cannot be established. However, there are sufficient indicators to show a good number of new industries were built.[29] During the Great War, Chinese capitalists in Hong Kong saw the effect of the disruption of supplies and used this opportunity to produce some simple industrial goods that Hong Kong used to import from Europe.[30] Both the scope and pace of industrial development continued to expand after the war.[31] Most of the new industries were founded by the local Chinese.[32] They received no direct assistance from the government though those industries that exported to the rest of the British Commonwealth, such as producers of rubber footwear, did benefit from the introduction of a system of imperial preference in 1932.[33]

In addition to the Chinese community's investments in the industrial sector, British-owned and generally larger manufacturing industries, such as shipbuilding, sugar refining and cement manufacturing, continued to flourish. They were also augmented by major new industries introduced by non-Chinese investors. The most notable of these were the founding of the Hong Kong Electricity Company and the China Light and Power Company that produced and supplied electricity commercially.[34] The building, running and maintenance of the Kowloon-Canton Railway might not have involved any major industrial production locally but they were a significant new factor in the local economy both as an employer of skilled and semi-skilled labour and in facilitating the movement of goods and people.

The range of new industrial establishments that came into existence in the inter-war years was significant in terms of products manufactured and the scale of operations. While most establishments were small and employed only a few workers, there were also at least three new major Chinese manufacturers that individually employed between 1,000 and 2,600 workers.[35] There were also at least 34 other Chinese industrial establishments, each with between 100 and 1,000 employees. These included factories making machine tools, mosquito incense, fireworks, tins for canning, perfume and for knitting and dyeing. Since most manufacturing facilities were established by Chinese entrepreneurs who preferred minimum contact with officialdom, they did not all register with the colonial administration, which did not, in any event, become a legal requirement until 1938. This applied particularly to smaller concerns. Even though the number of registered factories and workshops unquestionably understates the scale of industrial development, its growth from 403 establishments in 1933 to 829 in 1938 indicates how fast new factories were being created.[36]

Thus, Hong Kong was industrialising in the inter-war years though trade remained, at least as far as the British and the colonial governments were concerned, its economic *raison d'être*. By the end of the 1930s, the annual value of manufactured export was estimated at $90 million, which was roughly one-sixth of Hong Kong's total export and re-export trade.[37] According to the census of 1931, out of a total population of 850,000 and an economically active population of 471,000, over 110,000 were engaged in manufacturing, in contrast with only 97,000 in trade and finance.[38] These figures confirm the growing importance of industrial production.

The biggest challenge in the economic sphere that the Hong Kong government had to deal with was the fluctuation of the value of silver, upon which its currency was based. As a result of the Great Depression, the value of silver fell. This meant the Hong Kong dollar depreciated by some 50 per cent and led to a trade boom at the beginning of the 1930s. However, this was only a short-term advantage. The value of silver went up later and by 1935 the value of Hong Kong's trade had fallen back to its 1931 level.[39] Hong Kong's problems with the fluctuating value of silver had a parallel in China, which had also adopted the silver standard. Given the economic links between the two, which were even closer than Hong Kong's ties with Britain, Hong Kong worked on the basis that 'as long as China linked her currency to silver, so long must it... do likewise'.[40] The changing fortunes of their currencies in this period happened in large part because their other most important trading partners, Britain, Japan and the USA, went off the gold standard between 1931 and 1933.[41] The consequent depreciation of sterling, the yen and the American dollar meant an appreciation of the Hong Kong dollar and the Chinese yuan. The situation was aggravated by a new American policy to purchase silver in 1934. While Hong Kong suffered from the revaluation of its currency, China saw a rapid drain of silver that led to an 'acute deflationary crisis'.[42] The Chinese government responded by going off the silver standard in November 1935. Hong Kong immediately followed suit and created an Exchange Fund to serve as 'an exchange equalisation fund'.[43] It had the desired effect of restoring financial stability and economic growth.[44]

As the scope of government expanded and the importance of economic and financial matters became increasingly obvious, the colonial government elevated the office of Colonial Treasurer to that of Financial Secretary in 1937. This position was at first filled by an official seconded from the Colonial Office, Sydney Caine, but was subsequently taken by a senior cadet. In due course, as the management and supervision of Hong Kong's budget, finance and economic affairs became more important, the Financial Secretary replaced the Secretary for Chinese Affairs as the ranking officer behind the Colonial Secretary in the administration.

Although social life in Hong Kong in the inter-war years continued to be affected by some of the basic ills inherited from the Victorian era, particularly institutionalised racial discrimination, considerable progressive changes also took place. They partly reflected the rapid general progress during the twentieth century. Social legislation was becoming a feature of life in Europe and America, and the ideas underlining it were spreading, albeit slowly, to the rest of the world. The great advancements in transport and communication that enabled more people to travel and for information to be disseminated quickly and widely accelerated the process of social change even in colonial territories. Social legislation changed working conditions and altered the social environment in which people lived and interacted usually by reducing or even eliminating some social ills. Social progress also reflected a change in the way the colonial government looked at and treated its subjects. Its old attitude that the local Chinese community could largely be left to its own devices faded.

Whatever effect changes in government attitude might have had on social development in Hong Kong, the most basic factor that governed life among its Chinese community, which constituted over 95% of the total population at any point, was its unsettled nature. The Chinese community continued to be made up mainly of Chinese immigrants or sojourners. Hong Kong's population grew from 301,000 in 1901 to 463,000 in 1911, to 625,000 in 1921, and to 850,000 in 1931.[45] Although no census figure for 1941 is available because of the Pacific War, reliable estimates put it at 1,007,000 in 1937 when Japan invaded China, and at 1,639,000 at the outbreak of the Pacific War in 1941.[46] The fivefold increase in a period of 40 years or an almost threefold expansion during the inter-war period meant most of Hong Kong's adult Chinese population were first-generation immigrants, temporary workers or refugees. Just prior to the Pacific War, only 38.5 per cent of the Chinese population had lived there for more than 10 years and only 6.4 per cent for over 30 years.[47] Most had not thought seriously about whether they were immigrants or not. They generally took a merely short-term view about working in Hong Kong. They lived on the assumption that they would eventually return to their homes in China, though an increasing number ended up living in Hong Kong on a long-term basis. Settlement was, nevertheless, not an issue that most Chinese migrant workers thought they needed or wanted to address.

Their basic attitude and pattern of life were therefore governed more by what prevailed in their home country and in a poor and fluid immigrant society than by government policy or legislation in Hong Kong. Most of them went to work and live in Hong Kong not because of the rule of law or other good qualities of its British administration but because they could find work and opportunities not available at home. Indeed, despite low wages, long hours and harsh working conditions, they were still 'better off in Hong Kong than they were in China' with many 'able to remit money home to China monthly'.[48] This motive was reinforced and superseded by those who sought the safety of this British colony after a full-scale Japanese invasion of China started in 1937. Consequently, few of the new residents developed any sense of loyalty to the British Empire or to Hong Kong itself.

The colonial government did not try to turn them into citizens by instilling in them ideas like civic responsibility and political participation but it would have failed if it had tried. To most new Chinese residents in this British colony, these concepts were irrelevant. Instead, the minority among them who had more than a passing interest in politics were more influenced by Chinese nationalism, and more concerned with civil wars and Japanese imperialism in China than with local political developments. This is not to say that there did not exist, among the educated or critically minded Chinese, a growing recognition, even admiration, for the rule of law and relative integrity of the colonial government when compared with the situation in China.[49] The last group existed and was growing but it remained a minority even among the small number interested in politics.

The scale and pace of the expansion of Hong Kong's Chinese population also meant most found employment beyond the colony's nineteenth-century economic activities. Although expatriates and writers on Hong Kong continued to use a nineteenth-century local term, 'coolie' (literally meaning bitter labour), to describe Chinese working men, by then most of them were in reality workers in factories, workshops, transport services and other public utilities, or assistants in shops, catering establishments and other menial services rather than physical labourers. Their general level of knowledge and exposure to the modern world were substantially better than the illiterate and mostly inward-looking so-called coolie of the Victorian era. They were no longer satisfied with relying almost entirely on the local dignitaries like the directors of the Tung Wah to be arbiters of their lives or disputes.

The inter-war years were a transitional period when long-established institutions like the Tung Wah or the District Watch Committee continued to play important roles in the Chinese community, while increasing numbers of this community also ventured to seek help or redress of grievances outside of this framework. The Chinese community, or sections of it, had begun to make demands of the colonial government, the society or their employers. The economically driven strikes of the early 1920s illustrated how many changes had taken place since the nineteenth century. In the case of seeking help from the government, members of the Chinese community generally went through the Secretariat for Chinese Affairs, the Urban Council or occasionally even the court system in the urban areas, and through District Officers in the New Territories.

Social developments were also affected significantly by new legislation intended to deal with some of the social ills created as Hong Kong grew and some of those longstanding ones previously ignored by the government. The most notable batch of social legislation dealing with the former concerned employment as industries spread. The first labour-related legislation was the introduction in 1919 of a resolution in the Urban Council to enable itself to make by-laws regarding child labour.[50] This was followed by the appointment of a Commission to inquire into the conditions of industrial employment of children in 1921 and the passing of an ordinance to outlaw the employment of young children in dangerous occupations.[51] In the following two decades, a series of other labour laws were passed to deal with industrial accidents, employment of women, pensions and registration of factories, in addition to those that governed trade unions. The government now attempted to define the framework within which Chinese workers were to be treated. In support of the legislative efforts, a Labour section was created within the Secretariat for Chinese Affairs in 1927, and a Labour Officer appointed a decade later. Although enforcement of these laws was weak and working conditions for most Chinese workers remained appalling, the government's efforts limited abuse and improved the lot of the average worker.

Among the traditional social ills that caught the public imagination was the Chinese practice of keeping *mui tsai* (or *meizi*), a kind of domestic female bond servant better-off families secured, usually with a one-off payment and a deed of gift, from poorer families which could not afford to raise the girl concerned. Great discrepancies existed in how individual mui tsai fared. They varied from being reasonably well treated as an unpaid live-in young domestic helper who would be married off when she came of age to being abused practically as a domestic slave. Since no servile status was recognised under British law, a 'mui tsai was entirely free to leave her master at any time', but in reality long-established practice and ignorance of the law on the part of mui tsai meant they accepted their status as bond servants.[52]

A long drawn out campaign to end this practice started in 1917, when the British Member of Parliament John Ward noticed it. He saw it in terms of slavery and drew the attention of the Secretary of State to it, which caused the Colonial Office to question the Hong Kong government.[53] This private approach was followed up by a public campaign after the War, energetically pursued by Mrs Clara Haslewood, who arrived in August 1919 following her husband's appointment as Superintendent of the Naval Chart Depot in Hong Kong. As Clara's husband, Hugh Haslewood, was a government servant, Governor Stubbs reacted with a heavy hand and forced him to leave his post, and they had left for Britain by the end of the year.[54] Once back in London, Mrs Haslewood organised a major public campaign, enlisting the support of the Anti-Slavery Society, members of parliament, women's rights supporters and political grandees to seek its abolition.

Finding himself in the acutely embarrassing position of being required to defend what was publicly billed as slavery almost a century after its abolition in Britain, Secretary of State Winston Churchill reacted strongly. He ruled in early 1922 that Hong Kong must see to it that 'no compulsion of any kind will be allowed to prevent these persons from quitting their employment at any time they like'.[55] Although Governor Stubbs and the Chinese elite in Hong Kong objected to it and Stubbs tried to evade it, he had to publish a public proclamation and pass the Female Domestic Servants Ordinance in early 1923.[56] This dampened the agitation in London but did not bring about much improvement, as few mui tsai knew of their rights and the colonial government did not enforce the new law.

The issue was revived and gained wide publicity in 1929, an election year in Britain, by a report in the *Manchester Guardian* newspaper in Britain. The election produced a Labour government with Lord Passfield as Secretary of State for the Colonies. Like Churchill, Passfield overruled the reservations expressed by Governor Clementi and insisted on actual progress being made.[57] As a result, three inspectors were appointed in Hong Kong to enforce the 1923 Ordinance.

The real break happened after Sir Andrew Caldecott became Governor in 1935. Unlike his predecessors, he was 'convinced that the mui tsai system was a thoroughly nasty practice' and thus pushed through an amendment in the Legislative Council to add imprisonment as a penalty for offences under the 1923 Ordinance.[58] With the government now behind the abolition of mui tsai, much faster progress was made and it was largely eliminated as an institution by the eve of the Pacific War. In the end, mui tsai was abolished partly because the government pushed for it, and partly because enforcement of the new legislation 'helped to shift Chinese opinion from tolerance... to distaste for it'.[59]

Social legislation on this occasion was driven mainly by the devotion of a number of expatriate campaigners and pressure from the British government. Affairs among the Chinese in this British colony were no longer permitted to be handled virtually without intervention from either the expatriate community or public opinions outside of Hong Kong. The Chinese community in Hong Kong was willy-nilly becoming part of the wider community that interacted and was impacted upon by developments that happened elsewhere. Government-led social changes to the removal, reduction, or regulation of social ills like mui tsai, opium smoking or prostitution, were mainly a result of pressure from London.[60]

The colonial government also took very modest initiatives of its own to improve social conditions for its Chinese community. The most important of these was to improve the provision of education. In this respect, efforts to provide primary education or improve basic literacy had a much wider impact than the support of the few elite English-language government schools. Even though the government did not provide free education in the inter-war years, it did start to 'provide Chinese schools with strong central direction and to raise their academic standards'.[61]

The first major step was taken in the 1910s, when two Chinese graduates of Cambridge and Oxford were appointed Inspectors of Vernacular Schools. This was followed by a commission of inquiry in 1921 that recommended elementary vernacular education should be made compulsory and presumably free.[62] Nothing in fact came out of this particular recommendation, but active government encouragement and assistance, in contrast to benign neglect hitherto, helped the spread of basic literacy. Much of this was achieved by government subvention to grant-in-aid schools run by missionary societies and other charitable organisations such as the Confucian Society. By the late 1930s, there were 279 subsidised schools with 20,200 pupils who came mostly from working-class families and paid no or very low fees.[63] By 1931, 48 per cent of the 119,000 ethnic Chinese children aged between five and 13 claimed to be able to read and write in Chinese. This was the beginning of a major change as it improved the life chances of the young people born and brought up in the colony.

The flagship of the government's educational initiatives was the founding of the University of Hong Kong in 1911. At that time there were only 18 universities in Britain itself, and five were recent creations. Although the University was officially devoted to offering a higher education to a standard similar to other British universities, it was also intended to advance British interests and to 'promote a good understanding with the neighbouring empire of China'.[64] Its foundation had political overtones, as its most important sponsor, Governor Lugard 'looked on the University as an instrument of British foreign and colonial policy'.[65] While Lugard left in 1912, two months after the University had opened, and it did not become in any real sense an instrument for British policy, it did acquire an importance of its own.[66]

Its real value for Hong Kong was to train a small number of local people, usually from more privileged backgrounds. Its graduates constituted well-educated human resources for the expansion of Hong Kong's economy and their existence undermined the basis for the colonial government to resist localisation of the civil service. In the inter-war period, well-educated Chinese had started to be recruited as specialist or technical officers to the government to serve mainly in the medical, sanitary, education and public works departments, and a very small number were even employed at the sterling scale hitherto reserved for expatriate officers.[67]

Progress was significant but limited, as there remained a ceiling for their promotion and no ethnic Chinese would be considered for recruitment to the elite cadet service. It was against such a background that the government announced in 1935 that it had 'fully and frankly accepted the policy of replacing wherever possible European by Asiatic employees'.[68] Even though localisation at the more senior level did not in fact materialise until after the end of the Pacific War, the official change of policy happened before the might of the Empire was challenged successfully by the Japanese. The seeds for more progressive changes in the civil service were sowed but their growth would be gravely stunted, before being given a real boost, by the interregnum of Japanese occupation during the Pacific War.

The Calm Before the Storm

On 7 July 1937, Japanese army units deployed near Beijing started the full-scale invasion of China. This was quickly followed by a parallel massive attack on Shanghai. Although the Japanese High Command calculated that it would take no longer than three months to destroy the Chinese will to fight, Chinese forces of very diverse backgrounds rallied around their national leader, Chiang Kai-shek, and put up a stubborn fight.[69] Chiang deployed the best of his army, amounting to 700,000 troops, almost exclusively infantry, in Shanghai. They had to stop a Japanese seaborne invasion force of 300,000, supported by over 300 guns, 200 tanks, 200 aircraft and numerous warships.[70] Against all expectations, the Chinese held off the Japanese for three months.[71] To support and sustain their invasion the Japanese eventually deployed and maintained 1.2 million troops and 500 aircraft in China.[71] In October 1938, after a year's resistance and retreat, the Chinese government withdrew to its wartime capital of Chongqing in Sichuan province, while Canton fell to the Japanese after an amphibious landing in Daya Bay, just north of Hong Kong.

The beginning of full-scale war, even though undeclared, between China and Japan, had important consequences for Hong Kong. Chinese refugees flooded into the colony. It became an important lifeline to China.

Hong Kong's value to China was tremendous, since China was still essentially an agricultural country and had quickly lost most of its industrial base in the coastal regions. To sustain its war efforts, China had to secure as much equipment and strategic material as possible from the outside. In addition to supplies from the Soviet Union, Germany and Italy, the Chinese looked to Britain and the USA for support.[73] Overland deliveries were possible from the Soviet Union. However, because the Japanese navy controlled the China coast, supplies from other countries had to come through Hong Kong or over China's border with British Burma or French Indo-China. British support was therefore very important to China. The excellent port of Hong Kong played a key role before the fall of Canton. It also set up new industries to produce helmets, gas masks and other wartime supplies for China.[74] The new industrial and economic expansion stimulated by China's misfortune accounted for Hong Kong's ability to absorb a population increase of 63 per cent (over 600,000) in the first four years of the war.

The refugee- and war-driven boom created a strange situation and atmosphere. Its surreal nature became more acute but did not change in any fundamental way following the outbreak of war in Europe in September 1939. By then, Britain was no longer in a position to defend its empire in the East, including Hong Kong.[75] In the years when China desperately needed its support, Britain was preoccupied, first with the Nazi threat and then with war in Europe. On several occasions it was forced to appease Japan. The British government repeatedly turned down China's requests for British pilots to serve as advisers in the Chinese air force. It also had to, for example, refuse the Chinese permission to set up a secret aeroplane assembly depot in Hong Kong.[76]

Although the British government realised in private that 'Hong Kong could not be expected to hold out for long' against a Japanese invasion and that 'delaying action was the best to be hoped for', it put up a brave face in public as no British reinforcements could be spared for this imperial outpost.[77] Indeed, the general public in Hong Kong did not fully grasp the seriousness of the situation as the Sino-Japanese war dragged on, and continued to live under the false sense of security inherent in the grandeur and arrogance of the British Empire.

Complacency prevailed among both the expatriates and the Chinese, though for different reasons. For most expatriate Britons, longstanding arrogance based on racism and imperial privileges produced a state of mind that allowed them to accept incredible intelligence about their potential invaders. The government's assessment deemed the little yellow soldiers of Japan 'incapable of night movement', their pilots unable to cope with night flying, 'their bomb-aiming... bad' and 'they only seemed good because they had been pitted against inferior opponents'.[78] It was with such a mentality that the expatriate community released 'a torrent of criticism' against the government after it sensibly (though not equitably) evacuated expatriate British women and children in the summer of 1940.[79] The Chinese community shared the confidence of the expatriates as most still believed or preferred to believe in the might of the British Empire. The destitute refugees, preoccupied with making a living, had no choice but to trust in the protection of the British flag.

There was an irony about the serenity of *pax Britannica*. It is true that some top policymakers, like Sir Alexander Cadogan, Permanent Under-Secretary at the Foreign Office from 1938 to 1946, already recognised the Empire's bluff had been called, not least by the Japanese demands since 1937 that forced Britain to reduce its support for China's war efforts.[80] However, the perception in Hong Kong, and indeed in other European colonies in East Asia, was different.[81] There, the idea of *pax Britannica* still had the desired effect. There were also those who believed that war between Japan and the West was not inevitable.[82] War clouds were gathering and disaster awaited but Hong Kong remained remarkably calm, still basking in the residual glow of imperial splendour until December 1941.

Part III

A Colonial Paradox

Chapter 9

Japanese Invasion and Occupation

The centenary of the British occupation, 1941, was a landmark in the modern history of Hong Kong in more than one sense. It was the first time that its survival and continuation as a Crown Colony came under a serious threat, as it faced a full-scale invasion by the Japanese Empire. Even though its defence was poorly prepared and organised, its garrison put up a gallant though short fight. Thus began the ordeal of Japanese occupation that lasted three years and eight months. For the first time since Elliot claimed Hong Kong for Queen Victoria, the British were not the lord and master but prisoners and internees. Japanese rule did not last but the impact of Japan's successful invasion destroyed the myth of the invincibility of the British Empire. *Pax Britannica* was reduced from the basis of Hong Kong's security to a relic of history. The clock could not be turned back. In the meantime, both the expatriate British and the Chinese of Hong Kong did what they could to resist the Japanese. The British government also put together a small team in London to plan and work for the restoration of British sovereignty at the end of the war. There was a recognition among the planners that while Britain must restore its jurisdiction over Hong Kong, British rule would be different from what had prevailed before the war.

The Battle of Hong Kong

When Japan invaded China in July 1937, Nazi Germany under Adolf Hitler had already reoccupied the Rhineland in breach of the Versailles Peace Treaty and the Spanish Civil War had been raging for about a year. The British armed forces were in no state to fulfil its worldwide obligations in imperial defence and meet the rising challenge being posed by a rapidly rearming Germany at the same time.[1] This was due in large part to the British government's strategic assumption during the inter-war period that there would not be a general war for ten years.[2] The neglect of its defence consequently 'placed the British Empire in a position of the utmost danger by the later 1930s'.[3] This explained Prime Minister Neville Chamberlain's view following the Japanese invasion of China that 'to pick a quarrel with Japan at the present moment' was 'suicidal', because if Britain 'were to become involved in the Far East the temptation to the Dictator States to take action whether in Eastern Europe or in Spain might be irresistible'.[4] Even before the Second World War started in September 1939, British defence planning already worked on the basis that in the event of a war with Japan, 'delaying action was the best to be hoped for' in Hong Kong.[5] This was because the military admitted that problems of 'effective defence of Hong Kong' against Japanese air assault were 'virtually insoluble'.[6]

The situation grew worse when war started in Europe and the Royal Navy became fully occupied in keeping the sea-lanes open for Britain. By then, London had reluctantly considered Hong Kong expendable.[7] Although staunchly against giving up any British territory, Winston Churchill, who took over as Prime Minister in May 1940 at the critical time of the Dunkirk evacuation, accepted that Hong Kong would fall to the Japanese and that the peace conference would deal with its future.[8] To minimise losses there, Churchill preferred to reduce the garrison to a nominal size but refrained from doing so in order not to undermine the prestige of the Empire and China's will to resist and to tie down a large number of Japanese forces.

Hong Kong's defence in the summer of 1941 consisted of four regular infantry battalions, of which two were Indian, the reinforced battalion-strength Volunteers, four regiments of artillery, a flight of three obsolete Wildebeeste torpedo bombers, two Walruse amphibian planes, four destroyers (three would be away and one in dry dock when Hong Kong came under attack), four gunboats, a flotilla of eight torpedo boats and the local naval reserve.[9] Churchill allowed this force to be reinforced because Canada offered two infantry battalions. After their arrival in November, three weeks before hostilities started, they brought the total strength of the defence force to just over 10,000. The Canadian battalions had not yet completed their training, did not have all their equipment and were not combat ready. They were sent partly because they were not ready for service in Europe where the best-trained units were earmarked. They did not have time to know the terrain or train with the rest of the defence force before they saw action. They went to Hong Kong to deter the Japanese, encourage Chinese resistance and boost British prestige and morale in Asia.[10] There was no expectation that they could enable this exposed imperial outpost to be held indefinitely, though a handful of general officers and policymakers indulged in the wishful thinking that the reinforced garrison could hold out for at least four months.[11]

The arrival of the Canadians led British commander Major General Christopher Maltby to change the defence plan, which had previously focused upon the defence of the island but not the mainland. Maltby now deployed one of his two brigades on the mainland. The basic thinking was to hold the invaders in a prepared defence line, the Gin Drinker's Line in the southern part of the New Territories for a week before withdrawing to Hong Kong island, where the garrison would make a strong stand.[12] On the island, troops were again deployed for static defence of prepared positions. There was no mobile reserve of a meaningful size that could be sent quickly to counterattack and destroy a Japanese landing force. The involvement of the local Chinese in the defence was largely limited to about 450 who volunteered to join the local defence forces and a larger number in essential services, such as air raid wardens or auxiliary firemen.[13] The large pool of Chinese manpower was not utilised to any serious extent. The defence plan was unimaginative.

By the summer of 1941, the British had reached an understanding with the Chinese government under Chiang Kai-shek to coordinate their respective military operations in the event of a Japanese attack on Hong Kong.[14] The main agreement was that, once hostilities started, the Chinese Army would attack the Japanese forces from their rear to relieve the pressure on the British garrison.[15] The British also explored the possibility of cooperating with the Chinese Communist guerrillas, who operated in the vicinity of Hong Kong, though no agreement was reached as the Communists thought the British 'lacked sincerity in the common defence against the Japanese'.[16]

Poised to attack Hong Kong was the 23rd Corps of the Japanese Army under Lieutenant General Sakai Takashi, who was also given overall command of the air and naval units in support of the assault. The actual invasion force was Lieutenant General Sano Tadayoshi's battle-hardened 38th Division, which was generously reinforced by two brigades and six battalions of artillery, tanks, and other logistical units. They were supported by 63 bombers, 13 fighters and 10 other aircraft, as well as a light cruiser, three destroyers, four torpedo boats, three gunboats, two ancillary ships and five naval aircraft.[17] The invasion force as a whole was well over 20,000 strong and had a considerable edge over the motley assortment of the multilingual and multiethnic British defenders.[18] The Japanese forces also enjoyed the benefit of having the Corps headquarters assuming overall command, the confidence that Sakai could call on the two other divisions of the Corps deployed in Guangdong to reinforce or block any Chinese relief efforts if necessary and the advantage of having been put together and trained together for this specific operation for over a month.[19]

The Japanese also had superb intelligence about Hong Kong's defence, which they had gathered over a long period by placing their agents to work as waiters, barmen, hairdressers, masseurs and prostitutes to service British officials and military officers.[20] This included, for example, a naval commander who, for seven years, worked as a hairdresser and patiently listened to conversations among his British patrons, including two governors, senior army officers, the commissioner of police and the head of the special branch. It meant the Japanese had 'a full and accurate survey of the whole defensive position' before the invasion started.[21]

At 8am on 8 December, a clear and sunny morning, four hours after the United States Navy base at Pearl Harbour in Honolulu came under the most devastating attack ever mounted against the USA, Japanese bombers effectively destroyed British air power in one attack. Although two of the Wilderbeestes in fact escaped damage, they were never deployed against overwhelming odds and were themselves destroyed by the British before the airport was evacuated.[22] The battle for Hong Kong had started with the Japanese gaining complete air supremacy within the first five minutes. Two days later, the Japanese breached the Gin Drinker's Line at the Shing Mun Redoubt. Maltby concluded that unless he withdrew his brigade from the mainland immediately he would not be able to hold the island for long. Thus began the best-organised operation of the battle, under which the British disengaged from combat and evacuated their forces across the harbour with relatively little loss.[23]

The second and much more intense phase of the battle started under cover of darkness late at night on 18 December, when six Japanese battalions successfully crossed Victoria Harbour at its eastern side, after an unsuccessful attempt three days earlier. This was the beginning of the end but much hard fighting was waged by the defenders on the island.

Although Hong Kong's defenders were inadequately trained and poorly prepared they gave an honourable account of themselves, which differed greatly from what happened in Singapore or Malaya. The resolute leadership of Sir Mark Young, who took up the governorship on 10 September, and Maltby's tenacity, despite his other inadequacies as a general, left their marks. They saw to it that Hong Kong's completely outclassed defenders followed Prime Minister Churchill's order to resist with utmost stubbornness 'in spirit and to the letter'.[24] They put up a gallant though badly organised fight for 17 days, and did sufficient damage to the Japanese 38th Division to delay its redeployment to the Dutch East Indies.[25] Some units also demonstrated such courage, resolution and daring against overwhelming odds that they deserved to earn, in Churchill's words, the 'lasting honour' that was their due.

There was, for example, the stand of the 'Hughesiliers', a unit of the Volunteers, at North Point power station the night the Japanese crossed the harbour. The 'Hughesiliers' consisted of four officers and 68 men, all over 55 or too old for service but volunteered to serve under their commander Lieutenant Colonel Owen Hughes, a former member of the Legislative Council. They were, like 70-year-old private Sir Edward Des Voeux, mostly taipans or seniors in British hongs and were deployed at the power station to keep them out of the front line.[26] On the night of the engagement, 36 of them were on duty under Major John Patterson (Chairman of Jardine and member of the Legislative Council), and they were reinforced by technicians of the power plant and a small number of soldiers from the Middlesex Regiment who drifted there following the tide of battle elsewhere. The power plant happened to be in the way of one of the advancing Japanese columns. They came under fierce attack at 1:00am on 19 December and denied the power plant to the Japanese until 4:00am. They did not surrender and give up their position until they ran out of ammunition the following afternoon.[27] They halted the advance of a Japanese column for as long as was humanly possible.

There was also the charge of the motor torpedo boats (M.T.B.s) when the Hughesiliers were making their last stand. The Japanese were pouring across the harbour in small craft to consolidate their 'beach head' on the morning of 19 December. Six boats of No. 2 M.T.B. flotilla under Lieutenant Commander George Gandy were organised into three waves to speed across the harbour from west to east to disrupt and if possible stop the crossing.[28] They attacked in pairs in broad daylight, though the Japanese dominated the harbour, both by superior artillery and machine-gun fire on the north shore of the entire harbour, additional fire from the south side of the harbour, from North Point to the east, and from the air. The first wave, which enjoyed the benefit of surprise, disrupted the Japanese landing, though one boat was badly damaged.[29] The second pair charged courageously but met with concentrated and accurate fire, which sank one and severely damaged the other.[30] Since the Japanese had by then stopped sending any more landing craft into the harbour, the British naval commander ordered the third wave to abort. It is not clear whether Lieutenant D.W. Wagstaff, commanding M.T.B.26, did not receive the order or chose to ignore it.[31] His boat charged into a maelstrom of fire and bombs and was sunk with its last Lewis gun still firing off North Point, more than halfway across the harbour.[32] Whether the charges of the second and the third waves were heroic or, like the charge of the Light Brigade in the Crimean War, foolhardy, they had the effect of stopping the Japanese reinforcement of its forces on Hong Kong island for the rest of the day.[33]

Britain's new ally, China, did try to keep its promise. On the day the Japanese attacked Hong Kong, Chiang Kai-shek declared war on Japan – until then the Japanese invasion was resisted without either side declaring war. On the following day, he ordered three corps under General Yu Hanmou to march towards Hong Kong.[34] To relieve the Hong Kong garrison, he planned to launch a New Year's Day attack on the Japanese in the Canton region. However, before the Chinese infantry, which had no motor transport, could get into position to attack, the Japanese had shattered Hong Kong's defences.

The end came on Christmas Day. By then, one of Maltby's two brigade commanders, Canadian John Lawson, had already been killed. Organised defence had been reduced to pockets of resistance, some of which were out of contact with headquarters, and the Japanese were about a mile from Army and Navy Headquarters as well as from Government House. That morning, Young sent his Christmas message to what remained of the defenders in a language resembling Churchill's own. He urged them to 'hold fast for King and Empire... in this your finest hour'. [35] He also rejected for the third time an offer to surrender, and intended 'to add another twenty-four hours to the credit of the account'.[36] At 2:00pm Maltby checked with the Middlesex Colonel commanding the front in the central pocket and was told that in an hour or so useful military resistance would no longer be possible. Maltby telephoned Young with a recommendation to surrender an hour later.[37] Young asked Maltby to check the situation again and was informed that the remnants of the Middlesex battalion could hold out for another half an hour at most, with the remaining posts manned by remnants of the Punjabi battalion lasting a maximum of two more hours.[38] After checking with the naval commander who confirmed Maltby's assessment and who, like Maltby, assured Young that they were personally prepared to defend and perish with their respective headquarters, Young decided further resistance could no longer justify the costs involved. At 3:15pm, he accepted Maltby's advice in order to reduce further heavy loss of life and to avoid provoking the Japanese to brutalise the civilian population in attempting a repeat of the 1938 Nanjing Massacre.[39] Darkness descended on this outpost of 'the empire where the sun never sets'.

The human cost of the battle was high. The British suffered casualties amounting to 2,232 killed or missing and 2,300 wounded, while the Japanese reported 1,996 killed and 6,000 wounded.[40] The losses of the civilians, who suffered from Japanese brutalities, sustained bombardment and systematic looting by gangsters following the retreat of British forces and police, cannot be reliably estimated.

The Destruction of Imperial Invincibility

The myth surrounding the might of the British Empire ended when Young became the first British governor to surrender a colony to an enemy after the end of the American War of Independence in 1782. The battle of Hong Kong was in any event greatly overshadowed by the Malayan campaign and, above all, by the surrender in February 1942 of Singapore, the symbol of British imperial power in the East.[41] Hong Kong fell because its defenders were outnumbered at least two to one, vastly outgunned on land, in the air and at sea and outmanoeuvred. In Malaya and Singapore, 138,708 British servicemen were defeated and captured by 50,197 Japanese, who suffered, in comparison to the 17-day Hong Kong operation, merely 9,824 battle casualties over the ten weeks of the campaign.[42] The Japanese victory and the British defeat in Southeast Asia were nothing short of spectacular. They caught the imagination of Asia.[43]

The Japanese humiliated the British Empire and in the process destroyed the myth of the superiority of the white race. As a result, even long-time supporters of the Empire, such as the Secretary of State for India, Leo Amery, lost heart. He admitted that 'we were on the eve of very great changes in the relation of Asia to Europe' and it is doubtful 'whether in the future empires like our Asiatic empire' could subsist.[44]

The destruction of the supposed invincibility of the British Empire had practical implications for its claim over Hong Kong, as the colony lay inside the Allied powers' China theatre, which covered the whole of China, Indo-China and Thailand.[45] On US President Franklin Roosevelt's initiative, Chiang Kai-shek became supreme commander of this theatre in January 1942.[46] This arrangement was primarily a gesture to Chiang and at this stage was largely academic with regard to Hong Kong. Indeed, it was not clarified whether Hong Kong, as a British territory, was within Chiang's command. Nevertheless, Chiang was justified in considering it within his theatre. A shadow was cast over its long-term future as a British territory.

As the shock of the rapid collapse of the Allied defences in Southeast Asia sank in, responsible officials in both the British and Chinese governments began to think about Hong Kong's future. Now that the myth of British invincibility had been destroyed, the nationalistic Chiang pondered whether he could use the wider war to end, as soon as possible, the 'unequal treaties' to which China had been subjected since the 1840s.[47] Consequently, he instructed the Chinese Ambassador to Britain, Wellington Koo (Gu Weijun), to explore the British attitude towards Hong Kong.[48]

In London, the Colonial Office was the first to reflect on – and recognise the implications of – Britain's failure to defend Hong Kong for any length of time.[49] While Britain had no illusions about the difficulty of defending the colony, its rapid fall was a major blow. When David MacDougall, a cadet officer of the Hong Kong government, joined the Colonial Office after a daring escape to China on the day the colony fell, he immediately raised an alarm. He reported that all Chinese officials he met in China, up to the vice-ministerial level, assumed that Hong Kong would be returned to China after the war.[50] The Colonial Office accepted that 'the arrangements existing before the Japanese occupation would not be restored'.[51]

The question of Hong Kong's future became the subject of an intense internal debate within the British government in June 1942, which was when the Foreign Office took an active interest. The head of its Far Eastern Department, Ashley Clarke, initiated the debate after he visited the USA, where he engaged in lengthy discussions with State Department officials. His US colleagues, particularly Stanley Hornbeck, expressed strong pro-China and anti-British Empire sentiments. This troubled Clarke deeply,[52] for he believed that the US would reject the restoration of the *status quo ante* in Hong Kong. He thus urged the British government to prepare itself to give up Hong Kong 'in order to maintain the really important things'.[53] The Colonial Office officials, led by Assistant Under-Secretary Gerald Edward Gent, considered Clarke's view 'defeatist'.[54]

With the help of MacDougall and the blessings of his senior colleagues, Gent produced a policy paper to pre-empt an unacceptable one being put forward by Clarke.[55] The Secretary of State for the Colonies, Lord Cranborne, strongly supported Gent.[56] The issue was eventually referred to the War Cabinet, which preferred to avoid giving up Hong Kong. Churchill felt that 'questions of territorial adjustment could not be considered now and must be left to be raised at the peace conference'.[57]

The issue of Hong Kong's future, disguised in the form of the future of the leased New Territories, did come up when Britain negotiated with China in late 1942 to end extraterritorial and other privileges it enjoyed in China.[58] It became the sticking point preventing an agreement to be reached. A compromise was eventually devised. It was for the Chinese Foreign Minister to inform the British 'that the Chinese government reserves its right' to raise the issue of the New Territories lease again 'for discussion at a later date'.[59] Britain formally acknowledged the Chinese position.[60] What this meant was that Britain accepted for the first time that there was a 'Hong Kong problem' – a problem the Chinese could raise after the victory over Japan.

Occupation and Resistance

Although the spectacular defeat of Britain and the other Western imperial powers in Asia by Japan shattered once and for all the myth of the superiority of the white race, it did not enable the Japanese to build up a Greater East Asia Co-prosperity Sphere. The Japanese made two basic and interrelated errors. To begin with, they not only wished to dominate the region to achieve 'economic self-sufficiency' but also to 'satisfy a psychological craving – the recognition of Japan's ethical and cultural superiority... to play the part which the Chinese had once played in the great days of the Celestial Empire... when China was regarded... as exemplar and fountainhead of civilised life'.[61] The Japanese tried to achieve this primarily through the use of force. They did not understand that China could have done so in the past because she was so vastly richer and more powerful than all her neighbours that she could afford to be overly generous to them and thus earned her place. It was a position Japan did not enjoy and could not afford in the 1940s. The second mistake the Japanese made was a failure to recognise 'freedom for Asia' particularly if only achieved by the iron fist of a new hegemonic power, even if it was Asian, 'was not enough, that each national movement demanded its own freedom'.[62] The Japanese never intended to treat other Asians as equals or genuine partners.[63] Consequently, even though they technically liberated many Asian peoples from Western imperialism, they could not secure, with a small number of exceptions, their loyalty and support. They tried to pacify their new empire by repressive measures. This meant Japanese occupation in Asia was brutal. Hong Kong was no exception.

In its incarnation as the Captured Territory of Hong Kong, Lieutenant General Isogai Rensuke took over from Sakai and became Governor in February 1942. While the Japanese Prime Minister General Tojo Hideki deemed Hong Kong 'strategically vital for the defence of the Greater East Asiatic Sphere', its future status was not settled.[64] It was intended that it would be administered as a Japanese territory but its retrocession to China as part of the post-war arrangement was not ruled out.[65] As long as the war went on, Hong Kong's first and foremost function was to support the Japanese war effort.[66] This underlined Japan's occupation policy.

Although real power in occupied Hong Kong continued to rest with the military, a civil administration was set up and local collaborators were recruited to give the administration credibility and reduce the need for a sizable garrison. For this purpose, two councils were set up with established local Chinese elite being recruited, cajoled or forced to serve. At the top was the four-member Chinese Representative Council chaired by Sir Robert Kotewall. Below that were the 22 members of the Chinese

Co-operative Council under the chairmanship of Sir Shouson Chow. Kotewall was a member of the Executive Council prior to the occupation and Chow had served in the same capacity from 1926 to 1936. They were authorised to collaborate by the Secretary for Chinese Affairs R.A.C. North, Attorney General Grenville Alabaster and Defence Secretary J.A. Fraser in January 1942, as the British were no longer in a position to act on behalf of the local Chinese.[67] Although Kotewall was not as enthusiastic a collaborator as his two colleagues on the Representative Council, Chen Lianbo and Liu Tiecheng, and his loyalty to the British Crown was eventually accepted after the war, his apparent willingness to collaborate caused serious misgivings upon the Japanese surrender.[68] The same did not apply to Chow and, indeed, to a number of others like Li Shu-fan and Man-kam Lo, who had served against their own wishes on the Co-operative Council.[69] The two Chinese councils were in any event meant mainly to make Japanese rule easier for the Japanese and to help monitor the views of the Chinese community.[70] They were not powerful or influential organisations like the Executive and Legislative Councils under the British.

Given Hong Kong's place in Japanese strategic thinking and the logistics involved in feeding a population of over 1.5 million after its economy was broken, the Japanese assiduously worked to reduce the population. This was achieved by requiring all who did not have residence or employment to leave. Although this policy was odious, with brutal tactics employed to ensure its implementation, it was highly successful. By February 1943, the population had dropped to 969,000, falling further to 5–600,000 by the time the Japanese had surrendered in August 1945.[71]

Those who stayed behind suffered considerable hardship under a reign of terror. They had to suffer from the arbitrary and bloodthirsty behaviour of Japanese soldiers and their terror-instilling military police, the *Kempeitai*. Japanese sentries regularly and harshly punished and occasionally even shot or beheaded any passing Chinese who failed to bow in the required manner.[72] Some also frequently raided Chinese homes and took whatever they wanted.[73] Such behaviour reinforced the image of terror created by atrocities the Japanese committed during the battle, of which the most infamous was the St Stephen's College massacre in Stanley. This happened on the last day of the battle, when 56 British wounded, two doctors and seven nurses were murdered in cold blood in this wartime medical station. Even more terrifying to the local community were random atrocities committed against them, as some civilians 'were used for bayonet or shooting practice, or for jujitsu practice, being thrown heavily a number of times, and bayoneted when unable to move'.[74]

They also had to endure great shortages in all kinds of commodities, including rice. This was caused partly by Tojo's directive to find and export all valuable material kept by the British in this wealthy colony for use in Japan.[75] This resulted in the shipping from Hong Kong to Japan of the colony's large reserve of rice, among other valuables like vehicles and machinery. The result was a severe shortage and dramatic price increase for this the most basic of essentials for the local community.[76] The situation deteriorated further as the tide of the war turned against Japan and its navy could no longer secure the sea-lanes. According to one account, for much of the occupation between 300 and 400 corpses were routinely collected everyday from streets, though the highest recorded was 721.[77] How many of these died of starvation or privation cannot be ascertained. Whatever sympathy the Japanese gained from the Chinese in removing their British colonial masters was quickly destroyed and replaced by fear and hatred. The Kempeitai instituted a reign of terror by publicising its methods of torture and places for execution. Some of their favourite methods of torture were pumping water into a victim until it came out from other parts of the body or pulling off nails from fingers, both techniques regularly applied to anyone deemed to have committed minor offences like violating currency control.[78]

As for the British, the Japanese sought to destroy their presence by renaming streets and places, removing old records, replacing the currency when possible, changing the school curriculum by substituting Japanese for English and humiliating them in front of the Chinese.[79] British prisoners of war were kept mainly in the former army barracks in Shum Shui Po, while most of their officers were kept in the smaller Argyle Street Camp in Kowloon. Although a small number of the prisoners were able to escape, including Lieutenant Colonel Lindsay Ride of the Volunteers, most prisoners remained in their camps or were sent to Japan to work. Life in the camps was harsh, with food being kept to near starvation level and any able bodied men put to arduous work on construction projects like extending the local airport.[80]

British and other Allied civilians, numbering about 2,500, were interned in Stanley next to the local prison on the southern side of the island. Conditions there were marginally better than in the POW camps since the internees were not required to supply manpower for work parties.

The collapse of British power had different effects on the internees. Some Britons continued to indulge in racism and blamed the presence of Eurasians for the inadequate food, though it was often the Eurasians who secured extra food from their relatives in the city and sometimes shared it with others.[81] Others used their ingenuity and resourcefulness to produce additional food. A notable contribution in this respect was made by Geoffrey Herklots, a botanist at the university and an authority on local flora and fish. There was also Franklin Gimson, who arrived to take up the office of Colonial Secretary the day before the Japanese attacked and showed himself to be remarkably far-sighted and reflective. In Stanley, Gimson had to work hard to restore the reputation and credibility of Hong Kong officialdom, both in tatters as a result of the rapid collapse of the defence.[82] Above all, he had to battle the old establishment view, put strongly by Secretary for Chinese Affairs R.A.C. North, against introducing self-governing institutions to the people of Hong Kong as a whole.[83] In contrast, Gimson tried to persuade the others that 'in future the Chinese will have to play a bigger part in Hong Kong and that the Europeans will have to rely on their co-operation more than they have done in the past'.[84]

Hong Kong's resistance efforts were made mainly in parallel by two groups, though some cooperation did exist between them. On the one side were the British efforts to which young Chinese of Hong Kong like Francis Yiu-pui Lee and Paul Ka-cheung Tsui volunteered and made important contributions. They were carried out by the British Army Aid Group (BAAG), set up and commanded by Lieutenant Colonel Ride, the best-known escapee from Shum Shui Po. On the other side were the Chinese guerrilla efforts carried out mainly by Communist partisans.

After his escape in January 1942, Ride persuaded the British military representatives and the Chinese government to allow him to set up a unit to help others escape from Hong Kong, for which he was to recruit from members of the Special Operations Executive (SOE) and particularly from among those who had served in Hong Kong.[85] The BAAG operated in close liaison with the SOE but it also coordinated its work with the Chinese government and had limited contact with Communist partisans operating in and around Hong Kong.[86] In addition to its function in rescuing Allied personnel, including airmen shot down and essential workers trapped in occupied Hong Kong, the BAAG developed a major role in intelligence gathering. It enabled the British to secure not only regular military intelligence but also valuable information on the situation in Hong Kong, including the loyalty of prominent individuals.[87] Altogether, the BAAG helped 139 POWs, 33 American airmen, 314 Chinese in British armed services, and 1,400 civilians to escape and rejoin the war effort.[88]

Although technically part of the escape and evasion organisation M.I.9 and coming under the command of the Director of Military Intelligence, General Headquarters in New Delhi, the BAAG primarily represented Hong Kong's resistance efforts.[89] Its agents and runners were mostly ethnic Chinese even though most of its officers were expatriate British. This was the first organisation in which expatriate Britons, Chinese and other nationalities of Hong Kong served together without a clear and unbreakable racial divide, where ethnic Chinese like Lee and Tsui were, among others, commissioned as officers. Both rose to the rank of captain. Indeed, Tsui's war record was an important factor in his selection as the first ethnic Chinese cadet after the end of the war. In the resistance efforts of the BAAG, old colonial Hong Kong was beginning to give way to one that promised to be different.

The other main resistance was waged by Chinese Communist guerrillas, who were formally organised into the Hong Kong and Kowloon or the First Independent Group of the East River Column under General Zeng Sheng in December 1943.[90] The group was in fact formed in February 1942 with local residents Cai Guoliang as commander and Chen Daming as political commissar and armed with 30 machine guns and several hundred rifles left by defeated British forces.[91] Its strength numbered about 400 between 1942 and 1945.[92] The group operated mainly in Sai

Kung, its stronghold, and in Sha Tau Kok, Taipo, Yuen Long and Lantau
Island, though a special pistol unit operated in the urban areas of Hong
Kong and Kowloon.[93] Its first task was to rescue various prominent
Communist and leftwing individuals who were stranded in Hong Kong.[94]
It also developed a role for helping Allied escapees and downed airmen
to evade their Japanese pursuers, a role which was often shared or
coordinated with the BAAG and accounted for the safety of 89 individuals
including Ride.[95] In addition, the Communist cadres used the resistance
efforts to recruit supporters particularly from among the young and
educated people of Hong Kong.[96]

Wartime Planning in London

After the initial shock and problems associated with the collapse of British
power in East Asia had sunk in, the Colonial Office started to examine
what the future held for the British Empire there. The first issue for
Hong Kong concerned its post-war status, since the British government
had conceded that the Chinese government had a right to raise the future
of its New Territories after the defeat of Japan.[97]

At the beginning of 1943, Colonial Office thinking was that Britain
must try to avoid giving up sovereignty over Hong Kong. Should that
prove impossible, it would negotiate with China and treat Hong Kong
as Britain's contribution to a general settlement for a new order in the
Far East.[98] The Colonial Office insisted that, in such a situation, Britain's
contribution must be matched (though in still undefined forms) by China
and the USA.[99] Though official British policy separated sovereignty over
Hong Kong proper from that over the New Territories, officialdom dealt
with the two together in internal deliberations.

The following summer, Assistant Under-Secretary Gent produced a
paper to argue that Britain should retain the New Territories or keep
Hong Kong proper if it could not hold on to the New Territories.[100] In
the event of the latter, he suggested Britain use the early end of the lease
to negotiate with China for joint control over the airport, reservoirs and
other parts of the infrastructure in the New Territories essential for Hong
Kong's wellbeing. This was the first time in internal discussions that
British officials had seriously proposed examining the possibility and
implications of keeping Hong Kong proper without the New Territories.
Nothing came of this initiative, since the Foreign Office, which was still
inclined to use Hong Kong as a bargaining chip to secure other more
important British interests, refused to take part.

In the meantime, Gent made what arrangements he could within the
authority of the Colonial Office to strengthen Britain's ability to recover
Hong Kong. He proceeded to create a civil affairs staff for Hong Kong
even before the armed forces were ready to accommodate such a unit in
their organisations or, indeed, to plan an operation to recover the
colony.[101] Thus, a Hong Kong Planning Unit was created under the wing
of the Colonial Office. It was initially put under a recently retired Colonial
Secretary of Hong Kong, Norman Smith. From 1944 onwards, it was

headed by David MacDougall, the cadet who had escaped from Hong Kong. By setting up the Unit at such an early date, Gent tried to build up an implied acceptance at an official level that Britain would return to Hong Kong at the end of the war.[102] It also provided Britain with the human resources, the core of a civil affairs staff, it needed to take over the administration of the colony as soon as it could be liberated.

In addition to helping the Colonial Office work out specific policy directives on policing, education, prison, financial policy, immigration, Chinese Affairs and other matters, the Hong Kong Planning Unit embarked on a study of constitutional reform in May 1945.[103] Several proposals, ranging from reforming the Executive and Legislative Councils to establishing a new municipal council, were discussed though no conclusion was reached before the Japanese surrendered in August. In general, Gent felt 'there should be an extension of democratic forms in the new era'.[104] With Gent providing a guiding hand, the 'Colonial Office wanted a bold approach', preferring measures that would provide 'a sufficiently wide range of functions to attract responsible Chinese to serve on' the new or reformed councils.[105] Gent had taken to heart the lessons he learned defending Hong Kong as an imperial possession after the destruction of the veil of imperial invincibility.

The fortunes of war affected Britain's attitude towards Hong Kong. In 1944, China suffered a major reverse when it lost more than half a million troops to the Japanese offensive known as Operation Ichigo.[106] In contrast, the British counter-offensive in Burma, which was assisted by the Chinese, was making steady progress. Britain's successes in the war and the prospect of instability and weakness in post-war China hardened its attitude towards Hong Kong. In November, the deputy prime minister and leader of the Labour Party, Clement Attlee, declared in the House of Commons that Britain intended to return to Hong Kong.[107] The British government's attitude hardened further when the US Ambassador to China, Patrick Hurley, visited London in April 1945. In response to Hurley's suggestion that Britain should return Hong Kong to China, Prime Minister Churchill emphatically stated that it could only happen 'over my dead body'.[108] With the backing of the Prime Minister, the Colonial Office won the upper hand in its bureaucratic battle against the Foreign Office over Hong Kong's future.

The planning undertaken in London suddenly assumed urgency in July. Although the Americans in China, under Lieutenant General Albert Wedemeyer, had started planning an operation to liberate south China earlier in the spring, including the Canton–Hong Kong region, the British were not informed.[109] Until July, the British worked on the premise that 'nothing whatever has been settled' with regard to the manner of Hong Kong's liberation and 'no decision [was] likely for a considerable time'.[110] At the Potsdam Conference, the Americans told them Wedemeyer's plan.[111]

The prospect of the regular Chinese army reoccupying Hong Kong in the near future galvanised the British into action immediately. The idea of launching a British attack to liberate Hong Kong was considered but dismissed, because there were 'insufficient British forces available at present to oust the enemy'.[112] The consensus reached was that Britain should attach a civil affairs unit to the Chinese invasion force. In the event of Chinese irregular forces retaking Hong Kong, it was agreed that the SOE would send in a British civil affairs unit in a clandestine operation mounted outside China.[113] Such options were available thanks in no small part to Gent's earlier initiative to establish the Hong Kong Planning Unit. The Unit was put on standby for incorporation into the armed forces as civil affairs staff. Its head, MacDougall, was the first to be commissioned and was given the rank of brigadier.

The British felt they were working against great odds. They felt certain Wedemeyer was 'personally opposed to' their forces in China trying to recover Hong Kong.[114] This assessment was correct, because 'Wedemeyer regarded British intentions and plans as incompatible with American policy in China'.[115] Nevertheless, the Colonial Office explored every possible option to enhance the restoration of British sovereignty in Hong Kong. It arranged with the Admiralty to set aside 'two or three suitable fast moving fleet units to be so placed, if Japanese capitulation looks possible, that they may steam at once for Hong Kong under sealed orders on given signal'.[116] It also instructed the BAAG to smuggle a message to Gimson instructing him 'to restore British sovereignty and administration immediately' in the event of Japanese capitulation in Hong Kong.[117]

British officials were driven by the belief that the recovery of Hong Kong was very important for British 'prestige and future relations with China'.[118] There was also a feeling that, 'once in occupation [of Hong Kong], a Chinese force of whatever nature might prove difficult to extrude by ordinary diplomatic means'.[119] By then, the Foreign Office had come a long way from Ashley Clarke's 1942 position. In July, it modified and adopted as its own the position paper on Hong Kong that Gent had originally prepared in 1943. In the new circumstances, the Foreign Office sought to recover Hong Kong, including the New Territories, on three grounds.[120] These were:

- British enterprise and good government had built a barren island with a few thousand inhabitants into one of the world's great ports;
- with the removal of extraterritoriality and a probability of unsettled conditions in post-war China, Hong Kong was more important than ever as a base for British merchants and industrialists operating in China; and
- having lost the colony to the Japanese, it was 'a point of national honour... to recover it, and restore it to its normal state of order and prosperity'.[121]

Chapter 10

Return to Empire

The end of the Pacific War came when Japan accepted the terms laid down by the Allied powers in the Potsdam Declaration. The tremendous psychological shock of the devastating effects of the atomic bombs in Hiroshima and Nagasaki and the Soviet Union's entry into the war, as well as the Japanese government's 'almost paranoiac fear that, sooner or later, the people would react violently against their leaders if they allowed the war to go on much longer', finally persuaded it of the futility of further resistance.[1] On 14 August 1945, Emperor Hirohito announced Japan's unconditional surrender and ordered Japanese troops to lay down their arms.

Much as this earlier than expected end of the war was a godsend to the war-weary people of Britain, the British government found itself in a very awkward situation over Hong Kong. The Japanese surrender had transformed the internal deliberations and debates over the future of this imperial outpost in the previous three years into a live issue that required urgent attention. When the prospect of a military campaign to liberate Hong Kong had loomed earlier, the British government had accepted that it was 'within the operational sphere of Generalissimo Chiang Kai-shek'.[2] Furthermore, the US President's General Order No. 1, which laid down the principle for accepting the Japanese surrender, required all Japanese forces 'within China (excluding Manchuria), Formosa and French Indo-China north of 16 degrees north latitude' to 'surrender to Generalissimo Chiang'.[3] In line with the above, the Japanese should surrender Hong Kong to Chiang. However, the British government saw this arrangement as harmful to British interests, which required the restoration of British jurisdiction over all its Asian colonies. It therefore acted immediately. On the day the Japanese surrendered, the British proceeded to detach and form a special naval task group to sail towards Hong Kong.[4]

In China, Chiang had much on his mind in working out arrangements to accept the Japanese surrender, not least to minimise the scope for the Communist forces under Mao Zedong to use this opportunity to expand rapidly. He did not expect a dispute over Hong Kong. Nevertheless, he did not overlook Hong Kong and designated the Thirteenth Corps under Shi Jue, which had been issued with US equipment earlier in the summer, to take over Hong Kong.[5] Shi's corps was in the vicinity of Wuzhou, less than 300 miles from Hong Kong, when the news broke.[6] Sun Liren's New First Corps, which earned a reputation as the most combat effective unit in the Chinese Army in the Burma campaign was also in the same area, and was ordered to liberate Canton. The two forces, which together numbered more than 60,000, could have marched their infantries to Hong Kong relatively quickly even though the transportation of their heavy equipment would have taken longer in light of the terrain and badly damaged infrastructure in the region.[7] They did not proceed at all speed, as Chiang had not expected serious complications over the liberation of Hong Kong. He was wrong; Rear Admiral Cecil Harcourt lost no time in preparing a British fleet to steam towards Hong Kong.

The Race for Hong Kong

By seeking to pre-empt the prospect of having to ask a Chinese liberation force for the return of Hong Kong, the British provoked a major diplomatic dispute over its liberation. As soon as they had confirmation of the Japanese surrender, they sought the US naval authority's cooperation for the redeployment of naval units at that time assigned for operations under overall American command in the Pacific. On 16 August, the British government informed the Chinese of its plan, lest Chiang first hear the news from his American chief of staff Wedemeyer and take offence.[8] The British ignored the fact that Hong Kong was in Chiang's theatre and that they should have obtained his consent beforehand. London now took the position that 'irrespective of operational theatres, wherever the sovereign power has sufficient forces available it should resume its authority and accept Japanese surrender in its own territory'.[9] The British did not wish to provoke Chiang into a hostile response, but fully intended to retake Hong Kong before the Chinese army could get there. Britain started what could have become a scramble for the liberation of Hong Kong.

The Chinese government was offended when it was informed of the British action, which it deemed 'rather high-handed'.[10] It rightly suspected the British were concerned about Hong Kong's future. In the absence of Minister T.V. Soong, Vice-Minister K.C. Wu was in charge of the Foreign Ministry and negotiated with the British. He tried to assure the British that China had no territorial ambitions, that it would not take advantage of accepting the surrender to establish possession and that it regarded Hong Kong as a matter that would require eventual settlement through diplomatic channels.[11] The Chinese government also formally asked Britain to adhere to General Order No. 1, to act in concert with China as an ally to ensure peace and order in Asia in taking surrender from the Japanese, and to refrain from landing any forces in the China theatre without prior consent.[12] For its part, China pledged to respect all legitimate British interests and accord them every necessary protection. China tried to protect its interests by insisting on following the correct procedures. Its handling of the matter was reasonable and responsible.

Chiang did not order his army to race against the British fleet steaming towards Hong Kong. He stood by this decision, even after his insistence that the British should follow the agreed procedures proved fruitless and the British turned down his offer of compromise, which from his point of view would have protected the honour of both sides. This seems remarkable, particularly since he had at his disposal some of his best forces, which could probably have beaten the Royal Navy in the race.

Chiang's decision can only be understood in a wider context. His primary concern was China proper. To begin with, the Chinese Communist forces, which were in principle under his command, had openly disobeyed his orders about arrangements for the Japanese surrender.[13] Under Mao's leadership, they were preparing to 'struggle' against Chiang's hold over the country.[14] They were rushing to take over as much land and military hardware from the Japanese as possible.[15] To Chiang, this was a race he could not afford to lose. By comparison, the race against the British was of little consequence. Losing the former could pose a major problem for his post-war plans for the entire country. By contrast, he had few worries about Hong Kong, since he already had an agreement with the British over the future of the New Territories. He could raise the issue at any time. He also had to take into account the activities of the Communist East River Column, which had a guerrilla battalion operating in the New Territories.[16] By 20 August, the East River Column's main force had seized Shenzhen and was at the border of Hong Kong.[17] If Chiang had ordered his US-trained units to race against the British, he would have generated a nationalist fervour and provoked the Communists into competing. In such an eventuality, both he and the British would probably have lost the race to the East River Column. Indeed, the Chinese government felt that if its own forces could not liberate Hong Kong, it would rather this were done by the British than the Communists.

Also, Chiang could not afford to tie down his best units for garrison duties in Hong Kong. This would be unavoidable should he choose to confront the British. US Ambassador Hurley had informed Chiang of his conversations with Churchill the previous April. He believed the British would not give up Hong Kong without a fight.[18] The Chinese ambassador to London, Wellington Koo, confirmed that the new Labour government held the same view of Hong Kong as Churchill's government.[19] At that time, Chiang could not afford to use force over Hong Kong. With only 16 truly combat-effective divisions in the whole country – his remaining 250-plus divisions were of 'negligible' fighting value – he could not spare the New First Corps' three divisions.[20] These crack units were needed elsewhere – particularly for the reoccupation of Manchuria and north China, where the Communists were infiltrating. Thus, though in principle Chiang had some of his most powerful military units suitably located to back up a tough stand over Hong Kong, they were largely irrelevant to his diplomatic manoeuvres. He could not afford to commit them in a showdown with the

British. In any event, because China had just emerged as one of the five founding members of the United Nations, Chiang had no intention of confronting the British. His hands were tied.

As soon as the Sino-British diplomatic exchanges began to turn into a serious dispute, the British ambassador in Chongqing, Sir Horace Seymour, rightly assessed that Chiang did not want a confrontation, but was 'upset' because the British had ignored his prerogatives as the Allied commander of the China theatre.[21] He also correctly judged that Chiang would agree to a settlement for a British fleet to liberate Hong Kong if his authority as supreme commander were not compromised. In the ensuing dispute, the senior British officer in China, Lieutenant General Sir Adrian Carton de Wiart, also felt Chiang had justifiable grounds for his position.[22] The astute assessments of the British representatives in Chongqing proved to be of only marginal value, however, for they were overruled by London.

British officials in London were highly suspicious of Chiang's intention and were concerned that allowing Chiang to exercise authority of any kind in or over Hong Kong would be the thin end of the wedge and achieve his well-known objective for Hong Kong.[23] Chiang's predicament was not fully understood. More importantly, at this moment of victory, jingoism affected the judgement of the British in London. Chiang's responses were deemed 'unreasonable' because he 'could hardly have expected us not to wipe out the memory of the Japanese capture of Hong Kong'.[24] The obvious point, that Chiang was being publicly humiliated by an ally, did not catch anyone's imagination. British officials felt a sense of righteousness in their hardline approach.[25] Even Labour Foreign Secretary Ernest Bevin felt Britain must first recover Hong Kong from the Japanese.[26] Indeed, within days of the dispute emerging, he publicly committed his government in a statement to the House of Commons.[27] London was psychologically prepared to face down Chiang over Hong Kong. Its capabilities to do so were enhanced day by day, for a powerful naval task group was steaming towards Hong Kong.

As the British and Chinese were unable to agree on the arrangements for the Japanese surrender, they both appealed to the USA for support. Chiang did so in general terms through the normal diplomatic channels.[28] The British were a little slower off the mark, but were nevertheless more effective in securing US backing. Attlee, now prime minister, asked President Truman to instruct General Douglas MacArthur, supreme commander of the Allied powers, to order the Japanese in Hong Kong to surrender to the British.[29]

Unlike Roosevelt, Truman was not sentimentally attached to supporting Chiang over Hong Kong. In fact, he thought poorly of Chiang.[30] Truman told Chiang he saw the dispute as 'primarily a military matter of an operational character' and had 'no objection to the surrender of Hong Kong being accepted by a British officer, providing military coordination is effected beforehand by the British with the Generalissimo'.[31] The death of Roosevelt and consequent change of US president earlier that year ensured British success in Washington. Isolated diplomatically as well, Chiang had to compromise with the British.

Chiang proposed to Britain that, in his capacity as supreme commander, he would delegate authority to a British officer nominated by Britain to take the surrender in Hong Kong in the presence of a Chinese and an American officer designated by him.[32] He accepted the British wish to restore their military honour and reassured them that he respected legitimate British interests, including their return to Hong Kong.[33] To demonstrate his sincerity and to dampen jingoism from within his government, he made an announcement at the Supreme Council for National Defence categorically stating that he did not intend to send troops to Hong Kong.[34] In the meantime, appropriate orders were duly issued to his forces.[35] He even personally told Ambassador Seymour that he desired to have good relations with Britain, though he also insisted that he must defend China's legitimate rights.[36]

In return, Chiang asked the British to undertake not to accept the Japanese surrender in Hong Kong before he had done so in the China theatre as a whole. This would include the handing over of Japanese ships and mechanised transport equipment in Hong Kong, and making the port and related facilities there available for the transhipment of Chinese troops to north and north-east China.[37] Chiang bowed to the political and diplomatic reality and, in the light of the rising Communist challenge, to the military imperative as well. He was as accommodating to the British as anyone could reasonably have expected him to be.

Deeply affected by their prejudice against Chiang, British officials in London rejected his face-saving formula. They suspected that if Chiang were allowed to delegate authority to the British commander, Harcourt, he could continue to exercise military authority through Harcourt after taking the surrender.[38] Chiang would be asked to waive his authority in the case of Hong Kong. When Seymour approached Vice-Foreign Minister Wu about the situation, the latter strongly advised him against putting the matter to Chiang. Seymour believed that Wu was sincere when he advised, on a private and completely confidential basis, that if Britain could not accept a delegation of authority, it should simply 'leave the matter alone and go ahead with surrender arrangements as planned'.[39] As Wu rightly assessed, Chiang felt very strongly about the issue and stood his ground.[40] He could not be moved. The final compromise was a British decision for Harcourt to represent both Britain and Chiang, as supreme commander of the China theatre, when receiving the surrender from the Japanese, an arrangement in which Chiang acquiesced.[41]

As the diplomatic saga unfolded, news of the Japanese emperor's broadcast spread in the Stanley camp. The senior British officer Franklin Gimson was a courageous and far-sighted official who represented the best in the British Empire. Once he was certain that the Japanese were surrendering, he went to see the commandant. He informed the Japanese that, from then on, he would take charge of the administration. He asked for accommodation for himself and his officers and, pending the arrival of British forces, demanded that the Japanese troops continue to maintain order.[42] Shortly afterwards, on 23 August, an ethnic Chinese BAAG agent delivered the instructions London had ordered the BAAG to transmit to him.[43] Once he knew London's intentions, Gimson promptly asked the Chief Justice in the camp, Sir Athol MacGregor, to administer the necessary oath for him to take over as officer administering the government. Frail and undernourished, Gimson and some of his fitter colleagues reclaimed British sovereignty over Hong Kong by sheer courage, stamina and dedication.[44]

On 30 August, Admiral Harcourt led a powerful Royal Navy task force, consisting of two aircraft carriers, a battleship, three cruisers and a number of destroyers and minesweepers into Victoria Harbour to take over from the Japanese forces.[45] He was greeted by Gimson and his slender nucleus of a civil administration. On 1 September, Harcourt formally proclaimed the establishment of a British military administration with himself as its head and, on his own initiative, appointed Gimson lieutenant governor. London later disallowed this last act, for a military administration with full powers coexisting alongside a civilian government created a constitutional anomaly.[46] MacDougall, now given the rank of brigadier, and his civil affairs unit (formerly the Hong Kong Planning Unit) took over the administration when they arrived on 7 September. Gimson was repatriated for recuperation.

On 16 September 1945, in Government House in the presence of Major-General Pan Huaguo and a US colonel, Harcourt formally accepted the Japanese surrender. Hong Kong had finally returned to the British Empire's fold. Contrary to Foreign Office concerns, Chiang never made use of Harcourt having accepted the surrender on his behalf to attempt to exercise authority over him. Chiang handled the liberation of Hong Kong in good faith; it was the British who were high handed.

Military Administration

Hong Kong entered an unusual period in its history as it came under military rule for eight months. Although only a transition period to prepare for the restoration of civil rule, it was not a period of muddling through by professional soldiers who knew nothing of good governance. On the contrary, it was a period when the administration functioned remarkably efficiently in very difficult conditions. This was helped tremendously by the fact that Harcourt, the head of the Military Administration, and his Chief Civil Affairs Officer MacDougall worked well together.

Hong Kong and MacDougall were fortunate in having Harcourt as the division of duties and chain of command were complex and open to abuse by the senior military officer. MacDougall was responsible to Harcourt 'on matters in which the Admiralty' or War Office had an interest and to 'the Secretary of State for the Colonies with regard to other matters'. Even for affairs in the latter category, MacDougall had to report through Harcourt and the Admiralty as Harcourt was given the right 'to make such comment on such communication' as he saw fit on grounds of military considerations.[47] As it turned out, Harcourt resisted the effect of power corruption inherent in the trappings of near absolute power and did not interfere in areas beyond his professional competence. Instead, he gave generous support to MacDougall, which enabled MacDougall to focus his limited resources not in bureaucratic infighting but in dealing with Hong Kong's urgent needs.[48] Under MacDougall's able leadership, the civil affairs unit quickly restored the administration in Hong Kong to a level of efficiency that made it the most shining example of all the territories liberated from the Japanese.

MacDougall focused himself upon the urgent and vital tasks of getting supplies to feed the local population and maintain stability. He approached them in a pragmatic spirit and made the most of what resources he had at hand. Hong Kong suffered from all kinds of shortages, including not only food, but also administrators to work in the civil affairs branch. Even two months after the beginning of the military administration, he had merely 18 per cent of the established strength in civil affairs officers.[49]

MacDougall thus pressed on without regard to pre-war procedures, protocols, background of individuals or other formal requirements that could have given rise to bureaucratic delay.[50] The ultimate demonstration of his pragmatism was to remove a major bone of contention with the Chinese authorities in Canton over the right of Chinese to enter Hong Kong. Without clearing the matter with London or the British Embassy in Chongqing, MacDougall reached an understanding with the Cantonese that he would not enforce an immigration control that he had no officer to impose, in exchange for a Cantonese promise to supply Hong Kong with food that he knew the Cantonese could not spare.[51] On the whole, and as illustrated by his deal with Canton, MacDougall avoided consulting the Colonial Office even on major policy matters, went on to do what he felt was needed and reported to London with such a time-lag that it would in any event be too late for London to object.[52]

He inspired his colleagues to take initiatives and responsibilities in finding practical solutions to pressing problems that they encountered. This eight-month interlude was a period marked by administrative dynamism. To many who served in the military administration and stayed on to serve in the Hong Kong government, this was one of the most rewarding times of their careers as colonial administrators.

Among the many tasks the military administration had to deal with, the immediate military problems were relatively simple. The small British forces, consisting mainly of naval ratings, Royal Marines, and members of a Royal Air Force airfield construction unit in the early days, had to take over control and general police duties from the Japanese, and to disarm and intern them as soon as sufficient forces were available.[53] As a result, the British worked on a tacit understanding with the Communist East River Column that the latter would maintain order in those parts of the New Territories under its control until British reinforcements arrived in sufficient numbers to take over the policing in these areas.[54] British forces also had to liaise with the Chinese army units that used Hong

Kong as an embarkation point for redeployment to north and north-east China in the autumn and winter of 1945.

The civil affairs problems were more difficult to resolve. Instead of wasting his limited resources and time to restore the administration to its pre-war structure and undo the effects of the Japanese occupation, MacDougall and his team turned their attention to the immediate problems: currency, labour, public health, food, and fuel. In order to restore the economy to a sound basis, the military administration promptly substituted the Hong Kong dollar for the Japanese military yen, even though the quantity of dollars available was very small, and proceeded to put the dollar in circulation by paying 30–40,000 unskilled workers to clean up the city.[55] This also had the effect of averting the immediate threat of labour and general unrest as the jobless people were employed. A moratorium was also imposed on all debts incurred during the occupation. Banks and utility companies were given assistance to enable them to resume operation as soon as possible. In addition, the price of food and other essential goods was controlled, relief was provided to those who needed it, and ships were sent to Chinese and Southeast Asian ports for food and fuel.[56]

MacDougall also gave his blessing to a significant and fruitful attempt at self-help initiated by Geoffrey Herklots, the resourceful biologist who did much good in improving food supplies in the Stanley Internment Camp. Herklots devised and implemented a fishery cooperative scheme.[57] This made it possible for Hong Kong's fishing fleet to put to sea almost immediately, and thus secured an important source of food. Herklots was largely given a free hand and he later introduced a similar agricultural cooperative project.[58] These initiatives in fact made remarkable long-term contributions. They ended the traditional exploitation of fishermen and farmers by the *laans* – wholesaler and loan shark combined – who had previously had firm control over those industries.

It was with this kind of bold approach and initiative that Hong Kong managed to deal with the severe problem of shortages in supplies and keep one step ahead of disaster. The worst time was the middle of September 1945 when the stock of food reached the dangerously low level of only ten days supply, a situation that did not improve fundamentally for almost three months.[59] However, the apparent competence of the civil affairs unit kept public confidence.

Before the end of the year, the situation had improved so much that the banks were fully operational, public utilities were running and the colony was reopened to trade. The population had increased from less than 600,000 when the British returned, to well over one million by early 1946. However, this increase represented mainly the return of residents who had been forced to leave during the Japanese occupation rather than an influx of newcomers. Hong Kong was once again bustling with life and some of the worst fears of its inhabitants ended. The Herculean task of general rehabilitation and reconstruction of the economy and society of Hong Kong had barely begun, but this was a long-term problem for the post-war civil government.

The remarkable success of the British Military Administration should not be attributed entirely to MacDougall, Harcourt and their magnificent lieutenants. As MacDougall privately admitted to the Permanent Under-Secretary of the Colonial Office, while he 'would like still more to be able to assure you that our efforts are solely responsible for the gratifying transformation... the truth is a good deal simpler: if you give them half a chance, you cannot keep the Chinese down'.[60] What really enabled Hong Kong to recover so fast was the existence of a dedicated, hard-working and honest administration, ran by a small number of British officers who provided the political infrastructure, order and social stability as well as vital supplies that inspired confidence in the local Chinese, who in turn dedicated themselves to make the most of the situation. The resourcefulness of the Chinese referred to by MacDougall flourished more in Hong Kong than in any liberated Chinese city as members of the administration worked with and for the local people rather than for personal gains.

Although Hong Kong had unquestionably recovered sufficiently for civil government to be restored by 1 March 1946, the military administration was sustained until the end of April. While this provided some advantages in terms of enabling MacDougall and his staff to stay on military ration and utilise their military ranks to secure supplies, the real cause of delay was the need to wait for Sir Mark Young to recuperate sufficiently to resume his interrupted governorship. The Colonial Office took the view that it was 'particularly important, as a point of prestige and as a move which would have a striking effect on local opinion that, if at all possible' Young 'should personally take back the government of the Colony from the Service authorities'.[61] The effect intended was not to indicate a return to the status quo prior to the Japanese invasion. It was to assert the point that the Japanese occupation was only a rude interruption of continuous British imperial rule at a time of temporary British military weakness, which was supposed to have been relegated to the dustbin of history by the Royal Navy's triumphant return.

Status Quo Ante?

Young restored civil rule and reintroduced a Crown Colony system of government on 1 May 1946. MacDougall stayed on as Colonial Secretary. By then the urgent immediate post-war problems had largely been solved. Supply was still tight, but this was the situation worldwide. Allegations in the early days of collaboration with the Japanese had been potentially disruptive but had died a natural death.[62] At the time of the handover, Harcourt considered the main problems for the civil government to be the introduction of a new constitution, the placing of Chinese into positions of responsibility in the administration, the elimination of the colour bar, and the return of some old-timers who failed to realise the need for a new outlook.[63]

What Harcourt, MacDougall and a few others referred to as the '1946 outlook' in their reports to London arose as a result of the initial defeat of the British Empire at the opening stage of the Pacific War. The clock could not be turned back or the formal glory of the old colonial regime simply restored.

This situation was not immediately obvious, as the initial responses of the local population to the return of the British amounted to a mixed signal. When the Japanese surrendered the first and foremost concern of the Chinese inhabitants was that they should now be able to secure enough food to eat.[64] They saw the return of the British with both relief and indifference. Uninformed of secret wartime negotiations, they did not know the Chinese government's attitude towards the future of the colony. To them the British had always been in Hong Kong and their return was unexceptional. With the brutality and hardships of the Japanese occupation as a comparison they remembered the pre-war British administration as benevolent and efficient. This notwithstanding, in the city itself four times as many Chinese national flags as Union Jacks were displayed. In the euphoria of victory, the local people identified themselves with China. For them, as for the rest of the Chinese nation, the victory was a great moment. They saw not only the end of the war and misery but the beginning of a new era, one in which China had become one of the five great powers.[65]

The Chinese residents of Hong Kong developed the '1946 outlook' after the initial euphoria had subsided and some of the most pressing problems successfully tackled. It consisted not only of a sense of national pride in China, but also of a feeling that the *status quo ante* was anathema. Chinese national pride manifested itself in the columns of local newspapers and in the public reactions to local incidents. The leading local newspapers occasionally reminded the local people to behave in ways befitting citizens of a great power.[66] There was a strong and swift reaction to the death of a Chinese girl at the hands of a British sailor in early October 1945 and to similar incidents involving Chinese and Europeans.[67] Two local riots broke out when a police officer on street duty inadvertently caused the death of a hawker.[68] Significantly, the temper of the crowds was anti-European.

In sharp contrast to the pre-war days, a slap in the face was no longer meekly accepted by the Chinese. This happened as the immediate memory of the harshness of the occupation receded. As time went by the local people put things in better perspective and remembered the pre-war conditions as they actually were. There had been too much privilege, snobbery, discrimination, racial prejudice, corruption, and absentee exploitation against the local Chinese. They began to see the pre-war government as having failed to give due regard to their interests. This change in public attitude became an important factor in the socio-political scene of the immediate post-war period in Hong Kong.

What the more articulate local Chinese wanted was a new deal. They voiced their desire for better and fairer treatment, removal of corruption, the appointment of British officials who had at least some knowledge and understanding of the Chinese and free education for the children of the poor.[69] Above all they preferred not to see a return of the pre-war officials who were deemed a potential threat to the new order.[70] Some of the pre-war officials, who had not divested themselves of the treaty port mentality, were in fact keen to restore the old order. The articulate public made it clear, however, that any attempt to resuscitate the government machinery which had failed them so badly in 1941, would not be acquiesced in meekly.[71] They looked forward to a radical reform which would provide the people of the colony with a greater say in public affairs. They wanted the framework of the new constitution to be clearly defined so that the new civil government would be built on such a basis.[72] They were, however, not specific about what they wanted in the new constitution.

The British government knew about the '1946 outlook' as Harcourt and MacDougall's reports were collaborated by views expressed by non-officials. John Keswick, taipan of Jardine Matheson and a wartime political adviser at the British Embassy in Chongqing, went further than most. He strongly urged the British government to transform the Crown Colony into what he called the 'Free Port and Municipality of Hong Kong'.[73] Keswick thought that the governor's title should be changed and that he should be assisted by an elected council. He was concerned with the uncertainty over the future status of the colony. He felt reform was necessary both to fulfil the British policy of leading colonies to self-government and, more significantly, to take some of the wind out of the sails of the Chinese and American critics.[74] With an eye to relations with China, he further proposed to replace the Secretary for Chinese Affairs with a Secretary for Chinese and External Affairs.[75]

Although the re-appointment of Young, the head of the pre-war regime, as governor appeared to go against the spirit of the time, this was not the intention. It was indeed because the British government recognised that post-war Hong Kong needed a new deal that Young was given only one year before a new and younger man was to take his place, regardless of how well Young might perform.[76]

The irony of history was that Young was in reality remarkably forward-looking and far-sighted. On the day he restored civil rule, Young declared that the British government had 'under consideration the means by which in Hong Kong, as elsewhere in the Colonial empire, the inhabitants of the Territory can be given a fuller and more responsible share in the management of their own affairs'.[77] Admittedly the scheme he referred to was devised partly in accordance with the policy drawn up under Gent in the Colonial Office during the war, and modified on the basis of advice from Harcourt and MacDougall. It nevertheless put Young on the right footing with the local community as it assured them that Young shared the '1946 outlook'.

Young embraced the idea of political reform and pursued it energetically. It was partly because he believed 'given the Chinese Government's determination to recover Hong Kong... the only way to keep the colony British was to make the local inhabitants want to do so'.[78] In his view, this could be achieved by turning the local inhabitants from Chinese sojourners into citizens of British Hong Kong through popular political participation.[79] While Young's bold attempt to introduce representation into the local administration was linked to his wish to pre-empt the need to return Hong Kong to China, he also genuinely grasped the need for the '1946 outlook' and quickly ruled out a return to the *status quo ante*.

Chapter 11

A Fine Balance

As a British colony in Asia where the pivot of British imperialism, India, was moving rapidly towards independence, Hong Kong could not afford to develop regardless of the momentous changes unfolding in the region. As the war ended, the power balance also shifted between the British Empire, for which the resources of India had been crucial, and China, which had become one of the five permanent members on the Security Council of the newly founded United Nations. Britain had also lost its place as the premier power in China, a position now occupied by the USA, which had completely overshadowed Britain in China in the course of the war.[1]

The decline in the standing of the British Empire in China made it necessary for the British government to handle relations with China with much greater sensitivity than before. This meant the British had to maintain a balance between the desire to ensure the continuation of British rule in Hong Kong and the need not to provoke the Chinese government to demand the return of the New Territories, which was understood to imply raising the issue of the future of the colony as a whole.[2] It also meant the British sought to avoid getting caught up in the intricate power games in post-war China by maintaining strict neutrality in the intense and brutal struggle for supremacy between the ruling Kuomintang and its Communist opponents, as their wartime truce steadily gave way to a resumption of their long-standing civil war. After the end of the Pacific War, Britain's primary concerns in China were to rebuild its economic interests and, above all, to secure its position in Hong Kong at the lowest possible cost.[3]

Rehabilitation and Constructive Partnership

The restoration of civil rule did not remove Hong Kong's economic problems overnight, though it helped the process of rehabilitating the economy. The thorniest problem in May 1946 remained getting essential supplies, particularly rice and fuel. The shortage of rice was so serious that the daily ration was reduced to three ounces per person from the already low allowance of 12 ounces in December 1945.[4] There were also problems with the high cost of living and a severe shortage of housing. However, the end of military rule reinstated the normal legal framework for regulating commercial transactions, for protecting security of goods and investments and for the maintenance of general stability.[5] In other words, it recreated the environment for businessmen to resume their trade and production and to tap all sources of supply to meet the requirements of a market starved of basic essentials and consumer goods. It also furnished a secure base for Hong Kong traders to operate in East Asia where political instability prevailed. To illustrate the tremendous recovery Hong Kong had made: in 1946, it handled 50–60 per cent of the pre-war trade in terms of volume. Impressive as this was, it was not until the second half of 1947 that conditions for trade had been sufficiently restored for it to expand on a sustainable basis.[6]

In the meantime, Hong Kong had to live with being reduced to financial dependence on the British Treasury. In order to end Treasury control, Hong Kong had to free itself from British subsidy. With this in mind, Young set out to introduce income tax. It was strongly opposed by leaders of both the local Chinese and expatriate communities.[7] But the need to balance the budget left Young with little choice. The income tax legislation was based on the War Revenue Ordinance (1941).[8] It was pushed through despite the determined opposition of three unofficial members on the Legislative Council. As he did so, Young made it clear that he saw this as linked to his proposed political reform, which would enhance representation. As a result of the introduction of income tax and rapid economic rehabilitation, Hong Kong was able to end its financial dependency on Britain and thus secure the end of Treasury control in April 1948.[9]

Politically, Young moved quickly to mark the beginning of a new era. While he examined the introduction of a major reform to increase public participation in government, he promptly reconstituted his Executive Council.[10] Before the war, the Council comprised seven official, two expatriate unofficial and one ethnic Chinese unofficial members. Young added another ethnic Chinese unofficial member and thus gave equal weight to both the local Chinese and expatriate British communities.[11] This was an important departure from the pre-war era, when the idea that the much more numerous Chinese community could be given equal weight to the tiny expatriate community in the Governor's top advisory council was anathema.

Young also swiftly removed the symbol of the long-established colour bar by repealing the legislation that restricted the Chinese from residing in the Peak district.[12] To add substance to this gesture, Young not only reiterated the policy of localisation but actually appointed, for the first time in Hong Kong's history, an ethnic Chinese as a cadet officer.[13] He was Paul Ka-cheung Tsui, who demonstrated his loyalty to the Crown by his service in the British Army Aid Group.

Young further showed his willingness to cast away old bureaucratic ways by taking bold steps to meet the special requirements of post-war reconstruction and rehabilitation. As his administration was still short of senior officials, Young retained on one-year contracts a number of military officers who had served under Harcourt.[14] Above all, he broke with another pre-war practice of reserving the top positions for cadet officers. He appointed the resourceful Geoffrey Herklots, an academic, to head the new Secretariat for Development in order to ensure the good work in creating the fishery and agricultural cooperatives he had started under the Military Administration could be continued and institutionalised.

Young also recognised the importance and delicacy of Hong Kong's relations with China. He deemed it essential that his government should take a more positive approach to developments in China. Consequently, he pressed for the appointment of a political adviser who would be a specialist in Chinese affairs. He suggested seconding the first officer from the Foreign Service since most senior officials in Hong Kong were out of touch with events in China.[15] In spite of his title, the Political Adviser functioned as Hong Kong's secretary for external affairs with a special focus on relations with China. Young's original proposal that a diplomat be appointed as a temporary measure came to be accepted as the norm, as his successor felt Hong Kong fell more properly into the remit of the Foreign Office than the Colonial Office and thus welcomed the presence of a seasoned diplomat on his staff.[16]

These progressive changes were meant by Young to supplement his scheme for political reform. What he tried to create was 'a form of diarchy, or parallel government' under which the colonial government was 'to continue to control such vital functions of government as finance and security', while 'the creation of a municipal council would allow the inhabitants of Hong Kong a fuller share in the management of their affairs'.[17] When he restored civil rule four months later, he followed up on his forthright statement proclaiming the British government's intention to introduce political reform with a broadcast outlining his proposals in some detail in English and in Chinese.[18] His underlying thinking in fact 'reflected British colonial policy dating back to the lessons learned from the American Revolution: by giving colonial subjects a voice in their own affairs, they would be co-opted as collaborators in the imperial system'.[19]

Whatever his intention, by proactively consulting the local people and reporting to them the progress he had made, he had projected himself as a 'far-sighted and capable mandarin who knew the needs of his people and who would care for them like a father would care for his sons' – the image of the best official in the Chinese political tradition.[20] Together with the changes already being put in place, Young's handling of the proposed constitutional reform went a long way to dispersing any initial doubts the local community might have had concerning his return.[21] He tried to forge a constructive partnership between the colonial government and the local Chinese community while Hong Kong was being rehabilitated economically.

The responses of the local Chinese community disappointed Young, as they appeared apathetic. Even though Young did realise the passive reactions of the local Chinese 'may be flattering to the system… and to the Government itself', he felt this 'manifestly needs to be overcome by political education and by an insistence on the transfer of responsibility'.[22] The constructive partnership he wished to build depended on overcoming political apathy. While Young pressed on with his plan for reform, it did not outlast his short tenure. Ironically, the local Chinese community did not sustain their demand for a new deal expressed in 1945 because Young was accepted as a forward-looking governor who could be trusted to govern Hong Kong in the spirit of the new era. In the end, Young's ideas did not survive his term mainly because they did not get a sympathetic reception from his successor, Sir Alexander Grantham.

Grantham started his career as a cadet in Hong Kong, learnt the Cantonese language, and proved himself an able administrator in Bermuda, Jamaica, Nigeria and Fiji before he was appointed as the first truly post-war governor of Hong Kong. During his ten-year tour of duty, Grantham established himself as one of the greatest governors. He was progressive, dedicated to Hong Kong and willing to defend what he saw as the best interests of the colony. However, his experiences did not expose him to the kind of changes that Young and Gimson had personally lived through and keenly observed as the myth of the invincibility of the British Empire in Asia was shattered by the Japanese. Grantham's knowledge of Hong Kong and the Chinese people was gained between 1922 and 1935. In this period, the events that left the deepest mark on him were the strike-cum-boycott of 1925–6. They persuaded him that Young was naïve and misguided in his conception both for a diarchy and for making the local Chinese loyal to the British cause.[23]

To Grantham, the new colonial policy of the post-war Labour government leading colonies to self-government should not apply to Hong Kong, as it could 'never become independent' and must remain either a British colony or be absorbed into China.[24] He believed the cultural affinity of the Chinese was too strong and Hong Kong too close to China for the majority of the local Chinese to develop local loyalty to the colony, let alone allegiance to the British Empire.[25]

Grantham preferred an alternative to Young's approach: to build up a constructive partnership with the local community. He thought 'provided that the Government maintains law and order, does not tax the people too much and that they can obtain justice in the courts, they are satisfied and well content to devote their time to making more money in one way or another'.[26] This was essentially the direction which Grantham followed after he took office in July 1947. Grantham's alternative worked, as economic rehabilitation was by then well advanced, and the local Chinese had become increasingly preoccupied with matters of livelihood.[27]

In the meantime, China descended into chaos as civil war between the Communists and the Kuomintang resumed. Its debilitating effects deflated the sense of pride in mother China among the Chinese in Hong Kong, as their country was engulfed in fratricidal butchery and disorder. The conditions that gave rise to the enthusiasm for a new deal when Harcourt's fleet sailed in had been changed. Young had proved the post-war government embodied the '1946 outlook', and instability in China revived the traditional Chinese fear of chaos. With Grantham quickly demonstrating his competence and steering Hong Kong safely through a period of great regional instability and tension in the Cold War, they tacitly accepted Grantham's new conception for a partnership between the government and the people and focused their attention upon improving their living conditions.

The Question of Hong Kong's Future

While Hong Kong was busy with its rehabilitation, the governments of Britain and China pondered over its long-term future.[28] In London, the Colonial Office submitted a paper on Hong Kong's future for incorporation into a general document setting out Britain's post-war foreign policy, which the Cabinet Office's Far Eastern Planning Unit adopted in October 1945.[29] By so doing, the Colonial Office tried to pre-empt the Foreign Office and seize the advantage of providing the basis it itself had approved for interdepartmental consultation. The starting point of this paper was the need to prepare for the Chinese raising the question of the future of the New Territories. It listed four options:[30]

- Britain rejects any Chinese demand for the return of Hong Kong or the New Territories;

- Britain returns the New Territories with certain conditions;

- Britain enters into a leaseback arrangement whereby it cedes the sovereignty of Hong Kong proper to China, but leases the entire territory back for a specific number of years; or

- Britain retrocedes the entire colony.

Although the paper set out the arguments for each of these options, there was a preference that the last two should not be pursued if avoidable.

The Foreign Office shared the Colonial Office view that something had to be done. George Kitson, head of its China Department and an old China hand, thought Britain could not 'go on treating Hong Kong as a Crown Colony on an island off the coast of China'. He believed that political reform there would not stop the Chinese demanding its retrocession.[31] In February 1946, he produced a 14-page memorandum, which he hoped would form the basis of a Cabinet paper.

Kitson started by trying to explain Chinese feelings by an analogy with the Isle of Wight. He argued:

> Supposing the Chinese had taken the island against our will 100 years ago and covered it with pagodas, etc., and developed it by means which they had invented and we had not learned to use, doing all this for their own purposes, although talking a great deal about the material advantages to the United Kingdom, and all the time emphasising the value of this haven of good government, a protection against insecurity, in the Isle of Wight. Even if they had created a heaven on earth in that small island we should have only one feeling about it. We should want it back.[32]

While Kitson also restated the case for retaining Hong Kong he felt it was essential not to reject outright any Chinese request on the subject. He believed Chinese cooperation was crucial for the restoration of British economic interests in China, for international peace and security, and for avoiding problems on the China-Burma border, in Tibet and even among the Chinese community in Malaya. He was convinced that Sino-British relations could 'not rest on a fully satisfactory basis until the Hong Kong issue is faced and fairly dealt with'. He advocated that Britain take the initiative and raise the matter. The reason was that the 'right sort of gesture would... provide the Chinese government with an invaluable aid in overruling an opposition and keeping in check a public opinion which, in the absence of any encouraging sign from our side, might drive the government to extreme and inconvenient demands'. He urged the British government to declare publicly that it was prepared 'as a gesture of goodwill and in a spirit of friendship for the Chinese nation to enter into negotiations' for the return of the New Territories 'on suitable conditions'.[33]

Although Kitson demonstrated a good understanding of Chinese feelings, he showed remarkable *naïveté*. However apt his analogy with the Isle of Wight might have been, it was utterly unacceptable to the mainstream British view. Hong Kong or its New Territories' future raised issues with wider implications, such as Britain's dispute with Spain over Gibraltar.[34] The permanent secretary within the Foreign Office, Orme Sargent, rightly saw Kitson's assumption as 'a complete delusion and a very dangerous one', for its effect on China's policy towards Britain would 'either be nil or of very short duration'.[35] Indeed, Kitson's wish to win Chinese gratitude and thus secure their friendship and cooperation was unrealistic. Given their feelings about Hong Kong, the Chinese would at best see the gesture he proposed as correcting a wrong done to them. Furthermore, since the Chinese wanted to recover Hong Kong in its entirety, a gesture over the New Territories could hardly achieve Kitson's hope for Chinese gratitude, even in the short term. Sargent and Foreign Secretary Ernest Bevin felt Britain had only two reasons to give up Hong Kong or the New Territories... 'either because we have no longer the physical means (military and financial) to maintain our position or because we anticipate that sooner or later the Chinese Government will be able to hold us to ransom by paralysing our trade and administration in Hong Kong'.[36]

Undeterred, Kitson substantially revised the paper and presented it as a Foreign Office memorandum in July.[37] It listed four options:

- the return of the New Territories in exchange for Anglo-Chinese control over the airport, reservoirs and other infrastructures in the New Territories;

- to turn Hong Kong in its entirety into an Anglo-Chinese condominium;

- to place Hong Kong under international control with China and Britain having a predominant share in its administration; and

- to retrocede Hong Kong in its entirety, but for a new treaty to be signed by which Britain would lease Hong Kong (with or without the New Territories) for a period of 30 years.

The paper recommended the last option. It took no account of its implications for the local people or their views. It also excluded a key option advocated by the Colonial Office, which was to reject a Chinese demand for retrocession.

The Colonial Office and Young reacted against it strongly. The Under-Secretary for Far Eastern Affairs, Thomas Lloyd, shared Young's view against taking any initiative or accepting the leaseback proposal.[38] Lloyd attempted to counter the Foreign Office's greater weight in Whitehall by enlisting the support of other ministries likely to be sympathetic, including the Treasury, the armed forces, the Board of Trade and the Ministry of Civil Aviation. All Lloyd would concede was for the Colonial Office to provide an alternative draft paper, which would incorporate the views of the Foreign Office. The Foreign Office paper was unacceptable to the Colonial Office, even as a basis for further consultation.

Lloyd's opposite number in the Foreign Office, Esler Dening, was, unlike Kitson, not personally committed to the paper. He accepted Lloyd's proposal.[39] A joint paper, which listed the options and arguments for and against each one of them, was finally produced in the following year, but it was never submitted to the Cabinet. By then, in 1947, China was engulfed in a full-scale civil war and the government's position was rapidly deteriorating.[40] There was no longer an immediate prospect of the Chinese government raising the issue, and Foreign Secretary Bevin preferred to keep quiet about Hong Kong.[41]

Between the Japanese surrender and 1949, there was a considerable amount of Chinese nationalist agitation for the recovery of Hong Kong. The Foreign Ministry considered the issues involved and 'looked for the right moment' to open negotiations with the British.[42] It took the position that whether China should raise the question of the New Territories or of Hong Kong as a whole must depend on what circumstances prevailed when negotiations were started.[43] When the British were examining the possibility of building a new airport in Pingshan in the north-west of the New Territories in 1946, the Ministry of Defence recommended considering this issue together with that of the future of the New Territories.[44] Whenever there were disputes in Hong Kong, such as over the old fort of Kowloon, numerous petitions from county or provincial assemblies in different parts of the country demanding the return of Hong Kong were submitted to the central government.[45]

Despite the public agitation, the Chinese government did not formally raise the question of either the New Territories or Hong Kong. Chiang Kai-shek defined the basis of China's policy in August 1945 in the following terms:

> I wish to state here that the present status of Hong Kong is regulated by a treaty signed by China and Great Britain. Changes in future will be introduced only through friendly negotiations between the two countries. Our foreign policy is to honour treaties, rely upon law and seek rational readjustments when the requirements of time and actual conditions demand such readjustments. Now that all the leased territories and settlements in China have been one after another returned to China, the leased territory of Kowloon should not remain an exception. But China will settle the last issue through diplomatic talks between the two countries.[46]

The ties on Chiang's hands, which produced the restraint behind the above statement, got even tighter afterwards. Chiang had to face the grim reality that to reoccupy and rehabilitate a country the size of a continent he had a battered bureaucracy and, with the exception of the six US-trained divisions, a largely ineffective army supported by a war-torn economy suffering from hyperinflation.

The biggest problem Chiang faced was the Communist challenge in north China, which was spreading fast into Soviet-occupied Manchuria. However, most of his combat-effective troops were in south and south-west China. For the eventual dispatch of these forces to the north, he had to rely on Hong Kong's port facilities. Until they had all passed through Hong Kong in the spring of 1946, Chiang could hardly afford to create any tension over Hong Kong that might jeopardise the high-priority deployment of forces.

Chiang also learned a lesson from Britain's intransigent handling of Hong Kong's liberation: unless he had the resources to support a tough stand over Hong Kong, a robust British stance would backfire on his standing within China. The intelligence available to him also confirmed – in this case wrongly – that the British government would 'under no circumstances return Hong Kong'.[47] Consequently, Chiang understandably refrained from raising the issue of the New Territories. With the Communist challenge rapidly turning into a full-scale civil war, the last thing Chiang needed was an embarrassing diplomatic impasse over Hong Kong. Chiang did try to ascertain the British intention at the ambassadorial level on two occasions in 1946, which only confirmed his suspicion that the British would make a stand.[48]

From that point onwards, the Chinese government accepted that the issue would have to be tackled at a later date, perhaps when it had re-established control in China. The preferred solution was based on Chiang's idea that China would voluntarily turn Hong Kong into a free port after its return. Options that compromised Chinese sovereignty, such as turning Hong Kong into the Far Eastern headquarters of the United Nations, were deemed unacceptable.[49] In 1947, senior Chinese leaders close to Chiang announced China's decision to defer tackling the Hong Kong question.[50] As long as China's sovereign rights would be upheld, the Chinese government's primary concern was to reach an amicable settlement, as the country was descending into a national crisis.[51] Increasingly domestic events, not least the tide of the Civic War which was turning against Chiang's Kuomintang forces, prevented him from paying serious attention to the future of Hong Kong or its New Territories.[52]

By 1949, the back of the Kuomintang's military power had been broken by the Communists led by Mao Zedong. The latter crossed the Yangtze River from north China, captured the capital Nanjing and the financial centre Shanghai in April. By October, Mao had proclaimed the establishment of the People's Republic of China (PRC) in Beijing, and his forces had reached the Sino-British border. Britain recognised this new regime on 6 January 1950. For better or for worse, China had a Communist government and this now handled the Hong Kong question.

In the immediate post-war period, the Chinese Communist view of the world was based on the existence of the Cold War between the Soviet and US blocs.[53] Mao played a pivotal role in shaping this world view and in making foreign policy.[54] His thinking was deeply affected by his own experiences as a revolutionary and in the civil war. As a master strategist, he consistently emphasised the importance of holding the initiative.[55] This requirement was adopted as one of the PRC's basic foreign policy principles and was applied over Hong Kong.[56]

Hong Kong occupied an unusual place in Chinese Communist calculations, as it was at the same time a foreign policy and a domestic policy issue. In Beijing's view, the treaties that governed the status of Hong Kong and the New Territories were invalid 'unequal treaties',[57] and Hong Kong was therefore a domestic issue for China. With regard to the foreign policy complications, it saw Hong Kong as a matter 'left behind by history', which 'could be resolved through negotiations when the conditions were ripe'.[58] However, unlike most international disputes, it was an issue that Beijing maintained 'the United Nations had no right to discuss' as soon as it became a member of this international organisation.[59]

Mao first made known his views about Hong Kong to a handful of Western journalists at the end of 1946: he did not seek its early return.[60] According to Gordon Harmon, a British journalist in the group, Mao reportedly said:

China has enough trouble in her hands to try and clean up the mess in her own country, leave alone trying to rule Formosa, for us to clamour for the return of Hong Kong. I am not interested in Hong Kong; the Communist Party is not interested in Hong Kong; it has never been the subject of any discussion amongst us. Perhaps ten, twenty or thirty years hence we may ask for a discussion regarding its return, but my attitude is that so long as your officials do not maltreat Chinese subjects in Hong Kong, and so long as Chinese are not treated as inferior to others in the matter of taxation and a voice in the Government, I am not interested in Hong Kong, and will certainly not allow it to be a bone of contention between your country and mine.[61]

Preoccupied with the civil war, Mao did not at this stage pay much attention to Hong Kong. This was also because the British enclave was highly valuable to the Communists. For a short time, when it was unsafe for the CCP to operate in south China, it surreptitiously located its South China Bureau inside Hong Kong.[62] Even after the bureau had been re-established in China proper, a sub-bureau was maintained in Hong Kong.[63] Hong Kong was 'more a regional than a purely local centre' from which the Party sought to coordinate and aid the struggle for power on the mainland, and 'for transmitting directives to neighbouring countries'.[64] The CCP had learned from its lessons in the pre-war era. In the 1940s, it required its cadres not to break Hong Kong laws openly and to refrain from challenging or even criticising British imperial rule there. As they could find no evidence of any subversive activity against the government of China either, the British ignored its existence.[65]

As victory over all China loomed, the CCP sought to reassure the British of its policy towards Hong Kong. This was carried out in late 1948 by the local head of the Xinhua News Agency, Qiao Guanghua, an alternate member of the Party's Central Committee and its de facto representative in Hong Kong. Qiao told the British that 'it was not the Communist Party's policy to take the British colony by force when they come into power in China'.[66] He further 'inferred that his Party would not agitate for the return of Hong Kong'.[67] The rationale was based upon, as Mao admitted a few months later, Hong Kong's 'economic value to China'.[68]

The establishment of the PRC did not fundamentally change the Communist Party's policy towards Hong Kong. When their forces were about to reach the Hong Kong border in October 1949, the local commander was specifically instructed not to let any incident happen.[69] Hong Kong became even more valuable to the PRC as a result of the outbreak of the Korean War and the intensification of the Cold War in East Asia. Premier Zhou Enlai told senior cadres based in Hong Kong in the early 1950s that the PRC would not attempt to take Hong Kong, for it was a valuable instrument with which to divide the British from the Americans in their East Asian policies.[70] Zhou also stressed Hong Kong's value in helping the PRC break the embargoes the USA and UN had imposed on it as a result of the Korean War, in serving as a base to build up the widest united front against the 'American imperialists', and in being a valuable opening for the Chinese Communists to operate in the Western world, Southeast Asia, the rest of Asia, Africa and Latin America.[71] Zhou's instructions were echoed by Politburo member Peng Zhen, who explained to cadres within the PRC that it would be 'unwise for us to deal with the problem of Hong Kong rashly and without preparation'. This would 'not only bring unnecessary technical difficulty in the enforcement of our international policy but would also increase our burden'.[72] In 1954, Zhou admitted privately that, up to then, the PRC government had not deliberated on Hong Kong's future.[73] In 1959, Mao reaffirmed the policy of keeping the status quo there because of its value to China.[74]

The Party's Central Committee issued a directive sometime in the 1950s that Hong Kong should be fully utilised to further the country's long-term interests. This emerged as the guiding principle for the PRC's Hong Kong policy. It survived the upheavals of the Cultural Revolution and came to be reaffirmed after reviews in the 1970s and 1980s.[75]

From late 1948, the PRC continuously maintained that the Hong Kong question would be settled through negotiations at a time of its choosing. Unlike Chiang Kai-shek's government, the PRC rejected the relevance of a technical distinction in legal status between the New Territories and Hong Kong proper. It expected to recover Hong Kong in due course. When Sino-British relations were normalised in 1972, Premier Zhou told a British journalist that he expected to settle the question through negotiations and had 1997 in mind as the appropriate time for a solution.[76] Beijing could afford to take a relaxed attitude because, as I explain below, the British did not publicly challenge its position and thus allowed it to feel it had retained the initiative over Hong Kong.

When the Chinese civil war reached its turning point in December 1948, the British government rightly concluded that 'Communist domination of China' would 'only be a matter of time'.[77] It started to work out a new China policy. It recognised that the Chinese Communists were orthodox Marxist-Leninists on the basis of Communist documents captured by the Hong Kong police.[78] Consequently, it accepted that its relations with China would undergo fundamental changes. Nevertheless, it decided against abandoning their position in China and tried to keep 'a foot in the door'.[79]

As 1949 unfolded, British concerns about Hong Kong's future underwent a basic change. The prospect of Chiang's government raising the question had ceased to be relevant. The new consideration was whether the Chinese Communists would allow a 'well-organised, well-run British port convenient for their trade with the outside world' to exist, or whether they would seek to get it back by using 'every method short of war'.[80] The British did not doubt that the Communists intended to recover Hong Kong, but thought that it was not imminent. They did not expect an attack.[81] The British saw the most serious threat as internal unrest 'inspired by the Communist-dominated' trade unions.[82]

Before the end of the year, the British government nevertheless massively reinforced Hong Kong's garrison from one infantry brigade to about 30,000 troops. These were supported by tanks, heavy guns, a powerful fleet, including an aircraft carrier, and a sizeable air force.[83] This was not so much because of a changed assessment of the threat as because of an unexpected incident that occurred more than 700 miles away from Hong Kong.

On 20 April, a British frigate, HMS *Amethyst*, was shelled and badly damaged on a routine mission sailing up the Yangtze River to Nanjing. It was held captive by Communist artilleries massed on the northern bank of the river, which were preparing to attack Kuomintang forces on the south of the river. It was not until 31 July that HMS *Amethyst* eventually escaped after an ordeal lasting 101 days. The failure of the Royal Navy's attempts to rescue the ship was seen in Hong Kong as its greatest humiliation in the East since the sinking of HMS *Prince of Wales* and *Repulse* at the beginning of the Pacific War.[84] The incident also had a major impact on public opinion in Britain. The government tried to calm its critics and demonstrate its determination to protect British interests in East Asia by immediately dispatching a brigade to strengthen the Hong Kong garrison.[85]

Irrespective of the Communist threat, once the Hong Kong garrison had been doubled and the British had committed their prestige to its defence, it became vitally important not to risk losing Hong Kong and its defence force. In the view of the chiefs of staff, 'failure to do so would have a disastrous effect on morale in Southeast Asia'.[86] For a short time, Hong Kong came to be seen as the most exposed of a line of dominoes vulnerable to pressure from the Communist camp.[87] The British government felt it had to reinforce Hong Kong massively to deter a Communist attack.[88]

The reinforcement pushed the question of Hong Kong's future higher up the political agenda. A new policy was produced in August. By then, Hong Kong's future had come to be seen more from the perspective of the Cold War than from that of fending off a Chinese claim for retrocession. The British concluded that the situation they faced in Hong Kong was like that in Berlin. Just as Britain could 'not foresee with certainty how the future of Berlin' would develop, but were 'convinced of the necessity of remaining there', it felt 'impelled to remain in Hong Kong without any clear indication of the extent or duration of the military commitment involved'.[89] Such a policy was partly based on the armed forces' assessment of the situation. They took the view that the reinforced garrison had 'a good chance of holding Hong Kong against a full-scale attack by Chinese Communists unless the latter were receiving appreciable military assistance from Russia'.[90] It was also partly meant to enlist American support for Hong Kong's security.

The Cabinet paper outlining the new policy laid down that Britain 'should not be prepared to discuss the future of Hong Kong with the new Government unless it were friendly, democratic, stable and in control of a united China'.[91] It further explained:

> We cannot agree to negotiate about Hong Kong with a Government which is unfriendly, since we should be negotiating under duress. We should equally refuse to discuss the future of Hong Kong with a Government which is undemocratic, since we should not be prepared to hand the people of Hong Kong over to a Communist regime. Finally, we should be unwilling to discuss Hong Kong with a China which is not united, because its future would be likely to become a pawn in the contest between conflicting factions. Unless there were a stable Government we could not rely on it to preserve Hong Kong as a secure free port and place of exchange between China and the rest of the world.

Since it was obvious that the new Communist government to be set up in China could not meet any of the above conditions, the issue of discussing Hong Kong's future was treated as academic. The New Territories' lease, which was due to expire in 1997, posed a different problem. The Cabinet paper suggested:

> It does not seem likely that when that time comes any Chinese Government will be prepared to renew the lease. Without these territories Hong Kong would be untenable, and it is therefore probable that before 1997 the United Kingdom Government of the day will have to consider the status of Hong Kong. But we are surely not justified some two generations in advance of the event in attempting to lay down the principles which should govern any arrangement which it may be possible to reach with China at that time.

When the issue was put to the Cabinet, there was a strongly expressed view that Hong Kong could only be held in the long term with American support.[92] Furthermore, the Cabinet agreed to remove 'democratic' from the conditions to be met, for it precluded discussions with a Communist government in China. The British government expected the Communists to stay in power on a long-term basis and had resigned itself to dealing with the Hong Kong question prior to 1997.

Britain's attempt to secure American support for Hong Kong's defence proved problematic. To begin with, the two countries responded very differently to the Communist victory in China.[93] Furthermore, the US government had an ambivalent attitude towards Hong Kong. This was partly because of its colonial status, but there were also wider strategic considerations. On the one hand, Washington saw that, with its 'strongest ally... threatened with a state of war or a serious loss of prestige' over Hong Kong, its 'interests in the Far East would be involved'.[94] On the other hand, it recognised the disparity between its capabilities and worldwide obligations.[95] In the US assessment, defending Hong Kong 'would require the establishment of a military position well inland' and would involve 'a movement of large-scale forces into China', which would risk global war.[96] The USA decided against helping to defend Hong Kong. It did not 'expect to retain by force any foothold in continental China' in the event of a world war.[97]

By 1960, the military build-up during President Dwight Eisenhower's administration had considerably strengthened his confidence in American power. He now had the resources to contemplate military intervention to support a determined British attempt to defend Hong Kong.[98] Nevertheless, he refrained from making a firm commitment. American policy subsequently remained noncommittal, even in 1967 at the height of the Vietnam War and the Cultural Revolution, when local Communists challenged the Hong Kong government's authority.[99] Thus, though the British had at times expressed confidence that the USA would come to Hong Kong's aid should it come under attack and that American nuclear retaliatory power served as a deterrent to the PRC, they were always aware that there was no American undertaking to defend Hong Kong.[100]

The Impact of the Korean War

The failure of the British government to secure an American undertaking over the defence of Hong Kong made its position there more precarious as the Cold War in Asia turned into a shooting war in Korea. Even before the Korean War broke out in June 1950, Hong Kong was already delicately placed in the stand-off between the two Cold War blocs. As a result of British involvement as a leading member of the United Nations and the closest ally of the USA, Hong Kong found itself serving as a base to support British military and naval operations in Korea. Hong Kong was therefore understandably jittery in the early stages of the Korean War, even though both the Chinese and the British governments deliberately ignored the fact that their respective forces were engaged in combat in Korea when they dealt with Hong Kong.[101]

The outbreak of war in Korea did, however, have a major impact on Hong Kong as the USA promptly 'neutralised' the Taiwan Strait in order to prevent the conflict in Korea from spreading. This had the effect of preventing Chinese Communist forces from crossing the Taiwan Strait to destroy the remnants of the Kuomintang forces under Chiang Kai-shek and conclude the Chinese Civil War. The situation deteriorated when the PRC interfered militarily in Korea in October–November 1950.[102] Hong Kong held its breath and prayed that the Korean War and the Kuomintang-Chinese Communist struggle would not converge with an explosive outcome which might embroil it.[103]

With a stalemate imposed on the Chinese Civil War set in the wider context of the Cold War, Hong Kong found itself unwittingly caught up in the continuing struggle between the Chinese Communists and the Kuomintang. To the PRC, Hong Kong was central to its united front in isolating and weakening the Kuomintang's Republic of China (ROC) government in Taiwan, described by Mao as one of the 'running dogs of imperialism'.[104] The Kuomintang, for its part, saw Hong Kong as a crucial place to stage covert operations against the PRC. The colonial government had to devise a strategy to prevent, on the one hand, such activities from turning Hong Kong into a Chinese political cockpit and, on the other hand, to demonstrate its determination to hold the territory without provoking an irredentist response from the nationalistic PRC.

The Korean War also affected Hong Kong economically. The imposition of a trade embargo against the PRC by the USA in December 1950 was followed by a partial embargo on the export of strategic materials by the UN in May 1951, and by a tightening of British export control the following month. They put an end to Hong Kong's continuous economic boom, which had followed its successful economic rehabilitation.[105] More importantly, the Western trade embargoes against the PRC meant Hong Kong lost its long-standing role as the premier entrepôt between China and the West. Hong Kong's resourceful people had no choice but to face the challenge and attempt a transformation of its economy.[106]

Strategy for Survival

Finding itself vulnerably placed in the Cold War, caught between the unfinished Chinese Civil War and the risk of becoming a flashpoint, Hong Kong tried to separate the first two and deal with them with level-headed pragmatism. It minimised the effect of the Cold War by ignoring it. It succeeded because none of the Great Powers interested in Hong Kong in fact wanted a showdown there. The basic threat to Hong Kong's security and, indeed, its survival was the menace of Chinese irredentism on the one hand, and the danger of being sucked into the unfinished Chinese Civil War and turned into a battleground between the two protagonists on the other. The strategy for survival which Hong Kong devised in the 1950s was consequently predicated on this premise.

This involved upholding a policy of neutrality in Chinese politics. Its rationale was explained by Governor Grantham:

> The strength of our position in Hong Kong depends largely upon non-involvement in political issues. This can be achieved only by maintaining strict legality and impartiality in any issues with a political tinge. We have followed this attitude in relation to Chinese political activities in the Colony e.g. treating both [the Kuomintang] and Communists exactly similar and absolutely according to law. Any departure from this… would weaken our position, both externally and internally.[107]

To maintain strict neutrality when one is precariously placed between two parties engaged in a civil war is like walking a tightrope – one's real concern is not to maintain balance per se, but rather not to fall, though this in practice requires keeping the balance. This was the spirit behind Hong Kong's strategy. But to stay totally impartial in Chinese politics was a particularly difficult task for Hong Kong, since it was 'geographically and racially a part of China' and had in the 1950s 'no politics of its own but reflect[ed] the politics of China'.[108] Impartiality was enshrined as the basis for Hong Kong's policy but the colonial government never lost sight of the forest by focusing on the tree in upholding neutrality for the sake of it.[109]

In addition, the government also tried 'to administer the territory in the interests of the inhabitants, including those numbering nearly a million who have come from China in recent years' and to prevent it being used 'as a base for hostile activities against China'.[110] Increasingly, it fulfilled the expectations Mao set out for Gordon Harmon as requirements for the Communists not to raise the Hong Kong question at the end of 1946. In political terms, Hong Kong made it a point not to become a thorn in the PRC's side.

Economically, Hong Kong also made itself valuable to the PRC. In the 1950s, its existence helped procure certain strategic materials, which were smuggled into the PRC when the US and UN embargoes were in place.[111] Among the most valuable materials were penicillin, other medical supplies, petrol and tyres for motor vehicles.[112] In the early days, local residents' remittances to relatives on the mainland provided valuable foreign exchange. During the famine – caused by the failure of the Maoist policy, known as the Great Leap Forward, to increase steel and agricultural production without regard to common sense or the laws of physics and biology – in the late 1950s and early 1960s, food parcels and other support from the people of Hong Kong formed a vital lifeline for many in the PRC. Hong Kong's economic take-off in the late 1960s and early 1970s greatly enhanced its value, particularly after Hong Kong resumed its pre-1950 role as the PRC's main entrepôt in the 1970s.[113] This happened as the PRC embarked on its programme of 'four modernisation'. Hong Kong became the principal channel through which the PRC acquired modern technology, management skills and capital.[114] It contributed almost one third of the PRC's foreign exchange earnings.[115] It also provided crucial financial services that were unavailable in the PRC.[116] After 1949, Hong Kong turned itself into the goose that laid golden eggs for the PRC.

By deliberately avoiding the issue of Hong Kong's status, Britain gave the PRC no reason to feel concerned about Hong Kong. Indeed, there was a clear recognition among key British policymakers that there was 'a definite term set to the continuance of Hong Kong's quasi-colonial status'.[117] Sir Robert Black, who succeeded Grantham as governor shared Grantham's view that the year 1997 would be critical for the future of Hong Kong. During his term, from 1958 to 1964, Black worked on the basis that 'we hold our position in Hong Kong at China's sufferance', and recommended to the British government that it would be 'vital for Hong Kong's stability that there should be no official or authorised pronouncement on Hong Kong's future until and unless this becomes clearly unavoidable'.[118]

Until the end of the 1970s, the British in effect satisfied the most basic requirement Mao laid down in dealing with Hong Kong, which was to feel that it held the initiative over Hong Kong. The PRC government had no reason to disturb the goose that so obligingly laid bigger and bigger golden eggs. The people of Hong Kong also chose to ignore the fact that the New Territories' lease would expire in 1997 and that something would have to be done about it, at least about the expiry of British jurisdiction there. Because the PRC regarded the 'unequal treaties' as invalid, many people thought that the PRC might choose to ignore this particular appointment in history. Some even indulged in the comforting thought that the PRC might allow the status quo to continue for as long as it proved advantageous to it. Most people simply preferred not to look beyond the short term. The way the government and the people of Hong Kong dealt with its future was essentially built on this formula of not rocking the boat. It was not glamorous but it was Hong Kong's strategy for survival.

Chapter 12

Economic Take-off

The restoration of civil government by Governor Young in May 1946 was meant to mark a return to normality. It largely succeeded in the economic sphere, but not because the economy had by then been dramatically improved over the last stage of the Military Administration. It did so because the local people were determined to make the most of the situation and simply get on with life. The entrepreneurial spirit, resourcefulness and business acumen of the local Chinese that made pre-war Hong Kong what it was were quickly at work. With China's economic infrastructure in a sorry state and continuing to be devastated by the civil war, Hong Kong swiftly resumed its role in servicing the China trade. Old factories and workshops that existed before the war also resumed production as soon as the necessary workers, raw materials and other essentials could be found. The more enterprising added new manu-facturing facilities, as the disruption of trade and transportation by the war meant there were demands for basic everyday light industrial goods in East Asia.

Once the effect of the economic disruption caused by the war receded, Hong Kong's economy grew very fast. The number of registered industrial establishments increased quickly, from 972 in 1947 to 1,522 in 1950.[1] This amounted to an increase of 36 per cent over four years. This impressive industrial expansion notwithstanding, until after the Korean War started in June 1950, the ambition of Hong Kong was to restore itself as the leading entrepôt for the China trade. Although industrial-isation had already started before the Pacific War, the government and the colonial establishment still focused their attention mainly upon trade. Most workshops and factories were small to medium-size facilities. The overwhelming majority of them were founded and operated by the local Chinese who were not part of the establishment. The community of local industrialists was not represented in the Legislative Council and was not in a position to exert major influence on policymakers in the late 1940s.

Though large industrial concerns owned by expatriates were in a different category and were represented, their representatives did not put much emphasis on developing industry. Most of these large industrial establishments, like shipyards and sugar refineries were in fact part of large British hongs like Jardine Matheson or Swire Pacific. It is true that their chief executives or senior directors often sat on the Legislative Council and even the Executive Council, but the primary interest of these business conglomerates was trade not industries.

In any event, trade did grow very fast in the late 1940s. It rose from $HK2,767 million in value in 1947 to reach $HK7,503 million in 1950, representing an aggregate growth of 63 per cent.[2] This was much faster than the rate of industrial expansion. The colonial establishment was therefore not unjustified in hoping that Hong Kong would restore its place as the premier entrepôt of China, though its attitude mainly reflected bureaucratic inertia. This working assumption was not seriously challenged until the United Nations and the USA enforced a total embargo against trading with the PRC after the latter militarily intervened in the Korean War.

From Entrepôt to Industrial Colony

What marked out the economic history of the early post-war decades was the transformation of Hong Kong from its long-established position as China's main entrepôt to an industrial colony. From overwhelming dependence on the China trade in 1950, Hong Kong transformed its economy into a highly industrialised one within a decade and a half. According to the by-census of 1966, two-fifths of Hong Kong's labour force was engaged in manufacturing, and locally produced goods made up four-fifths of its exports.[3] As a source of employment, manufacturing accounted for less than five per cent of total employment in 1950, rose to about ten per cent in 1960, to about 25 per cent in 1970 and peaked at just over 40 per cent in 1980.[4]

This rapid industrial expansion should not, however, be mistaken to imply industrialisation started in this period. Although the growth in the post-war decades marked a quantum leap from the industrial develop-ments of the pre-war era, the already substantial industrial developments before the Japanese invasion should not be overlooked.

The most important driving force behind Hong Kong's industrialisation was the local Chinese. They accounted for most of the investments in production facilities. They also provided the bulk of managers and almost all the industrial workers.

The fast pace of industrial growth in the 1950s was not the result of a change in government policy. Just as the government did not have an anti-industry policy prior to 1950 it did not, and indeed could not, reverse itself and adopt a pro-industry policy either.[5] It recognised the spectacular boom of 1950 and 1951 was an economic bubble fuelled by speculation over the PRC's needs for reconstruction and for other supplies when the Korean War started.[6] In private, Acting Financial Secretary Arthur Clarke was not sorry when the bubble burst as he thought it distorted the local economy and was unsustainable. However, the consolidation he hoped to have seen as a result centred around putting Hong Kong's trade on a less speculative and therefore more sustainable basis.[7] Transforming Hong Kong from a trading centre to an industrial colony was not part of government policy in this period.[8]

The government's recognition of the shifting balance of importance between trade and industry came after the local people reacted to the changing economic environment and devoted themselves to industrial productions. Most of those who made this transition quickly in the early 1950s were Chinese entrepreneurs. The majority were recent immigrants who brought with them small capital from Guangdong. They knew there was no safety net for them in Hong Kong. To survive, they altered their investment strategies as soon as the economic climate changed. Some moved into small industrial production adroitly when the speculative trade boom busted in early 1952, and prospered. Others failed, lost what little capital they had and joined the labour force. They did not expect or get help from the government.

In parallel to the small entrepreneurs who were predominantly of Guangdong origin, Hong Kong's industrial growth also benefited from the arrival of Shanghai industrialists. They started investing significantly in Hong Kong as the Chinese civil war resumed. Some Shanghai industrialists, particularly in the spinning sector of the textile industry, went to Hong Kong to diversify their risk exposure. It was in the turbulent years of 1948 and 1949 that the real influx occurred when two-thirds of Shanghaiese-owned cotton spinning factories were set up in Hong Kong.[9]

Two characteristics distinguished Shanghai textile industrialists from their longer-established Cantonese colleagues in this period: the scale of their production facilities and their sophistication. Factories built by the Shanghai immigrants were usually much bigger and more advanced than the existing local ones. The influx of Shanghai spinners meant not only the creation of new and bigger production facilities, but also the injection of more sophisticated management and technology, as well as the introduction of more advanced and expensive machinery.

In the expansion of its spinning industry, Hong Kong also benefited from the existence in its warehouses of a large quantity of modern machinery imported from the West by Chinese spinners for their Shanghai factories.[10] With strict foreign exchange control in place and uncertainty during the civil war, some Shanghai industrialists arranged for their newly ordered machinery to be delivered to Hong Kong first.[11] Some of them subsequently used this machinery to start their new mills and production in Hong Kong as the political, social and economic conditions in China, including Shanghai, deteriorated.[12] Once Shanghai had fallen to the Communists, what remained of those valuable textile machinery and other equipment stored in local warehouses quickly found themselves used to fit out new factories in Hong Kong.[13]

The expansion of the Shanghaiese-owned textile production swiftly overshadowed the longer-established local factories. In 1947, before the Shanghai entrepreneurs started to invest heavily, Hong Kong already had 405 registered establishments in the textile industry employing 9,328 workers, with most engaged in weaving and knitting.[14] Five years later, Hong Kong's textile industry employed 27,394 workers in 502 registered factories. The cotton-spinning sector, where the Shanghai immigrants dominated, saw an expansion from five factories with 102 workers in 1947 to 13 factories employing 8,925 workers.[15] The textile industry became the most important economic activity. When Hong Kong became known for its textile industry in the late 1950s and the early 1960s, the image that was projected internationally was usually that of the larger mills owned and operated by the entrepreneurial immigrants of Shanghai. They played the leading role in building up Hong Kong's modern textile industry, particularly its spinning sector, after the war.

What really changed Hong Kong's attitude towards industrial development was the Western trade embargo against the PRC. American pressure on Hong Kong to enforce the embargo practically ended its role as China's premier entrepôt.[16] It is true that smuggling to the PRC of some banned material continued.[17] It should also be recognised that some of the imports the PRC secured through Hong Kong, such as 'pharmaceuticals (antibiotics and sulpha drugs), machinery and dyes' were particularly valuable as they could not be supplied by the PRC's Eastern European allies.[18] However, the quantity and monetary value involved were substantially smaller compared to the scale of the old China trade. Hong Kong's share in China's total trade fell 'from 32 per cent in 1951 to five per cent in 1959'.[19] American pressure and Cold War politics meant Hong Kong had to observe the embargoes.[20] As a result, exports to the PRC came under stringent control, though legitimate local trade of non-strategic material between Hong Kong and the mainland survived. With the bulk of the old China trade cut off, many entrepreneurs had no choice but turn to small-scale light industrial production.

Even for the export of Hong Kong's own products to the rest of the world, a system of certificate of origin had to be introduced by the government in order to assure much of the world, particularly the USA, that they were not re-exports from Communist China. The American embargo was vigorously enforced, though what constituted re-exports from the PRC was not always easy to define. Hong Kong officials had to reach an understanding with their American colleagues to devise mutually acceptable working guidelines. Some of the issues involved were as thorny as to decide whether meat products from chicken or ducklings hatched in Hong Kong from eggs imported from the PRC should be deemed to have sufficient capitalist pedigree for export to the USA. The certificate of origin system gained enough credibility to be accepted by the Americans to resolve such matters.

In its industrial development of the 1950s, Hong Kong's entrepreneurs had no master plan and received no leadership or direction from the government. Unlike some of the leading Shanghai immigrant industrialists who had long experience in cotton spinning, large quantities of modern machinery in place and expert knowledge of their chosen industry, most small local entrepreneurs simply tried to make the most of what they had and find the right niche for themselves. Hong Kong had limited land and few natural resources. What it did have was a cheap and highly flexible labour force, as well as excellent port facilities and a rapidly expanding domestic market for basic household goods generated by the presence of a large refugee population.[21] In their search for the right niche for manufacturing, most local entrepreneurs chose to engage in export-oriented, labour intensive, low technology, light industrial production or the manufacture of cheap basic household utensils. They made the most of Hong Kong's comparative advantages not because they had any understanding of this economic concept but because it made good business sense.

The government became more positive about industrial development after the dissipation of Hong Kong's prospect of restoring its role as China's main entrepôt when the Korean War ended in a stalemate in 1953. Around this time, Governor Grantham came to realise that the bulk of Hong Kong's recent immigrants and refugees would not return to the Chinese mainland as earlier waves of refugees had done in the previous century. Communism in China put an end to this historical pattern.[22] This recognition led the government to see the importance of industrialisation. Since its primary concerns were stability and prosperity, it accepted the need for industrial expansion to provide employment to the large immigrant population.[23]

The increasingly positive view the government took towards industrial development did not imply it became less supportive of trade. There was no shift from a policy of supporting trade to industry. The government did not see a need to choose between the two. Indeed, with fewer than 50 administrative officers, even at the end of the 1950s, the government simply did not have the resources to do strategic planning for promoting economic development in one or the other direction.

The greatest contribution by the government to Hong Kong's economic transformation in the 1950s lay in providing the conditions for industries to develop and grow. It maintained political and social stability at a time when neither could be taken for granted in East Asia. It provided a relatively efficient administration that sustained good order without impeding industrial growth through oppressive or unpredictable policies. It operated a credible certificate of origin system that allowed local manufacturers to export despite the trade embargoes against the PRC. It steadily improved the local infrastructures, building roads, for example, and improving water supplies that enabled industry and trade to grow.[24] It made land available for large factories to be built, particularly in new towns, and constructed low-cost, multi-storey industrial buildings in resettlement estates for light industries.[25] Its massive resettlement or housing programme, started after 1953, meant cheap and heavily subsidised housing was made available to workers. It also invested in human resources by providing heavily subsidised education and health services. As the decade progressed, the government gradually took on board the importance of industrial development and gave it what benign support it could.[26] It helped industries and businesses by minimising bureaucratic red tape and legal formalities in the setting up of new enterprises.[27] It should, however, be recognised that while these improvements helped to nurture industry, some were introduced because they were needed for maintaining stability and good order as well.

The government also balanced the desirability of regulating conditions for the employment of labour on the one hand, and the need to allow the greatest scope for proprietors to manufacture at the lowest cost on the other.[28] The former was more than just a matter of minimising the abuse of vulnerable workers, particularly children and women, by factory owners. As Britain established its own welfare state after the war, the colonial government came under pressure from London to follow the British lead in the promotion of labour rights.[29] Although it hosted labour advisors from London periodically and benefited from their advice in improving working conditions modestly, it resisted pressure that could have adversely affected the profitability and competitiveness of its industries.[30] In the 1950s and 1960s, the colonial government was undoubtedly guilty of not doing all it could to improve conditions for workers. It did so mainly to support industries in order to maintain economic stability, though it was also partly due to bureaucratic inertia.

What the government did not do was pick winners or losers in industries or, for that matter, among various economic sectors. Except in fish and agricultural distribution and over the supply of rice, it did not give industrialists and businessmen any directions or special inducements to develop particular industries or trade. It devoted its limited resources to its areas of core competence, which was to maintain a minimalist administration and to buttress the rule of law. It left business and industrial development to the entrepreneurs. Hong Kong focused heavily on the textile industry in the 1950s, because it was one area in which it actually enjoyed competitive advantages. Local entrepreneurs shifted to other industries when they sensed greater profitability. In so doing, they often followed each other but they did not rely on a shift in government policy or on government inducement.

Rapid industrialisation in fact reinforced and extended Hong Kong's role as a major trading centre. Industrial development and trade were highly complementary to each other, as Hong Kong's small population and limited natural resources could not in themselves sustain rapid industrial expansion. The industrial boom benefited tremendously from Hong Kong's long-established, extensive and efficient trading networks, since most of its industrial output was for export, and its industries relied on imported raw material and machinery for production.[31] Indeed, the end of the old China trade did not destroy Hong Kong's position as a trading centre. Rapid industrialisation generated new trade, and Hong Kong turned itself into an entrepôt for the East Asia region as a whole.

In Hong Kong's economic transformation in the 1950s and early 1960s, the Shanghai immigrant entrepreneurs, who had contributed so much to the textile industry, made a further significant break with traditional practice that had wider ramifications. Hong Kong's longer-established

Cantonese entrepreneurs historically turned to the local Chinese banks to finance their expansions, though some of the larger loans might have involved the local Chinese banks working with their bigger British counterparts in a syndicate. Few local entrepreneurs directly approached the leading British banks for loans. Those who came from Shanghai, which was a more cosmopolitan society than Hong Kong before the Pacific War, behaved differently. They were not deterred by the language barrier and the long separate and parallel existence of the local Chinese and the expatriate communities.[32] They took the lead in breaking the barrier and approached British banks for loans for their enterprises.[33]

The positive response of the British banks to the Shanghai entrepreneurs encouraged other Chinese entrepreneurs to approach British banks directly.[34] The old communal barrier came to be eroded steadily as Hong Kong's rapid industrialisation induced the local Chinese and the expatriates to work more closely together.[35] The involvement of British banks in financing the local manufacturing sector did not mean local Chinese banks were displaced. Growth was so fast that both the local Chinese and the international British banks expanded. The availability of this new and very large source of finance enabled the local entrepreneurs to expand even faster than they otherwise would have managed.

In time, a symbiotic relationship developed. The British banks had the financial resources, expertise and ready access to the rest of the world through their excellent international financial networks. They became available to the local Chinese entrepreneurs who surpassed the long-established British hongs in exploiting the economic opportunities. The British banks themselves benefited greatly as the business environment in Asia in the 1950s and early 1960s did not provide them with much alternative scope for expansion.[36] By taking the lead in lending to the local industrialists, the Hong Kong and Shanghai Bank benefited most from this symbiotic relationship. As the British banks helped the local industrialists to enter international markets and make considerable profits, Hong Kong prospered as it combined to good effect the resources of entrepreneurial industrialists, expert exporters, trade financiers and international bankers.[37]

The Immigrant Mentality

Hong Kong's population expanded from about 600,000 in 1945 to over 2 million in 1950, and to 2.5 million in 1955.[38] It is true that a large number of those who went to Hong Kong from China in this period had either previously lived in the colony or had families there. However, there was no dispute about the size of the immigrant population. Even as late as 1961, 33 per cent of the workforce had arrived after 1949 and 13 per cent had lived there for five years or less.[39] Whether they had lived in Hong Kong before the war or not, they went to this British colony again as either refugees or economic migrants.[40] The immigrant nature of the population, the uncertainty over whether they would make it their permanent home, and their lack of dealings with the colonial administration on policy matters left important marks on the society and the business culture of Hong Kong.

The Chinese community of post-war Hong Kong not only inherited the legendary entrepreneurial spirit of the Chinese people but also reacted to a desperate need to succeed in order to survive. The uncertainty that prevailed was captured by a visiting British labour adviser in the late 1950s:

> A feeling of insecurity colours nearly everyone's lives [sic] in Hong Kong – trade unions, and individual workers are never sure of work, housing, food or even the right to stay in Hong Kong. Capitalists (factory owners and house-owners) want quick returns – money back in 5 years, not 20 – for fear something happens before. No one knows how long Hong Kong will exist, or how long it will prosper.[41]

This reality induced the Chinese immigrants to make the most of what they had, be they entrepreneurs or unskilled working persons. Flexibility and ingenuity, whether in investments, nature of business or in employment, were the keys for survival. Post-war Chinese immigrants to Hong Kong developed their entrepreneurial spirit to the full because they felt they could only rely upon themselves in this foreign enclave.

While the British labour adviser's reference to a five-year investment cycle probably applied to the larger business and industrial concerns, it was in fact far too long a duration for most of the smaller entrepreneurs. In the early post-war decades, few of these had sufficient capital to invest in an enterprise without seeing a sufficient return to support their family within a much shorter time frame. Loans and their servicing costs were expensive. The local entrepreneur's single-minded determination to make money was driven by the need to survive in an environment in which the only alternative to success was financial ruin. An extremely short-term approach was therefore commonplace.

This reality forced most entrepreneurs, who were generally not well educated, to stay highly focused upon their core businesses. It meant that industrialists, for example, usually operated as contract manufacturers. They produced against firm orders for goods designed and to be marketed by the purchasers. They focused upon the task they knew best, which was to manufacture the specified goods within their capabilities to a designated quality in an agreed time frame, and leave the rest to others.[42] Where one manufacturer could not fulfil a large order it would sub-contract a reliable peer to share the work. Indeed, according to one account, about 24 per cent of orders for manufacturing came from peer sub-contracting.[43] Small factories could operate as a network of producers as they did not have to compete against each other in the design or marketing of the finished products.

Dealings with overseas buyers were usually left to the numerous trading companies. A relatively small number were part of the large British hongs, while most were small outfits operated by other local entrepreneurs. These trading firms not only served as the interface with the overseas purchasers, but would also handle shipping, insurance and the documentation required.[44] Thus, even though most Hong Kong industrialists devoted themselves to a narrowly defined scope of manufacturing activity, networks of trading and servicing firms provided them with excellent access to global markets.[45]

In Hong Kong's numerous small factories, productivity by conventional measure was low. Most industrialists and managers had little formal training themselves. They were also generally 'uninterested in any form of training other than the teaching of skills and actual workshop processes'.[46] Notwithstanding this and the low level of capital and technological input, production was cost effective.[47] In the 1950s and 1960s, most local factories and trading firms were run not by people with higher education or formal industrial or management training but by astute managers who kept a keen eye on the bottom line. The sense of insecurity and the immigrant mentality encouraged manufacturers to maximise output from capital investment. Allowing machines to stay idle because of poor maintenance or missing spare parts was an expensive folly that few could afford. Thus, in most factories practically every machine was manned and run while every square foot of space was utilised.[48]

The same mentality and low standard of formal training meant Hong Kong entrepreneurs also had to be willing to move on to alternative lines of manufacturing or business quickly. They had neither the capital nor the human resources to do any research and development work or to learn about the state of the market. Few could upgrade their products on their own. Functioning largely as contract manufacturers, they were highly vulnerable to changes in the international market place. To survive they had to be able to move to different kinds of production or even different lines of business, once profitability for their particular products fell significantly. What this meant in practice was that many of the smaller factories existed for a relatively short time for specific productions. When the time came, the enterprising ones would reinvent themselves and set up new factories or modify the old ones to produce the next hot commodity within their technical competence. Proprietors of factories often had to close down no longer profitable workshops and move on to the next profitable line of work. Those who failed to do so fell by the wayside. The competitiveness of Hong Kong's industrial economy rested on the survival of the fittest.[49]

The labour force was also employed to maximise production by allowing unskilled workers to do specific simple tasks, and by a brutal incentive regime. Wage differential between unskilled, semi-skilled and skilled workers was large and most workers were paid at piece rather than time-rate.[50] They were meant to provide incentives for individuals to upgrade their skills and to keep costs low. Working hours were extremely long and health and safety standards low. Despite the harsh working conditions, there were few complaints or industrial actions by workers in the 1950s.[51] Most preferred to work, which generally meant at terms offered by industrialists, rather than risk being dismissed and penniless. Even by the 1960s, the most important source of job satisfaction for the average working person was still the size of the pay packet.[52]

Trade unions generally did not help to improve the conditions of the working people much in the early post-war decades. The trade union movement was weakened by the polarisation of the bigger and more powerful unions into the Communist-dominated Federation of Trade Unions and the Kuomintang-dominated Trade Union Council.[53] Their political division and rivalry also gave the government reasonable grounds to resist the promotion of union activities, as they were seen to be potentially subversive to stability and good order. The subservient nature of these organisations, particularly of the left-wing Federation of Trade Union to the Chinese Communist Party, meant the union movement was often not directed with the interests of the local workers in mind.[54] Indeed, the Federation was known to have modified its programme to fall in line with the political situation or policy requirements of the PRC.[55] Their external political links also made union leaders fearful of being deported by the colonial government should they take too activist an approach.[56]

A weak union movement heightened the sense of insecurity among workers. It also made the tasks of well-intentioned labour advisers from London to persuade the Hong Kong government to take the lead in improving the conditions of workers more difficult.[57] It produced a vicious circle and inhibited the development of genuine unionism. It meant relatively little was done to improve working conditions in the 1950s. Apart from four or five days of paid holiday a year, workers generally did not have a weekly paid rest day in the 1950s. Sunday as a rest day only became the norm in the latter half of the 1960s as the effect of growing wealth filtered down to the workers.

The refugee mentality meant most entrepreneurs and workers saw this British enclave as the lifeboat with China being the sea. Those who had climbed into the lifeboat did not want to rock it.[58] Enterprising as they were, they did more than just stay passively on board and wait to be rescued. They used all their imagination, ingenuity, available resources, hard work and sheer single-minded determination to make sure the lifeboat sailed to safety. The foundation of Hong Kong's spectacular post-war economic miracle was built on the blood and sweat of its workers as much as on the resourcefulness, business acumen and spirit of enterprise of its entrepreneurs.

Take-off

With a solid foundation in light industrial production and export trade thus established, Hong Kong's economy truly took off towards the end of the 1960s.[59] This economic transformation roughly coincided with significant political changes that followed the Maoist-led confrontation of 1967.[60]

By the end of the 1960s and the beginning of the 1970s the Hong Kong government took on a more positive and proactive approach in social policies. This was partly because a generational change had occurred within the administration.[61] The older and more backward-looking senior officials had all been replaced by younger, more forward-looking and energetic ones. The colonial government had also realised how vulnerable it was during the Maoist-led riots of 1967 and the value of popular support.[62] It accepted the importance of turning itself into a government for the people and acted on this recognition.[63] Above all, rapid economic growth had given the government the necessary resources to expand the civil service and fund new expenditures for social purposes. Economic take-off had enabled the government to raise revenue substantially without increasing tax.[64]

The fundamental guiding principles behind the government's financial and economic policies did not change despite the economic take-off. They came to be popularised by Philip Haddon-Cave (Financial Secretary, 1971–81) as the positive non-intervention policy.[65] However, as a policy its origin should be traced back to his predecessor, John Cowperthwaite.[66] A man of considerable intellect and integrity, Cowperthwaite (Financial Secretary, 1961–72) is Gladstonian in outlook over public finance and a self-confessed 'Hong Kong chauvinist'.[67] His basic attitude to the management of Hong Kong's public finance and economic policy was to do everything within the means of the Treasury to help the economy and improve Hong Kong, provided he, as the controller of the public purse, was satisfied of the soundness of any proposed public expenditure.[68] He also worked on the basis that the private sector was better placed than the government in managing businesses. He publicly accepted that private enterprise in Hong Kong had 'a good record of productive re-investment' and professed 'a keen realisation of the importance of not withdrawing capital from the private sector of the economy'.[69] These principles were adhered to by Haddon-Cave, which ensured continuity in policy for two decades.[70]

What had also not changed was the importance of the government as a factor in the local economy. It remained the largest employer, the biggest developer of real estate, the leading constructor, the largest landlord and the biggest provider of education and health services.[71]

What had changed was the amount of resources at the disposal of the government. It had consistently maintained a budgetary surplus after the war in order to avoid financial control by the British Treasury.[72] However, it was not until the end of the 1960s that a comfortable safety margin, a reserve the size of two-thirds of annual government expenditure, had been secured.[73] As a result, the government could use the benefits of previous austerity for the good of the community. What were unaffordable luxuries in the early years of Cowperthwaite's tenure as Financial Secretary had become affordable by the time he handed over to Haddon-Cave.

Indeed, the government started to invest in highly desirable but non-essential major infrastructure projects like the Cross Harbour Tunnel and introduced a public assistance scheme for the poor as well as free compulsory primary education shortly before Cowperthwaite retired. It also expanded public expenditure substantially in housing, health services, higher education and the civil service on a scale unimaginable a decade earlier. Responding also to changes in the world, which had turned decidedly hostile to colonialism, the government put the additional resources available to improve local living and working conditions as a constructive step forward. This happened without a fundamental change in the ethos of the administration or a shift in economic policy.

The steadily increasing injection of investments into the local economy by the government itself stimulated growth. It also made another impact, as the government acted on its recognition of the value of a positive social policy and benefited from better communication with the people. It responded to the changes of the time by giving more positive help to trade and industries, improving working conditions and helping to raise the general standard of living. The establishment of the Trade Development Council in 1966, the creation of the Productivity Centre and Council in 1967 and the passing of various legislative amendments to reduce working hours for industrial workers were, for example, part of this process.

While these efforts brought real benefits to the economy, the government did not change its basic approach towards its management. The government played an important and positive role but did not direct the economy or produce a master plan for its transformation. The government's adoption of the positive non-intervention policy should not be confused with having a textbook laissez-faire policy.[74] It was the largest player in the local economy and regulated the allocation of essential economic resources, the most important of which was land. As such it was a significant factor that could and did influence the economy even though it did not seek to direct it. What the positive non-intervention policy meant in practice was to keep government small, restrict its scope to providing and improving the physical, economic and social infrastructures, and leave the private sector to make the most of them.

The conditions which produced a rapid rise in government revenue without increased taxation in fact reflected growth in the private sector. Its earlier success in manufacturing had made Hong Kong sufficiently attractive for foreign investors. The Americans and the Japanese led the way in the 1960s.[75] They provided additional capital investment though it took a decade before direct foreign investments accounted for 7.8 per cent of industrial employment and between eight and 11 per cent of value-added production.[76] More importantly, the earlier industrial success generated sufficient capital locally for further investment. At the period when manufacturing industries contributed most to Hong Kong's GDP, in the latter part of the 1970s, local capital funded over 94 per cent of industrial establishments, 87 per cent of industrial employment, and 80 per cent of production.[77]

At the same time, the local population grew from 2 million in 1950 to 3 million in 1960, 4 million in 1970, 5 million in 1980 and almost 6 million in 1990. Combining this with a rise in disposable income generated by the expanding economy, the domestic market itself became a major impetus for growth. With its economy being one of the most open in the world, a rise in consumption would have only a limited effect in stimulating local manufacturing, as Hong Kong imported most of its consumer goods. The expansion in the domestic market that really worked as an impetus for growth was in real estate development and in servicing.

Property prices had been high in post-war Hong Kong as the supply of land was limited, but demand for it rose steadily following population and industrial expansion. The almost continuous rise in property prices was, however, seriously disrupted by the Maoist-led confrontation of 1967. The fall in property value associated with the drop in public confidence in Hong Kong's future gave an opportunity for a whole generation of local entrepreneurs, many of whom had only limited property portfolios previously, to make fortunes and build up their business empires.[78] Indeed, with the exception of a couple of the long-established and successful British hongs like Swire and Hong Kong Land (part of the Jardine group), as well as a few large local landowners like the Hotung family and the Hysan group, most of Hong Kong's top business conglomerates of the 1990s were built on the basis of bold investments in real estate development in this period. Li Ka-shing's Cheung Kong empire is the best known example. The same applies to other conglomerates. Among the best known are the New World group, Henderson Land, the Hang Lung group and the Sun Hung Kai group.[79]

The substantial profits made by the pioneering entrepreneurs of these companies were turned into fortunes in the stock market boom of the early 1970s. The capital thus accumulated was, in turn, reinvested in a wide range of businesses and catapulted some of these astute entrepreneurs to rival long-established British hongs within a decade. Their spectacular rise was symbolised by the takeover of Hutchison Whampoa (originally founded in 1828 as John D. Hutchison) by Li Ka-shing in 1978.[80] As Li was acting with the blessing of the Hong Kong and Shanghai Bank, this takeover also revealed how far the symbiotic relations between British financial institutions and local Chinese entrepreneurship had developed in less than a quarter of a century. By the early 1980s, while venerable hongs like Jardine and Swire continued to prosper, companies owned by Li and his local Chinese colleagues had overtaken the hongs as the symbolic powerhouses for growth, taking over a few of the remaining hongs in the process.[81]

The property boom of the late 1960s happened not only because the confidence problem of 1967 quickly dissipated but also because a sufficiently large number of the working population had by then secured sufficient income to buy their own flats through mortgages. Hong Kong's per capita GDP passed the $US1,000 mark in 1969, though it was still only $US582 in 1961.[82] Unlike the beginning of the decade, when the ambition of most working people who lived in squatter huts was to move into a tiny spartan concrete cubicle in a government-built resettlement estate, by the end of the decade, the better-off working people increasingly pooled their family's income together to buy their own property.[83] In the second half of this decade real income began to rise steadily.[84] This enabled astute private real estate developers to make business fortunes relatively quickly.

The rise in disposable income and the emergence of a property-owning middle class in turn stimulated yearnings for improvement in the standard of living. The general rise in industrial productivity as the work force became better educated, increase in individual income and the introduction and steady tightening of government regulation over employment in the late 1960s resulted in a weekly day off becoming the norm.

As leisure ceased to be the privilege of the wealthy and the better-paid skilled workers, it fuelled demand for services and personal consumption. In the 1950s, the average worker's expenditures went mostly to pay for subsistence. By the late 1960s, wage or salary-earners could afford to eat in restaurants on social or family occasions, go to cinemas, dance halls, enjoy a day out or shop for consumer goods to improve their quality of life. As a result the local service sector expanded rapidly.

The advent of leisure also meant that ordinary people had the time and the resources to reflect on their living and working conditions, make their views known and generally play an active part in local society, politics and economy. It was instrumental in the emergence of a local popular culture as a rapid rise in demand for entertainment gave impetus to radio, television and cinema productions. The airing of public views on a fast-expanding basis encouraged the colonial government to turn itself from a paternalistic administration into a responsive government without the introduction of democracy.[85] This forced industrial employers to realise that the working people could no longer be treated merely as human parts of an industrial production line that could be exploited to ensure production at the lowest cost. Increasing productivity had become the key to improving profitability. Leisure also created the conditions for workers to organise themselves to seek further improvement in employment conditions without getting caught in external Chinese politics.[86] The ordinary working people had themselves become a factor in the economic development, either through collective bargaining or by putting pressure on the government to introduce new legislation.

The convergence of various favourable factors at the end of the 1960s produced sufficient momentum for growth to develop into a virtuous circle. The somewhat haphazard though spectacular economic expansion of the early post-war decades gradually came to be replaced by sustainable growth based on sound economic fundamentals. As the 1970s dawned, Hong Kong had a solid industrial base, excellent trade networks, modern international banking, insurance and other business servicing facilities, a vibrant domestically driven local economy, an increasingly educated workforce, and efficient public services to support and sustain a modern economy. It had also seen the transformation of its workforce from one made up of desperate immigrants or refugees struggling for survival into a modern labour force who were themselves consumers and a positive factor in further economic development. The gap between the rich and the poor had remained large but real wages had risen steadily since the second half of the 1960s. As a result, with a relatively small exception, even the desperately poor of the 1950s had seen sufficient improvements to have a relatively comfortable life by the 1970s.

Economic Maturity and the China Nexus

Although industries continued to grow and upgrade themselves at a very fast rate in the 1970s, the question of whether this could be sustained came to be taken seriously. The lack of land and natural resources, as well as lingering background doubts over Hong Kong's long-term political future, limited the kind of industries that could be developed. Hong Kong did not enjoy comparative advantages for developing capital-intensive or highly technological heavy industries. Thus, manufacturing growth was restricted largely to expanding and upgrading various light industries. It involved shifting from labour-intensive to higher value-added or knowledge-based production, as the cost of labour and production rose. The more successful and enterprising industrialists responded adroitly. They either expanded horizontally or vertically, or moved into different industries. Nevertheless, as the industrial sector matured the local economy needed to diversify to sustain a high rate of growth.

The main focus of Hong Kong's efforts to diversify its economy in the 1970s was to upgrade and develop its already impressive network of banks, shipping and insurance agencies into a modern financial centre and regional hub for business services. A major development was the lifting in 1978 of a moratorium on the issue of new banking licences, imposed after a series of bank runs in 1965.[87] As a result, major foreign and international banks, including leading international merchant banks, were able to open full offices. Their presence made Hong Kong more attractive to other major business servicing sectors, such as international law partnerships, accountancies and firms of consultants. They were essential to Hong Kong's success in turning itself into a leading modern international financial centre.

Hong Kong also sought to develop itself into a major capital market. It had had a stock exchange since the mid-1880s. Until the end of the 1960s, the Hong Kong Stock Exchange was under the control of the expatriates, even though ethnic Chinese made up a good percentage of brokers after it was reorganised after the war.[88] Its function as a capital market for local entrepreneurs was limited by the fact that, even though a local index for stocks and shares (the Hang Seng Index) was introduced in 1964, it was not made public until the latter part of the decade.[89] During this period, a generation of younger local entrepreneurs with modern Western educations aggressively pushed their way into the capital market. After they failed to get the Hong Kong Stock Exchange to expand significantly to accommodate themselves, they started their own exchanges.[90] They founded the Far East Exchange in 1969, the Kam Ngan Stock Exchange in 1971 and the Kowloon Stock Exchange in 1972. As a capital market, Hong Kong reached maturity when the four exchanges and the government regulator finally worked out the details for them to merge into 'The Stock Exchange of Hong Kong' in 1986.[91] By then, Hong

Kong had successfully developed into a capital market not only for the local entrepreneurs, but also for the region as a whole, particularly for the fast-growing economy of the PRC.

Hong Kong's new role as a financial centre was built on the demonstrated strength of its infrastructure in supporting the financial and servicing sectors. The integrity and efficiency of the administration and the rule of law underlined the existence of the basic political, social, legal and judicial infrastructure for a modern financial centre.

The local economy also benefited from the earlier heavy investment in education by the government and individual families. By the 1970s, the local economy enjoyed an abundant supply of school-leavers and an increasing supply of graduates from the local universities and institutes of higher education. Just as the school-leavers provided a flexible labour force for industries, shops and clerical positions, the graduates gave Hong Kong the human resources to take on the more knowledge-intensive jobs in finance, business servicing, as well as in marketing, design and product research in the maturing industrial sector.

Hong Kong's efforts to broaden its economic base received an unexpected major boost as the PRC dramatically eased tension with the USA by inviting President Richard Nixon to visit in 1972. This diplomatic breakthrough in fact followed the lifting of the US embargo on the trading of non-strategic goods in April 1971.[92] It also heralded the opening of the PRC to the outside world. As a result, Hong Kong's old role as the premier entrepôt of China could be restored. It added significant volume and value to Hong Kong's economic activities and made it more attractive as a regional base for finance and business services. The PRC's creation of Special Economic Zones in 1979 in locations clearly chosen to benefit from their easy access to Hong Kong's facilities further enhanced its attractiveness.[93]

Hong Kong succeeded in developing itself into a leading financial centre mainly through the efforts of its private sector, even though the government actually adopted a policy of encouraging this development. Largely in line with earlier decades, the government played a positive role. It did so not by giving incentives to foreign banks, management consultant firms, accountancies and international law firms to set up offices. It contributed by providing a reasonable regulatory framework, an efficient administration, a transparent and consistent economic policy, and a low taxation environment. They helped to make Hong Kong an attractive centre for multinationals engaged in finance and business servicing to locate their regional headquarters or at least open an office there. The government's desire to see Hong Kong develop into a leading financial centre would not have worked if Hong Kong did not have the right business environment and human resources.

The decline in the importance of the manufacturing sector since 1980 needs to be put in perspective. Although it has been steadily declining in importance as a contributor to the GDP, in real terms the value of manufacturing output continued to expand, from $US4.1 billion in 1980 to \$US12.7 billion in 1992, before starting to fall steadily.[94] In the meantime, as Hong Kong's manufacturing sector transformed itself into a high value-added production centre, it took the lead to turn the Pearl River delta into a low-cost centre for contract manufacturing. Production that could no longer be cost effectively done locally was transferred to the Chinese mainland. The scale and pace of Hong Kong's transfer of industrial production can be illustrated in general terms by the number of workers in the PRC employed by Hong Kong companies. It was estimated to number over 2 million in 1988 and shot past the 5 million mark in 1997.[95]

What at first appeared to be a major break that would simply revive Hong Kong's pre-1950 position as China's premier entrepôt soon turned into something more important. As the policy of economic reform pursued under Deng Xiaoping deepened in the PRC in the 1980s, a new symbiotic economic relationship emerged between it and Hong Kong. Hong Kong went beyond being the key entrepôt for the new China trade and the financial centre to support this trade and foreign investments on the mainland. It had taken the lead in building factories, first in the Special Economic Zone of Shenzhen and then more widely in Guangdong province.

The entrepreneurs of Hong Kong were among the first to make a success of industrial investments on the Chinese mainland. Their success did not come quickly or easily, as many of the problems that plagued major pioneering investors in industrial production in the PRC from the West affected them too. Three main reasons enabled Hong Kong entrepreneurs to succeed.

The first was the same brutal logic that underlay Hong Kong's own industrial success of the 1950s. It was the survival of the fittest. Many of the early Hong Kong investments in fact failed miserably. Their experiences had a cautionary effect but they were not sufficient to deter others. Hong Kong was the gateway for most foreign investments in the PRC and Western enthusiasm sustained Hong Kong entrepreneurs' interest. It took time, but the more astute Hong Kong entrepreneurs who invested on the mainland did learn how to operate in a quasi-command economy where bureaucratic corruption and the party machine distorted the market forces. Their successes, which attracted more attention than those who failed, encouraged others to invest. The eventual success of Hong Kong entrepreneurs was built on the experiences of failures of the pioneers.

The second reason was that there were genuine complementary conditions for industrial production between Hong Kong and Guangdong. As Hong Kong's economy boomed, once political uncertainty was removed by the signing of the Sino-British Agreement over Hong Kong's future in 1984, wage, rent and other production costs rocketed. By then Deng's economic reform policy had been in place long enough to improve the business environment in Guangdong, where the local people were keen to learn from Hong Kong. With a huge discrepancy in production costs, Hong Kong industrialists could cut their expenditure substantially by relocating their production facilities to Guangdong.[96] This was notwithstanding lower productivity per worker, and various bureaucratic red tape and extra-legal payments required to ensure the production process was not interrupted in the PRC. It worked, because most Hong Kong industrialists kept an office in Hong Kong to look after the non-production side of the industry. They made the most of Hong Kong's strength in marketing and design and of the low-cost production in the Pearl River delta.[97]

The third reason was closely related to the second one. It was the ability of Hong Kong entrepreneurs to grasp what would be needed to make the most of the complementary conditions on the one hand and to minimise the effect of the PRC system in disrupting production on the other. Most Hong Kong investments on the mainland started as small to medium-sized enterprises. Like the industrialists of Hong Kong a generation before, they were nimble and highly flexible. They were prepared to do whatever it took to clear bureaucratic red tape, secure the supply of raw material and ensure production at the quality contracted by overseas buyers. Owners of small factories in the Pearl River delta region frequently managed their investments in person or engaged Hong Kong managers, supervisors and foremen to ensure production went smoothly. The latter was particularly important in the early stages of transplanting Hong Kong factories to the Pearl River delta region. It could be done because the two shared the same language, and major improvements in communication (such as the introduction of a through train service between Hong Kong and Canton in 1979) made it possible to post Hong Kong employees on the mainland on a cost-effective basis. Once they had put their production facilities on track, it was relatively easy to train mainland Chinese staff to take over from lower-level Hong Kong supervisors and managers as the people of Guangdong had learned to admire Hong Kong and wanted to imitate their compatriots.[98]

What happened from the latter half of the 1980s to 1997 was the development of an intricate and mutually beneficial economic nexus between Hong Kong and mainland China, with Guangdong being the most important destination for Hong Kong investments. As Hong Kong continuously upgraded its own economy, it relied on the PRC as its economic hinterland while it served as one of the key locomotives pulling the Chinese economy on a fast track. The symbiotic relationship went far beyond the turning of the Pearl River delta into Hong Kong's external manufacturing base. By 1997, Hong Kong had become the largest source of investments in a very wide spectrum of economic activities and the most important capital market for the PRC. It was the PRC's key trading partner, middleman, financier and facilitator that underpinned the economic reform of Deng Xiaoping. It was the 'principal gateway to the Mainland for business and tourism'.[99] Its own economic dynamism was deemed to have 'activated market forces' on the mainland and forced the PRC government to decentralise its trade and other economic policies.[100] As 1997 approached, the process for closer economic integration that started after the reaching of an agreement over Hong Kong's future in 1984 gathered pace. After all, as its political future became tied to that of the PRC there was less incentive for investors in Hong Kong to hesitate staking their economic future with it as well. Hong Kong's economy did not merge into that of the PRC in 1997 but the two economies had by then become so intricately linked that the wellbeing of one had become crucial for the other.[101]

Chapter 13

The Rise of the Hong Kongers

Before the Pacific War, the overwhelming majority of Hong Kong's ethnic Chinese shared much more in common with their fellow countrymen living on the mainland of China than with their non-Chinese fellow residents in Hong Kong. They were either sojourners, economic migrants or refugees, and were not noticeably different from other Chinese living elsewhere in China.[1] Except for a small number who had taken root locally, most intended to return to their home in China for retirement or after making sufficient money for a more comfortable life back home. The Chinese community of Hong Kong did not have an identity of its own and the non-Chinese community was essentially an expatriate one.

This non-existence of a local sense of identity did not bother either the government or the local people until the end of the Pacific War. Although Governor Young already saw the need to instil among its residents a British Hong Kong identity and citizenship in 1946, his ideas were never put into practice as his successor, Grantham, disagreed with them. Nevertheless, a Hong Kong identity did eventually emerge. This process started with the Communists gaining power in China in 1949.

A Settled People

The changes brought about by the establishment of the PRC were much more profoundly felt in Hong Kong than was the case with any previous regime change in China. For a century, Chinese had sought sanctuary in Hong Kong in time of crisis and disorder but most returned once the situation had stabilised in their home country. The creation of a Communist regime in China as the Cold War intensified caused a basic change, though this was not immediately recognised by the colonial government.[2] Unlike previous waves of refugees, the overwhelming majority of those who arrived in the late 1940s chose not to go back to the mainland to live under Communism. It was only after the prospect that they would return to China started to fade in 1950 that the colonial government imposed permanent immigration restrictions at the Sino-British border.[3] The PRC government responded by enforcing its own border control.

This was a major break from the previous practice by which governments on both sides of the border permitted Chinese persons to enter Hong Kong freely or leave for China without restrictions except in time of crisis.[4] Until 1950, there was free and regular movement of people to and from China. This produced a sojourner mentality and largely accounted for the non-development of a sense of local identity. After the founding of the PRC, movement of people between the two was reduced to a trickle, except for short periods when a relaxation of border control by the PRC for domestic reasons led to an influx into Hong Kong, as happened in 1962 and in the latter half of the 1970s. Communist rule deterred most Chinese refugees from returning to their homeland. Although many had not originally intended to settle in Hong Kong, the overwhelming majority of them could not emigrate elsewhere. It took some time for many of them to accept this as a reality but like the other migrants to Hong Kong, they worked, lived and raised their families there. The closing of the border in 1950 turned the Chinese population of Hong Kong into a settled one.

Those born and bred in Hong Kong since 1950 by and large had no first-hand experience of the PRC until the latter opened up in the 1970s. It was this separation that provided the conditions for a political culture and an identity of its own to build up in Hong Kong.

The divergent development models followed by capitalist Hong Kong and Communist China left their marks on their respective people. In its first quarter century the PRC followed the Communist policies of Mao Zedong and launched massive mobilising campaigns like the land reform and its associated campaigns, the Great Leap Forward and the Cultural Revolution.[5] They brought untold sufferings to its citizens and reduced the Chinese legal system to a shambles. According to Hu Yaobang, when he was the General Secretary of the Communist Party, about 100 million of the PRC's citizens suffered from some form of prosecution in the first three decades of Communist rule. The same period also witnessed the most systematic and virulent attempt by any Chinese regime to destroy its Confucian heritage in two millennia.[6] The result was that the PRC remained an underdeveloped country with one of the world's lowest per capita incomes when Mao died in 1976. The Maoist development model and the Communist ideology shaped the outlook and the way of life of the mainland Chinese people.

In sharp contrast, social, economic and political developments in Hong Kong unfolded in an orderly fashion. The Confucian tradition was allowed to continue among its Chinese residents, though it had to coexist and accommodate changes brought about by rapid modernisation in a fast-growing and increasingly cosmopolitan port city and industrial economy. As the colonial government accepted that its continued existence was at the sufferance of the PRC, it became more responsive to the needs and wishes of its people and in delivering good governance, though this fell short of introducing democracy. The basis that underlay the government's approach was the constructive partnership advocated by Governor

Grantham. With the government slowly but steadily getting rid of the pre-war discrimination against the local Chinese and putting emphasis on education, the rule of law came to be highly valued. The contrast with the lawless horror in the near-totalitarian political system of the PRC made this Anglo-Saxon concept particularly attractive. By the 1970s, Hong Kong people of all ethnic origins had embraced the concept of the rule of law. Together with the routine safeguarding of freedom in this British enclave these basic changes set the people of Hong Kong apart from the people of the PRC and produced the conditions for a sense of local identity based on a way of life and a world view different from that in the PRC.[7]

Hong Kong's colonial capitalist road of development gave its local people distinctive experiences that contributed crucially to the rise of a local identity. In the 1950s, those born or brought up in Hong Kong since 1945 had, by and large, not come of age and were therefore irrelevant. The bulk of the adult Chinese population were immigrants and had experiences of living in China, particularly in the Pearl River delta region. Their own life experiences often involved making a decision to leave their home in China for Hong Kong in search of stability, good order and the prospect for a better life. Most were also affected, to various degrees, by the life and death struggle between the Kuomintang and the Communist Party. This often had the effect of making them think of politics in Hong Kong in terms of an extension of the brutal power struggle between these two Chinese parties. Hence, the overwhelming majority of them preferred not to get involved in what they saw as politics. In any event, most of them were so poor and life in Hong Kong still so hard that they had to focus their attention on earning a living. The 1950s thus passed without the issue of identity being raised seriously. However, this changed as the locally educated post-war generation left schools for work.

The coming of age of the first post-war generation occurred in the 1960s. By then economic conditions had improved considerably and the government's efforts to provide education to as many as possible had produced some thoughtful and articulate young people. They started to search for their own sense of identity. This involved much agonised soul searching. A member of this generation explained the dilemma he (and many of his generation) faced succinctly: although a Chinese person and keen to do something for his country, he was not prepared to 'give up the freedom and dignity befitting every human being to return to the mainland', nor to go to Taiwan, where he thought life was dominated by the patronage of the Kuomintang under Chiang Kai-shek.[8] In a local magazine he made a public appeal:

> Since we all intend to continue to live in Hong Kong, we should change our attitude from being sojourners and visitors to considering ourselves the local people and to caring about the political affairs of Hong Kong and helping to reform them. This is the proper attitude when one faces reality.[9]

It was in the 1960s that more and more of the younger locally born and educated ethnic Chinese came to see Hong Kong as their home and considered themselves citizens of the territory. However, this was not an issue that formed the focus of attention for most of them, who were generally more concerned with getting out of poverty and building a career. Even those who thought about their identity most were uncomfortable associating themselves with the colonial government. After all, they came of age in the decade which opened with the British Prime Minister, Harold Macmillan, publicly acknowledging that 'the wind of change' was blowing through the British Empire.[10] It was the decade when 'colonialism' or 'imperialism' came to be accepted in Britain as out of tune with the spirit of the era.[11] Indeed, it was a time when the British found themselves under pressure over the maintenance of colonial rule in Hong Kong from the anti-colonial lobby in the United Nations.[12] The 1960s was an important transitional period in the eventual emergence of a Hong Kong identity.

The genesis for a Hong Kong identity was ironically helped by the traumatic disturbances of 1967, a series of events that could have posed a fundamental challenge to the survival or at least the legitimacy of the colonial regime. When the local community was forced to choose between supporting the politically inspired disturbances orchestrated by the local Maoists and the colonial government, its sense of identity, loyalty and calculation of its interests was put to a severe test.

The Test of the 'Confrontation'

Large-scale and sustained disturbances occurred in Hong Kong from the middle to the end of 1967. Its beginning was marked by the turning of a labour dispute, which started at a factory of the Hong Kong Artificial Flower Works owned by Li Ka-shing in April, into riots on 6 May. Disturbances started in the larger of the two factories run by this company at San Po Kong in Kowloon, where it employed 686 workers. Although Hong Kong had already seen seven other major industrial disputes earlier in the year, it was this particular bickering that was seized on by the local Communists to mark their joining of the Cultural Revolution.[13] The working conditions and management style in this factory were, in general terms, neither significantly better nor worse than in most other factories of similar size and nature. The industrial dispute in San Po Kong merely provided the occasion, the real cause for the disturbances had to be found elsewhere.

The disturbances were organised and directed by the Hong Kong and Macao Work Committee, which was the local branch of the CCP that existed clandestinely, as Hong Kong banned foreign political parties in 1949. It operated in public under the guise of the Xihua News Agency, and was directly answerable to the Hong Kong and Macao Group of the External Affairs Office in the State Council, the head of which was Liao Zhengzhi for almost three decades .[14] It cannot as yet be proved that the Work Committee directed the original labour dispute in San Po Kong from the beginning and pushed for a showdown, though it is likely that

that was the case. What can be established is that the labour activists involved were members of the Communist-dominated Federation of Trade Unions, and they answered telephone calls from Hong Kong officials who tried to mediate by quoting 'from the works of Chairman Mao'.[15] After the labour dispute turned violent in early May, the head of the Work Committee, Liang Weilin, 'ordered a full scale assault by way of mobilising workers to take part in demonstrations and processions'.[16] The disturbances came to be known in Hong Kong as the 'confrontation' and was primarily a spill-over from the Cultural Revolution.

The Cultural Revolution was essentially an attempt by Mao Zedong to reaffirm his power and authority in the CCP by ousting his top lieutenants and their close subordinates, who were deemed to have deviated from his policy line.[17] Mao was worried that the steady consolidation of power by senior leaders around his number two, Liu Shaoqi, might eventually lead to him being ousted from power or completely sidelined. As a result, Mao bypassed the party apparatus and appealed to the young people to organise themselves into Red Guards to launch a massive attack against 'the capitalist roaders inside the party'. This was meant to destroy his real or potential challengers within the party, and to immerse the younger generations in new 'revolutionary' experiences so that they would protect his 'revolutionary legacy'. There are scholarly disagreements as to when the Cultural Revolution started, usually ranging between the making of an important speech in September 1965 by Lin Biao, Mao's close ally in the early stage of this movement, and the branding of senior leaders Peng Chen and Lu Dingyi as members of an anti-party group by Mao on 16 May 1966.[18] Whenever it actually started, by May 1967, the Cultural Revolution had engulfed mainland China in the largest-scale turmoil since the founding of the PRC in 1949 for over a year.

As far as members of the Work Committee in Hong Kong were concerned, the intensification of the political campaign and struggle for power in China from the middle of 1966 to early 1967 were watched closely and carefully. Given the prevailing chaos, no one in the Work Committee could be sure what was the right course to follow. What everyone was most concerned about was to avoid stepping into the shoes of those comrades who had fallen from power on the mainland. Although the Work Committee had received repeated assurances from Premier Zhou Enlai in the autumn of 1966 that the Cultural Revolution was not to be practised in Hong Kong, the leadership of the Work Committee remained worried about their own future.[19] The situation only got worse as the Cultural Revolution entered its even more radical and volatile stage in early 1967.

The concern of the Hong Kong-based cadres was understandable, as numerous top-level leaders, including Liu Shaoqi and Deng Xiaoping, had by then become targets of vicious political struggles, and the Foreign Ministry appeared to have come under the sway of the Red Guards. In fact, the Red Guards who seized power in the Ministry in January 1967 had done so under the encouragement of Zhou Enlai who was therefore able to exercise influence over them and thus over work of the Ministry in general terms.[20] Zhou did not really lose his authority over the Foreign Ministry until August, when Wang Li of the Central Cultural Revolution Small Group launched an attack on him.[21] The fact that Zhou had not in reality lost control in May was, as far as can be ascertained, not known to the leadership of the Work Committee in Hong Kong, who worked on the basis that the radical Maoists had already taken over the Ministry.[22] This explained the strong reactions of the Work Committee in Hong Kong once the San Po Kong labour dispute turned into a physical scuffle. Its members launched their version of the Cultural Revolution in Hong Kong to show how loyal they were to Mao as a means to protect themselves from being portrayed as not sufficiently 'revolutionary' in their reactions and made a target of the Maoist purge.[23]

This instinctive desire for self-preservation thus led the leaders of the Work Committee take the initiative to depart from the PRC's established policy of leaving Hong Kong alone, and spread the Cultural Revolution to this British enclave. Once they adopted the radical rhetoric and posture of the Cultural Revolution in organising a large public struggle against 'the British imperialist capitalists' who were allegedly oppressing the local Chinese workers, they provoked a general confrontation. On the one hand, the colonial government could not afford to be successfully challenged in public by the local Maoists without losing credibility, as had happened to the Portuguese authorities in neighbouring Macao. On the other hand, the Chinese leaders responsible for Hong Kong policy could not afford to be seen as less 'revolutionary' than the Work Committee in this struggle against the British colonial oppressors. Thus, even though the matter was referred to Zhou Enlai in Beijing, and he disapproved of the Work Committee's initiatives, he went along with the more radical reactions of the Red Guards and only exercised a moderating effect, such as rejecting a proposal to use assassination to support their political campaign in Hong Kong.[24]

The original labour dispute in Hong Kong was quickly subsumed by a series of large-scale demonstrations, marches, noisy street protests and stone throwing in the city and outside of Government House. They were organised, directed and supported by the Work Committee, though a committee to struggle against oppression by the British authorities was formed at the end of May.[25] Communist-controlled organisations in all sectors were mobilised in this endeavour. Both the core Communist newspapers such as the *Dagong Bao* (*Ta Kung Pao*) and the *Wenhui Bao* (*Wen Hui Pao*) and fringe ones like *Xianggang Yebao*, *Tianfeng Ribao*, *Xinwu Bao* and *Jing Bao* were instructed to launch sustained propaganda attacks on the colonial authorities. Workers in the transport sector, waterworks and other essential services that the Communist-run unions could control were called out to strike. Communist-controlled schools were also mobilised to send young students to support the public demonstrations and drill the youngsters in Cultural Revolution songs and slogans while some school laboratories were used to make explosive devices. The top leadership of the Work Committee wished to reduce Hong Kong to a state of paralysis. Such dissenting voices as existed among their colleagues and appealed for a more rational approach were quickly silenced.[26]

This challenge to its authority did not surprise the Hong Kong government, as local Maoists in Macao had already launched a similar attack upon the Portuguese colonial government there at the end of 1966.[27] When the disturbances did occur in Hong Kong, Governor Sir David Trench chose to deal with them by taking firm but measured responses, in order to avoid provoking an escalation or appearing weak and indecisive. The relative confidence of the government was partly based on the assessment that the confrontation was largely the result of local initiatives rather than the product of a carefully worked out policy of the PRC government.[28] The disposition of the People's Liberation Army (PLA) in Guangdong and regular intelligence the British had on the local Communists supported such a view.[29] The intentions of the government in Beijing was also reflected by the fact that, while it adopted harsh rhetoric, it made no specific reference to what action it might take to support the local Maoists.[30] The British thus worked on the basis that Beijing did not intend to force a solution over the future of Hong Kong at this moment, though no one could rule out such an eventuality if the confrontation were to escalate out of control.

The Hong Kong government also benefited from reforms introduced to the police after the large-scale anti-Communist riots that had happened a decade earlier in October 1956. By the middle of the 1960s, all police officers received regular anti-riot training and the police had three companies of anti-riot officers on standby at any one time.[31] This central mobile reserve could also be reinforced quickly, as standing instructions and contingency plans were in place for each division to mobilise and deploy one company of riot police if the need should arise. In other words, when the confrontation started the government had in place an organised, equipped, well-trained and efficient anti-riot police.[32] As a result of the so-called non-politically motivated Star Ferry Riots of 1966, the police also had an occasion to put the new anti-riot training and structure to the test and make further improvements.[33] The capability of the police to restore order enabled the government to avoid calling for a large-scale deployment of British troops to aid civil power, a key factor that allowed it to make measured responses, maintain public confidence and keep a high degree of normality that was not possible when it had last faced an organised challenge to its authority, staged also in part by the CCP, half a century ago in 1925 and 1926.

Despite having a clear policy of restraint, the police did use force to disperse the rioters. This included the fairly widespread use of tear gas and baton charges, as well as the very occasional discharge of firearms. For their part, the Maoists resorted to violence like throwing stones, setting vehicles alight and storming police lines. There were casualties on both sides, and one protestor died under police custody. On this occasion, an inquiry was conducted, and the three police officers responsible were charged and tried in a court of law. If this upholding of the law in any way weakened police morale in the short run, it had the effect of demonstrating the confidence of the government and helped it win the battle for the hearts and minds of the local people.[34]

Although both sides took the propaganda war seriously, it sometimes descended into farce. In order to back up their allegation of police brutality, Maoist rioters sometimes came equipped with bandages stained red, to be put on as soon as the riot police tried to clear them from the streets. There was also a battle of the loudspeakers, with noisy propaganda broadcast out of huge loudspeakers on top of the Bank of China and other Communist-owned buildings. The government responded by jamming the Maoist loudspeakers and setting up higher power loudspeakers on nearby buildings to play Cantonese operas or other music.[35] With greater technical competence, the government won this battle easily.

The steadfast yet, on balance, measured response of the government and its police meant the local Maoists did not gain much ground in the early stages of the confrontation. The frustration of the local Maoists, who were emboldened by supportive statements by the radicals in Beijing particularly through the *People's Daily* (*Renmin Ribao*), led them to escalate the disturbances into a stage of 'armed' conflict in July.[36]

The highpoint of this new challenge took place in the border village of Sha Tau Kok, when a sizeable detachment of Chinese militia crossed the border, attacked the police post and killed five and wounded 11 policemen. The police post was relieved by the British Army, while the regular PLA avoided direct involvement.[37] The main 'armed' struggle waged by the Maoists was through the launching of a campaign of indiscriminate bombing. This involved the planting of 8,352 suspected bombs; among these were 1,420 genuine explosive devices.[38] They also murdered the critical presenter of a popular radio programme, Lam Bun, and his clansman in August and let it be known that they had a blacklist of local notables to be eliminated.

The Maoist intimidation backfired. Their indiscriminate bombing campaign and attempts to paralyse the city caused great inconvenience and posed a threat to the life and property of ordinary residents. They antagonised public opinion and encouraged the general public to support the colonial government and the police in restoring order and maintaining essential services. The lack of support from Beijing for the Maoists' armed struggle was revealed by the non-involvement of the PLA, either in the border incident of early July or in supplying gunpowder or arms for the bombing campaign.

A further escalation happened in August, after the Hong Kong police responded to the indiscriminate bombing campaign by raiding Communist-owned premises, arresting some known advocates of the confrontation and closing three fringe Communist newspapers. The Maoists in Beijing retaliated by burning down the British embassy compound and kept Reuter's Beijing correspondent Anthony Grey under house arrest.[39] Anglo-Chinese relations reached a nadir and the British

Foreign Secretary formally proposed to his Chinese counterpart that it might be best 'if while maintaining diplomatic relations, both sides withdrew their missions and personnel from each other's capital for the time being'.[40]

Just as the confrontation started in response to developments on the mainland of China, it reached a turning point when the Cultural Revolution entered a less volatile phase towards the end of the year.[41] By December, despite the public rhetoric, the Chinese Foreign Ministry indicated that it was prepared to ease the tension.[42] In reality, Beijing instructed the Maoists in Hong Kong to end the confrontation, even though its own demands over Hong Kong made through diplomatic channels were mostly not met. By then, Zhou Enlai had had an opportunity to secure from Mao Zedong a reaffirmation of the PRC's long-standing policy towards Hong Kong.[43] The confrontation ended in December 1967, after Zhou ordered Liang Weilin to abandon what Zhou described as an ultra-leftist policy.[44]

The colonial government played as peripheral a role in ending the confrontation as it did in provoking it. However, its firm and, on the whole, carefully calibrated responses helped it to win over public support. As a challenge to the colonial authorities, even one of the more liberal-minded senior local Communist cadres admitted in retrospect that it had failed miserably.[45] The confrontation nevertheless imposed heavy costs. In seven months of disturbances, 51 people were killed. They included 10 police officers, an army sergeant investigating a suspected bomb, a fireman, 23 rioters, 4 bombers and 12 civilians, who were all victims of violence or the bombing campaign.[46] Among 1,172 injured, 340 were victims of the bombing campaign while 832 others received injuries as a direct result of the riots.[47]

The political nature of the confrontation and the government's success in dealing with it should not distract from the fact that Hong Kong was in any event facing serious social problems that were conducive to rioting in the mid 1960s.[48] Indeed, it suffered two days of serious riots in April 1966, though they were unrelated to the confrontation. They were called the Star Ferry Riots, as the immediate cause was a protest started by one young man, So Sau-chung, against the raising by five cents of the first-class fare for the cross-harbour ferry run by the Star Ferry Company. According to the report by the Commission of Inquiry into this incident, among 905 people who were arrested and charged 'the predominant age group is that of 16 to 20 years' who constituted 'the main source of violence'.[49] Most of the boys were employed but mainly in jobs that 'held little for them by way of future security or advancement'.[50] What is significant is that the protest was started and supported mainly by young people of the lower social and economic strata who would usually not have travelled first class on the Star Ferry. Most took part in the riots not because the fare increase directly affected their own livelihood but because they were frustrated and bored, and they resented the idea of businesses appearing to make excessive profits while their own lots were neglected.

The riots of 1966 revealed the existence of considerable social discontent. They were caused by a mixture of dissatisfaction towards the gap between the government and the people; the arrogant, overbearing and corrupt behaviour of a majority of government functionaries, who were normally the only officials the local Chinese residents dealt with on a daily basis; and the social injustice that existed between the rich and the poor and between the expatriate and the local communities.[51] The discontent was particularly pronounced among younger people because they, ironically, had benefited from the massive expansion of education, at first mainly at the primary level, funded by the government after 1949.[52] As an indication of the scale of the expansion, Hong Kong had 118,000 children in schools before the Pacific War in 1941, merely 4,000 in 1945, but 983,500 or 99.8 per cent of children of primary school age in 1966.[53] The receiving of a basic education and the settled nature of Hong Kong's young people in the 1960s made them different from the pre-war generations or from their parents. They had enough education and sufficiently secure livelihoods to desire improvements in their life chances, rather than just meekly accepting what life had in store for them. However, the social and political setting in the mid 1960s appeared to give them little scope to fulfil their modest and reasonable ambitions. They rioted because they were frustrated, though the heavy concentration of population in a small urban area also allowed riots to break out and spread quickly.

What was truly remarkable was that, despite the continuation of the same basic social problems in Hong Kong a year later, the Maoists had so little success in recruiting the frustrated local people, including the young rioters of 1966, to join them in the confrontation. In the battle for the hearts and minds of the local people against the Communist-dominated unions, banks, schools and media groups, the colonial government was able to enlist the public support of numerous civic organisations over a very wide spectrum.[54] Students receiving higher education were among the first to support the government publicly. The Hong Kong University Students Union and the Federation of Hong Kong Students appealed for an end to the disturbances as soon as the middle of May, shortly after the disruptions started. They stressed the need to maintain stability and order and condemned actions that would upset the economy and create unemployment.[55]

The Maoists failed to win general public support for two reasons. To begin with, the violence and chaos of the Cultural Revolution made their appeal to create a similar state of instability and savageness in their alleged struggle against the British colonial oppressor at best hollow and at worse highly repulsive. Their indiscriminate bombing campaign and disruption of economic life were made even more repugnant by the discovery of corpses with their hands tied behind their backs floating into the Hong Kong waters from the Pearl River. This hammered home the senseless brutality of the Maoist regime, from which over half of the local population had chosen to avoid or escape less than two decades earlier.[56]

In 1967, the local Chinese had to choose between supporting Communist China and the colonial government, which had provided stability, good order and the general conditions for them to live and work without facing persecution or overt oppression. In the process, they reflected on their sense of identity.[57] It was not an easy decision but they overwhelmingly chose to uphold their own way of life. It was as a result of being forced to choose that for 'the first time in Hong Kong's recent history, the inhabitants believed that the British-Hong Kong government was "their" government', however wanting it might be in other ways.[58] This change in attitude was critical to the forging of an 'imagined community' of Hong Kong in the long process entailed in the emergence of a local identity.[59]

The Emergence of a Local Identity

Realising the political significance of public support in defeating the Maoist challenge, the government under Governor Trench quickly sought to remove some of the basis for the social discontent that existed.[60] It tried to improve communication between itself and the people by introducing a City District Officer (CDO) scheme which was inspired by the work of the District Officers in the New Territories for half a century.[61] The new City District Officers were meant to function as political officers. They were required to 'make themselves as accessible as possible to the people in their districts', to assess 'the overall impact of government policies' and 'to explain these policies as well as the difficulties and the achievements of the Government to ordinary people'.[62] The government also introduced compulsory free primary education and reviewed its work in connection with the local Chinese community. As a result, it improved social welfare and took initiatives to involve young people and others in public events such as the Festival of Hong Kong.

Ironically, the flagship of the reforms, the CDO scheme, was essentially similar to an idea that Trench had had when he previously served as Deputy Colonial Secretary in Hong Kong, just before he left to become High Commissioner for the Western Pacific (1961–3).[63] He did not push for its introduction immediately when he returned as governor in 1964, as any such reform required the active cooperation and support of the Secretary for Chinese Affairs. This critical office was held by the last of the remaining senior pre-war officials, John McDouall. McDouall had previously been senior to Trench and continued to resist any such reform. After becoming governor, Trench envisaged introducing it after McDouall's retirement in 1966, but the confrontation intervened. After the confrontation, not only had McDouall retired, what remained of other resistance within the bureaucracy had also been removed.[64]

Trench thus started a process of transforming the government from an old-fashioned Crown Colony system into a modern administration responsive to public opinion. This process started with little fanfare but it marked an important change in policy. One of the most important of these understated reforms was the retitling of the Secretary for Chinese

Affairs as the Secretary for Home Affairs in February 1969. It was much more than a long overdue administrative rationalisation. It marked a recognition on the part of the government that it was no longer appropriate to treat the overwhelming majority of Hong Kong's citizens as a group that required the specialist attention of a department of its own, distinct from the rest of the administration. This subtle acceptance by the government that a Hong Kong community existed became a positive factor in the forging of a local identity.

The confrontation also provoked students, particularly those in higher education, to think hard about social and political issues. Their attitudes began to change. This became discernible as China stabilised after the active phase of the Cultural Revolution was formally concluded by the Ninth Congress of the CCP in April 1969. Their antipathy towards the Maoist regime subsided. The subsequent rise of the PRC, which took from the ROC government in Taipei one of the five permanent Security Council seats at the United Nations in late 1971, provoked much interest among the student activists. Their imagination was caught when American President Richard Nixon visited the PRC in early 1972. If the same event ignited enormous interest in the PRC and things Chinese in the USA and the Western world, it hit most Hong Kong people, especially the undergraduates, like a bombshell.[65]

Suddenly the Hong Kong students were confronted with the fact that the government in Beijing had catapulted China into the ranks of the great powers, a long-cherished dream of Chinese intellectuals since the nineteenth century. A surge of a sense of national pride in being a Chinese person swept many off their feet. Out of this was born a movement among students of higher education to 'know the mother country' and embrace the regime which gave them back their pride as Chinese people.[66] As part of their search for an identity, they also started a movement to have the Chinese language recognised as the second official language in Hong Kong, a demand to which the increasingly responsive government acceded in 1974.

The almost euphoric enthusiasm among Hong Kong's students did not last, however. Their understanding of the PRC was highly superficial. They too readily accepted Maoist propaganda at face value as they were driven by a kind of blind patriotism towards 'mother China', which many in this period equated with the PRC. A critical few were bewildered by various political campaigns in the PRC such as the 'Anti-Lin Biao and Anti-Confucius campaign' which really had the widely respected Premier Zhou Enlai as the target, and by the second fall of Deng Xiaoping from power in 1975, but most tried to put a positive gloss on such events and avoided or ignored the reality.[67] As the vicious nature of the power struggle in the PRC was unveiled, and their *naïveté* exposed by the dramatic fall from power of the Maoist 'Gang of Four' shortly after Mao's death in 1976, their illusions were shattered.[68] Their blind enthusiasm ended, and they entered another phase of reflection. This time they focused themselves more upon trying to understand the society in which they lived.

In the meantime, the torch of reform lit by Governor Trench burnt more brightly as it was passed on to his successor, Sir Murray MacLehose, at the end of 1971. A career diplomat and a former political adviser to Governor Black, MacLehose knew Hong Kong but did not carry the heavy baggage of the colonial civil service.[69] He was much more sensitive to the benefits of projecting the right image of the government, which required changes, than respecting the norms and established practices of the colonial administration. He therefore took a much higher-profile approach as he built on the reforms started by Trench. A classic and particularly important example concerned the attempt to tackle bureaucratic corruption. This started under Trench when he introduced the Prevention of Bribery Ordinance in December 1970. However, it was MacLehose who publicly established the Independent Commission Against Corruption that caught the imagination of the public.[70] As will be explained in Chapter 14, the success of the anti-corruption campaign greatly enhanced the credibility of the government. When the 1970s drew to a close, the success of the anti-corruption campaign gave the people of Hong Kong, of whatever ethnic origins, something to be proud of for being its citizens.

At the same time, the economy was expanding at breakneck speed, which made its previously fast growth rate look modest. Per capita GDP grew by five times between 1971 and 1981, in comparison to 2.8 times in the preceding decade.[71] This produced a generation of self-made billionaires. It raised the profile and self-respect of the local Chinese. By the end of the 1970s, the most successful of the local Chinese entrepreneurs were joining the boards of British hongs, and some of their companies were overtaking the hongs as the premier business conglomerates of Hong Kong. If the successes of entrepreneurs like Li Ka-shing demonstrated to the local Chinese what the most able among them could do, the swelling of the ranks of the middle class, the spread of professional training and their maturing as middle managers gave them confidence and pride.[72] A Hong Kong way of life was becoming visible.

The rapid improvement in living standards and conditions and the changing attitudes of both society and government further led to the rise of a vibrant local popular culture. It was one that increasingly mixed ideas and techniques from Western music and movies with the local culture and concerns of everyday life. The musical genres which came out of this process generally combined three elements: concern for the plight of the common folk, resonance with Chinese heroic times and their characters, and a soft touch for personal liberation and romantic love.[73] The same happened with locally produced movies and, more importantly, television programmes. They departed from the earlier mainstream cultural productions, which were dominated by the more traditional Chinese art form, and those imported from Taiwan or the PRC.[74] This indigenisation of popular music, film and television programmes further reinforced the outlooks, aspirations and expressions of a steadily more distinctive culture.[75]

The popular culture that emerged was based on the Cantonese language, but its liveliness, vibrancy and readiness to borrow from other cultures also modified the language. By introducing new terms and usage, the Cantonese spoken in Hong Kong became recognisably different from the Cantonese then in use in Guangdong. This new Hong Kong culture was not only embraced by the younger generations but was also accepted by the older generations generally across the social classes. As a largely immigrant society in which many new fortunes were made in a generation or less, the class barrier against the spread of this new culture was in any event weak. Television, radio and popular music in particular, helped to break the barriers and promote its new popular culture.

Rising affluence also enabled its people to travel. Those who went overseas for holidays often acquired a point of reference for comparison. This helped them to put Hong Kong's progress in perspective, and gave them a sense of the great achievements that Hong Kong had made and of the idea that Hong Kong was a community with its own character.[76] Those who went to the PRC, particularly young students seeking to learn about 'mother China', found themselves confronted with a harsh reality. The PRC that they saw did not tally with the image of 'mother China' they had previously had. The backwardness and the imprimatur of Maoist rule could not but make an indelible impression on them. From first-hand experience, most Hong Kong visitors came to realise that despite the common ethnic and cultural background they, the Chinese of Hong Kong, were different from the Chinese of the PRC. They had different ways of and outlooks on life.

The differences between the two peoples were reinforced by the influx of illegal Chinese immigrants from 1978 to 1980. Although the Sino-British border was closed in 1950, the Hong Kong government operated on a fairly liberal basis towards illegal immigrants from China during most of the following three decades. In general, an illegal immigrant from China who reached the urban areas and settled there, either by being united with family members or by successfully obtaining gainful employment, would be permitted to stay and gain citizenship after seven years of residence.[77] This was popularly known as the 'touch base policy'. It was abandoned in 1980, when the sustained nature and scale of the influx was 'seen to be eroding the improvement in standards that the people of Hong Kong have worked so hard to achieve'.[78]

The scale of the influx, which amounted to over 400,000 people in a period of about three years, created problems with assimilation in the short term.[79] The overwhelming majority of the new immigrants were young male farmers from rural communes.[80] They had been cut off from the world and brought up in a Maoist ideology and thus found 'Hong Kong's pace of life and multicultural energies most perplexing' in the early days.[81] The difficulties they had in assimilating into Hong Kong society led to discrimination and mockery from the locally born, who created negative stereotypes of them, such as 'Ah Chan' and 'Dai Huen Chai', which quickly gained general currency through the mass media, particularly the television.[82] The presence of these new immigrants was at first seen by the more established residents as incongruent with their newly acquired middle-class way of living, though most of these new immigrants did get assimilated in due course. The ending of the 'touch base policy' and the gap between the established residents and the new immigrants thus created a sense of us – Hong Kong people – and them – country bumpkins from mainland China or Ah Chan. The recognition of this distinction was essential for the emergence of a Hong Kong identity, the existence of which became unmistakable by the beginning of the 1980s.[83]

In this process, the younger and mainly locally born, bred and educated generations played the primary role. The distinction between them and their mainland compatriots was clear. However, the older generations, themselves immigrants, also shared the experiences of the younger people, watched the same television programmes, listened to the same new indigenous music, and became, though to a lesser extent, noticeably different from their mainland compatriots.

The success and affluence of Hong Kong, which came to be driven increasingly by local capital and talents, also reduced the old gap between the expatriate and the Chinese communities. Social interactions between members of the two remained limited, but they were by then regularly working together in business and in government. The policy of localisation and the breaking of the colour bar for recruitment to the Administrative Service that Governor Young affirmed in 1946 finally produced senior ethnic Chinese officials in significant numbers. The percentage of local Chinese who reached the top level, at the directorate, reached 41 per cent in 1979 and 49 per cent in 1983.[84] The old privileges and arrogance of the expatriate British community were eroding, but it happened more by the local Chinese rising to the standard of living and achievements of the expatriates than by the expatriates actually losing ground. The antipathy of the pre-war era or the aloofness of the immediate post-war period that both communities held towards each other had by the early 1980s largely been replaced by something else.

What governed relations between the two communities was a tacit mutual acceptance of a parallel existence, while they shared a sense of pride in the success of Hong Kong.[85] The local Chinese community did not include the expatriates among themselves when they referred to 'we, the people of Hong Kong', but they did not specifically exclude them either. Westerners who adopted Hong Kong as a home were accepted by the local Chinese as fellow Hong Kong 'belongers' in its wider rather than its narrower sense, and they were expected to share only some of the core values inherent in the local identity.

The Hong Kong identity that emerged was based on a shared outlook and a common popular culture which blended traditional Chinese culture with that imported from overseas, with the influences of the USA, Britain and Japan being particularly noticeable. This shared outlook incorporated elements of the traditional Confucian moral code and emphasis on the importance of the family, as well as modern concepts like the rule of law, freedom of speech and of movement, respect for human rights, a limited government, a free economy, a go-getting attitude and pride in the local community's collective rejection of corruption.[86] A Hong Kong person of the early 1980s would identify with Hong Kong and, at the same time, feel at ease both with his Chinese heritage and, for those who claimed British nationality, with travelling on a British passport issued by the Hong Kong government.[87] However, he was 'not British or western (merely westernised)' and at the same time 'not Chinese in the same way that citizens of the People's Republic of China' were Chinese.[88] He belonged to Hong Kong and was intensely proud of it.

The emergence of this Hong Kong identity among Chinese residents at the beginning of the 1980s did not mean they no longer felt Chinese as well. A sense of identity is inherently a complicated and complex matter, as it ultimately relies on people in a community choosing to identify with a country or a territory, and it does not need to be totally exclusive. Given the lack of any serious attempt by the colonial government to turn its locally born ethnic Chinese citizens into yellow Englishmen or even require them to adopt British nationality, most people in Hong Kong were fairly relaxed about their nationality. Indeed, as a general practice, a locally born Chinese would be asked to choose between the British or Chinese nationality upon reaching the age of 18, when one was required by law to acquire an identity card. For someone born in Hong Kong, claiming Chinese nationality at this stage would not preclude one from changing one's mind in later life and registering as a British subject. The fact that one was born in Hong Kong was under British law sufficient to entitle the person to claim British nationality. This relaxed attitude of the colonial government allowed a local Chinese to have a dual sense of identity – feeling both a Hong Kong person and a Chinese person at the same time.

The Chinese identity that most residents of Hong Kong subscribed to in the early 1980s was a complex and convoluted one. Except for new immigrants who had not yet been assimilated, being Chinese in Hong Kong was primarily an ethnic and cultural affiliation and generally did not mean being a Chinese citizen or national of the PRC. To understand the meaning of being Chinese in Hong Kong, one needs to recognise that:

'China' was to the Chinese what Christendom was to the West. 'China' was ideology and religion. He or she who is a Chinese believes in China. But that is not all. To be Chinese, he or she has also to be part of China.[89]

On how to meet the last requirement there was no consensus. To some, the fact that this British Colony was 'a borrowed place living in borrowed time'[90] secured from China was sufficient proof that Hong Kong was a part of China. To others their own provincial origins in China, whether it meant being Cantonese, Shanghaiese, Taiwanese or something else, entitled them to claim to be part of China. A minority continued to identify with either of the two Chinese governments, in Beijing or in Taipei, which continued until the end of the 1980s to claim itself the sole legitimate government of China. Thus, feeling Chinese and at the same time developing a Hong Kong identity did not produce a crisis of identity in the early 1980s. As a result, when a Hong Kong person of Chinese origins referred to 'China' he was not always clear what he had in mind. Sometimes it meant China in a geographical or cultural sense, for which Hong Kong, Taiwan and Macao were deemed as much a part as the PRC. In other times it meant the mythical China that did not have a clearly defined territorial confine. On yet other occasions, it meant the PRC. The average Hong Kong person did not make a clear distinction between these concepts and did not refer to them consistently.

Chapter 14

The Making of a Colonial Paradox

British imperial rule in Hong Kong transformed itself from an improved version of the pre-war benevolent autocracy into a government that met all the requirements for the best possible government in the Chinese political tradition by the early 1980s.[1] The British did not set out to fulfil this Chinese aspiration. The method of delivering it, as prescribed by Confucius and his disciples over two millennia, namely the setting up of a government composed of Confucian gentlemen-officials, was irrelevant to the British. Nonetheless, building on the basis of its own record and responding steadily to changes after 1945, the government produced a paradox. While it remained an essentially British colonial administration, it also fulfilled the basic conditions for such a government, namely, efficiency, fairness, honesty, benevolent paternalism, and non-intrusion into the lives of ordinary people. This was an achievement that had no match in over two thousand years of China's history as a unified country, and could be rivalled only after Taiwan successfully transformed itself into a democracy in 1996.[2]

The Nature of British Colonial Rule

British colonial rule in Hong Kong was first and foremost meant to serve British interests. This basic consideration does not mean the British were opposed to their presence being beneficial to the local Chinese residents. Since Hong Kong was an imperial outpost intended primarily to promote trade and profit, the first concern of the colonial government was to maintain the best conditions for trade and economic growth at the lowest possible costs. Whether its particular system of governance met the requirements of the best possible government in China was in itself of little concern to the British. What did matter was to ensure the government should maintain stability, good order and a general environment for Hong Kong to flourish, mainly as an entrepôt for the first century, and as an industrial and exporting economy from the early 1950s to the early 1980s.

The British started a process of reform of the colonial administration seriously in the late 1960s, after its inadequacies were revealed by the social disturbances. It reflected in part the British acceptance of 'the wind of change' within the British Empire. It was also because the presence of a powerful and nationalistic regime in mainland China seeking the eventual retrocession of Hong Kong created in the colonial government what can be called an 'inhibited political centre'.[3] The colonial government increasingly exercised greater self-restraint domestically, despite its autocratic system, as it became aware that should it provoke a major anti-colonial movement it would risk its own existence, since the PRC would almost certainly intervene and Britain could not be sure of support from the outside world, including the USA.[4] This was the beginning of a process that would slowly but steadily transform the Hong Kong government into one highly responsive to public opinions.

Whether the changes started by Governor Trench should be seen as progressive or not depends on one's standpoint. As far as the government was concerned, reform was the most sensible, responsible and cost-effective way to protect the British interests that were the *raison d'être* for the continuation of British rule. This happened to require changes to bring the Crown Colony system to meet the standard of governance in a modern multi-ethnic metropolis in the late twentieth century without democratisation. In the process of this reform, the British eventually produced in Hong Kong an administration that met the five conditions of good government in the Chinese tradition. From the mid 1960s onwards, Trench, his successors and other senior officials saw the promotion of British profit and the welfare of the local Chinese community as complementary. The fact that the reforms produced a government beneficial to the local Chinese was welcomed by the British, as the conditions required to sustain British profits by then included making the ethnic Chinese part and parcel of a contented and affluent citizenry sharing the fruits of economic progress.

Among the five requirements for good government in the Chinese tradition, three of them were met within the first century of British rule. The impact of the Pacific War on British colonialism in Asia generally encouraged the Hong Kong government to improve on them, but they were in place before the war. They are the existence of a non-intrusive, efficient and fair government. The remaining two conditions, honesty and benevolent paternalism, were not really met until the end of the 1970s.

From its earliest days, the colonial government was largely non-intrusive, adopting a policy of benign neglect towards the Chinese. It was primarily concerned with maintaining the basic political and legal infrastructure for all residents. Although institutional discrimination existed against the Chinese before 1946, they were mostly passive provisions to encourage segregation rather than active measures that interfered with the lives of the ordinary Chinese. Since the fluid Chinese population in any event preferred to keep to themselves, their own lives were generally not disrupted by such legislation.

Active intrusion by the colonial government was in fact limited by its small size and the aloofness of many of its senior officials. Until as late as

1941, for example, the government had an establishment of 35 administrative officers, which meant merely 26 officers were available for running the administration at any one time after taking account of training and long home leaves in the era before the jet airliner.[5] Among them, the Secretary for Chinese Affairs, the Labour Officer and two District Officers were the only senior officials specifically responsible for the Chinese community.

The degree of intrusion also declined after the first 50 years or so of British rule. Colonial rule was at its most intrusive in the middle part of the nineteenth century, when poorly qualified magistrates often meted out summary justice against members of the Chinese community brought in front of them. It also became more intrusive than usual when it had to enforce sanitary control at the time of the bubonic plague in the 1890s. However, such intrusions need to be put in context. Those who suffered most from it were people who had had a brush with the law or had to deal with the police, district watchmen, the fire service, the sanitary department, licensing offices and registration of various kinds. Most Chinese residents in fact had little to do with the government. This remained the situation until the mid 1960s, when Governor Trench started the reform process.

The degree of government intrusion in colonial Hong Kong also needs to be compared with the conditions that prevailed in China. Political and social stability as well as the colonial government's non-reliance on direct taxation from land or labour put it in a good light in contrast to the heavy and often arbitrary taxation imposed in China, particularly during the Republican era when in one region 'taxes had been collected 74 years in advance'.[6] The creation of a totalitarian state that reached to the farthest parts of China after 1949 made the Hong Kong government appear even less intrusive. On the whole, British Hong Kong had a record of non-intrusion not rivalled by any government in the recorded history of China.

In terms of the efficiency requirement, the Hong Kong government also basically met this from its foundation. The colonial administration was small and simple but was efficient for what was required of it in the first century of British rule. The demands the local Chinese made of the government were minimal, because they were used to a system where formal government stopped at the county level,[7] and they were themselves a largely transient population. They were not used to and did not expect the colonial government to do much for them. Thus the local Chinese generally did not find the administration inefficient before the Pacific War.

After the war, the colonial administration steadily expanded in size and in scope. A Resettlement Department, for example, was created when the government realised that the recent influx of refugees would stay on a long-term basis, and it started to provide public housing to victims of disasters and the destitute in 1954.[8] By 1969, the government re-housed over 1.5 million people, out of a total population of about 4 million.[9] However inadequate and problematic Hong Kong's education system was in the immediate post-war decades, the government's success in physically building numerous schools and training the teachers to staff them in little over a decade could not but be deemed efficient.[10]

A legitimate question to ask is whether the riots of the mid 1960s proved that the government had failed in some significant ways. As explained in Chapter 13, public expectations in Hong Kong had risen by that time, and this was partly responsible for the non-politically motivated Star Ferry Riots of 1966, but the riots reflected more a frustration against the lack of communication between the people and the government than dissatisfaction over government inefficiency. Once Governor Trench invigorated the process to review the work of the government proactively after the end of the confrontation, reforms were introduced to redress administrative bottlenecks and improve efficiency.[11] The changes made on the basis of the MacKinsy Report (1972) were just the best-known example of this process.[12] With a massive expansion in the recruitment of specialists and professionals to join the administration, the government continued to earn a reputation for being both efficient and effective.

As far as fairness is concerned, the local Chinese came to feel satisfied before the centenary of British rule. This took time to materialise and, unlike the other two conditions, was not met shortly after Hong Kong came under British jurisdiction. In the nineteenth century, the government treated the local Chinese unfairly. But even such unfair and sometimes harsh treatments compared well with what the Chinese would have expected from officialdom across the border in their own country.

Notwithstanding racial and other prejudices, particularly before 1945, the British courts generally treated the Chinese brought in front of them according to the law of the time. If the alien nature of the British legal system provoked negative Chinese reactions at first, by the twentieth century 'the English spirit of the rule of law' came to be 'deeply admired' by many local Chinese.[13] Even left-wing Chinese critics of Hong Kong, who disliked it for being 'a commercial centre where there was no culture', admitted that the British 'colonists were mostly members of the Conservative Party [sic] who [would] invariably... abide by the law'.[14] Compared to the conditions prevailing across the border in China since 1841, the independent judiciary in Hong Kong became steadily better appreciated by the local people.

The fulfilment of three out of the five requirements of good government in the Chinese tradition enabled the Hong Kong government to enjoy the passive support of the local Chinese community, but it fell short of winning their loyalty, even less affection, in the first century of British rule. This was reflected in their failure to rally the local Chinese around the colonial government to defend the colony against the Japanese in 1941. The improvements made after Young restored civil government in 1946 on the one hand, and the rise of the radical Maoist regime on the Chinese mainland on the other, helped the colonial government to win greater popular support when it next faced a potential challenge to its survival in 1967. The overwhelming majority of the local people supported the colonial administration in defence of their way of life but only relatively few felt a sense of loyalty to it. The colonial government needed to meet the last two remaining conditions of a good government in the Chinese tradition, honesty and benevolent paternalism, before it finally became one that most residents of Hong Kong were proud to call their government.

Corruption, Credibility and Benevolent Paternalism

Before it could meet the two remaining requirements, the Hong Kong government had to tackle the problem of corruption and change its policy on social welfare. It was in the late 1960s that the government started to make a determined attack on corruption, and the economy became buoyant enough to sustain an expanding social welfare programme. The attack on corruption was critical to establishing the credibility of the government, while a high-profile approach to welfare helped to meet the condition of benevolent paternalism. They were undertaken not with a view to fulfilling the requirements of a good government in the Chinese tradition but because they were deemed sensible by policymakers at the time.

Although corruption had long existed in Hong Kong and there were a few senior officials, such as William Caine and Daniel Cardwell in the middle of the nineteenth century, whose probity was in serious question, the higher echelon of the government was not as a whole corrupt before 1941. The problem of corruption among senior officials declined after the first two to three decades of colonial rule as the general quality of senior officials improved.

The real break happened as a result of the introduction of the cadet officer scheme in 1861.[15] It had the effect of building a meritocracy from recruits who came from a professional background. The average cadet came from 'a solid, though not rich, upper middle-class family, went to a public school, but not to the most prestigious, and then went up to one of the older universities'.[16] He was not brought up with expensive tastes or habits but was, instead, instilled with a spirit that valued hard work and 'healthy recreations'.[17] After initial training, mainly in the Chinese language, he would be put on a fast track for promotion to a senior position that carried a generous remuneration package.[18] He and his colleagues formed the elite of the administration and came under strong peer group pressure to live up to the standard of behaviour expected of gentlemen in the Victorian and Edwardian eras.

A similar programme was introduced in 1904 for the recruitment of senior police officers as Police Probationers, sometimes informally called Police Cadets.[19] They were again selected on a competitive basis from candidates of similar backgrounds in the UK. Once a probationer had passed all the examinations associated with his training, he would be appointed to a senior position on generous terms.[20] Since he would start his career as Assistant Superintendent of Police, without first serving as a constable or inspector, he would not normally have worked in a local police station dealing with members of the public on a daily basis. Nor would he be involved in running squads of policemen or detectives. Instead, his main tasks were to discharge managerial or senior command responsibilities.

Like his cadet colleagues, police superintendents from the early twentieth century onwards belonged to the upper echelon of the administration. They were well provided for and were not normally directly exposed to situations conducive to taking bribes. Above all, they shared an *esprit de corps* as the elite of the government, distinctly separate from the functionaries or the lower order of the administration.

The government was not surprised that junior police officers and government runners, who were poorly paid and were usually recruited from the lower classes, would succumb to the temptation and become corrupt.[21] Petty corruption was rampant in the lower levels of the administration. A different standard and code of behaviour was expected of senior officials. The stiff class distinction of England was even more rigidly upheld in the colonial context. Cadets and other senior officials, including police superintendents, generally looked down on their underlings and considered it beneath them to fall to the same level of their underlings and get caught up with corruption, though this does not imply that none of them ever did.

The fact that most senior officials were in fact honest was, however, of little relevance to the ordinary Chinese residents. The latter did not normally deal with senior officials. They drew their conclusions on the basis of their contacts with government functionaries. The rampant corruption of petty officials was sufficient to project a popular image of widespread corruption within the bureaucracy.

While the government after 1945 made considerable improvements on almost all fronts over its pre-war record, it did not do so as far as corruption was concerned. Shortly after the restoration of civil government, it admitted that corruption was a serious problem.[22] In recognition of this, the government introduced for the first time a specific law, the Prevention of Corruption Ordinance, to deal with this problem in 1948.[23] Despite the personal antipathy of most governors and top officials towards corruption, they generally continued to look at it with a certain ambivalence, preferring to see it as more of a problem in the business world.[24]

Although another major step against corruption was taken in 1960, when a standing committee on corruption was created, the government still worked on the basis that it was 'largely confined to the Inspectorate and lower grades, though it does on occasion reach higher levels'.[25] A better understanding of the problem was, however, gained. It came to be recognised that corruption had become organised within government departments. However, as Governor Black observed, he did not believe a consensus would be in place to launch a full frontal attack on corruption until 'there were a particularly fragrant case, or series of cases, well known to the public where the offender or offenders had escaped punishment because of the inadequacy of our control'.[26]

Despite greater attention being paid to it, the problem of corruption deepened in the 1960s. Ironically, this was at least in part enhanced by the more progressive spirit of the post-war era. The old rigid barrier between senior and junior officers was eroded steadily after the war. This applied to the police in particular. The practice of recruiting police probationers ended.[27] From the early 1950s on, all new superintendents, or the gazetted officers, were appointed on the basis of promotion from the inspectorate, excepting a few who were transferred from other colonies. This was in general a positive change as it meant senior officers, at the rank of Assistant Superintendent and above, would have hands-on experiences in day-to-day police work, before taking on senior command or management positions. It enabled them to have a much better understanding of modern policing and encouraged bright junior policemen to distinguish themselves with a view to promotion to the higher posts. Since the inspectorate and the other ranks of the police remained widely corrupt, it meant an increasing number of superintendents who rose through the ranks by the 1960s had previously been involved with organised or syndicated corruption. For those thus tainted, they would not and, indeed, could not suddenly stop being corrupt upon promotion. Towards the end of the decade, corruption was reaching the upper echelons of the police.

It was Black's successor, Governor Trench, who made the fateful decision to deal with this problem earnestly. The old inherent problem in stamping out corruption in a common-law jurisdiction remained: it is a vicious circle. All corruption cases involve at least two parties, but since both parties have broken the law and are often 'satisfied', they share a common interest in keeping quiet about it and will not testify against each other in court.[28] Conviction is therefore extremely difficult. When this particular issue was reviewed at the beginning of the 1960s, the Solicitor General reminded the government of the importance of maintaining a balance between protecting the human rights of suspects and the need for draconian powers to make successful prosecutions.[29] Trench decided to tip the balance in favour of more draconian power, and the result was the Prevention of Bribery Ordinance of December 1970. Armed with such new powers, the police investigated the conduct of one of its chief superintendents, Peter Godber, up to then the most senior official under suspicion in the post-war era. It was this case that set off a chain of events resulting in a dramatic change in the public perception of the integrity of the government.

The investigation took two years to gather sufficient evidence for action to be taken against Godber, who had earned a reputation for being an efficient and courageous officer in the confrontation. As he had in the recent past been in command of the police at the airport and still had a pass for the restricted area when he came under investigation, Godber used his privileged access at the airport and fled for England. His escape turned out to be the 'particularly fragrant case' Governor Black envisaged a decade earlier, and inflamed public opinion. A 'fight corruption, catch Godber' public campaign, organised by local activists of the post-war generation, attracted wide general support.[30] By then, Trench had been succeeded by MacLehose as governor, who responded to this groundswell of public opinion by creating an Independent Commission Against Corruption (ICAC) in February 1974.

The foundation of the ICAC was a landmark event, though the arguments for doing so rather than allowing the Police Anti-Corruption

204

A MODERN HISTORY OF HONG KONG

Office to continue its work just after a change of the law finally enabled it to function effectively were not decisive at the time.[31] In retrospect, it turned out to serve Hong Kong's interest well as it was an astute political move that made the right psychological impact on the general public. In the local Chinese community there existed a widespread and well-entrenched idea that the colonial government was corrupt from the bottom right up to the very top, and that it would only, in a graphic local description, 'swat the flies, not catch the tigers'. The high-profile establishment of an independent commission answerable directly to the governor challenged this particular piece of local folklore. In time, it would create a new one, which marked the beginning of the government's break with the past when corruption was tolerated. In 1974, it was merely a highpoint in the campaign against corruption, but the public perception of the government changed as a result.

This institutional change was insufficient on its own to ensure the anti-corruption campaign would succeed. It did succeed because the government shared the public conviction that corruption was no longer acceptable. There was no resistance in the higher echelons because most if not all top officials were not themselves corrupt, and had no vested interests to protect. On the contrary, they saw the success of this campaign as crucial to the well-being of Hong Kong, since the Godber case had 'done so much to denigrate Hong Kong in the eyes of the world'.[32] The success of the ICAC depended on the extradition of Godber. This happened in 1975. Bringing him to justice with wide media coverage was critical in dispelling the popular belief that the government was corrupt to the core; it demonstrated the government's determination.

By around 1980, the back of syndicated or organised bureaucratic corruption was broken, and public opinion on this subject had changed fundamentally. Unlike the pre-Godber days, corruption was no longer tolerable, even though corruption by individuals or small groups continued covertly as it did in most societies.[33] The success of the anti-corruption campaign finally established the credibility of the colonial administration as an honest government.

The last requirement for a good government in the Chinese tradition, that of benevolent paternalism, was met in roughly the same period. Until the early 1950s, the colonial government had a policy of not feeding or housing the destitute, lest it would encourage even more of China's teeming millions to cross the border. This policy continued until a disastrous fire among squatter huts in Shek Kip Mei rendered 50,000 people homeless at Christmas 1953. It was this disaster that persuaded Governor Grantham that the large Chinese refugee population were in Hong Kong to stay.[34] An emergency public housing scheme was introduced in response. Once the pressure for emergency relief ended, this initiative was unceremoniously turned into a massive resettlement programme. It was not meant to be the start of a welfare programme but it was. In parallel to the housing scheme, the government introduced a rudimentary but efficient and universal health service for a nominal charge, which could be waived for the destitute.[35] This was complemented by the rapid expansion, albeit in a poorly planned and somewhat haphazard manner, of public education.

Despite these changes, the government continued to affirm in public its commitment to a non-interventionist policy in social as well as in economic matters. Governors Black and Trench, who shared the same basic career background and outlook as Grantham, upheld the approach of providing welfare without a formal welfare policy. They did not want to commit the government to a formal policy, as they were keen to keep the government's commitment limited to what it could prudently afford. Given Hong Kong's status as a Crown Colony, any welfare programme that might put an unbearable burden on the colonial treasury would put at risk Hong Kong's financial independence from London. The flexibility of not having a formal welfare policy made it easier for the government to keep spending within an affordable level in the event of an economic slowdown.

A break from this policy happened after MacLehose succeeded Trench as governor. A career diplomat, MacLehose did not share the outlook and reticence of his colonial service predecessors. To him 'welfare' was an appealing policy, provided it meant a system that was economically sustainable and whose provisions were not abused. He could afford to work on this new basis as the economy had by then taken off, and his tenure (1971–82) coincided with a period of very high economic growth. He governed at a time when rapid expansion in welfare provision was affordable without new taxes. He was also politically astute and was interested in projecting a positive image of himself and his government. He thus directed his administration to devise impressive welfare programmes and gave them massive publicity.

The flagship of MacLehose's welfare programme was the Ten Years Housing Scheme, which he boldly claimed 'would lead to the virtual disappearance of squatter areas, eliminate overcrowding and sharing in both private and public housing... and would also keep pace with the natural expansion of the population'.[36] Although it was presented as a new initiative, this massive project was in fact built on foundations laid by Trench. Nevertheless, it was MacLehose's high-profile approach that caught the imagination of the local Chinese. As real progress was made on the welfare front, including the introduction of a public assistance scheme and universal free education for nine years, the public perception of the government changed in the 1970s.

Since the local Chinese were not used to the idea of a welfare state, they did not feel they had a right to receive welfare. The new policy under MacLehose, with its astute publicity campaigns, gradually earned it a caring reputation. As welfare was provided on application only, their provision did not make the government appear to ordinary people to be intrusive into their lives either. Under MacLehose, the Hong Kong government finally met the condition of benevolent paternalism, about the same time as it established its credibility as an honest government.

The Best Possible Government in the Chinese Political Tradition

By around 1980, the Hong Kong government had cast off its pre-war colonial image, although it remained undemocratic. Its constitutional structure was still that of a Crown Colony. It continued to be run by bureaucrats and, like all governments, made specific policy blunders occasionally. However, as it limited its span of control more than its counterparts elsewhere, the Hong Kong government also made fewer mistakes than many other governments in the modern world. On the whole, it was efficient, effective, conscientious, fair, honest and responsive to public opinion. Its limited span kept it non-intrusive to the ordinary people. Its widespread though limited welfare provisions and its ability to stay one step ahead of public opinion most of the time had also made it paternal in the traditional Chinese sense. It is therefore reasonable to conclude that, after almost a century and a half, the British colonial government of Hong Kong reached the best standard of government practicable in the traditional expectations of the Chinese.

If it is paradoxical that in over two millennia only British colonial rule managed to create such a government in an essentially Chinese society, then it is a double irony that, shortly after it had done so, this same government found itself at risk of falling short of local public expectations. In the 1980s, a distinct Hong Kong political culture had emerged and local expectations had changed. The people of Hong Kong by then increasingly wanted democracy.[37] Meeting the standard of the ideal government in the Chinese tradition, which did not include democracy, soon became inadequate.

The non-development of democracy, despite the otherwise impressive achievements in governance delivered by the colonial government up to around 1980, requires an explanation. The oft-repeated view that it did not happen because the PRC government would not accept democratisation in Hong Kong is too simplistic.

In the early years of the PRC, the reverse was closer to the mark. As explained in Chapter 11, Mao Zedong's main concern over Hong Kong in the late 1940s was that the local Chinese should 'not [be] treated as inferior to others in the matter of taxation and a voice in the Government'.[38] Even in the midst of Grantham's long drawn-out manoeuvre to neutralise the Young Plan in the early 1950s, the Foreign Office was not worried that the PRC would object to democratic changes in Hong Kong.[39] Its concern was that Grantham's alternative would give the Chinese 'ample grounds for charging that the reforms [were] undemocratic'.[40]

There is no record in the declassified British archives of the 1950s of any British official or diplomat being told that the PRC would not tolerate democratisation in Hong Kong.[41] This remained the situation in 1962 when Governor Black explained in passing to the Colonial Office that there was 'emphatically no emotional popular support' for a movement towards self-government; he did not mention objections from the PRC.[42] If the PRC changed its views towards democratisation in Hong Kong shortly afterwards, it had no impact on British policymakers. There was little focused discussion on this matter in official circles. It was not until 1965 that the Hong Kong government seriously re-examined the question of local government in the colony. At that time, Governor Trench took the view that, while the PRC government would not welcome any initiative that would lead to independence for Hong Kong, it would not object to the reform of local government he had in mind.[43] It was an assessment with which the Foreign Office concurred.[44]

Nevertheless, in the middle part of the 1960s, the idea that the PRC would not tolerate democratisation in Hong Kong gained currency among senior British and Hong Kong officials. It was closely linked to their assessment that the PRC would not allow Hong Kong to become independent.[45] It was also based on the British colonial experience that the introduction of democratic government was part of a process to give a colony self-government leading eventually to independence. Putting the two together, some British officials came to assume that the PRC would object to democratic reforms in Hong Kong, though none had been told this by their Chinese colleagues.[46] With these issues being discussed only a few weeks before the outbreak of the confrontation of 1967 dominated the official agenda, this idea came to be taken as an article of faith afterwards.[47]

There were, in fact, two main reasons why democratic development did not happen in Hong Kong between 1947 and 1982. These were insufficient public demand from below and the existence of a government that had largely met public expectations. This last was the result of the colonial administration increasingly meeting the conditions of good government in the Chinese tradition. The two factors mutually reinforced each other.

When Britain finally abandoned Governor Young's modest proposals for political reform in 1952, the first major post-war economic slowdown had hit the territory and Chinese refugees struggling to make a living had swollen Hong Kong's population.[48] Furthermore, most of the new arrivals had just escaped from political chaos and bad government in China. Their top priority was to feed themselves and their families, and they had little incentive to become involved in politics. By the mid 1960s, when there was considerably less destitution and a locally raised generation had come of age, demands for greater participation grew.[49] However, a huge gap separated the government from the governed. Most people were unaware that the government was actually increasingly prepared to respond to public demands. Then fate, or rather the confrontation, intervened.

After the disturbances, the government took the lead to improve the channels of communication and introduced City District Officers. Subsequently, public demands for participation rose. The government responded by opening even more channels, eventually building up a wide network of advisory committees and district boards to provide scope for increasing public participation.[50] The Hong Kong government's approach to meeting its local people's political aspirations has been described as an 'administrative absorption of politics'.[51] This involved 'the co-option of established and emergent Chinese elite into the colonial regime'.[52] In fact, public demands for a greater role in the management of their own affairs were fairly modest. Up to the early 1980s, they could be and were met without democratisation.

Three factors were mainly responsible for this extraordinary development:

- the irony of maintaining a colonial administration in an international city in an era when imperialism had become a nasty word;
- the existence of a healthy democracy responsive to world opinion in the metropolitan country that supervised the colonial government. This meant that while the Hong Kong government enjoyed power that would allow it to run the territory as a police state, it could not abuse such power. The watchful eyes of London and the rest of the world were on it.[53] And, finally,
- the presence of a powerful government in the PRC with clear irredentist ambitions, which heightened Hong Kong's vulnerability.

These three factors together produced the 'inhibited political centre' effect described above. It was a powerful force to ensure good and responsive government in the absence of democracy.

In time, such an awareness became an integral part of the Hong Kong government's ethos. As one retired senior civil servant recounted, between the 1950s and 1980s there gradually emerged a common wish to transform 'benevolent authoritarianism to wider consultation and a concern with achieving "consensus government"'.[54] With such an attitude, and the expanding network for collecting and responding to public opinion, the government avoided public agitation for democratisation. Such a demand would have normally been expected as Hong Kong transformed itself into a prosperous and well-educated community in the 1970s.[55] In an important sense, the people of Hong Kong did not do so because they did not need to demand democratisation. They were already enjoying many of the benefits usually associated with a working democracy – freedom, the rule of law, the protection of human rights, stability and the existence of a government responsive to their views.[56]

What prompted the people of Hong Kong to desire democratisation in the 1980s was the opening of negotiations between Britain and China over their future. With their right to direct participation in the talks denied, they became deeply frustrated and concerned about their own future. This drove them out of the complacence inherent in having as good a government as possible in the Chinese tradition. It might be too late to get the local people a seat at the negotiating table, but it was not too late to clamour for the democratisation that would give them a say in the future governance of the territory. The ultimate irony must be that, as will be examined in Chapter 16, it was the Chinese government in Beijing that firmly denied democracy to the people of Hong Kong when the British colonial administration was finally ready to democratise.

Part IV

Securing the Future

Chapter 15

Fateful Decisions

Having stood firm and held their ground during the confrontation of 1967, the British and the Hong Kong governments then re-examined the long-term future of the colony. In the late 1960s, Governor Trench took the view that:

- Britain had to 'recognise that Hong Kong's future must eventually lie in China and that our objective must be to attempt to negotiate its return, at a favourable opportunity, on the best terms obtainable for its people and for our material interests there';
- 'Withdrawal should not be contemplated' until Britain could 'negotiate terms that would take care of our responsibilities towards the people or our material interests';
- Britain 'should look for a suitable opportunity to negotiate our withdrawal with China, as soon as a more moderate regime emerges there', as it was 'important to do this before the economy of the Colony starts to run down in the 1980s'; and
- in the meantime, Britain 'should show firmly that we intend to maintain our position there, giving no indication that we contemplate withdrawal'.[1]

British policymakers had by then gone further than the Cabinet's decision in late 1949 that did not rule out, at some distant future date, Britain having to negotiate with the PRC over Hong Kong's future. They also moved one small but significant step further from the position taken when Black was governor (1958–64). Black thought that 1997 was a 'terminal date' for British jurisdiction and it was 'vital for Hong Kong's stability that there should be no official or authorised pronouncement on Hong Kong's future until and unless this became clearly unavoidable'.[2]

The real break of the late 1960s was coming to terms with the need to take the initiative to open negotiations when the radical Maoist regime gave way to a more moderate one in the PRC. In reality, there was little that the British could do while Mao continued to dominate Chinese politics.

It was only after the extremist policies of the Cultural Revolution finally ended with the death of Mao and the fall of the 'Gang of Four' in 1976 that politics in the PRC took on a new direction.[3] This direction was one

A MODERN HISTORY OF HONG KONG

of pragmatism and relative moderation with clear emphasis being put on revitalising the economy. It allowed relations with Britain to improve. By the late 1970s, China had changed sufficiently for Governor MacLehose to give public blessing to the Xinhua News Agency's presence for the first time. In October 1978, he attended the PRC's national day celebration.[4] The British were beginning to wonder whether a moderate government in the PRC with which Britain could negotiate Hong Kong's future was emerging.

Prelude to Negotiations

The year 1979 proved to be a crucial one in Hong Kong's history.[5] An official visit by MacLehose to Beijing heralded the beginning of a process that led to the opening of formal negotiations between Britain and the PRC in September 1982. At that time, MacLehose's intention was more to test the water than to start negotiations. However, although the visit received wide coverage in the media, very few people recognised its real significance.

The visit originated in an invitation by the Chinese minister for foreign trade, Li Qiang. The Chinese intended to use it to improve Sino-Hong Kong relations generally and, in particular, to enhance Hong Kong's contribution to the PRC's programme of 'four modernisations'. MacLehose had an additional idea: he wanted to find out the PRC's real design for Hong Kong's future.

Aware of the delicacy of such an operation, MacLehose opted to keep his intentions secret. It was to be a trial balloon. In Hong Kong he consulted Sir Yuet-keung Kan, a particularly trusted senior non-official member of the Executive Council, but kept Kan's colleagues in the dark. Among the civil servants, only David Wilson, his political adviser on secondment from the diplomatic service, was closely involved. MacLehose also informed the chief secretary, Sir Jack Cater, but does not seem to have consulted him. In the wider context of British policymaking, the key figures engaged in the planning were Sir Edward Youde, former ambassador to Beijing and at that time deputy under-secretary supervising Far Eastern affairs at the Foreign Office, and Sir Percy Cradock, then ambassador in Beijing. The operation received the blessing of Foreign Secretary David Owen.[6]

MacLehose cleverly devised his bold initiative. He had a general idea of what the Chinese intended to derive from his visit and reasonable grounds to believe that they would discuss Hong Kong's prosperity and value to the PRC. He planned to use such a discussion to raise the question of individual land leases in the New Territories.[7] These were all due to expire three days before the New Territories lease itself. He hoped to persuade the Chinese that if they could do something to blur the 1997 deadline, this would sustain confidence in Hong Kong, which would then be able to continue to assist the PRC's modernisation.[8]

A positive Chinese response would imply their consent to a non-offensive British effort to amend the Royal Order in Council of 1898 on which the extension of British jurisdiction in the New Territories depended. If successful, this scheme would remove the terminal date on the future of the New Territories, and therefore of Hong Kong, without provoking the PRC to take a nationalistic stand. The latter would be unavoidable if either side raised the question of the New Territories' lease itself. The success or failure of the MacLehose initiative depended on four factors:

- whether the Chinese leaders understood the subtle differences between the Crown and New Territories leases;
- whether they would treat the two as being distinct and separate if they understood;
- whether it would be possible to produce the perfect interpretation required to ensure that the subtle but vital differences were not lost in translation; and, most important,
- whether the Chinese were so committed to achieving their economic objectives that they would formally agree to put aside a matter involving what they saw as national dignity and integrity until an undefined date in the future.

It is important that Youde, Cradock and Wilson, who were among the best China hands in the Foreign Office, all went along with MacLehose's idea.[9] The British did not fully understand Chinese feelings about Hong Kong – which remained essentially the same as those captured in Kitson's Isle of Wight analogy of 1946.[10]

The longest-serving governor since Grantham, MacLehose by this time dominated Hong Kong's politics. He no longer felt he always needed the advice of his aides and was becoming increasingly autocratic. He seemed to suffer from what Grantham had privately called the long-serving colonial governor syndrome – excessive self-confidence produced by being 'next to the Almighty' for too long.[11] It gave people whose subordinates had reassured them of their infinite wisdom every day for many years a sense of infallibility. MacLehose also felt a sense of responsibility to the people under his charge. He was aware of the delicacy of the subject matter, but his great self-confidence and desire to crown his governorship with an historic achievement clouded his judgement.

MacLehose's personal role and the sense of responsibility shared by those involved were not the only factors, but they were the most important. In 1979, some people in business circles began to express concerns about Hong Kong's future.[12] Because only 18 years remained before 1997, the time was approaching for banks to consider altering their usual 15-year mortgage term. However, it was a good two years before the banks actually had to decide, and Hong Kong operated on the basis of five-year money back investments. On the whole, Hong Kong was unconcerned about its future. The local stock market indicator, the Heng Seng Index, increased from 495 at the end of 1978 to 879 in 1979. Even more telling, from a base index of 100, domestic property prices continued to rise to 121 in 1979 and further to 148 in the following year, before dropping in 1982.[13] It was only then, three years later when formal negotiations began, that the '1997 factor' emerged and had a significant impact on economic confidence and performance.[14]

MacLehose and his colleagues planned a pre-emptive strike. They took the initiative because they shared a sense of 'moral responsibility' towards the local inhabitants. To sit on their hands and do nothing about the future of the more than five million people under their charge was simply unacceptable. They felt that the responsible thing to do was to seek a solution before a crisis developed: a crisis would limit the options available to them and, by implication, to the people of Hong Kong. It never occurred to them that they should have sought the views of the people with whose future they were dealing.

This might seem to be incredibly arrogant and presumptuous: but they acted as paternal figures and thought they were doing so in the best interests of the people of Hong Kong. Although most of these ethnic Chinese were British subjects by birth, British officials did not regard them in the same light as they did the citizens of the British Isles. Indeed, the officials' sense of 'moral obligation' to the people of Hong Kong is indicative of this mentality. If the British officials had thought of Hong Kong's British subjects as British rather than Chinese, they would have spoken of their obligations rather than their 'moral obligations' to them.

At that time, the policymakers further believed that with the pragmatic Deng Xiaoping in charge of the PRC, Hong Kong, the metaphorical goose, had the best chance of getting what it wanted. This was a stay of execution in return for producing more and bigger golden eggs for the PRC.[15] Except for the conviction of MacLehose, who enjoyed the support of his senior diplomatic colleagues, as yet Britain had no compelling reason to take a bold initiative.

While MacLehose's visit was presented to the public as very successful, his attempt to find a solution for Hong Kong's future backfired and turned into a disaster. When the Chinese Foreign Ministry learned of his intentions, it was taken by surprise. According to a Chinese insider, the Foreign Ministry specifically asked the British not to raise the issue when they met Deng Xiaoping.[16] At that time, Deng had not yet firmly established himself as the paramount leader, but he was assiduously consolidating his power and took the official position of vice-premier.[17] In any event, nobody had briefed him of MacLehose's intention. In the meeting, Deng said:

> It has been our consistent view that the People's Republic of China has sovereignty over Hong Kong while Hong Kong also has its own special position. A negotiated settlement of the Hong Kong question in the future should be based on the premise that the territory is part of China. However, we will treat Hong Kong as a special region. For a considerable length of time, Hong Kong may continue to practise its capitalist system while we practise our socialist system.[18]

MacLehose used this opening to raise the question of the Crown leases, which seem to have been confused in interpretation with the New Territories lease. Wilson interfered to correct the mistake and this annoyed

Deng. Deng responded by asking the governor to tell investors in Hong Kong to put their hearts at ease, but reiterated that the PRC would recover Hong Kong.[19] In line with PRC practice, once the most senior leader has spoken, no one contradicts him.[20] MacLehose and his colleagues' subsequent discussions with other Chinese leaders produced no softening of Deng's stand.

On his return to Hong Kong, MacLehose put the best gloss on this secret fiasco and skilfully encouraged the media to produce an optimistic illusion. Retrospective popular belief in Hong Kong and most accounts do not do justice to MacLehose. They generally charge him with either lying or being economical with the truth about his meeting with Deng.[21] They accuse MacLehose of omitting half of Deng's message – that the PRC would recover Hong Kong – and of merely reporting that investors had nothing to fear. The truth is more complicated. The day after his return, MacLehose made a public statement, in part of which he said:

> You know the long-standing Chinese position on Hong Kong, that it is part of China and a problem that will be solved when the time is ripe. But the point that was repeatedly stressed to us at all levels was the importance which the Chinese leaders attach to the value of Hong Kong, to the contribution that it could make to the modernisation programmes, to the importance of maintaining investment and confidence in Hong Kong, and of increased Hong Kong investment in China. Indeed Vice-Premier Deng Xiaoping formally requested me to 'ask investors in Hong Kong to put their hearts at ease'; he also asked for encouragement of investment in Guangzhou [sic] Province and the rest of China.[22]

In the rest of his press statement, by emphasising the good news, MacLehose effectively encouraged the journalists and local people to focus on the more positive side of his visit. He did not omit the bad news: he gave it almost by way of a preamble, and the media and the people of Hong Kong preferred to ignore it. Their response to Deng's message of assurance almost amounted to euphoria.[23] They did not want to worry about the future. They chose to celebrate the good news and avoid studying the governor's full statement carefully. This reflected the mentality of the people at that time.

Cruel as it was to let the local people continue to live in a fool's paradise, the governor must have deemed it irresponsible to set off a panic by being candid. A panic before working out a plan to pre-empt such an eventuality might have gravely undermined public confidence and thus damaged the economy. It is unclear whether or not MacLehose also felt concerned about the impact on his personal reputation.

Understandably, this disappointed the British. In the two following years they took every opportunity to probe the Chinese attitude further. The Chinese did not wish to give away anything while they were working out their Hong Kong policy. They kept the initiative in their own hands.

The one result MacLehose's visit delivered was to put Hong Kong on the Chinese political agenda.[24] Deng Xiaoping had thought about Hong Kong and about the reunification of China, but until then he had not put the two together.[25] Hitherto, his thinking had mainly been about how to utilise Hong Kong to the full to support the PRC's modernisation. With respect to unification, Deng had Taiwan in mind.

When MacLehose visited, Deng had just made a major foreign policy breakthrough that promised to provide an opportunity to resolve the Taiwan issue. This was the reaching of an agreement in December 1978 to normalise relations with the USA.[26] It involved terminating the US defence treaty with the Republic of China or Taiwan in a year's time.[27] This meant that the USA would remove its Seventh Fleet, which had been a major obstacle in the way of the PRC gaining control of Taiwan since June 1950. From Beijing's point of view, this heightened threat might persuade Taipei to respond to China's wooing.[28]

These endeavours culminated in one of Deng's close political allies, Ye Jianying, issuing a nine-point statement in September 1981. An intensive campaign to elicit a positive response from Taipei followed but hit a brick wall.[29] Before the end of the year, Deng decided to alter the PRC's priority in the unification plan. He now wanted to take advantage of the British initiative over Hong Kong, implying a willingness to compromise. He resolved to seek the return of Hong Kong and use it as an example to persuade Taiwan to rejoin mother China.

Though it was originally devised with Taiwan in mind, he thus applied the idea of 'one country, two systems' to Hong Kong. Its genesis can be traced to Ye's statement. This pronounced that, 'after reunification of the country, Taiwan could become a Special Administrative Region, enjoy a high degree of autonomy and keep its armed forces'.[30] It adds that 'the central government would not interfere in the local affairs of Taiwan'.

The PRC rebuilt its bureaucratic infrastructure to deal with Hong Kong in late 1978, when Deng planned to make the most of Hong Kong for the modernisation of the country. He entrusted this matter to a close colleague and veteran 'Hong Kong hand', Liao Chengzhi. In 1978, Liao had already been rehabilitated from being a victim of the Cultural Revolution to membership of the Communist Party's Central Committee.[31] He became Director of the Hong Kong and Macao Affairs Office (HKMAO) under the State Council, which enjoyed ministerial rank. Under Deng's supervision, he was largely responsible for Hong Kong affairs until his death in 1983.[32]

Liao's two principal assistants were Li Hou and Lu Ping, who later became closely involved in the formal negotiations between the PRC and Britain, and in the drafting of a Basic Law for Hong Kong. Until 1981, the focus of HKMAO's work was on building up a broad united front in Hong Kong rather than on working out a scheme for its return. It is impossible to say with certainty whether the PRC on its own would have raised the Hong Kong question later in the 1980s. However, it is beyond doubt that the PRC's decision to tackle the issue was a reaction to the British initiative.

The CCP Politburo made the first major decisions on Hong Kong during a meeting in March 1981. It decided to recover sovereignty in 1997, ensure Hong Kong would continue to serve the PRC's economic and political interests, and devise an appropriate arrangement to fulfil the first two requirements.[33] Over the rest of the year, Liao and his office tried to work out the details on the basis of this Politburo decision. However, there was resistance from within the top leadership to the suggestion that the idea of 'one country, two systems' should apply to Hong Kong.

Li Xiannian, a senior leader who headed the party's Foreign Affairs Leading Small Group, was the most ardent opponent. He felt that permitting a capitalist enclave to continue within the PRC would leave the Communist revolution incomplete. He also worried that it might become the first step towards the restoration of capitalism. Others suggested exploring the option of turning Hong Kong into a socialist society.[34] In the end, Deng, who had by then fully established himself as paramount leader, prevailed over his colleagues. To him, the starting point was the reality in the PRC. To his mind, since the PRC had both 'a Hong Kong problem and a Taiwan problem', the only way out was 'to seek a peaceful resolution' by implementing the idea of 'one country, two systems'.[35] He assured his colleagues that tolerating capitalism in Hong Kong would not affect the upholding of socialism in the PRC. Deng had intended the 'one country, two systems' policy to benefit, not undermine, Communist Party rule in the PRC.

By January 1982, Deng had carried his colleagues with him, and the Chinese government was therefore ready to respond to the gentle prodding of the British. It did so during a visit by the Lord Privy Seal Humphrey Atkins, who was responsible for Hong Kong in the Foreign Office. Premier Zhao Ziyang told Atkins that the PRC had evolved general plans for Hong Kong, which would maintain its prosperity and safeguard the PRC's sovereignty over it.[36] The British were also advised to consult Ye's nine-point statement for Taiwan. Since Atkins had instructions to enquire into Chinese intentions for Hong Kong and to prepare for a visit the following autumn by the Prime Minister, Margaret Thatcher, he responded positively. The ground was now clear to open negotiations.

At that stage, however, the Chinese had not worked out more than the basic framework for their Hong Kong policy. For the following nine months, Liao headed an interdepartmental task group to turn the general principle laid down by Deng into a clear policy. The Chinese appeared to wish to improve their understanding of Hong Kong by inviting a stream of prominent Hong Kong citizens to visit Beijing. In reality what they wanted was to persuade the Hong Kong visitors to help to ensure the continued prosperity of Hong Kong on the basis that it would be handed over to the PRC.[37] Whatever most Hong Kong visitors had in mind when accepting the invitations, most lost their resolution to speak frankly in the presence of Chinese leaders who did not welcome negative comments about the prospect of a Chinese takeover.[38]

When three eminent members of Hong Kong's Executive Council led by Sir Sze-yuen Chung spoke their minds at a later stage, Deng humiliated them.[39] He dismissed their positions in Hong Kong society, told them they represented no one but themselves and stressed that the Chinese leadership knew what Hong Kong really wanted.[40] This exercise of inviting influential Hong Kong figures to visit Beijing was standard practice in the Chinese Communist United Front.[41] The PRC government sought to win them over and increase its influence in Hong Kong, which would strengthen its position in the forthcoming negotiations with the British.

By August 1982, a month before Thatcher's planned visit, Liao's group produced a draft paper and submitted it to the Politburo. The paper contained 12 points, mostly on arrangements to maintain Hong Kong's stability and prosperity, but also included measures to uphold public confidence. It formed the basis for discussions among the top leaders. The paper's final draft after Thatcher's visit underlined the importance of protecting Chinese sovereignty over Hong Kong.[42] It also became the Chinese team's basic brief for formal negotiations with Britain.[43]

The Sino-British negotiations (1982–4)

Margaret Thatcher's September 1982 visit to Beijing was originally meant to reciprocate Premier Hua Guofeng's visit to London in 1979. It took on new significance after Atkins' visit early in the year. Thatcher now toughened Britain's position over Hong Kong, since she felt both her personal standing and Britain's position in the world had been greatly enhanced as a result of the Falklands war.[44]

She planned to make a stand in the first instance on the grounds that treaties protected British sovereignty over Hong Kong island and the tip of the Kowloon peninsula.[45] The foreign secretary of the day, Francis Pym, did not play a significant role, for he did not enjoy the prime minister's confidence or respect.[46]

The debates among the British policymakers focused on what Britain could hope to achieve and the best way to approach the Chinese. The British based their position on the understanding that Hong Kong was militarily indefensible and that the permanently ceded territories were not viable without the New Territories.[47] Thus, reverting the whole territory's sovereignty in 1997, in exchange for terms most acceptable to the British government and to the people of Hong Kong, was a matter of a negotiated settlement. To Thatcher, it meant 'continued British administration of the entire Colony well into the future'.[48] The British did not fully understand the strength of Chinese feelings about Hong Kong.

Deng Xiaoping defined the Chinese government's position. To him there were three issues: the question of sovereignty; how China would administer Hong Kong after 1997 to maintain its prosperity; and how to ensure an undisturbed transition.[49] He was absolutely rigid over the question of sovereignty. While he desired an agreement for cooperation with Britain and valued highly Hong Kong's prosperity and stability, he refused to achieve them by making any concession over sovereignty. The old anti-imperialist jingoism of the Communist movement in its early days affected Deng. He was determined to use Hong Kong to wipe out China's humiliation by the West in the preceding century.

To his mind, making any concession over Hong Kong's sovereignty would put him in the same category as those he called traitors. Deng felt very strongly that if the PRC's resumption of sovereignty over Hong Kong would bring about cataclysmic results, then the PRC 'would courageously face up to this catastrophe'.[50] At heart, he did not believe Hong Kong's prosperity could only continue under British administration, and was confident that the PRC could somehow successfully take it over even without British cooperation.[51] Thatcher's bottom line, which was a kind of leaseback arrangement, was unacceptable to Deng.

When Thatcher visited Beijing in September, she affirmed that Hong Kong's prosperity depended on confidence, which in turn required continued British administration.[52] She tried to entice the Chinese to accept her proposal. She did this by stressing that she would consider the question of sovereignty if they agreed to an arrangement that was acceptable to the British Parliament and to the people of Hong Kong.

The Chinese did not know enough about how Hong Kong worked to see the force of her argument, which they in any event did not accept. Deng stated the Chinese position, which was that the PRC would recover Hong Kong in 1997 and make suitable arrangements to assure its prosperity.[53] He rejected the British position, particularly the validity of the treaties. He said that he would allow a year or two to reach an agreement with Britain but would then announce a unilateral solution should the negotiations prove fruitless.[54]

The PRC government under Deng was by then determined to have its way. It was so confident of its ability to force the British to accept its position that it leaked the gist of the 12-point policy paper to the Hong Kong media. This was even before formal discussions with Thatcher began.[55] This public statement that sovereignty over Hong Kong belonged to China and was not negotiable demonstrated how rigidly the Chinese government held this position.

The main achievements of Thatcher's visit were to open negotiations over Hong Kong's future and to make known to each other their respective views. Apart from the common wish to maintain stability and prosperity in Hong Kong, a great gap separated the two. If there had been any illusion that subsequent negotiations would be anything but tough, it was shattered.

In Hong Kong the mood changed in 1982. Once it was clear that the Chinese government was devising a policy on Hong Kong's future, an air of anxious anticipation prevailed. Sir Sze-yuen Chung, the Executive Council's unofficial leader, greeted MacLehose's successor as governor, Sir Edward Youde, with a clear request when he took office in May. Chung voiced the public wish that the new governor should put the future of Hong Kong on the top of his agenda, and maintain public confidence while he resolved the issue.[56] The local people had very mixed views on the subject.

On the one hand, Chinese nationalist writings and Communist propaganda had made most local residents believe that the British acquired Hong Kong through the so-called 'opium wars' and that colonialism was inherently bad. They felt they should be proud of being Chinese and should desire the early departure of the British 'imperialists'. On the other hand, the idea of being handed over to a Communist regime, whose atrocious record some had experienced first-hand and others knew of through relatives and friends, terrified them. The effect of having as good a government as possible in the Chinese tradition was being felt in Hong Kong. Most of them had seen the tremendous differences between the Hong Kong and the Chinese governments at work.

The economic miracle of post-war Hong Kong had also given them vested interests to protect. They had a way of life different from that in the PRC. Only a handful dared to say it publicly, but the overwhelming majority clearly did not want a PRC takeover. However, most were realistic enough to recognise that independence was not an option, for the PRC would never accept it. What they hoped for was similar to Thatcher's bottom line – a kind of leaseback arrangement. Instead of attempting to control their own destiny actively, they responded in the first instance as they had always done. They looked to the British and the Hong Kong governments to secure their future.

Most Hong Kong citizens naïvely thought that Deng's pragmatism would prevent the Chinese leaders' irrational reactions based on nationalism from destroying Hong Kong – the goose that was laying the golden eggs. They were themselves affected by Chinese nationalism, but could not believe that the Chinese leaders would put nationalism above Hong Kong's economic value. They therefore watched Thatcher's visit with intense interest. They became very jittery about their future when they saw Thatcher failing to deliver an upbeat report, as MacLehose had done in 1979. The stock market, the property market and the value of the local currency reflected their hidden fears.[57] Within ten days of Thatcher leaving China, Hong Kong's stock market had lost 25 per cent of its value and, within a month, the Hong Kong dollar had depreciated by 12 per cent. Nevertheless, most people in Hong Kong continued to hope that a diplomatic miracle would somehow be possible and an acceptable agreement eventually reached. This latent sense of optimism or *naïveté* was an important element of Hong Kong's resilience as it entered a period of considerable uncertainty.

The so-called first phase of negotiations defined the basis on which to conduct the talks and set out the agenda.[58] It lasted from October 1982 to June 1983. To the Chinese, the object of the exercise was to secure British cooperation to maintain stability and prosperity in Hong Kong. Since the Chinese refused to accept the validity of all three treaties that governed Hong Kong, they declined to discuss its sovereignty. They simply ignored the convention in international law by which a territorial cession implemented by a treaty remained valid unless and until superseded by a new one.[59] Before getting down to serious negotiations, the Chinese demanded that the British acknowledge their sovereignty over Hong Kong. This was a precondition. The British resisted it. Ambassador Cradock debated repeatedly with Vice-Foreign Minister Zhang Wenjin, and later with his successor, Yao Guang, but there was no real progress for eight months.[60]

In the meantime, the PRC's policymaking establishment and propaganda machine shifted into high gear. Under Liao Chengzhi, Chinese officials revised the 12 points and, as part of their United Front work, released more and more details to the media of their blueprint for a post-1997 Hong Kong.[61] In December 1982, the Chinese National People's Congress (NPC) also passed a new constitution, which contained an article intended for Hong Kong, Taiwan and Macao. Article 31 specifically provided for the establishment of 'special administrative regions when necessary'.[62] Thus, as diplomatic talks ground to a halt, the Chinese seized the initiative to shape Hong Kong's future. By spring 1983, Cradock had concluded that Britain was facing 'the danger that we could be locked out of meaningful discussion, while Hong Kong's fate was decided, and promulgated, in Peking'.[63]

It took a series of what Cradock called 'finesses' to overcome or set aside the many areas of major disagreement in the Sino-British talks, which lasted until September 1984. The first was a letter from Thatcher to Premier Zhao in which she slightly modified her previous position. She did not formally accept the PRC's precondition of Chinese sovereignty, but wrote that if the people of Hong Kong accepted the outcome of the negotiations, she 'would be prepared to recommend to Parliament that sovereignty over the whole of Hong Kong should revert to China'.[64]

From China's point of view, Thatcher's démarche – delicate policy and diplomacy – meant that the British had accepted the precondition in disguise.[65] Since the negotiations were only about practical arrangements, the Chinese interpreted the British prime minister's undertaking as implying that she no longer contested whether or not the precondition was acceptable.[66] Given their own experiences of the rubber-stamping NPC, the Chinese leaders believed that the British Parliament would accept an agreement. The gap that originally separated the two sides appeared to have been bridged when Deng decided to use Thatcher's letter to let the British climb down with a semblance of dignity. This was to secure their cooperation in transitional matters.[67] To the British it was finesse, but to the Chinese it was British capitulation. As a result, the Chinese allowed the negotiations to enter a second phase in July 1983. Only then did detailed discussions on matters of substance start.

The two governments thus assembled their negotiating teams. The Chinese team consisted of diplomats from the Foreign Ministry's Western European Department, a legal adviser, Lu Ping of HKMAO and Li Jusheng, a deputy director of the Xinhua News Agency in Hong Kong. Its leader was Vice-Foreign Minister Yao Guang, who was later replaced by Assistant Foreign Minister Zhou Nan.

On the British side, Cradock headed the team until his retirement at the end of 1983, at which point Ambassador Sir Richard Evans took over from him. Governor Youde, Hong Kong's political adviser Robin MacLaren, four diplomats from the embassy and the Hong Kong government's main interpreter supported the British leader. There was an unspoken understanding in British and Hong Kong circles that Governor Youde would represent Hong Kong. However, when Youde confirmed this in a press interview, the Chinese government challenged his role. The Chinese Foreign Ministry then issued a repudiating statement saying that Youde did not represent Hong Kong and was acceptable to the PRC only as a member of the British delegation.[68] The PRC government considered the negotiations to be strictly between itself and the British government.

The people of Hong Kong took no part in the negotiations: they had no elected representative to speak for them. Nonetheless, their views and concerns were constantly conveyed to the British team. Under the leadership of the highly conscientious and utterly incorruptible Sir Sze-yuen Chung, the unofficial members of the Hong Kong Executive Council tried to fill the void.[69] The governor relied on Chung and his colleagues as confidential advisers. Although they were mostly from business or professional backgrounds, their fellow citizens basically shared their preferences for the outcome of the negotiations. Chung also felt a personal sense of responsibility to his fellow citizens and to his place in history. With Governor Youde's support, they were briefed and consulted regularly in the course of the negotiations. They actively involved themselves in internal debates and played a significant role in working out Britain's policy.[70]

Although the PRC government openly dismissed the idea of a 'three-legged stool', and thus denied Hong Kong a direct role in the negotiations, it nevertheless claimed to represent the local people. Just as the talks were entering the second phase in July 1983, the Chinese government appointed Xu Jiatun to become its de facto representative in Hong Kong. He was a member of the CCP Central Committee and a ministerial rank cadre. In public, he was director of the local Xinhua News Agency. In private, he was the secretary of the party's local branch. He was not only the most senior PRC cadre ever appointed to Hong Kong, but he was also an exceptional one.

Despite his own limited and sometimes faulty understanding of Hong Kong, Xu recognised that Beijing held a highly distorted picture of public opinion there. It was almost the exact opposite of the actual situation.[71] In trying to rectify the misconception, he encouraged Chung and two of his Executive Council colleagues to call on Deng and speak their minds.[72] Xu also thought the British were manipulating public opinion in Hong Kong, and took it upon himself to counter it. A great master in the art of the United Front, he tried to win over public opinion by mobilising the media and by meeting and talking to a wide spectrum of Hong Kong society.[73] His United Front work was very successful and considerably reduced local antipathy towards the PRC.[74] Though Xu improved the PRC's understanding of Hong Kong, there were limits to his positive influence. These became apparent when he arranged for Chung and two other Executive councillors to visit Beijing, only to be rebuked and publicly humiliated by Deng for very politely speaking the truth.[75] Deng insisted that he knew the Hong Kong people better than they did themselves and that he acted in their best interests.[76] The Chinese government remained convinced that it and it alone represented the people of Hong Kong – whatever the latter thought.

The rigidly structured formal negotiations were mainly conducted by the leaders of the two teams. In keeping with British tradition, a major input came from the person on the spot – the forceful and sharp-minded Cradock. Evans carried less weight when he took over.[77] Although Cradock had reached retirement age, his services were considered too valuable to lose. So, contrary to the usually strict Foreign Office retirement rules, the prime minister installed him as a deputy under-secretary in the Foreign Office and made him a special adviser on foreign affairs. He in effect became the supremo of officialdom and took charge of the negotiations on a daily basis.

The leader of the Chinese team had much less flexibility or influence than his British counterpart. In line with Chinese Communist negotiating practice, he spoke mainly from a prepared brief from which he rarely departed.[78] The change from Yao Guang to Zhou Nan made no difference other than that Zhou argued the PRC's case more forcefully. Although the Foreign Ministry was formally responsible, the CCP's Central Foreign Affairs Leading Small Group headed by Li Xiannian, with Premier Zhao as his deputy, supervised the negotiations. Ultimate authority rested with Deng himself. In accordance with established practice, the Chinese also fully utilised the fact that they were hosting the negotiations.[79] They selectively leaked the contents of the negotiations to the media to strengthen their negotiating position.

From the beginning, the second phase of the negotiations ran into serious difficulties. The stumbling block was Britain's role in the administration of Hong Kong after 1997. The basic British position was not to retain sovereignty but to relinquish it in exchange for continuing to administer Hong Kong for as long as possible beyond 1997.[80] The Chinese rejected the idea that it was possible to separate sovereignty and administration. As Zhou Nan saw it, to do so meant replacing 'an old unequal treaty with a new one'.[81] His government was 'determined to recover complete sovereignty and administration of Hong Kong'.[82]

Hong Kong and its financial market reacted with mild panic to the impasse, which continued into the autumn of 1983. By late September, the Hong Kong dollar had fallen to a low of 9.5 to the US dollar, as compared with 5.9 in the previous year, before the negotiations had begun. Local residents started to stock up on essentials.

In October, with the help of the Bank of England, the British and Hong Kong governments finally came up with an arrangement to restore public confidence. They linked the local currency to the US dollar, and this did the trick.[83] Though a major economic crisis was averted because nobody wanted it to happen and the British made the right gesture, the Chinese saw the near crisis as a result of deliberate British manipulation.[84] They did not understand that Hong Kong's government could not control its entirely open economy. The PRC government announced that, unless they reached an agreement within a year, it would impose a unilateral solution.[85] It remained firm and unshakeable in its insistence on ending British administration in 1997.

In the face of Chinese intransigence, the British eventually accepted that they would be unable to administer Hong Kong after 1997. Since avoiding a breakdown in the negotiations then became their overriding objective,[86] they authorised Cradock to attempt what he called 'the second finesse'. In November 1983, the British formally conceded that they 'intended no link of authority between Britain and Hong Kong after 1997'.[87] While Cradock justifiably called the first British climbdown a finesse, this was much more like a major retreat, for Britain actually abandoned its previous bottom line. However, it created a breakthrough in the negotiations because it finally cleared the way for serious discussions that could lead to an agreement.

After their orderly retreat, the British regrouped and worked out a new strategy. This was aimed at 'extracting concessions of substance from Peking and enshrining them in a binding agreement... within the Chinese timetable'.[88] Cradock rightly believed that 'pressure of time would in the end work for us as well as for the opposition'. Otherwise, the British would have 'little chance of inserting our substance and details into the outline [of] Chinese principles'.[89] Cradock was right because there were few if any details in the Chinese plan for post-1997 Hong Kong: the Chinese government did not in fact wish to have a detailed agreement.

The eventual compromise was a short agreement with three annexes; the longest of these, Annex I, sets out China's policy towards Hong Kong after 1997. The British made a significant input by providing ideas and explaining how the Hong Kong system worked. As the deadline imposed by Deng approached in the summer of 1984, the Chinese negotiators acted as Cradock predicted. In order to meet the deadline, they became more willing to cooperate with the British in reaching agreements on what remained of the so-called matters of detail.[90]

Until the late summer of 1984, the negotiations continued to be very tough. The most difficult issue concerned the Chinese proposal to set up a joint commission in Hong Kong to oversee the transition.[91] Deng suspected that the British would strip Hong Kong of its assets and create an undesirable political fait accompli before 1997 and it was he who suggested the proposal.[92] Deng and most of his colleagues found the idea of British 'imperialists' seeing it as a matter of honour and moral responsibility to run Hong Kong as well as possible too alien to take seriously. He wanted to create a special agency or commission to supervise the 13 years of the transition.[93]

Although the Chinese did not intend the commission to become a shadow government, when news of it leaked out most people in Hong Kong feared that this was exactly what would happen.[94] Governor Youde himself found the creation of such an institution unacceptable: he thought it would make Hong Kong ungovernable.[95] Hong Kong's initial resistance softened as negotiations over the commission dragged on and the Chinese again proved adamant.

Hong Kong's governor and Executive Council turned their attentions towards devising compromises to make the commission less objectionable.[96] In the end, Britain's counterproposals amounted to setting up a Sino-British Joint Liaison Group (JLG), which would be an institution for consultation and not an organ of power. This was acceptable to the Chinese, as they had never planned to take over the administration of Hong Kong immediately. Xu Jiatun, who understood Hong Kong's situation better than most of his colleagues, helped by explaining the need to neutralise Hong Kong's anxiety.[97] The final compromise was for it to come into existence when the Sino-British agreement came into force and to last until the year 2000. This was agreed when Foreign Secretary Sir Geoffrey Howe visited Beijing at the end of July. With this major hurdle removed an agreement became possible.

Other details in the final agreement defined the scope of political developments in the period of transition and the basis for Hong Kong's future: they were in fact important provisions. The main emphasis was on securing the territory's prosperity and stability. The final agreement also settled any questions that touched on sovereignty, as defined by the Chinese in line with the PRC's demands. The most notable example here was Deng's decision to station a Chinese garrison in Hong Kong. He announced this in May, in front of a group of Hong Kong journalists, who immediately broadcast the news in Hong Kong. Not surprisingly, it had a very negative impact on public confidence.[98]

Though the Chinese government was keen to protect public confidence in Hong Kong, its top leader had little real understanding of what engendered confidence. There was more give and take over practical arrangements that did not involve sovereignty. The British persuaded the Chinese to abandon their original idea of making parallel announcements of their agreements and to opt for a joint declaration. Many of the details of the arrangements were agreed in the final months of the negotiations. In a few cases, these were written in language that later laid them open to different interpretations. In any event, the negotiators met Deng's deadline and produced the final draft of an agreement towards the end of September.

The Joint Declaration

On 26 September 1984, Ambassador Evans and Zhou Nan initialled the agreement known as the Sino-British Joint Declaration in Beijing. The relatively short Joint Declaration has three annexes, which are all as equally binding as the main document. Together they make up a formal international agreement registered at the UN. The Joint Declaration was formally signed in Beijing on 19 December by Prime Minister Thatcher and Premier Zhao Ziyang. After ratification in May 1985, the agreement came into force and the transitional period began.

Under the Joint Declaration, both sides agreed that sovereignty over the whole of Hong Kong would be transferred from Britain to the PRC on 1 July 1997. It provided that, in the transitional period, Britain would be 'responsible for the administration of Hong Kong with the object of maintaining and preserving its economic prosperity and social stability' to which the PRC would 'give its cooperation'.[99]

The Chinese government defined its basic policies towards Hong Kong, which were elaborated in Annex I. The Chinese government commited itself to establish 'a Hong Kong Special Administrative Region [SAR] upon resuming the exercise of sovereignty over Hong Kong'. This would come 'directly under the authority of' the Chinese government. The SAR would 'enjoy a high degree of autonomy, except in foreign and defence affairs'. It would be 'vested with executive, legislative and independent judicial power, including that of final adjudication', where the 'laws currently in force in Hong Kong would remain basically unchanged'. Its government would 'be composed of local inhabitants' and its chief executive would be appointed by the Chinese government 'on the basis of the results of elections or consultations to be held locally'.

The SAR's principal officials would be 'nominated by the chief executive... for appointment by' the Chinese government. 'Foreign nationals previously working in the public and police services in the government departments of Hong Kong may remain in employment'. It would keep the existing social and economic systems as well as the existing lifestyle, whereby 'rights and freedom, including those of the person, of speech, of the press, of assembly, of association, of travel, of movement, of correspondence, of strike, of choice of occupation, of academic research and of religious belief will be ensured by law'. Private property, ownership of enterprises, legitimate rights of inheritance and foreign investments would also be protected by law.

As an SAR, Hong Kong would remain 'a free port and a separate customs territory'. It would 'retain the status of an international financial centre, as well as its markets for foreign exchange, gold, securities and futures'. It would continue to enjoy the free flow of capital and a freely convertible currency. It would not be subject to taxation from China and would have independent finances. It would have the right to 'establish mutually beneficial economic relations with the United Kingdom and other countries', and 'conclude relevant agreements with states, regions and relevant international organ-isations' for economic and cultural purposes. Its government could 'on its own issue documents for entry into and exit from Hong Kong' and would have responsibility for maintaining public order there. Finally, the Chinese government pledged to implement its commit-ments in a Basic Law for the SAR to be promulgated by its NPC, which would 'remain unchanged for 50 years'.[100]

As elaborated in Annex I, the Joint Declaration enshrined China's blueprint for a post-1997 Hong Kong. It provided the future basis on which Hong Kong and its people would depend. Although the Joint Declaration contains specific provisions or omissions that are open to criticism, as a whole it was acceptable to the people of Hong Kong. This is so long as it is enforced honestly and in full, which was a responsibility both signatories were to share equally. However, implementation of the Chinese promises ultimately depended on the promulgation and enforcement of a PRC law, which Beijing saw as a domestic affair and permitted no foreign interference.

The intransigence the Chinese government demonstrated in the negotiations towards any issue remotely connected with sovereignty pointed to problems ahead. It implied a non-cooperative Chinese approach to any British attempt to enforce the Joint Declaration in the event of a major disagreement over interpretation. The British approach to the negotiations also revealed a harsh fact of reality. While the British government could be expected to try to enforce the agreement and to use every available negotiating means to do so, it did not have the will or might to require the Chinese to abide by the agreement should the latter deviate from it.

Implementation of the Joint Declaration ultimately depended on Chinese goodwill, sincerity and the ability to interpret its terms correctly. There is no need to doubt the first two factors. The Chinese government would not have gone into such lengthy and difficult negotiations only to reduce its final product to a worthless piece of paper. However, interpretation remains a major problem, not least because the Chinese did not understand what made Hong Kong tick when they signed the agreement. In an important sense, they did not really know what they had committed to maintain unchanged for 50 years. The Joint Declaration was supposed to assure Hong Kong's future, but it has not – at least not entirely or securely.

When, after two years of inordinate tension and uncertainty, the contents of the agreement were announced in the autumn of 1984, Hong Kong responded with relief. Though some individuals expressed reservations, the majority of local people accepted it – after all, their only alternative was to have no agreement at all.[101] One might have expected stronger expressions of doubt about the value of the Joint Declaration. After all, the nature of the Communist regime in the PRC, on which the enforcement of the document depended, had not changed. However, the citizens of Hong Kong wanted to look forward to a bright tomorrow rather than a future with a dark cloud hanging over their heads. Serious doubts and the re-emergence of uncertainty and fear belonged to a later time. The end of September 1984 was a time when most people in Hong Kong bravely looked forward to building a future on the basis of the Joint Declaration.

Chapter 16

The Beginning of the End

When the Joint Declaration came into effect in 1985, it opened a new chapter in Hong Kong's history. This was the beginning of the transition leading to the retrocession in 1997 of this rich, successful British colony, deeply embedded in Western capitalism, to the PRC, one of the most powerful Communist states in the world.

There were two inherent contradictions in the arrangements for this transition agreed in the Joint Declaration. The first was its stipulation that Hong Kong's existing non-elective Crown Colony system would be replaced by a government with its 'legislature... constituted by elections' by 1997, though the Joint Declaration was intended to keep Hong Kong's system unchanged for fifty years.[1] The second was that Britain would 'be responsible for the administration of Hong Kong with the object of maintaining and preserving its economic prosperity and social stability', to which 'China [would] give its cooperation'.[2]

What this meant in practice was that democratic Britain was charged with reforming Hong Kong's legislature, but only in a way that the Leninist regime in China could support. In light of their opposing political persuasions, the agreement in effect put the two on a collision course but forbade them from crashing into each other. The situation was further complicated by the fact that introducing elections to the legislature would involve handing over certain political power to the local people in Hong Kong. The politics of transition therefore involved a realignment of power between Britain, China and the people of Hong Kong.

Realignment of Power

As far as the Chinese government was concerned, the transitional period served only one purpose, which was to prepare Hong Kong to rejoin mother China undamaged. It was willing to exercise as much flexibility as possible and made considerable concessions in the agreement of 1984, because it was in its own interest to do so.[3] It believed the proper role for the British government was to serve as its custodian in Hong Kong, which implied not attempting anything disapproved of by itself. The reality that the transition was to enable it to take over Hong Kong gave it increasing weight in the local political scene. This steady tipping of the balance of power in the PRC's favour was not foreseen, but it was welcomed by Chinese leaders, including Deng Xiaoping himself.[4]

Once the Chinese realised the realignment of power underway would in effect give them a pocket veto over political developments in Hong Kong, they used it to force the British to converge to their position. Nevertheless, the PRC's need and desire for a successful takeover, which could not be achieved without the cooperation of Britain, imposed a limit to its ascendancy in the power alignment. The same also applied to the local people, whose feelings the Chinese could not completely ignore. Most Hong Kong people were concerned that 'their freedom, way of life and standard of living' would not be preserved and that the Chinese would not refrain from interfering in the territory's domestic activities.[5] The Chinese had to reassure the local people or win their hearts and minds in order to ensure a smooth transition. Since this was needed in order to further their own interests, it provided a powerful incentive to exercise self-restraint. This allowed scope for the people of Hong Kong to play a role in local politics, and for the British to direct political developments in Hong Kong.

When it signed the Joint Declaration, Britain did see its role as that of a custodian, but of its own and Hong Kong's rather than Beijing's interests.[6] It recognised the need to secure the blessings of Beijing for its policies in Hong Kong during the transition but resisted being reduced to being the latter's hatchet man. From London's point of view, the agreement was intended to safeguard British interests and enable Britain to withdraw from Hong Kong with honour.[7] As the sovereign power until 1997, Britain at first felt it had considerable latitude to run the territory as it saw fit through the colonial government. To the British, the transition was to ensure that the pieces would remain in place for the Chinese takeover. As far as they were concerned, the governor would not abdicate his authority, though he would have to be sensitive to the wishes and needs of China, the prospective new sovereign.

Indeed, the British government and parliament and the Hong Kong government engaged themselves in serious wishful thinking for a short time. In Hong Kong, a major political reform was being examined during the last stage of the negotiations. When the British parliament debated the draft agreement, a majority supported it on the understanding that democratisation would be introduced in Hong Kong as part of the deal.[8] The British establishment proceeded on the basis that Britain would be able to reform the political system of Hong Kong within the framework defined by the Joint Declaration.[9] It deluded itself by refusing to recognise that by signing the Joint Declaration the old alignment of power between Britain and China over Hong Kong had been changed fundamentally.

This remarkable display of British confidence did not last, however. Once the PRC had publicly challenged the British over the proposed Hong Kong reforms in late 1985, the Chinese had to be accommodated lest a public confrontation shatter the fragile public confidence. The reality was that Britain demonstrated it lacked the will and power to stay in Hong Kong when it signed the Joint Declaration. Despite the public rhetoric, backed up by an exercise ostensibly to assess public acceptability of the agreement, the British also admitted that there was 'no possibility of an amended agreement' because the Chinese would not reopen negotiations.[10] This implied that, while Britain had tried to secure the best deal it could, it had conceded British pre-eminence in the politics of Hong Kong was coming to an end when Prime Minister Thatcher put her name on the Joint Declaration. That it took the British a year to accept it did not mean the alignment of power had not shifted.

However, there was a limit to Britain's decline as a political force in Hong Kong. This was mainly based on the fact that it was responsible for the administration until 1997 and was very good at it. The record of the colonial government had earned Britain admiration from the local people, though many of them also resented it for different reasons.[11] The Chinese accepted the continuation of British rule because it was beneficial to them, since a premature end to British rule would gravely damage Hong Kong's stability, good order and, above all, prosperity.[12]

In fact, the Sino-British negotiations of 1982–4 epitomised the political impotence of the people of Hong Kong.[13] Their future was decided without their direct input. This generated much frustration that gave rise to a new desire to have a say over their own future, though they were divided as to the best way forward. To some, democratisation was the obvious answer.[14] Others preferred to cultivate the new prospective sovereign and seek to be co-opted into the power structure by the Chinese. Some of the establishment figures also tried to fight a rearguard operation to protect their vested interests. In this new changed political situation, the people of Hong Kong wanted to assert themselves as a force in local politics.

Their desire to take their fate in their own hands notwithstanding, the people of Hong Kong merely played a peripheral role in determining the direction of political development in the 1980s. This was out of step with the fact that Britain was willing to open the local political arena to public participation, and 'the colonial government had displayed tremendous capacity to adapt its methods of government to social changes'.[15] The reality was that the PRC, the rapidly rising political force in Hong Kong, would not tolerate any development that might allow Hong Kong to move towards independence.[16] In Beijing's conception, the 'high degree of autonomy' it promised Hong Kong did not mean democratic self-government.[17] However, it was willing to make some concessions if it would not feel threatened as a result. The absolute limit of China's tolerance was not tested because Hong Kong did not have an indigenous leadership pushing for it. In the 1980s, Hong Kong had conspicuously failed to produce 'a group of popular and organised *indigenous* [italics original] leaders as the guardian of its interests, as confidence-boosters and as guarantors of the success of the vaunted "one country, two systems" approach to Hong Kong's political future'.[18] These two factors accounted for the limited role played by local people in the politics of the transition.

The increasing importance of the PRC and the decline of Britain in Hong Kong politics were inherent in the logic of the transition. A triangular power alignment among Britain, the PRC and the politically active people of Hong Kong existed in practice. It was not a static relationship. This new alignment of power provided the context in which the British attempted to democratise the colonial administration.

Flirtation with democracy

The British embarked on democratisation in Hong Kong during the Sino-British negotiations, before they recognised a realignment of power would follow the reaching of an agreement. This was meant partly to build as strong a safeguard for Hong Kong's way of life as possible when it eventually came under the jurisdiction of a Leninist regime.[19] It was also because the nature of British politics was such that any agreement to hand over two to three million British subjects, albeit of Chinese origins, to a Communist state would be more acceptable to parliament if it included giving these people some kind of democratic future.[20] The democratic experiment of the 1980s was, like the attempt of the 1940s, the result of an initiative from above, even though it coincided with the emergence of a modest public demand for democratisation locally.[21]

In July 1984, two months before the Joint Declaration was initialled, the Hong Kong government published a consultative document, a green paper on political reform.[22] It made the boldest statement since Governor Young's similar attempt 38 years earlier. It stated that the government aimed 'to develop progressively a system of government the authority for which is firmly rooted in Hong Kong, which is able to represent authoritatively the views of the people of Hong Kong, and which is more directly accountable to the people of Hong Kong'.[23] The timing allowed the PRC an opportunity to see what the Hong Kong government was thinking before the negotiations for the Joint Declaration were completed.

This was meant to be a genuine review of 'how the central institutions of government in Hong Kong might be made more representative in a way which will make the Government more directly accountable to the people'.[24] This document not only provided for the introduction of a substantial, albeit indirectly, elective element to the legislature, but also for the introduction of a quasi-ministerial system. Nevertheless, it kept to Hong Kong's political tradition by proposing to move forward cautiously. The imperative of maintaining stability and prosperity was fully accepted.

The green paper set off lively debates on both the scope and pace of democratisation. There was broad public support for its main objective. On the basis of the consultation, the government published a policy document or white paper on the subject in November – again, a month before the formal signing of the Joint Declaration. This document set out provisions for admitting 24 indirectly elected members to the 56-seat Legislative Council in 1985. It also committed the government to review, in 1987, the introduction of directly elected members in the following year, but sidetracked the idea of a ministerial system.[25] The British tried to strike a balance between the desire for reform and the need to remain in control of the pace and scope of change. This was not least because of the need to dovetail the Basic Law for the SAR to be enacted by the PRC in due course.

Though the British presented their ideas about democratisation as openly as possible, Chinese cadres found it very difficult to grasp what they were attempting. Consequently, the PRC reserved its position on the subject and stressed that 'it was a matter for the British, for which it was not responsible'.[26] By the Joint Declaration, and by their acts in the summer and autumn of 1984, the PRC government appeared to have passively endorsed Hong Kong's democratisation scheme. This was provided it did not subvert the objectives and principles laid down in the Joint Declaration. However reasonable such an interpretation, it was emphatically not what the Chinese intended or understood.

In 1985, the Chinese came to see the democratisation attempt as an underhand British plot to regain what they had lost in the negotiations.[27] From the PRC's point of view, the British were trying to create a situation that would allow them to continue to run Hong Kong after 1997.[28] Firmly convinced that this was the British objective, the PRC organised a counter-attack.

This came in November when Xu Jiatun, Beijing's de facto representative in Hong Kong who enjoyed ministerial rank, held his first-ever press conference. On this occasion, he pointedly accused the British of violating the Joint Declaration. In effect, he demanded that they follow the still-undrafted Basic Law as the basis for political reform.[29] Xu and his colleagues could not believe that the British had primarily intended democratisation to protect the existing way of life in Hong Kong and to secure parliamentary support for the Joint Declaration. They never explained how the British could hope to retain control by stealth after 1997 through introducing genuine democracy.

The Chinese also failed to see that much would have to change to preserve Hong Kong's dynamic capitalist system and way of life.[30] This was because its 'political, social, and economic arrangements depend for their efficacy both on strict legal rights and on legitimate expectations habitually upheld by the authorities in accordance with well-established and credible rules of self-restraint'.[31]

With the end of democratic Britain's supervision in sight, introducing democratisation was the most effective way to ensure that the local government upheld the existing rules of self-restraint. This was too alien a concept to be comprehensible to the Chinese cadres. They took the accuracy of their own interpretation of Britain's motive for granted. Once Xu's initiative received Deng's backing, the PRC was set on a new course. This was to oppose liberal democracy publicly and to restrict the scope and pace of democratisation in Hong Kong.[32]

Convergence

China's rejection of democratisation gave the word convergence a new meaning for Hong Kong.[33] Previously, the British position had been that, while they planned for political developments, they would 'keep in mind the fact that the Chinese Government will be considering the future Basic Law for Hong Kong, and the provisions of the Sino-British agreement, which provides for an elected legislature by 1997 and an executive accountable to it'. They would therefore do 'nothing... inconsistent with those aims'.[34] In other words, convergence meant both sides would start on the basis of the Joint Declaration and meet each other halfway.

From the British point of view, their reform of Hong Kong's authoritarian system would dovetail with China's plan for the SAR as both would be guided by the Joint Declaration. It was like laying down new railway tracks from opposite ends and joining them up in the middle as they met. The Chinese demand of late 1985 was that the British should stop, or slow down drastically, their building work. They could recommence when the Chinese had rethought the plan for laying the track and had completed the groundwork on their own section.[35]

This Chinese view of convergence put the British in an awkward position. They had publicly stated that the Hong Kong government would review the progress of reform in 1987, particularly over introducing directly elected members to the Legislative Council in the following year. They could not break this promise without gravely undermining the Hong Kong government's credibility. The British also recognised that convergence would only happen if their reform plans were acceptable to the Chinese.[36]

Once the Chinese government had formally reaffirmed Xu's public position in January 1986, the British felt they had no choice but to accept the Chinese definition of convergence.[37] They wanted to ensure that whatever was in place by 1997 would survive the handover. It was not, however, a complete capitulation. The British reached an understanding with the Chinese that there would be no major reform until the Basic Law was promulgated in 1990, and that nothing the British introduced would breach the Basic Law. The British also expected to have an input into drafting the Basic Law by offering their views as part of the Chinese consultation process. In return, they expected the Chinese to let the Hong Kong government, including its Legislative Council, be formed in line with the Basic Law in 1995, to continue to function after the handover in 1997. This became popularly known as the 'through train' arrangement.

It was against such a background that the Hong Kong government proceeded with its political reform review in 1987. In contrast with 1984, when it boldly stated its objective was to develop a government that could authoritatively represent the local people, in 1987 it tried to obscure the issue and mentioned no objective in the green paper.[38] As Foreign Secretary Geoffrey Howe admitted, the exercise was conducted to keep the government's promise to have a review.[39] It was not to explore the way forward for developing a representative government.

To satisfy members of the general public that their opinions were given due consideration in the review, for a period of four months the Hong Kong government set up the Survey Office to collect and collate public responses. The most important question was whether direct elections for the Legislative Council should be introduced in 1988 – an option the PRC had rejected. The Survey Office eventually produced a report of over 1,500 full pages, but it misrepresented the thrust of the public view.

According to the report, there were 125,833 individual submissions on the question of whether to introduce direct elections in 1988.[40] Of these, 84,202 (or 67 per cent) opposed them, even though most of them supported direct elections in principle. Included among these were 69,557 form letters, most of which were originally handed out to employees by the managements of PRC-owned banks and enterprises in Hong Kong. What the Survey Office did not count as submissions were the results of 21 different signature campaigns, for which individuals were asked to sign and write down their identity card numbers after reading various letters. In all, these contained 233,666 signatures, of which 233,371 supported and 295 opposed direct elections in 1988.[41]

By excluding the signature campaign submissions, but including the form letters, the Survey Office concluded that there was overwhelming support for introducing direct elections to the Legislative Council in principle, but not in 1988. It unjustifiably implied that the people of Hong Kong had changed their minds since 1984. In the white paper of 1984, the Hong Kong government actually correctly reported that 'with few exceptions the bulk of public response from all sources' supported 'introducing a very small number of directly elected members in 1988 and building up to a significant number... by 1997'.[42]

In the 1988 white paper, the government claimed on the basis of the survey report that public opinion on the subject was 'sharply divided'. However, it admitted that there was strong public support for introducing direct representation.[43] On this basis, the document provided for the introduction of ten directly elected members to the 56-seat Legislative Council in 1991. By the time the white paper was published, it was already known that the PRC intended to allow at least ten directly elected members to be admitted to the SAR legislature. The whole exercise was blatantly based on the wish to make Hong Kong's political system converge with the Basic Law, which would not be finalised until 1990.

Although it might seem improper for the Hong Kong government to have manipulated the results of the opinion assessment, its justification for doing so was on the grounds of Hong Kong's best interests. As Foreign Secretary Howe explained, Britain's key objective was 'to design a structure that will not be temporary or fallible but one that will endure beyond 1997'.[44] Convergence – as defined by the PRC – had become the political imperative. In 1987 and 1988 the British government deemed manipulation the lesser of the two evils. The other was provoking the PRC to commit itself to dismantle whatever reforms the British might introduce. By slowing down the pace of democratisation, Britain hoped to persuade the PRC to include provisions in the Basic Law for limited direct representation at the legislature.

The British and Hong Kong governments could get away with manipulating the opinion survey results because the people of Hong Kong did not assert themselves strongly enough.[45] Had the majority of those who supported holding direct elections in 1988 organised a campaign against the Survey Office report's findings, it would have been gravely discredited. The British and Hong Kong governments would have had to respond. The reality was that there was still public ambivalence about democratisation. Not even those most in favour of it were prepared to work for it actively. Hong Kong had not produced leaders with sufficient political skills to force the government's hand or to mobilise the general public to do so.[46] No political party organised an effective campaign to press the British to stand by their 1984 commitment to democratise. Indeed, the first true political party, the United Democrats, was not founded until almost three years later, in April 1990.[47]

Because of Britain's acceptance of China's definition of convergence, the Hong Kong government acquired the public image of being a lame duck. This was remarkable for a government that still had a tenure of almost ten years guaranteed by an international agreement. It was particularly remarkable given that this was essentially the same government that had met the requirements of as good a government as possible in the Chinese political tradition only a few years earlier. What it really reflected was the new alignment of power after 1984.

The British relied on secret diplomacy to assure Chinese cooperation in securing the through train. This was widely misunderstood or not considered credible in Hong Kong. An increasing number of Hong Kong people felt that the British government was betraying them and that the Hong Kong government was letting them down. Their sense of frustration and powerlessness increased and their confidence in the future fell. As a result, an increasing number of Hong Kong residents planned and prepared to leave, or at least to seek the security of a foreign passport.

Convergence was a double-edged sword. On the one hand, it harmed the credibility of and public confidence in the Hong Kong government and this reduced its vitality in facing the longer-term challenges of retrocession. On the other hand, convergence provided the best chance to minimise the impact of the Chinese takeover, given the attitude of the Chinese leaders, which is examined in detail below.

The alternative – to democratise Hong Kong's political system as permitted in the Joint Declaration – would only have led to the PRC dismantling what it disapproved of in 1997. Obsessed with the idea of sovereignty and 'face', Beijing would deem all political reforms introduced in Hong Kong without the PRC's tacit approval as unacceptable. Ignoring the Chinese completely because their interpretation of the Joint Declaration was ill based would have been detrimental to Hong Kong's long-term well-being. The Joint Declaration would be worth less than the paper on which it was printed if the Chinese should decide not to abide by it because of a difference in interpretation. The British adopted convergence as a policy not because they liked it but because they believed it was, on balance, the lesser of two evils.

In the period of transition, the Hong Kong government needed to steer a course and devise policies that would both be supported by the local people and be tolerable to Beijing. Up to 1989, it tried to find such a course, but erred more on the side of accommodating Beijing.

China's Hong Kong Policy

Policy towards Hong Kong for the PRC combined elements of both foreign and domestic policies. Until 1997, it was partly a foreign policy matter, because it was under British rule and its status could not be altered without British cooperation. However, because it was regarded as Chinese territory, it also fell within the domain of domestic policy.[48]

As a matter that involved sovereignty, national dignity and the future of economic reform within the PRC, their Hong Kong policy was of great importance to Chinese leaders. There could therefore be no major policy decisions or changes without the top leaders' approval. This meant when he was alive and physically fit, paramount leader Deng Xiaoping had the final say.[49] The PRC's basic policy towards Hong Kong rested on the principle of exercising maximum flexibility in practical matters but maintaining complete rigidity over sovereignty.[50]

Deng and his comrades had no love for condescending Hong Kong capitalists who profited as middlemen between the PRC and the rest of the world.[51] However, they knew they 'needed those capitalists for their knowledge of business and technology, their access to finance, their skill in managing large projects, and their control of the transportation and telecommunication infrastructure'.[52] Within the first decade of the opening of the Chinese economy, Hong Kong had become one of the most important drivers behind Deng's ambitious economic reforms.

It was to reconcile the conflicting requirements of recovering sovereignty and utilising Hong Kong for the Communist Party's own purposes that the PRC devised the policy popularised as 'one country, two systems'. The Chinese considered it an ingenious idea that would enable the PRC both to have its cake (reclaim sovereignty) and eat it too (retain Hong Kong's economic utility).[53] This was essentially a modification of and, from the PRC government's point of view, an improvement on the policy that Mao had advocated after 1949.

The guiding principle behind it has, however, remained essentially the same. It is to further the interests of the PRC as defined by the Communist Party. This is the most powerful factor in inducing PRC leaders to adhere to the Joint Declaration. This also meant, in the words of senior cadre Lu Ping, that if Hong Kong should 'be of negative value instead of positive value to China', it 'would be disastrous for Hong Kong'.[54]

This raises a basic problem, which is that capitalist Hong Kong can only run its own affairs with 'a high degree of autonomy' within the framework of a socialist PRC if the latter feels confident enough to allow an *imperium in imperio* to practise a system fundamentally hostile to its survival. In the mid 1980s, Deng had the necessary confidence. He believed that the PRC's Communist system was superior to Hong Kong's capitalist system.[55] However inherently self-contradictory this might sound, he also conceded that it would be advantageous to let Hong Kong capitalism supplement the superior PRC system. It was, in any event, for a limited period only. Deng never intended to let Hong Kong be the catalyst to set off a chain reaction to change, let alone subvert or supplant, the socialist system in the PRC.[56]

As will be explained in the next chapter, if or when the Communist leaders felt threatened, they would either pre-empt or eliminate such a threat, regardless of the cost. If Hong Kong were to be deemed the source of such a menace, it would be dealt with accordingly. Deng emphatically told Prime Minister Thatcher that if, in trying to protect its sovereignty over Hong Kong, the PRC should bring about catastrophic results, he would face them.[57] But then Deng felt confident that the PRC would take over Hong Kong successfully.

The PRC's approach to the recovery of sovereignty severely restricted whatever 'high degree of autonomy' Hong Kong expected to enjoy. Deng himself told the drafters of the Hong Kong Basic Law that they 'should not think Hong Kong affairs should all be handled by Hong Kong people': 'this was impossible, and such an idea was unrealistic'.[58] He added that, should it become necessary for Beijing to interfere, 'it would in the first instance be done through the executive branch without involving the Chinese garrison'. This would only need to be called out in the event of disturbances.[59] Behind its rhetoric about autonomy, the PRC's policy was to allow the SAR government to run its own affairs only so long as the Communist Party or its leaders did not see its actions as contrary to their interests.

The very nature of the Communist system influences its Hong Kong policy. Organised along Leninist lines, the CCP is interventionist in its ethos. When he re-emerged from political oblivion after the Cultural Revolution, Deng reaffirmed the basic principle that the party must play a leading role in all matters.[60] As he put it, 'one should never depart from the leadership of the party and praise the initiative of the masses'.[61] Deng's directive was very much in character with the party tradition that transformed 'what Sun Yat-sen described as a "sheet of loose sand" into one of the most highly organised societies in the world'.[62]

Deng then instructed his party to go against its tradition and make an exception of Hong Kong. While he was undoubtedly sincere, he gave the party a very tall order. The party was to keep the promises it had made in the Joint Declaration. In principle, this was an easy task to perform – all it required was to do nothing and let the Hong Kong government continue as before after retrocession. In reality, the Communist Party was being asked to contradict its very nature – the most difficult task for any individual or organisation.

The PRC's Hong Kong policy was also influenced by a basic distrust of the British and of their supporters in the territory.[63] This derived from

China's tendency to adopt a doctrinal and nationalistic view of the British colony. It coloured their judgement. PRC leaders and officials remained convinced that the British were engaged in a conspiracy, at the expense of the territory and its future sovereign, to spirit wealth from Hong Kong to Britain before 1997.[64] They could not believe that the public tender system and the overseers of various public bodies, including the Legislative Council's Finance Committee, would not allow Britain to do so.

Their view is partly explained by Hong Kong and the PRC having very different bureaucratic cultures and practices. PRC cadres assumed that British imperialists had always exploited Hong Kong and had done so with the cooperation of local civil servants. They did not realise that the Hong Kong civil service had developed a very strong commitment to the territory and had at times fought London in defence of local interests.[65] They could not and did not accept that, by the 1980s, the colonial administration had become as good a government as possible in the Chinese political tradition. The PRC's failure to grasp this is an indication that it really did not understand what made Hong Kong tick.[66]

The Basic Law

However important the Joint Declaration may have been as an international agreement to protect Hong Kong's way of life, its implementation required the promulgation and enforcement of the Basic Law for the Hong Kong SAR.[67] According to the terms of the Joint Declaration, this new constitutional instrument had simply to stipulate the terms of its Annex I in an appropriate legal form.[68] Although the PRC leaders had no intention of breaching the Joint Declaration, they did not accept such an interpretation when they started to work on the Basic Law. They deemed the Basic Law a subsidiary of their own constitution and not of the Joint Declaration.[69] To the Chinese leaders, the important issue was how to make the Basic Law serve their best interests rather than to dovetail with the Joint Declaration.

Both Hong Kong and the PRC regarded the drafting of the Basic Law as a matter of great importance. To the people of Hong Kong, for whom it was the litmus test of the PRC's sincerity, it was about how to preserve their 'system' and way of life for 50 years. To the PRC, it provided an opportunity to lay down the parameters of Hong Kong's autonomy after retrocession. It was also pivotal to its United Front work among the local residents in order to win over their support and retain Hong Kong's utilities.

The PRC leaders realised that, in the mid 1980s, the people of Hong Kong were sceptical about their sincerity and ability to take over Hong Kong and preserve its way of life. They were prepared to go a long way towards persuading the local people of their sincerity. To allow their cadres sufficient time to do the United Front work properly, they set aside a long period for drafting. They tried to enhance public confidence by arranging for the National People's Congress (NPC) to appoint a committee of specially co-opted Hong Kong members to draft the Basic Law.[70] The Basic Law Drafting Committee (BLDC) came into existence on 1 July 1985 with 59 members.[71] To ensure that it would be seen as having been drawn up 'democratically', the PRC also appointed a consultative committee of local residents.

The composition of the BLDC was carefully worked out. It had to contain a sufficiently large representation of Hong Kong residents to give it a democratic façade, but not large enough to oppose the PRC's will. In accordance with usual CCP practice, the local party branch or the Hong Kong and Macao Work Committee compiled the list, which the top leaders approved before the individuals in question were invited to serve.[72] On the Work Committee's recommendation, 23 of the members, or just under 40 per cent, were selected from among Hong Kong's residents. This gave what was deemed an appropriate representation from different sectors of the local community.

The PRC chose this percentage because it only just provided a two-thirds majority. This was what Hong Kong members would need to oppose the mainland members on important matters.[73] However, at least two of the 23 Hong Kong members were under Communist Party control. They were the publisher of *Ta Kung Pao* and the deputy head of the Federation of Trade Unions.[74] In other words, on matters of importance only 21 members could not always be counted on to vote for the Party. The members also disagreed with each other on many issues, which was partly why they were selected. In some cases, their backgrounds and political persuasions were so different that it was more difficult for them to work with each other than with PRC cadres.[75]

The PRC's concern to sustain Hong Kong's economic utilities also influenced its choice of local members. Ironically, of the 23 Hong Kong members only two were union leaders. The Communist Party preferred to give the business tycoons a stronger say. After all, it needed to secure their investments. Furthermore, in line with United Front practice, the party also offered membership to its most vocal local critic, Martin Lee. Xu Jiatun of the Work Committee was confident that including Lee would be preferable to excluding him.[76] It would be easier to contain his criticisms inside than outside the BLDC's confidential working atmosphere. Making Lee a party to the drafting process would also make it easier to persuade the rest of the Hong Kong community that the Basic Law was good for them.

Ultimate control of the BLDC rested in the hands of senior Chinese cadres normally responsible for Hong Kong policies. This was despite the fact that, strictly speaking, the BLDC was an NPC and not a State Council special committee. Ji Pengfei, the director of the HKMAO, chaired the committee and his deputy, Li Hou, headed the BLDC secretariat. The other members of the secretariat were also senior cadres from the HKMAO and the Work Committee. Not surprisingly, the head of the Work Committee, Xu Jiatun, was a deputy chairman of the BLDC. In other words, excepting the foreign minister, the other two ministerial-rank cadres, Ji and Xu, who were responsible for Hong Kong policy, occupied leading positions on the BLDC. Their dominance was unquestionable, however much they claimed to be willing to listen to other members. They were assured of the support of the numerically superior mainland drafters, who were mostly members of the CCP and, as such, had to observe party discipline. There was no danger of errant Hong Kong drafters violating them over matters that threatened the basic interests of the Party.

The guiding hand of PRC cadres was also behind the formation of the Basic Law Consultative Committee (BLCC). Like the BLDC, it too was intended to be a major instrument for United Front work. The Work Committee therefore carefully planned its size and composition.[77] As a purely consultative body, the CCP could afford to fill its 180 seats with Hong Kong residents. The Work Committee even invited prominent local citizens it could not trust on the BLDC to join the BLCC. The BLCC also provided a means of reaching out to Hong Kong's so-called pro-British and Kuomintang elements. Although the Work Committee's attempt to neutralise their open opposition failed, those who were invited found it difficult not to soften their stand towards the BLCC.

Despite the Chinese cadres' deliberate efforts to give the selection of the BLCC a democratic façade, the true nature of the exercise was revealed in December 1985. This occurred during a meeting to prepare for the inauguration of the committee. To counter the impression that Communist cadres ran the whole process, they entrusted the Hong Kong vice-chairman of the BLDC, Sir Y.K. Pao, to chair the preparatory meeting. Its purpose was to elect an executive board of 19 from among the members; they considered Pao to be sound. Their strategy backfired. To begin with, Pao was not a member of the BLCC and therefore, according to its charter, had no authority to chair the meeting.[78] His high position in the BLDC was completely irrelevant because, as Ji Pengfei put it, 'there was no question of one [committee] being subordinate' to the other.[79] Furthermore, Pao ignored the agreed procedures and proceeded to read out a list of 19 names and directed the meeting to elect them with a round of applause.[80]

The process revealed the invisible hand of the Communist Party. The list had been agreed beforehand and, as was usual practice inside the PRC, those elected had already been consulted. They unwittingly ignored the due process because, as Xu Jiatun admitted in retrospect, those concerned, including himself, lacked any appreciation of the democratic procedure.[81] They later tried to rectify the problem by holding another meeting during which they produced the same list and duly elected those whose names appeared on it. While this showed the PRC leadership's willingness to respond to public outrage, it also demonstrated the extent of the Party's influence. Once the Party had publicly invested its reputation, albeit unintentionally, in its choice of the BLCC Executive Board, members of the BLCC felt they had no choice but to acquiesce.

To ensure that the BLCC behaved responsibly and did not damage the vital task of recovering Hong Kong, the CCP kept it under its own guidance, though not always directly. The first instrument was the BLDC, despite Ji's public statement that the BLCC was not subordinate to it. Notwithstanding its rhetoric, the PRC tried to ensure that leading BLDC figures would steer the BLCC towards supporting the Basic Law. Hence, six of them were appointed to the BLCC's Executive Board, one of whom (Dr T.K. Ann) was even 'elected' chairman.

The vital task of handling the paperwork was first entrusted to Mao Junnian, a member of the Work Committee and deputy secretary-general of the BLDC. The intention was clearly that the BLCC should support rather than be independent of the BLDC. Once the CCP felt more confident in its ability to direct the BLCC's work, it allowed a non-Communist to replace Mao. Although the new secretary-general of the BLCC, Leung Chun-ying, was born in Hong Kong, he had by then built up a reputation as a staunch opponent of democratic change.[82] Leung's own political conviction was such that the Party regarded him as a safe pair of hands in which to entrust the Basic Law.

The principle behind the procedure for drafting the Basic Law, the so-called 'two ups and two downs' approach, was based on Mao Zedong's idea of 'from the masses to the masses'. The Maoist axiom requires the Party to:

> take the ideas of the masses (scattered and unsystematic ideas) and concentrate them (through study turn them into concentrated and systematic ideas), then go to the masses and propagate and explain these ideas until the masses embrace them as their own, hold fast to them and translate them into action.

It then needs to repeat the process 'so that the ideas are persevered in and carried through'.[83]

By combining this principle with that of the United Front and adapting the end product to Hong Kong's circumstances, the PRC leaders devised a basic policy for drafting the Basic Law. This entailed having the local people conduct the drafting process with the invisible hand of the CCP guiding them. They would produce a draft for submission to Beijing, which the PRC would then send back to Hong Kong for public consultation. The local people would then complete the drafting work and resubmit the Basic Law to Beijing for formal promulgation.

The Communist cadres did, however, considerably adapt their work style to make the whole drafting process acceptable to their Hong Kong colleagues. In the early stages of the drafting process, the BLDC secretariat, which Communist cadres controlled, followed standard PRC procedure.[84] They prepared an important document about the structure of the Basic Law and circulated it among leading BLDC members. When this came to the attention of a Hong Kong member (Dorothy Liu), who had no such privileged access, she openly criticised the practice as undemocratic. In response, the Communist cadres agreed to change the procedure and appoint two co-convenors to each of the BLDC task groups, one of whom would always be a Hong Kong person.[85]

This accommodation to the specific demands of Hong Kong members did not mean that the PRC cadres were prepared to relinquish control. What they did was give the impression that both co-convenors were equal. The Hong Kong convenors were encouraged to appear as the more dominant in public. The relationship between the two co-convenors was similar to that between a military commander and a political commissar in the PLA.[86] In this analogy, the Hong Kong convenor is the military commander and the mainland convenor the commissar. While both have the same institutional status, the first is expected to 'command', whereas the latter is there to ensure that political mistakes are not made.

For the actual drafting of the Basic Law, the BLDC was divided into five task groups. To the PRC, the two most important of these were the ones responsible for the political system and for working out relations between the central government and the SAR.[87] The BLDC members allocated to these specific task groups were also senior cadres. Li Hou, Lu Ping, Zhou Nan and Ke Zaishuo, who were of deputy ministerial or at least ambassadorial rank, were all assigned to these two groups and not to any of the others.[88] The remaining three groups dealt respectively with the rights of the residents of the SAR; economic and financial matters; and education, science, technology, culture, sports and religion. These groups were also important, but since they did not deal with matters of sovereignty, the PRC leaders could afford to be more relaxed about them.

The task groups working on central government-SAR relations and on the political system had to define the exact scope of the autonomy Hong Kong was to enjoy. This was a testing task for all the Hong Kong members, who had to play the more active role. It was particularly demanding of the two Hong Kong co-convenors, Rayson Huang and Louis Cha. There was a tacit understanding that Hong Kong would have relatively little room for manoeuvre in relations between the central government and the SAR. There was no such understanding over the question of political developments. Thus, as co-convenor of the political system task group, Cha had the most difficult and sensitive job. He and his group had to function while the Hong Kong government was introducing an element of representative government and then reviewing the progress of its reforms. This was also a time when the rest of Hong Kong was openly debating democratisation. Cha and his group needed to balance local demands against what Beijing would actually tolerate.[89]

The torrent of public criticism levelled at Cha when he tried to steer the BLDC towards accepting a compromise illustrates how difficult his task really was. When the Hong Kong members of the BLDC were unable to resolve their differences over the pace and scope of democratisation in late 1988, Cha attempted to find a compromise solution. He did not aim to resolve the Hong Kong drafters' differences. The compromise he sought was one that would give Hong Kong sufficient democratisation to sustain its existing way of life and yet prove acceptable to Beijing. As a realist, he saw the latter as being of primary importance, since Beijing would never permit the SAR to introduce a system of which it disapproved.

Consequently, he produced a set of proposals that included as many democratic elements as possible but just short of touching the PRC bottom line, which he ascertained from senior PRC cadres, including Xu Jiatun.[90] His proposals would not give democracy to Hong Kong until at least 2011, when a referendum would be held to decide the matter.[91] Meanwhile, they would allow Hong Kong's existing system to become more representative and would commit the PRC to respect such a development. Although the BLDC adopted his proposals – with an amendment to make the conditions for the referendum more restrictive – they provoked vehement attacks from the Hong Kong media.[92] By the late 1980s there was already a strong undercurrent favouring democracy in Hong Kong.[93]

Though the majority of local people remained silent, they undoubtedly shared the broad sentiments of the media's opinion leaders, who generally supported democracy. They felt that Cha had let them down. An important difference divided them from him. They saw democracy as a goal permitted in the Joint Declaration and were less sensitive to what Beijing would allow. They simply wanted democracy for Hong Kong and expected Beijing to tolerate it. Cha believed Hong Kong's best interests lay less in developing full democracy (which he judged intolerable to Beijing) than in tying down the PRC to respect a political system in the SAR that would permit at least some democratic representation. The public's criticism of Cha reflected the great gap that lay between the PRC leadership and Hong Kong people's wishes.

The political crisis that erupted in Beijing in the spring and early summer of 1989 briefly interrupted and significantly affected the drafting process. The Tiananmen incident and its general ramifications for Hong Kong are examined in the next chapter. Suffice to stress here that it badly shook the PRC leadership's previous confidence in the 'one country, two systems' model. When Communist Party rule in China became threatened, the PRC expelled Martin Lee and Szeto Wah from the BLDC. These two men were the BLDC's leading advocates for a faster pace of democrat-isation. The CCP responded to the blow to its confidence by tightening its control over the drafting process and by adding provisions to enhance the PRC's control over the SAR in the Basic Law.[94]

The president of the PRC promulgated the Basic Law after the NPC had adopted it in April 1990. Its legality is based on Article 31 of the PRC constitution of 1982. This permits the state to 'establish special administrative regions when necessary' and to do so 'by law enacted by the National People's Congress in light of the specific conditions'.[95] Strictly speaking, whether this can provide the necessary constitutional authority is doubtful. Article 1 of the constitution states that 'the People's Republic of China is a socialist state' and adds that 'sabotage of the socialist system by any organisation or individual is prohibited'.[96] Article 5 further stipulates that 'the state upholds the uniformity and dignity of the socialist legal system' and 'no law or administrative or local rules and regulations shall contravene the Constitution'.[97]

In the common-law tradition, the three articles together suggest that the NPC can establish an SAR, but that the SAR must nevertheless practise and uphold the socialist system. Article 4 of the Basic Law, which stipulates that 'the socialist system and policies shall not be practised in the Hong Kong Special Administrative Region', must therefore be unconstitutional. However, since the PRC is still a Communist party-state and considers the Hong Kong question above all a political issue, such a legalistic view is merely of academic importance. Indeed, none of the PRC's four constitutions since 1949 contains an effective procedure for independent review of a law's constitutionality.[98] More important, the entire PRC establishment holds that the Basic Law is completely in line with the constitution.[99] Since Hong Kong wishes to minimise interference from the PRC, it does not serve its interests by challenging the constitutionality of the Basic Law.

The Basic Law's drafting process is a good illustration of how the PRC's approach to allowing maximum flexibility within a rigid framework works in practice. While much of the thinking behind the PRC's approach originated in Communist practices, these were adapted whenever possible to meet Hong Kong's demands. This was done so skilfully that most people, including politicians and political analysts in Hong Kong, did not realise that the guiding principles behind the drafting process were based on Mao's ideas of the mass line and the United Front. The PRC's bottom line was that it could not allow its ultimate control to be undermined. Once it was satisfied on this front, the PRC was prepared to consider all other demands made by the local people.

By and large, the PRC has committed itself in the Basic Law to recreate in the SAR a Chinese version of the British Crown Colony system of government that existed in Hong Kong in the 1980s. This may have fallen short of public expectations, for by then the people of Hong Kong wanted a more democratic system of government. There are also specific provisions in the Basic Law that are problematic. However, the drafting process demonstrated the amount of flexibility Beijing was willing to exercise to ensure a successful takeover of Hong Kong.

Chapter 17

The Final Chapter

As Hong Kong was preparing its transition from British colony to Chinese SAR, its history came to be affected in a fundamental way by events in China. In 1989, Deng Xiaoping's post-Mao reforms, encapsulated in the policy of the four modernisations – agriculture, industry, science and technology and national defence – stalled and entered a critical stage. This policy had always been meant to be a limited one, introducing 'economic improvement without systemic change'.[1] In other words, it was to import capitalist methods to help enrich the PRC and entrench Party rule but not to allow Western ideas to infiltrate the PRC and challenge the Leninist system.[2] However, China was an organic entity like any other country. It was impossible to modernise specific parts of it without this having some impact on the rest of the structure. By 1988, Deng's economic reforms had already run out of steam and created serious imbalance. They produced high unemployment, high inflation, conspicuous inequalities and a demand for political changes. As 1989 dawned, the PRC was 'a tinderbox of suppressed anger, mounting despair and corrosive envy'.[3] A crisis was in the making.

The death of Hu Yaobang in April 1989, Deng's right-hand man until he was sacked as Party general secretary in 1987 and one of the very few top leaders who had a public reputation for not being corrupt, offered an opportunity for the disaffected, particularly university students, to use his funeral to test the Party's reactions to a protest movement.[4] They demonstrated at Tiananmen Square in Beijing in the spring and were later joined by ordinary citizens who shared their discontent. The Communist leadership appeared restrained at first, as it was paralysed for a short time by an intense power struggle at the top.[5] This paralysis unwittingly heartened the protesters and the whole process quickly escalated.[6] In the meantime, the power struggle among the top leaders unfolded.

Although more than a million demonstrated in the streets and there was some dissent within the military leadership over the use of force against them, it was only a matter of time before the CCP would unleash the full force of its might against the protesters. Once he himself became a subject of protest, Deng took a hard line.[7] He believed that the protesters 'had two objectives – to overthrow the Communist Party and to topple the socialist system'.[8] He and a powerful group of top leaders had come to see the protest movement as 'a life and death' struggle for the Party.[9] With Deng giving his backing to the hardliners, the relatively moderate general secretary of the Party, Zhao Ziyang, who resisted suppressing the demonstrators by force was ousted from power.[10] A forceful suppression was in the making.

When the student movement erupted in Beijing, an increasing number of people in Hong Kong came to identify with what the local and Western media portrayed as a 'democracy movement'. They themselves were frustrated by the PRC sidetracking the Joint Declaration and restricting democratic developments after 1984. They were developing a sense that 'as long as freedom, human rights, and democracy cannot be guaranteed in the PRC, they cannot be protected in Hong Kong after 1997'.[11] Consequently, an unspoken common front emerged between the people of Hong Kong and the Beijing demonstrators. Admiration and support, including generous donations, built up quickly. Many became so emotionally involved they could not see the reality. Others, like many foreign journalists in Beijing, chose to ignore the dark side or inadequacies of the student movement.[12] They wanted to believe in a bright future for the PRC and thus for Hong Kong too.

When the movement in Beijing came under serious threat, the already strong support of the people of Hong Kong mushroomed. Premier Li Peng's imposition of martial law on 20 May galvanised them into action. On the following day, they showed their solidarity with the Beijing protesters. They staged an unprecedentedly massive sympathy demonstration of over 500,000 residents (out of a total population of fewer than 6 million at that time).[13] Even Communist cadres and their close supporters in Hong Kong gave their backing to the protesters, seeing the unfolding events as a great patriotic movement.[14] In Hong Kong, there was a general feeling that what was happening in Beijing would have major (though as yet not clearly defined) implications for its own future.

On the night of 3–4 June 1989, the PLA executed the orders of the top Communist leaders led by Deng. It used excessive and indiscriminate force to suppress the protest movement centred on Tiananmen Square.[15] The Communist leaders intended not only to disperse the demonstrators, but also to teach them and the rest of the nation a lesson. Their message was that the Party had the might to maintain power and the will to use it. This public and bloody suppression was designed to pre-empt any similar protest movement in the future.[16]

The PLA's ferocity was captured on film and immediately relayed around the world. The whole world was stunned and dismayed by the massacre they saw on their television sets. The people of Hong Kong were utterly devastated. As soon as they recovered from the initial shock, horror and disbelief, over half a million people went on a march in Hong Kong to mourn the dead and to express their anger at the PRC regime. The spirit of the time was captured in the editorial of a local newspaper:

> In supporting the Beijing student movement, the people of Hong Kong had identified themselves completely with it. The recent marches, [fund-raising] concerts, sit-ins, and hunger-strikes have reflected the Hong Kong people's yearning for liberal-democracy – both for China and for Hong Kong.[17]

If the earlier successes of the Beijing students had given the people of Hong Kong a ray of hope for the future, the tanks that rolled into Tiananmen Square shattered it. The brutal military crackdown raised the spectre that what happened in Beijing could well be the future for Hong Kong in less than a decade, after the PRC's resumption of sovereignty.

The Impact of the Tiananmen Incident

To understand Hong Kong people's feelings about and reactions to the Tiananmen incident, they need to be put in the context of the local people's changing sense of identity.[18] This has a bearing on what they saw as Tiananmen's implications for Hong Kong. When the peaceful demonstration in Beijing ended in a savage tragedy, it forced the people of Hong Kong to confront the problems of who they really were and what would be in store for them.

The process of reflecting on their sense of identity started with the signing of the Joint Declaration. The people of Hong Kong gradually accepted the prospect of retrocession. In 1997, all Hong Kong residents of Chinese origin would become Chinese nationals. Since only a very small number of them enjoyed the right of abode in the UK, after the coming into effect of the British Nationality Act in 1982, many began to feel they had no choice but to identify with China. The upshot was a new sense of a dual identity – they belonged both to Hong Kong and to China.

This lack of clarity in their minds had important implications. On the one hand, as Hong Kong citizens, they wanted to preserve their own way of life under the 'one country, two systems' formula. This should have implied non-intervention in each other's affairs by both the PRC and Hong Kong. On the other hand, feeling that they were Chinese too, they believed they had a right to have a say in vital matters affecting the future of the nation, which in practice meant PRC politics. Few Hong Kong people could see the inherent contradiction between asserting their right to have a say in the politics of the PRC and their demand that the PRC should not interfere in Hong Kong's domestic affairs.

The confused identity of most Hong Kong people and their resultant contradictory view of Sino-Hong Kong relations made it easy for them to make a vital transition in the first half of 1989. They swiftly shifted from a position of wanting to forestall PRC interference in Hong Kong affairs to wanting to play a meaningful though essentially supportive role in the Chinese 'democracy movement'. They became emotionally committed. When they stood behind the students they felt they were not just Hong Kong citizens, but Chinese ones as well. It made them feel righteous about demanding changes within the PRC in 1989.

Most Hong Kong people's identification with the 'democracy movement' turned them, in their own minds, into the student protesters' instant comrades. When the PLA massacred protesters in Beijing, many in Hong Kong, watching on their televisions, saw *their* comrades fall. They felt just as anguished and outraged as Beijing citizens. They felt frustrated that there was little they could do to help. They could only watch in agony. However, they were also thankful that the Union flag flying over their heads in Hong Kong had saved them from their comrades' fate. This security and protection, which they craved, also gave them what one may call survivor's guilt. Consequently, they wanted to do something to ease their conscience. They overwhelmed collection centres in their scramble to donate blood in Hong Kong. They also tried to force a run on PRC-owned banks by withdrawing their deposits.[19] None of these actions could help the hapless protesters in Beijing or save the movement from being ground to dust. However, to an extent, they eased the intense pain brought about by their own failure to stand by their comrades under fire.

Their emotional commitment and sense of guilt weakened their ability to put matters in perspective. Most people in Hong Kong found it difficult, if not impossible, to envisage that the PRC government could justifiably see their support for the 'democracy movement' as subversive.[20]

For those living under the protection of the British flag, giving material support to people across the border to overthrow the legitimate PRC government was subversive. The latter could justifiably take it as an attempt to interfere in its domestic affairs and a clear violation of the principle of 'one country, two systems'.[21] Technical definitions of 'subversion' apart, self-interest should have encouraged the people of Hong Kong to insulate themselves from volatile PRC politics to avoid provoking the wrath of 'big brother'. The CCP had shown its true colours. Hong Kong's best chance of maintaining its system after 1997 lay in persuading the Communist leadership that it neither intended nor would try to become such a menace. In the event, the people of Hong Kong were far too emotionally involved to consider such an option calmly.

The Tiananmen incident both brought the Hong Kong people's identity problem to a head and destroyed their confidence in the future. As the British House of Commons Foreign Affairs Committee observed, a visible collapse of public confidence had led to 'calls to tear up the agreement, reneging on the Joint Declaration and breaking off all negotiations with China'.[22] To illustrate the scale of the crisis, 75 per cent of respondents to opinion surveys were optimistic about the future in January 1989, but this dropped to 52 per cent by September, three months after the massacre.[23] Another survey conducted a month later suggested that 70 per cent of the respondents had no confidence in the PRC honouring its pledge not to interfere in Hong Kong affairs after 1997.[24]

Whatever happened around Tiananmen Square, the realignment of power after 1984 meant it was unrealistic to think that the PRC regime would make more concessions to Britain or Hong Kong if the Joint Declaration were to be annulled, especially so shortly after the military crackdown. This did not mean nothing could be done to prevent the crisis deepening. Indeed, three measures quickly came to be seen as essential for such a purpose.

The first and most important was for the local people to have an opportunity to leave should the Chinese takeover turn into a disaster.[25] The idea was to provide the people of Hong Kong with a home of last resort in what came to be known as the 'Armageddon scenario'. This involved asking Britain to restore full citizenship, including the right of abode in the UK, to Hong Kong's 3.25 million British subjects and to help the remaining 2.5 million secure a chance of settlement elsewhere if necessary.[26] The thought was that with an escape route provided, those who did not really want to leave could have the confidence to stay and the exodus of individuals essential for the territory's well-being could be reduced. This proposal was also meant to discourage the PRC government from importing Tiananmen-style solutions to Hong Kong.

Whatever the merits of this proposal, the British government rejected it firmly.[27] This was due to the powerful resistance led by Norman Tebbit, a political heavyweight in Margaret Thatcher's ruling Conservative Party, and opposition from the Labour Party.[28] The upshot was a classic British compromise. It was to give UK citizenship to 50,000 key people holding essential positions in Hong Kong and their dependants to provide sufficient reassurance to persuade them to stay.[29] The British government's handling of the citizenship issue demonstrated the limit of its commitment to Hong Kong.

The second requirement, which the British adopted, was to revive and accelerate the process of democratisation.[30] Over this matter, Hong Kong's interests did not contradict those of Britain. The British hesitation before the Tiananmen incident was due to the perceived need to accommodate the PRC in exchange for the 'through train' arrangement. The real obstacles to democratisation since 1984 had been the PRC's attitude and the lack of a strongly expressed common view among the people of Hong Kong. This situation changed during the student movement in Beijing. The strong public emotions expressed in support of democracy left their marks. Any lingering doubt about whether the people of Hong Kong were ready for democracy was removed.[31]

The outburst of public emotion pushed unofficial members of the Legislative and Executive Councils to reach a consensus. They asked for direct elections for half the Legislative Council by 1997 and for the whole Council by 2003. They also asked for the chief executive of the SAR to be popularly elected no later than 2003.[32] They hoped that the common front they had obtained might persuade the PRC government to revise the draft Basic Law to accommodate the strongly expressed public wish. Those who supported this consensus proposal did not intend to use it to confront the PRC authorities. However, the Chinese leadership viewed their firm stand, on a matter Beijing had already rejected, with suspicion.

With the swing of public opinion in Hong Kong and the British media putting pressure on it to give Hong Kong as much democracy as possible before handing Hong Kong over to the PRC, the British government raised the matter with the Chinese government. It did not, however, push very hard. While sympathetic, Thatcher thought instinctively 'that this was the wrong time'.[33] Her government worked on the basis that a powerful push 'could have provoked a strong defensive reaction that might have undermined the Hong Kong Agreement'.[34]

Consequently, the British government tried to get the best deal possible within the framework of convergence. It pleaded for 'sufficient flexibility in the Basic Law to accommodate the new situation'. The Chinese were tough, unyielding and deeply mistrustful of the British. Nevertheless, an understanding was reached in February 1990. It was for the British 'to limit to 18 the number of directly elected seats to be introduced in 1991'. In return, China would agree to extend to '20 directly elected seats in the SAR legislature in 1997, 24 in 1999, and 30 in 2003'. It would also 'observe the 1991 legislature in operation' and on that basis consider a faster pace of democratisation.[35] This understanding fell significantly short of the consensus reached among Hong Kong's legislative and executive councillors, but represented a step forward. The net gain for Hong Kong was to increase the number of directly elected seats in the Legislative Council from 10 to 18 (out of a total membership of 60) in 1991. Its terms were duly incorporated into Annexe II of the Basic Law.

The third measure to restore confidence was to introduce a bill of rights to enhance the legal basis for the protection of human rights. The Joint Declaration requires the SAR government to 'protect the rights and freedoms of inhabitants and other persons in the Hong Kong Special Administrative Region according to law'.[36] However, the collapse of confidence meant that such a provision was no longer deemed adequate. The Hong Kong government therefore introduced a bill of rights 'to incorporate provisions of the International Covenant on Civil and Political Rights as applied to Hong Kong into the laws of Hong Kong'.[37] As a safeguard against Tiananmen-style repression, the bill of rights is no more effective than a glazed door against a determined intruder. Nevertheless, the need to restore confidence was so acute that this was a welcome gesture in Hong Kong.

In the immediate aftermath of the massacre, the PRC government also tried to stop Hong Kong's confidence crisis deepening. HKMAO Director Ji Pengfei stated: 'I, on behalf of the Chinese government, solemnly declare that the Chinese government's policies towards Hong Kong and Macao, which have been formulated in line with the conception of "one country, two systems," will not change.'[38]

This public reaffirmation of its basic policy did not alter the fact that the PRC leadership was very angry at and resentful of the support the people of Hong Kong had given the student protesters. Thus, even when he tried to dispel the fear among the people of Hong Kong, Ji reminded his audience that they had 'done something that is impermissible by the state Constitution and law and has in fact added fuel to the flames of turmoil'.[39] The PRC leadership believed the people of Hong Kong attempted to subvert it even though, in line with the United Front approach, it only accused a small group of 'reactionaries' of having done so. After the massacre, it wanted to restore public confidence in Hong Kong, not because it thought the local residents there deserved help but because it was in the Communist Party's interest to do so – Hong Kong was still the goose laying badly needed golden eggs.

The Chinese leadership was also bitter about Britain being the first to impose sanctions in response to what it saw as a purely internal affair.[40] It could not believe that Britain had not intended to let Hong Kong be used to subvert the PRC.[41] It could not understand the feelings of the people of Hong Kong.[42] Deng Xiaoping himself decided that the PRC should take a tough stand towards the British.[43] The PRC leadership therefore only gave limited cooperation to British attempts to restore confidence in Hong Kong.

Two other basic problems dampened the PRC leadership's willingness to cooperate. First, to endorse any of the three British confidence-boosting initiatives would have been an admission on its part that its actions in Tiananmen caused fear in Hong Kong. Second, and more fundamentally, the popular challenge to its authority in Beijing gravely weakened its self-confidence, which was further undermined as Communism collapsed in Eastern Europe in the winter of 1989–90.[44] Its tremendous faith in the superiority of its own system previously had enabled it to exercise maximum flexibility towards Hong Kong, albeit within a rigid framework. Now that this confidence was seriously undermined, it reduced the scope of flexibility and looked at Hong Kong with suspicion.

In policy terms, after the military crackdown, PRC leaders sought to neutralise anyone in Hong Kong who posed a challenge or appeared disloyal during the protest movement. Their first task was to purge the Communist organisations in Hong Kong, which had wavered in their support for the top leaders. This was on the whole carried out secretly. It involved, above all, the removal of Xu Jiatun as head of the Work Committee.[45] Xu was seen as having been too soft during the Tiananmen incident and too close to Zhao Ziyang, the ousted Party general secretary.[46]

Another urgent task for the CCP was to destroy the main Hong Kong organisation that had supported the Beijing protesters. This was the Alliance in Support of the Patriotic and Democratic Movement in China founded by Szeto Wah and Martin Lee. The Chinese asked the Hong Kong government to proscribe it, but the latter politely refused on the grounds that there was no legal basis for such an action.[47] They then tried to intimidate the organisation's supporters into abandoning it and attempted to isolate Szeto and Lee by naming them as subversives.[48] The two were also expelled from the BLDC. The intimidation backfired, for it actually encouraged many local people to rally around the two men and their organisation. Thus, when work on the Basic Law was resumed, the PRC leaders introduced new provisions, including a clause on subversion, Article 23, to strengthen their ability to control events in the SAR before they finalised the Basic Law.[49] In the interests of maintaining confidence, the PRC authorities decided not to punish Hong Kong any harder for its involvement in the Tiananmen incident.

In terms of Sino-Hong Kong relations, the Tiananmen incident gave rise to more confrontational politics. The British confidence-boosting measures reminded everybody of the massacre. The PRC government responded by becoming more confrontational than at any time since 1984. It denounced the British scheme to give 50,000 Hong Kong families the right of abode in the UK, and opposed the introduction of a bill of rights.[50]

British officials handling Hong Kong affairs for their part tried to repair Sino-British relations once the dust had settled. Sir David Wilson, who had taken over as governor from Sir Edward Youde in 1987, stressed in his first post-Tiananmen state of the territory address that Hong Kong and the PRC 'need to restore mutual trust as the necessary cornerstone for the unprecedented political experiment that will begin in 1997'.[51] However, the scars on the people of Hong Kong were too deep for them to accept a restoration of the *status quo ante*. Their true feelings were put to the test in the first-ever direct elections, for 18 of the 60 legislative councillors in September 1991.

The elections dissipated any hope of the Hong Kong people putting the Tiananmen incident behind them. The single most important electoral issue was candidates' attitudes to the PRC and the Tiananmen incident.[52] All the candidates who campaigned on a pro-PRC platform were defeated.[53] The pro-democracy parties and groups won a landslide. They secured 58 per cent of the votes and 15 of the 18 seats.[54] The United Democrats, which Martin Lee and Szeto Wah had organised into a political party only a little over a year earlier, did particularly well. It alone won 12 seats.

The message Hong Kong's voters delivered was that they were still emotionally committed to the causes championed by the Tiananmen protesters. They had voted against the restoration of the *status quo ante*. While they dared not confront the PRC government publicly, their strong feelings were disclosed. The Chinese leadership emerged convinced that democratic developments in Hong Kong were against their own interests and should not be allowed to spread uncontrolled. The electoral fiasco of the pro-PRC forces had destroyed any hope of the PRC agreeing to any British proposal to quicken the pace of democratisation in Hong Kong after 1991.

The Tiananmen incident left another important legacy that made the idea of restoring the *status quo ante* meaningless. In October 1989, Governor Wilson announced the Hong Kong government's plan to build a massive infrastructure project known as the Port and Airport Development Strategy (PADS). The entire project was scheduled to be completed in 2006 at a cost of $HK127 billion, but the first phase, including the building of a new airport, would be finished in 1997. Wilson stressed that it was 'to show clearly how, despite the shocks we have experienced during the year, your government is continuing to plan for the long-term future of Hong Kong'.[55] Whatever the strength of the economic case, it was primarily intended to rebuild public confidence.[56]

Although the PRC government did not object to this at first, it became increasingly suspicious of the British intention. Since neither the proposed new airport nor the main port expansion would be completed much before the scheduled British departure in 1997, Chinese cadres could not understand the British rationale. They looked at PADS with the suspicion that Deng Xiaoping first expressed when the Joint Declaration was being agreed in 1984. He thought the British would conspire to use Hong Kong's financial resources to buy goodwill from the local people, and to spirit Hong Kong's wealth to Britain before the handover.[57]

As Communist Party General Secretary Jiang Zemin saw it, PADS was a British plot to host a lavish dinner party and leave the Chinese to pay the bill.[58] It is indicative of the PRC mentality that Jiang already considered that Hong Kong's financial resources belonged to the PRC seven years before retrocession. When the Hong Kong government granted the contracts to build and run two of the four berthing places for a new container terminal to a leading British-Hong Kong company and not a PRC consortium, the PRC leadership found confirmation of their suspicions.[59] Plagued by suspicion of corruption in their own bureaucracy, Chinese leaders doubted the integrity of Hong Kong's public tender system. Driven by self-interest and a conviction that the British – being imperialists – must have ulterior motives, the PRC blocked PADS. Since such a massive project required public borrowing on a large scale, the PRC's hostility meant it could not be built without its blessing.

When the PRC government took a public and high profile stand to block PADS, it changed the nature of the dispute. The crux of the matter had become the assertion by the PRC of its 'right to be consulted on all matters that straddled 1997'.[60] The PRC position in fact amounted to exacting the power to veto major Hong Kong economic policies or public projects if they should have significant implications for the SAR.[61] Conceding this demand would have reduced the Hong Kong government to lame-duck status. The government therefore resisted it.[62] It was not until June 1991 that the PRC finally indicated any willingness to compromise, because it was by then eager to break the diplomatic quarantine imposed by major Western powers following the Tiananmen incident.[63] Premier Li Peng, whose reputation was particularly badly tarnished by the Tiananmen incident, was personally keen to have a summit meeting with the British prime minister in Beijing.[64] For such a British concession, Li and the PRC government were willing to reach an agreement over building the proposed new Hong Kong airport.

John Major, who had taken over as prime minister from Thatcher less than a year earlier, duly visited Beijing in September 1991 and signed a memorandum of understanding over the airport. The British tried to limit the scope of the veto demanded by the PRC but this compromise created a precedent. It gave the PRC grounds to demand prior consultation on other major policy matters.[65] By its actions over PADS, the PRC government actually acquired a far greater say over Hong Kong affairs than it had enjoyed prior to 1989.

The Last Governor

The countdown to Hong Kong's handover to the PRC entered a new phase in 1992. The year started with an announcement that Governor Wilson would retire after the British general election later in the year for which no date had yet been set.[66] No successor was named. Despite public disclaimers, Wilson, who was more than three years from the statutory retirement age of 60, was removed by being elevated to a life peerage. A few months later, Prime Minister Major also retired Percy Cradock, his most senior official adviser handling Hong Kong affairs. Although Cradock served beyond the normal call of duty by staying on for ten years after his retirement, this went unrecognised when he left office. The changing of the guard reflected Major's dissatisfaction with the way policy towards Hong Kong and China was handled.[67]

Unlike his predecessor, Margaret Thatcher, who demonstrated a commitment to Hong Kong, Major took very little personal interest in it.[68] He lost faith in the old China hands after he reluctantly visited Beijing in 1991 on their advice that as 'the first Western leader to do so after the massacre' in Tiananmen he would be able to resolve the dispute over the PADS, but achieved little.[69] Consequently, he decided to stiffen Britain's policy towards the PRC over Hong Kong. He did not, however, have a clear idea of what to do. All that was decided was that Wilson would be succeeded by a politician, and therefore the choice would have to wait until after the general election. When he announced Wilson's retirement he had not thought through its implications. He had unwittingly reduced Governor Wilson to a lame duck.

The results of the British general election caught many by surprise. As chairman of the Conservative Party, Christopher Patten had played a crucial role in steering the Party from a widely expected defeat to victory. Ironically, he lost his own seat in Bath, which was 'a devastating shock' to him.[70] Fresh from his electoral triumph, Major showed his gratitude by trying to 'find a proper job for someone who had, in effect, laid down his constituency for the Party'. He offered Patten Hong Kong, after the latter turned down the options of returning to the Cabinet as a member of the House of Lords, or to fight a by-election in due course.[71] Patten became the last governor of Hong Kong as an accident of history.

With no meaningful experience in dealing with Hong Kong or China, Patten prepared himself before heading east by talking to a range of China experts from the political, diplomatic and academic worlds.[72] Among the many issues he explored was the question of what the PRC would do if Britain granted democracy to Hong Kong. He was advised on at least one occasion that, while the Communist leaders would prefer not to have to do it, they would undo any political reform in Hong Kong that challenged what the PRC saw as its sovereign authority.[73] When he took up the governorship in July, Patten was aware of the delicate and difficult position in which Hong Kong found itself.

Patten wanted to better his diplomatic predecessor and to leave his own mark. Arriving in Hong Kong, where Wilson was unkindly but widely denigrated for his alleged readiness to yield to pressure from the PRC, Patten intended to restore credibility to the governorship in the eyes of the local people.[74] He did not set out to antagonise the PRC, but he knew that his standing would be gravely undermined if he were to be seen to kowtow to Beijing, particularly in his early days. He had to balance the PRC leadership's expectation that he would pay homage to it in Beijing and the wish of the Hong Kong people that he would represent them and stand up for them. A skilful politician, Patten tried to finesse a compromise between these requirements, but he placed greater emphasis on securing the support of the local people.

Patten was a political heavyweight. He was a friend and close political ally of Prime Minister Major and Foreign Secretary Douglas Hurd. As Governor of Hong Kong, he enjoyed more leverage than any of his predecessors in the twentieth century.[75] Though he had direct access to the top, the Foreign Office continued to handle most contacts between the Hong Kong and British governments through its normal channels of communication. He had a mandate from the prime minister to review Britain's Hong Kong policy, and played a pivotal role in revamping it.[76]

Apart from his close personal and political links with the prime minister, there was another reason for vesting so much power in him. There was a general feeling in British political circles that the last governor would need clout in Westminster and political skills in the final stage of the transition.[77] This resulted in shifting the locus of policymaking from the old China hands or career diplomats versed in Chinese idiosyncrasies to the politician governor after the summer of 1992.[78]

In October, Patten announced his agenda in his first policy address to the Legislative Council. He produced a political reform package that would give the local people as much democratisation as possible without breaching the Basic Law. To sweeten the deal for the PRC, he adroitly removed a major political irritant to Beijing. He tried to finesse the irreconcilable demands the PRC government and the people of Hong Kong had put on the governor.

More than anything else, the people of Hong Kong expected their new governor to speed up the pace of democratisation.[79] They included expanding the representative aspects of the Legislative Council and appointing a couple of directly elected legislative councillors to the Executive Council. The most popular candidates were Martin Lee and Szeto Wah, leaders of the United Democrats, which won most of the directly contested seats in the election the previous September.[80] However, the PRC would not tolerate Lee or Szeto being appointed to the Executive Council.

Patten came up with an extremely cleverly devised set of proposals to reconcile the conflicting requirements. First, by claiming that the existing overlap of membership between the Executive and Legislative Councils would 'inhibit the effective development of the Legislature as an independent check on Government', he proposed their separation.[81] It was a masterstroke that diffused the intractable problem over the appointment of Lee or Szeto to the Executive Council. This also in fact did the PRC a favour by giving it what it wanted – a strengthening of the executive branch at the expense of the legislature. (If Hong Kong had followed the more usual process of democratisation in a British colony, it would have developed towards a Westminster model with parliamentary supremacy.) To compensate for the severing of links between the two councils, the governor gave up the presidency of the legislature. Instead, he introduced a question time during which he would, as chief executive, answer questions from legislators.[82] He supplemented this by establishing a 'Government-LegCo Committee' through which to maintain 'an effective working relationship between' the executive and the legislature.[83] All the above proposals were deemed unlikely to be objectionable to Beijing and were implemented without delay.

Patten also suggested introducing changes to electoral arrangements for the Legislative Council in 1995. He stressed that, as far as possible, he wanted the 'reforms to be compatible with the Basic Law and, accordingly, to transcend 1997'.[84] There were seven specific recommendations:

- to reduce the voting age from 21 to 18, which was the voting age in the PRC as well as in Britain;
- to increase the number of directly elected seats from 18 to 20, which was the number laid down in the Basic Law for the first SAR legislature in 1997;
- to change multiple-seat geographical constituencies into single-seat ones;
- to replace 'all forms of corporate voting... by individual voters' in the 21 existing functional constituencies.[85] This meant giving a vote to the individuals working in professions or specified business sectors rather than their companies. It would make this archaic type of representation more in tune with modern times, and its voting less susceptible to manipulation;
- to add nine new functional constituencies so that people who did not belong to existing categories would be represented in the new functional constituencies. This was needed to enable the Legislative Council of 1995 to dovetail with the arrangements laid down in the Basic Law, which provided for 30 functional constituencies in the SAR legislature in 1997;[86]
- to devolve some power over local matters and give more financial resources to district boards. Also, direct elections would replace all appointments to these boards and to the municipal councils; and
- finally, he suggested that the Basic Law's requirement for ten members to be elected by a selection committee of 400 should be chosen in a different way as a stopgap measure in 1995.[87] In Patten's conception, instead of having the governor appoint a similar committee – the composition of which would probably be objectionable to Beijing – he would ask all the directly elected members of the district boards to elect ten among themselves as a one-off arrangement.[88]

In making these proposals, Patten pushed the grey area in the Basic Law to its limit, but did not actually violate it. The Basic Law does not specifically prohibit anything in his scheme. This is in line with the common law tradition whereby anything not prohibited is permitted. In this sense, his scheme was a masterstroke. It did not contravene the constitutional position to which the PRC had committed itself in the Basic Law. Yet, it delivered to the people of Hong Kong the largest possible step in the direction of democracy. In reality, this step remained a modest one. However, Patten did a first-class job in packaging and marketing it as a major step forward. He played down the fact that, even if his scheme were implemented *in toto*, Hong Kong would still only have one-third of its legislature returned by direct elections. His scheme was seen as a major step forward because the people of Hong Kong and PRC cadres accepted his democratic rhetoric at face value.

While it was obviously important to persuade the people of Hong Kong, Patten should have also ensured that the Chinese government understood what his scheme really entailed. This was vitally important, for Chinese cadres were well known for their inability to understand how Western democracies work. A Chinese failure to understand his scheme would cause them to overreact.

Before finalising his plan, Patten became aware that the PRC government was unhappy about it. Two weeks before announcing his proposals, Foreign Secretary Hurd had given his Chinese counterpart an outline of the scheme when they met in New York.[89] It took the Chinese a week to respond. Patten was asked to defer announcing his objectionable proposals until he had discussed the matter with the Chinese government.[90] Patten must, therefore, have calculated that, despite its dissatisfaction the PRC would not jeopardise confidence and stability in Hong Kong over his proposals.[91] He himself openly stated that he expected to hold 'serious discussions with Peking' over them.[92] For this purpose, he planned to visit Beijing shortly afterwards. He could not have expected the PRC to accept his proposals in full, but he must have intended to make the PRC justify the rejection of any of them in public. Had he been operating within the framework of British politics, this would have been a clever pre-emptive manoeuvre to seize the moral high ground and force his political opponent to negotiate publicly from a weak moral position. However, as a means of neutralising PRC objections, Patten's adroit move turned out to be as clever as waving a red flag at a bull one is trying to induce to leave a china shop.

The PRC leaders looked on with suspicion at the appointment of this politician who, from the very beginning, expressed a wish to further Hong Kong's freedom.[93] They wondered whether the new man – who had no understanding of Chinese thinking and was probably primarily concerned with British interests – would introduce any basic changes to Britain's policy. They reserved judgement at first. However, as the summer progressed, their original suspicions were confirmed. To begin with, unlike their 'old friend' Wilson, who from a Chinese point of view duly paid his respects upon assuming the governorship five years earlier, Patten did not visit Beijing before announcing his political agenda. Furthermore, he did not get along with the top Chinese cadre in Hong Kong, Zhou Nan, which exacerbated their misunderstandings. To Beijing, it appeared that a sinister plot was being hatched, either by Patten personally or by the British as a whole.

The PRC found Britain's handling of Patten's plan at least as objectionable as its contents. The Chinese believed they had had an understanding with the British since late 1985 over the meaning of convergence. As they saw it, they would define the scope and pace of the democratisation in Hong Kong towards which the British would converge.[94] As explained in the previous chapter, the Chinese made what they believed to be a major concession in allowing the number of directly elected seats to the Legislative Council to be increased from 10 to 18 after 1989.[95] This was achieved by secret diplomacy, which to the Chinese meant their 'sovereign authority' over Hong Kong was respected. Since the Patten plan was being hailed as a major political reform with implications beyond 1997, the Chinese expected the British to have consulted them first and to have provided them with an opportunity to reject any unacceptable elements. However, the British merely informed them on this occasion and, according to the director of HKMAO, Lu Ping, completely ignored the Chinese comments.[96]

The Chinese also believed that, by announcing the plan publicly, the British intended to present them with a fait accompli. They considered it at best a deliberate affront and at worst a sly move to undermine Chinese sovereignty. The Chinese also wondered whether this modified approach marked a fundamental change in British policy. Since convergence had worked well for their interests, they were eager to nip in the bud any change in British policy.[97] Hence, they made a very strong and swift negative response to warn the British to return to the policy of convergence.[98]

The skilful way in which Patten made his modest proposals look as if they were a major democratic reform also backfired. It so confused the Chinese cadres that they gave Patten much more credit than he deserved for 'democratising' Hong Kong. The Chinese saw the plan to fill the ten Legislative Council seats by means of elections among elected municipal councillors and district board members as direct elections in disguise. They mistakenly equated them with the electoral colleges in US presidential elections. Following this logic, Patten would indeed have taken a major step towards democratisation through the back door, for half the Legislative Council seats would for all practical purposes be open to direct elections. The Chinese did not understand the subtle yet vital differences between Patten's proposal and the US electoral college system. In the US, electoral colleges have no function other than to elect the president and each delegate is by convention returned on the basis of his or her declared choice of presidential candidate. In the Hong Kong case, the local-level elections would have to be contested on the whole range of issues handled by the municipal councils and district boards.

Furthermore, there would be a year between the local elections and the Legislative Council elections. During the 1994 local elections, no one could know who the candidates for the 1995 Legislative Council elections would be, and the latter therefore could not be an issue in the local elections. Hence, turning the municipal councils and district boards into an electorate for 1995 was not a direct election in disguise, but this was something the Chinese did not understand.

The Chinese further exaggerated the effect of Patten's proposed reforms. They also counted the nine new functional seats as if they were direct election seats.[99] They therefore wrongly thought that 'the number of directly and in effect directly elected legislative councillors would amount to 40 [sic]'. This was two-thirds of the council's total membership – a percentage that could allow the United Democrats (the predecessors of the Democratic Party) to win a majority.[100] They saw the Patten plan as 'an attempt to let the "anti-Chinese democratic party" which represents British interests to win, and enable it to take "the through train" into the first Legislative Council after the return of Hong Kong's sovereignty in 1997'.[101]

The Chinese also raised serious objections to other aspects of the Patten proposals. These included:

- substituting corporate voting with individual voting in the functional constituencies;
- ending appointments to (or more realistically gubernatorial patronage in) municipal councils and district boards; and even
- ending overlapping membership in the Executive and Legislative Councils.[102]

They failed to understand that the last proposal was a sweetener for them. They did not realise that it removed the public pressure on the Hong Kong government to appoint Martin Lee to the Executive Council. They also failed to understand that it took away the most powerful influence the Legislative Council traditionally exercised over the Executive Council. For more than a century, the Executive Council had tended not to push a controversial policy if its unofficial members, who also sat on the Legislative Council, could convince it that such a policy would be unacceptable to the legislature.

Patten's uncoupling of the two councils therefore turned the Hong Kong system into a much more 'executive-led' one.[103] It was exactly what the PRC wanted, but the Chinese cadres failed to grasp it. It reflected their inadequate understanding of how the political system in Hong Kong actually worked. It was also because they started from the assumption that Patten had ulterior motives. By focusing on every conceivable negative implication, they overlooked those that were positive to the PRC. As Lu Ping saw it, because the Chinese had already set out their plan in the Basic Law, they even found Patten's appeal to produce counter-proposals offensive.[104] The PRC government's basic objection to Patten's plan lay in the belief that it intended to introduce democracy to Hong Kong in open defiance of its stated policy.

Since Chinese cadres misread the nature of Patten's plan, their inaccurate assessments became the basis for decision-making. Seeing it essentially in terms of a British challenge to Chinese sovereign authority, the reaction was to take a tough stand.[105] The old mistrust expressed by Deng was revived – 'someone would not implement in full' the Joint Declaration.[106] Building on such a suspicion, the Chinese even saw it as part of a wider conspiracy.[107] As Zhou Nan explained, the British mistakenly believed that 'after the dissolution of the Soviet Union, China would also face the same kind of changes'. They thus wanted to 'use proxies installed with their help to extend British colonial rule, turn Hong Kong into a semi-independent political entity, and unrealistically wish to influence political developments in China'.[108] The PRC leadership thus decided to face this British challenge squarely and win at all costs.[109]

The PRC hardened its position after the Governor visited Beijing in October. This was the only occasion when Patten was received as Governor of Hong Kong by senior Chinese leaders like the foreign minister and the director of HKMAO. To Patten, it was an occasion when he could have serious talks with the Chinese about his proposals. To the PRC leaders it was an opportunity for Patten to admit his mistake and return to convergence.[110] There was no meeting of minds.[111] The PRC leaders felt they had confirmation that the British were attempting a volte-face and consequently prepared for confrontation. For months the Chinese ignored British démarche to open negotiations to resolve their differences over the Patten reforms.

The PRC leadership was still keen to make a success of the retrocession. It thus applied its well-tested United Front tactics to divide the British-Hong Kong camp and neutralise the Patten initiative. Used for this purpose, United Front tactics require one to isolate one's principal antagonist and destroy it by rallying one's supporters, winning over those wavering and neutralising the opponent's natural supporters. Once this is completed, one moves on to the next target and repeats the exercise until one establishes full control. In the winter of 1992–3, the Chinese saw Patten as the principal target. The people of Hong Kong were the wavering elements, and the British government and Hong Kong civil service were the opponent's natural supporters. Hence, despite seeing the Patten plan as a wider British conspiracy, the PRC propaganda machine singled out Patten for attack. In public, the PRC argued that one person, who was the cause of all the troubles, was destroying Hong Kong's interests and Sino-British cooperation. Its message to both the British government and Hong Kong was that once Patten had been removed, the *status quo ante* could be restored and Hong Kong would not have to see its stability and prosperity threatened.

This virulent attack on Patten provoked the British to close ranks. The British government felt that if it replaced Patten under overt heavy-handed PRC pressure, it would lose all credibility and authority in Hong Kong in the run-up to 1997. It was therefore not an option. The barrage of verbal abuse the Chinese heaped on Patten also made him appear like a great champion for democracy in Hong Kong. Some people there were intimidated and many wealthy capitalists asked the governor to defuse the crisis for the sake of stability and prosperity. The majority of ordinary folk, however, rallied around him for standing up for them. When the PRC propaganda campaign intensified in the winter, his popularity ratings rose to their highest point.[112] To most Hong Kong people, strong Chinese hostility was sufficient proof that Patten's plan must be a major democratic reform. The world media, which was still influenced by the legacy of the Tiananmen massacre, shared the same sentiment. Ironically, through the eyes of the international media, the high-profile PRC propaganda attacks quickly turned Patten into Hong Kong's English hero. The PRC had badly miscalculated the reactions of Britain, the people of Hong Kong and the international media. Its United Front tactics had backfired.

The confrontation between Britain and the PRC over the Patten plan was a tragedy that neither side wanted. The changing of guards and the new team's well-intentioned though naïve wish to recover some of the lost ground on the British side, led to its failure to anticipate the likely responses from the Chinese side.

The End of Cooperation

In March 1993, the Chinese finally but reluctantly realised that the British would not replace Governor Patten.[113] They therefore agreed to enter into negotiations with Britain, which started in earnest the following month. Deputy Foreign Minister Jiang Enzhu represented the Chinese in the talks with the British ambassador Sir Robin McLaren. Throughout the 17 rounds, the PRC kept up the pretence that the governor was not a party to the negotiations, though Patten remained the key figure behind the scenes on the British side. The negotiations were tough and progress was slow.[114] Though both sides had entered the talks partly to secure popular support in Hong Kong, they also wanted to reach an agreement to ensure a successful transition. However, they remained suspicious of each other's intentions.

The Chinese starting position was that the Patten plan violated the Joint Declaration, the Basic Law and various understandings over political developments reached after the Tiananmen incident.[115] General Secretary Jiang Zemin defined their basic stand. He said that the PRC 'would not make any concession on matters of principle'. It would be 'guided by the one country, two systems' policy and would 'take into account the basic interests of the Chinese people, who include the Hong Kong and Macao compatriots'.[116] In other words, he reaffirmed the policy of exercising maximum flexibility within a rigid framework.

An acceptable compromise would require considerable back-peddling on the part of the British to bring Patten's plan into line with the PRC's interpretation of the two documents and of various understandings. While Chinese sincerity was not in doubt, it was unclear whether they were keen to reach an agreement quickly. As the Chinese knew only too well, time was on their side. To introduce the changes proposed in the Patten plan, the Hong Kong government would need to pass one or more new laws. From Beijing's point of view, this was largely a British problem, for it was they who had provoked the dispute in the first place. The Chinese were unsympathetic to the time pressures the British side faced.

Governor Patten essentially defined the British position. As he himself put it, the crux of the matter was 'not about the pace of democratic development', which was 'set out in the Basic Law'.[117] The British sought to secure two basic principles. The first was to ensure that 'election arrangements in Hong Kong should be fair, open and acceptable to the community'.[118] The other 'was to agree on arrangements which would provide continuity through 1997'.[119] The British were therefore willing to reach a compromise by revising the 1992 proposals. In October 1993, the governor publicly stated the main thrust of the concessions the British were willing to make:

> First, we have devised a new proposal for the nine new functional constituencies, based on organisations as the Chinese have argued and with a total eligible electorate of about a third of that in my original proposal. We continue to insist that electors should vote individually, not corporately. Secondly, we have tried to meet China's preference for a four-sector Election Committee of the kind set out in the Basic Law for the post-1997 Election Committee. We continue to argue that all members of the Election Committee should themselves be elected.[120]

The governor also made clear, however, that 'there is a point beyond which I do not believe that we could justifiably go, even in pursuit of an agreement to which we genuinely aspire'.[121] The limits of the British concession were not only about the substance of the plan, but also about the timing for an agreement. The British had set a time limit because the necessary legislation had to be put in place to implement the proposed changes for the September 1994 local elections.

In Governor Patten's judgement, time ran out in late November 1993. The British gave the PRC a few days' warning before gazetting the draft bill they later introduced into the Legislative Council, though they also stressed their wish to continue negotiations.[122] Patten appeared to have felt a sense of frustration and resentment over the PRC's heavy-handed approach and verbal abuse of him personally. Because such a move would be so obviously against the PRC's own interests, he seemed reluctant to believe that the PRC would honour its own threat to demolish his reforms. Patten's assessment revealed his own ignorance and misunderstanding of the PRC's policy. The point of no return was reached in June 1994 when the Legislative Council passed his remaining reform proposals of 1992 into law in full.

The Chinese acted on their previous warning and declared the talks terminated.[123] They saw the British move as confirmation of their insincerity in the talks and held them fully responsible.[124] They were only prepared to resume negotiations if the British discontinued their unilateral action. From their point of view, the British move amounted to a return to challenging their sovereign rights over Hong Kong. They could not back down and their reaction was predictable. Whether justifiable or not, their certainty that the Patten plan violated the Joint Declaration, seriously weakened their sense of commitment to it and 'provided a perfect pretext for tinkering' with it.[125]

'Building a New Kitchen'

The breakdown of the talks marked the abandonment by the Chinese of the policy of a 'through train'.[126] Instead they devoted themselves to an alternative policy described in terms of 'building a new kitchen'.[127] The most important activity in a Chinese community is feeding the people and, in this respect, families function as the basic unit. The family kitchen is therefore the hub – the vital place in which to turn raw materials into nutritious food to sustain the family and enable it to prosper. Building a new kitchen symbolises the splitting of a family or the assertion of independence. The implication was that, with a 'new kitchen' in place, it would not need to rely on the existing one. As an analogy to Hong Kong, its existing 'kitchen', or political system, would remain under British control, but the PRC would build a new one that would take over the functions of the British 'kitchen' in 1997.

This threat to build a 'new kitchen' was first made by HKMAO Director Lu Ping in October 1992 when Patten was visiting Beijing.[128] Lu merely meant to warn Patten to abandon his scheme. Beijing had not yet committed itself to 'build a new kitchen'. The idea only developed after its initial attempts to force the removal of Governor Patten had failed. When the PRC opened negotiations over the Patten plan in April 1993, it also planned for the worst and strengthened its hand in the talks by preparing the ground for a 'new kitchen'. It announced its intention to set up a preliminary working committee (PWC) as a first step towards the eventual appointment of a preparatory committee for the Hong Kong SAR.[129] This was a clever move and in a sense was in retaliation against Britain's claim that the Patten plan had not breached the Basic Law. Although there is no provision for a PWC in the Basic Law, one of its appendices does require the forming of a preparatory committee sometime in 1996.[130] Since the Basic Law does not prohibit the setting up of a PWC, its creation did not violate the terms of the law.

The PRC had two objectives in forming the PWC in July 1993. The first was to put pressure on the British to make concessions over the Patten plan. The possibility of the PWC becoming an alternative centre of authority generated a certain amount of concern in Hong Kong. Its creation by slow but steady steps gave the PRC a useful additional bargaining chip.[131] Should the British decide to abandon the Patten plan, the PRC could then make a grand symbolic gesture. It could either suspend the appointment of the PWC or, if already formed, give it purely honorific functions. Such considerations lay behind the PRC's decision, while talks were underway over the Patten plan, to allow a long interval – three months – between announcing its intention and actually naming the committee.

The other, and at first secondary, objective was to provide the infrastructure to 'build a new kitchen'. All its 57 members were either senior cadres from relevant departments within the PRC establishment or Hong Kong residents who had taken a pro-PRC stance over the Patten plan. If it should prove unnecessary to build a 'new kitchen' the PWC could still serve as a useful interdepartmental coordinating body. Hence, it was headed by Vice-Premier and Foreign Minister Qian Qichen. It was represented at the vice-ministerial level by the Ministry of Public Security, the PLA, the Communist Party's United Front Department, and various economic, trade and financial ministries in addition to the Foreign Ministry and HKMAO. To make it non-offensive to Hong Kong opinion, 30 of its 57 members were carefully selected from among Hong Kong's residents.[132] With a membership on which the PRC leadership could count to safeguard its interests, it became a useful organisation in case a 'new kitchen' really needed to be built.

Until the Sino-British talks collapsed in December 1993, the PRC kept its promise not to make the PWC into an 'alternative centre of authority or a shadow government'.[133] On its inauguration earlier in July, the PRC gave the PWC rather general terms of reference, with no specific instructions to 'build a new kitchen'. It was only after the talks ended that the PRC asked the PWC to carry out serious and specific research into what could actually be done to prepare the PRC to resume sovereign authority.[134] The originally secondary purpose of the PWC, which was to 'build a new kitchen', had become the primary one. Once the Legislative Council passed into law the Patten reform plan, Jiang Zemin directed the PWC to 'rely on our own resources as the basis and staunchly follow the directive of upholding our interests to ensure the stable transition' in Hong Kong.[135] Construction work for a 'new kitchen' started in earnest.[136]

This change in PRC policy in 1994 was very important. Marked by Jiang's directive on self-reliance, the PRC acted as if the British had irretrievably abandoned convergence as a policy. It ceased to count on Sino-British cooperation to ensure a stable transition and minimised making public references to 'Hong Kong people ruling Hong Kong'.[137] Instead, it emphasised relying on itself to implement the 'one country, two systems' policy. Beijing accepted that Patten's reforms would be introduced, but was determined to reverse them. Furthermore, by preparing to nullify all legislative changes implemented through the bill of rights during Patten's tenure, the PRC aimed to counteract the impression that he had improved Hong Kong's human rights situation. Once conciliation failed, the PRC sought to destroy Patten's reforms and to lay the blame entirely on him for causing the retrogression.

The British, for their part, had not abandoned convergence as a policy in 1994. They still wanted a smooth and successful transition and therefore continued to cooperate with the PRC over practical arrangements. After their spectacularly unsuccessful stand over the Patten plan, the British conceded that 'further contests with China' on most other matters had become 'a thing of the past'.[138] Although the British did not capitulate on all issues, they accepted that, by July 1997, the PRC would be able to do whatever it wanted. If they believed that the PRC was misguided over some issue, they were prepared to argue and try to persuade it otherwise. However, apart from the Patten plan, they did not take a stand on other issues. This even included the Court of Final Appeal – vital for maintaining judicial independence. Patten faced great pressure from some of his former Cabinet colleagues who were more interested in promoting trade with the PRC.[139] Since the PRC mistakenly thought the British had abandoned convergence and no longer expected almost automatic British cooperation, their public disputes became relatively less acrimonious. An ironic situation was thus created in which Sino-British cooperation appeared to improve after the talks over the Patten plan collapsed.

In September 1995, Hong Kong elected a new Legislative Council along the lines of the Patten plan. Although the elections proved beyond any reasonable doubt that it was possible for fair, open and democratic elections to flourish there, Hong Kong was not turned into a democracy. Martin Lee's Democratic Party failed to gain power, despite its electoral successes. Contrary to the PRC's understanding, there was simply no scope for such a development in the Patten plan. The PRC allowed its supporters to take part in the elections, but they did badly. They won only 16 seats from different types of constituencies in a council of 60. It was a slap in the face for the PRC. It removed what residue of hope there was that the Chinese leadership might allow the last Legislative Council to continue basically as it was after retrocession.[140] This led to a difficult problem. Arrangements had to be made either for new elections in 1997 or for an interim measure to be taken.

In light of the shift in PRC policy from seeking Sino-British cooperation to relying on itself, and the electoral defeat of pro-PRC forces, the PRC leadership decided to keep a tighter rein over the first SAR legislature. It thus resolved not to hold new elections but to form a provisional Legislative Council by appointments. Such an arrangement breached the Basic Law and the Joint Declaration, both of which required the first SAR legislature to be elected. Justifying its creation on the grounds that this had become unavoidable following the British violation of these two documents by implementing the Patten plan, the PRC turned the provisional Legislative Council into a key feature of the 'new kitchen'.[141]

In the meantime, the PRC also proceeded to form a preparatory committee chaired by Qian Qichen in January 1996. This was 'responsible for preparing the establishment of the Selection Committee for the First Government' of the SAR.[142] The selection committee itself was duly constituted in November 1996. It was entrusted with selecting the provisional Legislative Council and with electing the chief executive for the SAR.

As the PRC had by then committed itself to 'build a new kitchen', Britain had become irrelevant to its endeavours to set up the SAR's political institutions. In its own way, however, the PRC did try to assuage public opinion in Hong Kong. The provisional Legislative Council finally appointed in December 1996 was constituted with this requirement in mind. Hence, of its 60 members, 33 were in the existing Legislative Council.[143] Allocating more than half the seats to incumbent legislators was meant to suggest that, had the British not implemented the Patten plan, Hong Kong could have had a 'through train'. In other words, the 1995 legislature could have served out its four-year term until 1999.[144] Though the 60 did not include anyone from Martin Lee's Democratic Party, which condemned the selection process, four members of the Association for Democracy and People's Livelihood, one of the smaller pro-democracy parties, were included.[145] This was supposed to suggest a balanced representation of the local community's different political persuasions.[146]

These two arrangements were designed to reassure the more sceptical elements of Hong Kong society. Seats were allocated both to reward groups closest to the PRC and to guarantee the PRC's ability to dominate the council. Ten of those who campaigned (but were defeated) on pro-PRC platforms in the 1995 Legislative Council elections were appointed, and 85 per cent of all appointees were themselves members of the selection committee.[147] With an appointed council making a mockery of the 1995 election results, the PRC had forced democratisation in Hong Kong to take a step back. Also, because Governor Patten was held to be responsible for derailing the 'through train', it was he who was meant to get the blame.[148] The composition of the provisional Legislative Council suggested that, for the PRC, the more important consideration had remained the safeguarding of its interests.

In December 1996, before the appointment of the provisional Legislative Council, Premier Li Peng appointed Tung Chee-hwa – a local shipping magnate whose company was previously financially beholden to the PRC – chief executive of the SAR. He was to take office formally on 1 July 1997.[149] A chief executive would probably have been selected around this time even without the dispute over the Patten plan. Given the decision to 'build a new kitchen', however, the PRC needed to handle the matter differently. When convergence was still in place, there was a general expectation that, to ensure continuity, the British would appoint the chief executive elect as a lieutenant-governor, or to a similar position, in the run-up to the handover. This prospect was removed when conciliation failed. In picking Tung, the PRC again ignored the British as a factor. This was in sharp contrast to the drafting of the Basic Law, when British comments were taken into account. In other words, although the idea of electing the chief executive pre-dated that of 'building a new kitchen', Tung's appointment turned him into the most important part of this new creation.

Once appointed, Tung proceeded to name his Executive Council in early 1997. In so doing, he had to defer to the PRC's wish to reverse Patten's 1992 initiative to separate the Executive Council from the legislature. Apart from two members of the SAR Executive Council being chosen from members of the provisional Legislative Council, the same rationale governing the formation of the provisional Legislative Council applied. Tung and the PRC government tried to appoint an Executive Council that would enjoy credibility among the people of Hong Kong, provide a degree of continuity and, most importantly, safeguard the PRC's interests.

To satisfy the first two requirements, Tung nominated two members of Governor Patten's Executive Council to serve on his 11-member SAR Executive Council. They would provide continuity. Furthermore, Tung appointed Sir Sze-yuen Chung as convenor of the SAR Executive Council. Chung had been the senior member of the Hong Kong Executive Council for much of the 1980s, particularly during the negotiations for the Joint Declaration. He had become acceptable to the PRC because he opposed Patten's reforms. Although Chung has continued to put Hong Kong's interests before all others, the PRC regards him as a repentant 'patriot'. As a respected elder statesman, his appointment was meant to lend credibility to the SAR Executive Council. To meet the requirement of safeguarding the PRC's interests, Tung allowed the PRC's invisible hand to guide him. He dropped two of his original choices and appointed a few whose names had been gently suggested to him.[150] It was not purely accidental that four convenors of various subgroups in the preparatory committee were appointed. Three of the 11 members are believed to belong to the Chinese Communist Party.[151] The composition of the SAR Executive Council reflected the PRC wish to strike a kind of balance between reassuring the local people and protecting its own interests.

By the spring of 1997, with the Chief Executive, his Executive Council and the provisional Legislative Council in place, the PRC had completed the 'new kitchen'. It had been built largely without taking British views into account. Now the PRC had an institution with which to take over Hong Kong on the appointed date, with or without British cooperation. The transition had reached a point at which the British had only limited room for manoeuvre. Foreign Secretary Malcolm Rifkind admitted in early 1997 that 'both the British Government and Hong Kong people were realistic about the scope for action by Britain at this stage in the transition period'.[152] Although the British government continued to discharge its responsibilities, it had accepted that the Patten reforms would not survive retrocession. The Chinese were convinced that the British would try to further their interests by seeking a confrontation over Hong Kong.

Conclusion
Full Circle?

At midnight on 30 June 1997, Hong Kong, the last great imperial possession of the British Empire, became the first Special Administrative Region of the PRC. In the context of modern Chinese history, this marked the completion of a full circle, from Hong Kong being ceded by the declining Chinese Empire in 1842 to its peaceful and successful retrocession to resurgent and powerful China 155 years later.

British rule, however, left indelible marks on Hong Kong. It had developed a history of its own, about which its people felt a sense of pride. It had transformed itself from a collection of sleepy fishing villages into a great modern metropolis. In the context of British imperial history, it had changed from an outpost of the Empire to its richest and most successful non-settlement colony.

British Hong Kong was handed back to the successor state of the Chinese Empire not because it had failed or its people had voted to do so, but for essentially the same reason that it had come under British rule in the first place. This was the result of the changing balance of power between Britain and China. The main difference being that this time this was recognised and acted on by its sovereign power, Britain, without fighting a war that it could not win. Both Britain and China accepted that Hong Kong had become too valuable to risk its destruction. In this sense the peaceful and successful transfer of its sovereignty represented the triumph of reason and responsible behaviour over emotion and dogma.

Hong Kong rejoining mother China was not a matter of putting the clock back. Both Hong Kong and China had changed fundamentally since the 1840s. Reintegrating modern Hong Kong into a rapidly modernising China was not a simple or straightforward process but a highly delicate affair. The adoption of the 'one country, two systems' formula by the PRC government for reunification underlined its tacit admission that British Hong Kong was such a spectacular achievement that it would need to be preserved essentially as it was, despite the need to satisfy Chinese nationalism and irredentism, and to safeguard 'socialism with Chinese characteristics'.

Hong Kong had indeed acquired a sense of identity, way of life and value system in its British period that set it apart from those prevailing in mainland China. Hong Kong's history under the British was, on the one hand, closely linked to developments in China. Economic imperatives, close social links, human ties and the sheer force of geography saw to that. British protection and values, on the other hand, insulated Hong Kong from the worst turbulence of modern Chinese history. The British presence kept Hong Kong out of great upheavals like the Taiping Uprising or the Boxer movement under the imperial dynasty, large-scale civil wars during the republican period and madness like the Great Leap Forward or the Cultural Revolution under the Communists. The history of British Hong Kong was both an important history in its own right and, at the same time, part of the history of the British Empire and an extramural part of the history of modern China.

Handover

The lowering of the British flag at Government House on 30 June 1997 for the last time marked the end of an era. It was an emotional moment for all concerned.

To the departing British, Hong Kong was their last major imperial possession and its handover to the PRC effectively symbolised the end of the British Empire built up in the heyday of Queen Victoria.[1] Had there been no appointment with China, Hong Kong would have been the greatest success story of modern British imperial rule. Britain was leaving behind a vibrant modern economy with a higher per capita GDP than that of the metropolitan country itself, a well-educated population admired for its resourcefulness and entrepreneurial drive, a law-abiding and human rights-respecting society, as well as a stable, liberal and efficient government. The transfer of power had worked so well that the British could claim that they left their last major colony with honour.[2] A dignified and graceful departure and handover was intended.

For the PRC, the handover symbolised the end of what it calls a century of humiliation by Western imperialism. It represented a great triumph for the pragmatism of Deng Xiaoping's approach in building 'socialism with Chinese characteristics'.[3] Since Deng had died earlier in the year, it was President Jiang Zeming, finally the top leader in reality as well as in name, who presided over this historic event with the national flag metaphorically draped all over him.[4] The retrocession of Hong Kong was a grand moment not only for the government, but also for a good number of Chinese who lived in big urban centres. Public emotion was high in the capital, Beijing, where a street party of gigantic scale was held to mark the occasion. For those Chinese who could afford the time to pursue an interest in either nationalism or Hong Kong, they by and large accepted the official Communist view of the history of Hong Kong and shared the sentiments of their leaders. To them, Hong Kong's retrocession was the greatest occasion for a public celebration since the founding of the PRC in 1949.

The local Chinese in Hong Kong, in contrast, had mixed feelings. While many shared the nationalistic sentiments of their compatriots, others displayed emotional, even melancholic, attachment to the era that was ending. In public, most citizens of Hong Kong expressed their confidence in the future and welcomed the retrocession, but in private many held their breath about their future and hoped for the best. Bearing in mind the well-known but unspoken sensitivity of the PRC establishment and their emotional commitment to the handover, Hong Kong society as a whole was ready to play its part in the great celebration.

What the people of Hong Kong were celebrating was not as clear-cut as that for their compatriots in the PRC. They celebrated for different reasons in Hong Kong. Some did so because they believed in Chinese nationalism, others because it was a politically correct and astute move. Still others, probably the overwhelming majority, took the occasion in the spirit that had made British Hong Kong the miracle it was. It was the spirit of resourceful resilience. The transfer of sovereignty was a foregone conclusion and it was vital to the people of Hong Kong that it should succeed. For this they must secure the goodwill of the new sovereign power. Many in Hong Kong celebrated to ensure they would have a future worth celebrating.

On the day of the transfer of sovereignty, both the British and Chinese governments were represented by their top leaders. The British delegation was headed by the Prince of Wales, as the personal representative of Queen Elizabeth II. It was constituted, in order of precedence, by Prime Minister Tony Blair, Foreign Secretary Robin Cook, Governor Patten and the Chief of the Defence Staff General Sir Charles Guthrie.[5] A long list of British dignitaries, including all the former prime ministers, foreign secretaries and ambassadors involved in the negotiations of Hong Kong's future since 1979 were among the 4,000 guests from all over the world.

The PRC delegation was headed by President Jiang Zemin himself. It was also made up of Premier Li Peng, Vice-Premier Qian Qichen, Deputy Chairman of the Central Military Commission General Zhang Wannian and Chief Executive designate Tung Chee-hwa. The ranking of the Chief Executive designate below the senior PLA representative made a contrast to the British arrangement by which the Governor took precedence over the Chief of the Defence Staff. It reflected the difference in importance accorded to the offices concerned by Britain and the PRC.

The absence of the third ranking leader of the PRC, Chairman of the National People's Congress Qiao Shi, on the Chinese side was noteworthy. In strict constitutional terms it is the NPC, not the Presidency or the Premiership, which took over from the British Crown as the ultimate source and arbiter of Hong Kong's constitution as a Chinese SAR.[6] Given that the SAR was founded on the authority of the NPC, his absence at the handover should have been a matter of significance; subsequent developments within the PRC suggest otherwise. Qiao's absence was connected with the consolidation of President Jiang's position as successor to Deng as paramount leader and Qiao's being eased out of the centre of power. It was not meant to undermine the constitutional links between the SAR and the NPC. Nevertheless, this should remind everyone that in the context of the political reality of the PRC, the real holders of power, rather than the constitutional repository of authority, are the ultimate arbiters of the SAR's scope of autonomy and future.

Whether Governor Patten, or for that matter anyone, represented the people of Hong Kong at the transfer of power was a moot point. The people of Hong Kong had previously been excluded specifically from the negotiations for their future in accordance with the PRC's policy. They were also not represented in the handover. Their last governor effectively left office after the Union flag was lowered at Government House in the afternoon, though the formal transfer of sovereignty and his authority did not take place until midnight. The handover ceremony was officiated by the Prince of Wales, heir to the throne for the British, and President Jiang for the Chinese. At this, the most formal and important part of the proceedings, Governor Patten had no official role to play. The only public roles he did play in the day were at the British farewell ceremonies, not at the handover ceremony. By the time of the handover he was, for all practical purposes, merely a member of the British delegation. Hong Kong was handed over with its people reduced to spectators and providers of entertainment for the day's celebrations.

Although the handover was treated by the two governments concerned as a bilateral issue, the world community and the international media devoted much attention to it. It is not clear whether such attention and high-level government representation primarily reflected a recognition of Hong Kong's economic importance or underlined the international community's support for the continued upholding of human rights and freedom in the SAR. The two considerations are in any event not mutually exclusive. As it turned out, the several thousand journalists from all over the world shared a moment of history and a grand party with one of the most spectacular firework displays in human history while the ceremonies of the day went largely as planned, except for the torrential rain.

When the PRC flag and the SAR flag were raised after the British had transferred sovereignty, Hong Kong was symbolically put in its place. With the SAR flag visibly smaller and raised half a pace slower than the PRC flag in the ceremony, the people of Hong Kong were shown quite clearly that the SAR was created with 'a high degree of autonomy' by the grace of the PRC. It left no doubt that the 'one country, two systems' policy was meant to further, first and foremost, the PRC's national interests. The existence of this new political imperative was acknowledged by the SAR's Chief Executive, who said at the ceremony to found the SAR:

Our foremost task is to enhance Hong Kong's economic vitality and sustain economic growth. Only through the creation of wealth can we improve the living of the people of Hong Kong, and continue to contribute to our country.[7]

Shortly after the formal handover ceremony, the new SAR government was sworn in by the new Chief Justice, Andrew Li. Tung Chee-hwa took office as Chief Executive of the SAR. Police and other uniformed officers kept their British-style uniforms but discreetly changed their cap badges and other insignia of the old colonial regime. Administrative power was transferred in an orderly, efficient and uneventful fashion.

Much as the transfer of sovereignty and power went smoothly, significant though subtle realignment of power also took place as Hong Kong started its first day as a Chinese SAR. This involved much more than introducing a series of measures required to put into legal effect the handover of power from Britain to the PRC.

As a reaction to the acrimonious disputes during the tenure of Patten as governor, the Chinese adhered to their policy of 'building a new kitchen'. As a result, the SAR introduced a wholly appointed provisional Legislative Council to replace the partially directly elected last British Legislative Council immediately after the handover ceremonies. In turn, this new Council promptly introduced and passed the Reunification Bill, which gave effect to 13 bills it had previously passed during sittings in Shenzhen, across the border.[8] They had the effect of annulling some of the changes introduced by Governor Patten.[9]

This did not mean the PRC intended to claw back from the 'high degree of autonomy' it promised the SAR. However, there was doubt at first whether the SAR government was prepared or able to exercise fully its 'high degree of autonomy'. In addition to the uncertainty inherent in a transfer of power of this nature, it was also because the PRC's assumption of sovereignty meant the power relationship among authorities in Hong Kong, the PRC government and other power centres such as the PLA, the Communist Party and other regions in China were changed.[10]

The most immediately relevant aspect of this new power alignment was the relationship between the Chief Executive and the head of the Hong Kong and Macao Work Committee of the Communist Party. After 1949, the latter used to operate as the PRC's de facto representative in colonial Hong Kong under the guise of the local Director of the Xinhua News Agency. The PRC government made a special effort to give the SAR government a good head start. The senior Party man Zhou Nan was retired. His multiple responsibilities were divided. His quasi-diplomatic duties were transferred to the Foreign Ministry's Special Commissioner stationed in Hong Kong, a cadre at ambassadorial rather than ministerial rank. The office of the Director of Xinhua was kept. However, Beijing did not appoint Jiang Enzhu to this office immediately after the handover. It gave the SAR government a month to settle in before Jiang's appointment was announced. As Jiang was elevated to membership of the Central Committee in the Fifteenth Party Congress in September, he undoubtedly also took over as Secretary of the Work Committee. This office carried ministerial rank. After 1997, the importance of Hong Kong would be at least equal to that of Shanghai or Tianjian. The Party Secretary of these two special municipalities usually carried membership of the Politburo.

That Jiang was only given Central Committee membership and a bureaucratic rank below that of the Chief Executive could not have been accidental. It meant the PRC government really intended 'to let the Chief Executive have a freer hand in the management of domestic affairs'.[11]

Indeed, the PRC government gave the SAR Chief Executive an important lever to enable him to defend himself and his administration against other Chinese power centres. He was given a bureaucratic rank higher than that usually granted to a provincial governor or mayor of a special municipality. He was given more than ministerial rank. His specific rank has not been clarified, but it is equivalent to either a State Councillor or a Vice-Premier.[12] This was meant to make him less susceptible to pressure from heads of provincial governments or heads of ministries. To reinforce this position, Jiang Zemin powerfully stressed at the founding ceremony of the SAR that 'no central department or locality may or will be allowed to interfere in the affairs' of the SAR.[13] Indeed, subsequent events and testimonies by top SAR officials confirm that senior PRC cadres visibly interfered less in the affairs of Hong Kong than they had before the transfer of sovereignty.

The continued adherence to a policy of exercising maximum flexibility within a rigid framework by the PRC government notwithstanding, the SAR government under Chief Executive Tung has not pressed for the widest scope of autonomy permissible since 1997. The most blatant example was over the dispute involving the right of abode of a large number of children of recent PRC migrants to Hong Kong.[14] When the number of children involved appeared dauntingly large, the Chief Executive abandoned his public commitments to the rule of law and subverted the ruling of the Court of Final Appeal, which ruled in the children's favour. In response, Tung invited the NPC Standing Committee to make an interpretation over such a matter that would be binding on the Court of Final Appeal, and thus forced the latter to reverse its ruling. Tung did not do so under pressure from the PRC. He took the initiative himself. In so doing he breached the terms of Article 158, the interpretation article in the Basic Law, which reserved the right to seek clarification or a ruling from the NPC to the Court of Final Appeal and not to the Chief Executive.[15]

British Legacies

By 1 July 1997, the British Empire had wound itself up in Hong Kong but its legacies live on, at least for the moment. The economic successes of modern Hong Kong should not be allowed to distort the real legacies of British administration for a century and a half. Although Hong Kong was transformed from a collection of fishing villages to a great metropolis and one of the world's leading financial centres, this should not be attributed to the efforts of the British. In its first century of British rule, Hong Kong in fact lagged behind Shanghai as an economic centre. In any event, Hong Kong's economic achievements owed more to its Chinese community than to its expatriate community after the first two or three decades of British administration. The greatest contribution of British rule in this regard was to provide the political framework and social stability that enabled Hong Kong's economy to flourish. However, the vibrant and highly capitalistic economy of Hong Kong at the time of the handover was not an export from socialist Britain. The management of Hong Kong's economy in the 1980s might have made it look like the only place where Thatcherism was applied in its purest form, but it was in place well before Margaret Thatcher came to power in Britain in 1979. The real legacies of the British Empire in Hong Kong need to be found elsewhere.

While the most significant British legacies are easy to identify, it is inherently controversial to rank their relative importance. However much one may try to be objective in a matter of judgement like this, one's assessments cannot but reflect one's personal values and background. To myself, an academic historian of the British liberal tradition who grew up in Hong Kong and witnessed first-hand its transformation from the 1960s, the most important inheritances the British passed on to the SAR are an independent judiciary and the rule of law. More than any other British legacies, they are not indigenous to the Chinese tradition and are fundamental for the protection and advancement of the rights and dignity of the individual.

In spite of the notable shortcomings inherent in the system, the integrity and standard of the judiciary in Hong Kong in 1997 was, in general terms, as high as most in British common law jurisdictions. The exorbitant charges of the legal profession in Hong Kong – one of its shortcomings – also ensured that Hong Kong's judiciary regularly saw the service of the best common law lawyers. The regular import of lawyers and judicial officers, even if only for short duration in relation to specific cases, helped a small jurisdiction like Hong Kong to maintain a high standard in its legal profession and judiciary. A competent and entrenched judiciary whose independence enjoyed institutionalised protection was handed over to the SAR in 1997.[16] Its independence has so far been upheld by the Court of Final Appeal since the transfer of sovereignty. Even in the controversial cases involving the right of abode for children of recent PRC immigrants, the Court of Final Appeal has maintained its own independence, though the SAR government improperly invited the Chinese NPC to change the law that became binding on the Courts.

The rule of law is more than an Anglo-Saxon political idea or legal concept. It is a way of life. It diverts completely from the Chinese legal tradition and remains an alien concept in the PRC, where it is routinely confused with 'rule by law'. It took Hong Kong a long time to understand and appreciate its value. By the 1990s, this idea had generally been accepted among the people of Hong Kong as a great gift from the British. They were proud that the rule of law prevailed in Hong Kong. In the first two years after the handover, commitment to it even appeared to have 'become an article of faith' in the SAR. It was so much so that 'no major speech by its senior officials has seemed complete without a passage explaining the importance of this idea to the territory's wellbeing'.[17]

Notwithstanding such value being put on it, whether the rule of law has really become an enduring part of the social and political fabric of Hong Kong remains to be tested. The first SAR government has so far, as revealed in the right of abode controversy, failed to show a real understanding and acceptance of this concept. If it did it would have accepted the Court of Final Appeal's ruling in January 1999, despite the economic costs for granting the right of abode to a large number of children of recent immigrants, and then sought to introduce new laws to rectify the situation. The acquiescence of the local community in the SAR government's effort to subvert the decision of the Court of Final Appeal suggests it has not fully understood the true implications of the rule of law either. In the long term whether this particular British legacy will prove enduring will depend first and foremost on whether it will indeed become part of the social and political fabric of the SAR, though pressure from the PRC to violate it may also become an issue at a later stage.

Another important British legacy is the politically neutral professional civil service, which largely functioned like a meritocracy. Although the colonial civil service suffered from many of the problems common to large bureaucracies of 180,000 employees, it was by any standard a modern, efficient, effective and honest one. It was indeed the existence of such a civil service that enabled the colonial authorities to deliver as good a government as possible in the Chinese tradition by the early 1980s. Its being handed over to the SAR virtually intact was also a key factor underlying the viability of the 'one country, two systems' policy. At the time of the transfer of sovereignty, the civil service had the trained human resources, structure, ethos and experience and sufficient public confidence to operate effectively on its own without political direction. If Hong Kong could be compared to a modern jumbo jet, its civil service would be the best autopilot or fly-by-wire system available. It worked so well that it could and did enable an inexperienced new captain to take over control smoothly.

In an important sense, the police force stands out as a particularly significant element of this British legacy. It is a critical instrument for maintaining social stability and good order, as Hong Kong has been highly susceptible to urban rioting since 1949. The SAR is one of the world's most densely populated urban centres, where people living in high-rise buildings can congregate and take part in urban riots with virtually no advance warning. It needs and has inherited a police force that is not only very well drilled and equipped in suppressing riots but is also trained to disperse gathering crowds through the minimum use of force to pre-empt a minor disturbance from escalating into a major riot. The police can do so because it enjoys public confidence. This was, in turn, based largely on the removal of organised corruption and the introduction of community policing in the 1980s. The existence of a credible, efficient and honest police force is therefore an important instrument left behind by the British underpinning good public order.

An equally important element of this British legacy is the Independent Commission Against Corruption. While the general achievements of the

ICAC in tackling corruption are notable and significant, its most important long-term contribution rests in being the symbol of a key basis of the local political culture. By the 1980s, the ICAC had managed to instil in the local population the value that corruption had no place in Hong Kong society though it in fact continued to exist, mostly on an individual basis. The change in general public attitude from tolerating corruption as a widespread 'ugly practice' in old Hong Kong to an arrogant assertion that Hong Kong was above such a despicable practice rampant in the PRC or elsewhere in Asia in the 1980s is highly significant. Just as the dramatic breaking of syndicate corruption established the credibility of the colonial government in the 1970s, a visible failure of the SAR government to uphold the integrity of the public service or to support the ICAC at its work can have much greater impact than any immediate failing. The public hostility towards corruption within Hong Kong, symbolised by the general public support for the ICAC certainly represents one of the best parting gifts from the colonial government.

While the civil service as a whole is an invaluable British legacy, its value also needs to be put in context. The colonial administration was well regarded because it was essentially a small government and the general public did not expect much of it. The span of government activities in British Hong Kong had traditionally been confined to providing mainly the regulatory framework for businesses and individuals to maximise their own potential. The colonial government had, for example, a very modest social welfare programme for a society more wealthy than the UK on a per capita basis. It did not take it upon itself to attempt social engineering or to direct the economy. The small span of the colonial administration and its basically non-interventionist ethos enabled it to avoid a lot of controversial public debates and attacks by politicians commonplace in democratic countries. This worked well for the non-elected colonial government which was contented with being a small government.

Although the SAR government benefited tremendously from inheriting a well-oiled civil service machinery, the demands on governance in post-colonial Hong Kong in fact go beyond what the old civil service was prepared to do. As a government of the local people, as distinct from being a colonial administration, the SAR government is expected to take a more proactive role in dealing with Hong Kong's economic and social problems. The inherited civil service, particularly at the policymaking level, was not used to taking a proactive approach over such matters. This problem is more pronounced as policies to direct the economy or to rectify social inequality, for example, are inherently political in nature. This is not an area in which the colonial civil service ever demonstrated any particular aptitude.

Furthermore, the end of colonialism also resulted in a basic change in attitude. One of the key factors that produced a non-interventionist government in British Hong Kong was the existence of the inhibited political centre.[18] After the handover, 'the paradox of maintaining a formal colonial regime in a world hostile to colonialism, which gave rise to the inhibited political centre effect, disappeared', and the SAR government felt it had a 'much greater scope than its predecessor for bold policy initiatives'.[19]

Equally importantly, with top civil service positions reserved for local officers, senior SAR officials also became more confident, assertive and arrogant. This was partly a reaction to the end of colonialism. It was also partly the result of a steady rise in 'an exaggerated assessment of one's ability... and a kind of Hong Kong chauvinism' that had become commonplace as Hong Kong achieved spectacular economic successes in the last decades of British rule.[20]

Moreover, the head of government was changed from the hands-off former British Cabinet Minister Patten to the former patriarchal head of a Chinese family business, Tung Chee-hwa, who was determined to show that the SAR could do better than the old British colony. They together caused a change in the ethos of the government, which shifted from the old 'positive non-interventionist' approach into a positive policy of actively managing new economic or social developments.

This basic change in the ethos of the administration underlines the SAR government's new willingness to support the property and equity markets and 'punish' currency speculators during the Asian financial contagion, and to require the Courts to deny children of immigrant Chinese from poor backgrounds from gaining residency in Hong Kong. This new approach goes beyond the grounds familiar to the civil service the SAR inherited from the British.

Another significant British legacy in the socio-political area is related to the ways the last British governor discharged his responsibilities. Although most of Patten's political reforms were undone after the handover, he did leave an indelible mark on the people and politicians of Hong Kong.

Although only a colonial governor, Patten continued to behave like a politician in a democracy. The way he handled Governor's Question Time in the legislature, members of the Legislative Council, the media and the general public gave the people of Hong Kong first-hand experience of how senior politicians in a democracy actually behave. He gave 'the Hong Kong people a taste, albeit a limited one, of what politics was like in a democracy with a first rate politician in power'.[21] He left a benchmark against which electoral and other politics has come to be measured in Hong Kong.

This applied even to the leading local political party set up with the blessings of the CCP, the Democratic Alliance for the Betterment of Hong Kong. It realised that it must become 'a full participant in conventional democratic politics' in response to Patten's impact on local politics.[22] Although the dismantling of much of Patten's reforms in 1997 set Hong Kong back in its democratic development, it did not destroy the local people's faith in democracy.[23] Patten's record of behaving like an elected chief executive while he was governor was like forbidden fruit to the people of Hong Kong. They had tasted it. Whether its effect will prove endurable or not remains to be seen.

Ultimately, the durability of the British legacies depends on whether they have become part of the fabric of the society and politics of Hong Kong. The attitude and policy of the PRC government are also important, but its continued adherence to the principle of exercising maximum flexibility within a rigid framework implies that much still rests with the government and people of the SAR. Their continuation does not in any way infringe the PRC's sovereignty over the SAR or challenge the continued domination of politics by the Communist Party in the country as a whole. The most important legacies from the British are all in fact essential for making Hong Kong the tremendously successful place it is, the *raison d'être* behind the Chinese policy of 'one country, two systems'.

Notes

Chapter 1: War and Peace

1. Hobsbawn, *Industry and Empire*, 48–9.
2. Stokesbury, *Navy and Empire*, 238.
3. Swanson, *Eight Voyage of the Dragon*, 37–8.
4. Loewe, *The Pride That is China*, 152.
5. Elvin, *The Pattern of the Chinese Past*, 312.
6. Banister, *China's Changing Population*, 3–4.
7. Peyrefitte, *The Collision of Two Civilisations: The British Expedition to China in 1792–4*, 544–5.
8. Huang, *China: A Macro History*, 193.
9. Schurmann and Schell (eds), *Imperial China*, 103.
10. Hsu, *The Rise of Modern China* (4ᵗʰ ed.), 150–1.
11. Blake, *Jardine Matheson: Traders of the Far East*, 59.
12. Wong, *Deadly Dreams: Opium and the Arrow War (1856–1860) in China*, 336.
13. Ibid. 346, 351.
14. Trocki, *Opium, Empire and the Global Political Economy*, 164–5.
15. Wong, *Deadly Dreams*, 406.
16. Ibid. 398.
17. Blue, 'Opium for China: The British Connection', 32; Spear, *A History of India*, vol.2, 113.
18. Hamashita, 'Foreign Trade Finance in China, 1810–50', 387–435; Blake, *Jardine Matheson*, 80–1.
19. Hamashita, op. cit., 398–400.
20. Polachek, *The Inner Opium War*, 104.
21. Fairbank, *Trade and Diplomacy on the China Coast*, 76.
22. Waley, *The Opium War Through Chinese Eyes*, 25.
23. Polachek, *Inner Opium War*, 109–10.
24. Ibid. 1–135.
25. For Macartney's embassy, see Peyrefitte, *Collision of Two Civilisations*.
26. Waley, *The Opium War Through Chinese Eyes*, 35.
27. Hsu, *China's Entrance into the Family of Nations*, 5.
28. Wong, *The First Chinese Minister to Great Britain*.
29. Fay, *The Opium War, 1840–1842*, 68–79.
30. Blake, *Jardine Matheson*, 78–9.
31. *Chinese Repository*, xi, no.4, 22 July 1836.
32. Fay, *The Opium War*, 82.

33. Huang, *Civil Justice in China*, 63.
34. For a survey, see Keeton, *The Development of Extraterritoriality in China*, vol.1, 27–88.
35. Polachek, *Inner Opium War*, 123–5.
36. Ibid. 128.
37. Ibid. 129, 134.
38. Fay, *Opium War*, 193–4.
39. Graham, *The China Station: War and Diplomacy, 1830–1860*, 113.
40. Morse, *International Relations of the Chinese Empire*, 622 (Palmerston to Minister of Chinese Emperor, 20 February 1840).
41. FO17/40, Elliot to Palmerston, 18 July 1840.
42. Fay, *Opium War*, 195.
43. Costin, *Great Britain and China, 1833–1860*, 74.
44. Spence, *The Search for Modern China*, 154. In this period, British warships were in general terms rated by the number of guns they carried. A first-rate man-of-war would carry about 120 guns. Each third-rate man-of-war used in the China campaign, except HMS *Cornwallis*, carried 74 guns.
45. Hoe and Roebuck, *The Taking of Hong Kong: Charles and Clara Elliot in China Waters*, 151.
46. Morse, *International Relations of the Chinese Empire*, 650–2 (Elliot to Auckland, 21 June 1841).
47. Blake, *Charles Elliot RN*, 55.
48. Ouchterlony, *The Chinese War*, 342–3.
49. CO129/1, Extract from Stanley to President of Board of Control, 31 December 1841.
50. Morse, *International Relations of the Chinese Empire*, 648 (Elliot to Auckland, 21 June 1841).
51. Fay, *Opium War*, 361.
52. Morse, *International Relations of the Chinese Empire*, 658–9 (Palmerston to Pottinger, 31 May 1841).
53. Ibid. 668–9 (Aberdeen to Pottinger, 4 January 1843).
54. Ouchterlony, *The Chinese War*, 384–93.
55. Smith, *China's Cultural Heritage: The Ch'ing Dynasty, 1644–1912*, 41, 50–1.
56. Huang, *Zhongguo gudai bingzhi*, 161–2.
57. Morse, *International Relations of the Chinese Empire*, 642 (Palmerston to Elliot, 21 April 1841).
58. CO129/1, Treaty between Her Majesty and the Emperor of China, 29 August 1842.
59. Blake, *Jardine Matheson*, 104.
60. Teng and Fairbank (eds), *China's Response to the West*, 37–40.
61. Wakeman, *Strangers at the Gate*, 74–80.

Chapter 2: Foundation of a Crown Colony

1. Belcher, *Narrative of a Voyage Around the World*, vol.ii, 147.
2. Sayer, *Hong Kong, 1841–1862*, Appendix II.
3. Ibid. Appendix I (Elliot's proclamation, 2 February 1841).
4. CO129/1, Minute of conference among Elliot, Gough and Bremer in Macao, 27 March 1841.
5. Bernard, *The Nemesis in China*, 205–6.
6. FO17/60, Chief Superintendent's Establishment from 1 June 1842.
7. Blake, *Jardine Matheson*, 110.
8. Bernard, *The Nemesis*, 206.

9. FO17/60, Pottinger to Aberdeen, 20 May 1842.
10. Morse, *International Relations*, 642 (Palmerston to Elliot, 21 April 1841).
11. Ibid. 663 (Aberdeen to Pottinger, 4 November 1841).
12. Ibid. 650–1 (Elliot to Auckland, 21 June 1841).
13. Blake, *Jardine Matheson*, 111.
14. Morse, *International Relations*, 657 (Palmerston to Pottinger, 31 May 1841).
15. CO129/1, Treaty of Nanking.
16. CO129/2, Aberdeen to Pottinger, 6 April 1843.
17. Both documents are readily accessible in Tsang, *A Documentary History of Hong Kong*, 19–30.
18. CO129/2, Stanley to Pottinger, despatch 11, 2 August 1843; Hamilton, *Government Departments in Hong Kong, 1841–1969*, 75.
19. CO129/2, Royal Instructions, 6 April 1843.
20. CO129/2, Letters Patent, 5 April 1843.
21. CO129/2, Stanley to Pottinger 8, 3 June 1843.
22. Ibid.
23. Grantham, *Via Ports*, 105.
24. CO129/2, Stanley to Pottinger 8, 3 June 1843.
25. Morse, *International Relations*, 642 (Palmerston to Minister of Chinese Emperor, 20 February 1840).
26. Ibid. 628 (Palmerston to George Elliot and Charles Elliot, despatch 1, 20 February 1840).
27. CO129/55, Labouchere to Bowring 82, 29 July 1856.
28. Morse, *International Relations*, 651 (Elliot to Auckland, 21 June 1841).
29. CO129/13, Gladstone to Davis, 7 March 1848.
30. Sayer, *Hong Kong, 1841–1862*, additional notes 6 (Elliot's circular to British subjects, 20 January 1841).
31. CO129/3, Aberdeen to Pottinger, despatch 4, 4 January 1843.
32. Morse, *International Relations*, 663 (Aberdeen to Pottinger, 4 November 1841).
33. Bruce, *Second to None*, 4.
34. Ibid. 9.
35. Richardson, *The Royal Marines and Hong Kong, 1840–1997*, 4.
36. The other major occasions when HK proved valuable to British forces as a base for operations in China were during the Boxer War (1900) and the Shanghai Crisis (1925).
37. CO129/3, Aberdeen to Pottinger, despatch 4, 4 January 1843.
38. Sayer, *Hong Kong, 1841–1862*, 201 (Elliot's proclamation of 2 February 1841).
39. See Chapter 4.
40. CO129/4, Treasury minutes of 19 December 1843.
41. Tsang, *A Documentary History of Hong Kong*, 144.
42. CO129/4, Treasury minutes, 19 December 1843.
43. CO129/569, N.L. Smith to M. MacDonald 2, 13 September 1938.
44. Income tax was not introduced in Hong Kong until the First World War.
45. CO129/5, Pottinger to Stanley 11, 30 January 1844.
46. Tsang, *A Documentary History of Hong Kong*, 107.
47. Hamilton, *Government Departments in Hong Kong*, 62.
48. CO129/13, Memorial to Stanley from British mercantile community, 13 August 1845.
49. CO129/13, Gladstone to Davis, 7 March 1848.
50. CO129/274, Chamberlain to Robinson, despatch 119, 29 May 1896.
51. CO129/222, Bowen to Stanley 348, 5 September 1885.
52. CO129/209, Bowen to Derby 60, 14 May 1883.

53. CO129/80, 'Hong Kong Cadetship' (paper submitted to Sir T. Roger, 2 July 1861).
54. Munn, 'Colonialism "in a Chinese atmosphere": the Caldwell affair and the perils of collaboration in early colonial Hong Kong', 12–37.
55. Tsang, *A Documentary History of Hong Kong,*, 148–60; Lethbridge, 'Hong Kong Cadets, 1862–1941', 36–56.
56. Endacott, *A History of Hong Kong*, 125.
57. CO129/55, Bowring to Labouchere 49, 26 March 1856.
58. CO129/55, Labouchere to Bowring 82, 29 July 1856.
59. CO129/187, Pope-Hennessy to Hicks Beech 4, 19 January 1880.
60. CO129/187, R. Meade's minutes, undated (*c.* end of March 1880).
61. CO129/187, Herbert's minutes, 2 April 1880 and Hicks Beech's minutes, 3 April 1880.
62. CO129/187, Hicks Beech to Pope-Hennessy 39, 20 April 1880.
63. CO129/209, Derby to Bowen 158, 7 August 1883.
64. CO129/263, Petition (enclosure 1 from Robinson to Ripon 133, 5 June 1894).
65. CO129/263, Ripon to Robinson 135, 28 August 1894.
66. CO129/263, Enclosures 2 and 3 from Robinson to Ripon 133, 5 June 1894.
67. CO129/263, Ripon to Robinson, despatch 135, 28 August 1894.
68. Endacott, *An Eastern Entrepot*, 285 (Chamberlain to Robinson 119, 29 May 1896).
69. Tsang, *A Documentary History of Hong Kong,*, 79–80.
70. CO129/256, Robinson to Ripon, confidential despatch, 6 December 1892.

Chapter 3: Imperial Expansion

1.   Wakeman, *Strangers at the Gate*, 71.
2.   FO17/210, Clarendon to Bowring 2, 13 February 1854.
3.   Morse, *International Relations*, 677 (Encl. from Bowring to Clarendon 164, 2 October 1854).
4.   Wong, *Deadly Dreams*, 264–5.
5.   FO17/210, Clarendon to Bowring 2, 13 February 1854.
6.   Morse, *International Relations*, 687 (Bowring to Clarendon 260, 21 August 1856).
7.   Tong, *United States Diplomacy in China, 1844–60*, 3, 174–5.
8.   Ibid. 177.
9.   FO17/274, Clarendon to Elgin, draft 7, 20 April 1857.
10. Morse, *International Relations*, 684–5 (Bowring to Clarendon 200, 1 July 1856).
11. Ibid. 688 (Bowring to Clarendon 260, 21 August 1856).
12. Wong, *Deadly Dreams*, 69–70.
13. Ibid. 266–75.
14. Wakeman, *Strangers at the Gate*, 73–80.
15. Polachek, *The Inner Opium War*, 244.
16. Hurd, *The Arrow War: An Anglo-Chinese Confusion, 1856–60*, 19.
17. Wong, *Deadly Dreams*, 121–3.
18. Ibid. 123–4.
19. Hurd, *Arrow War*, 16.
20. Wong, *Yeh Ming-ch'en*, 164.
21. Ibid.
22. Bonner-Smith and Lumby (eds), *The Second China War, 1856–1860*, 7 (Parkes to Ye, 8 October 1856).
23. See Wong, *Deadly Dreams*.

24. Bonner-Smith and Lumby, *Second China War*, 15 (Parkes to Bowring, 10 October 1856); 18 (Bowring to Parkes, 11 October 1856).
25. Quoted in Hurd, *Arrow War*, 28.
26. Bonner-Smith and Lumby, *Second China War*, 35–6 (Yeh to Bowring, 21 October 1856).
27. Hurd, *Arrow War*, 45–6.
28. Bonner-Smith and Lumby, *Second China War*, 190–1 (Clarendon to Bowring, 25 March 1857).
29. Tong, *United States Diplomacy in China*, 196–8.
30. Bonner-Smith and Lumby, *Second China War*, 195 (Clarendon to Elgin, 20 April 1857).
31. Ibid. 210 (Elgin to Clarendon, 9 July 1857).
32. Charles S. Leavenworth, *The Arrow War with China*, 67.
33. Graham, *The China Station*, 327–8.
34. Hsu, *China's Entrance into the Family of Nations*, 93.
35. Morse, *International Relations*, 575.
36. Graham, *The China Station*, 373–7.
37. Mann, *China, 1860*, 5.
38. Knollys, *Incidents in the China War of 1860*, 223–5.
39. Gregory, *Great Britain and the Taipings*, 156–7.
40. For the original exposition of this concept, see Gallagher and Robinson, 'The Imperialism of Free Trade'. An expanded and updated discussion can be found in their *Africa and the Victorians*.
41. Liu, *An Outline History of Hong Kong*, 44.
42. CO381/35, Royal Order in Council, 4 February 1861.
43. Tsang, *A Documentary History of Hong Kong,*, 32 (Russell to Elgin, secret despatch 11, 25 April 1860).
44. Costin, *Great Britain and China*, 337.
45. Quested, *The Expansion of Russia in East Asia, 1857–1860*, 260–1.
46. Wesley-Smith, *Unequal Treaty, 1897–1997*, 11.
47. CO537/34, Encl. from Robinson to Ripon, secret despatch 23, 9 November 1894.
48. CO537/34, Robinson to Ripon, secret despatch 23, 9 November 1894.
49. Quoted in Wesley-Smith, *Unequal Treaty*, 17.
50. Welsh, *A History of Hong Kong*, 318.
51. Quoted in ibid. 320.
52. Schrecker, *Imperialism and Chinese Nationalism*, 23.
53. Quoted in Welsh, *A History of Hong Kong*, 320.
54. Joseph, *Foreign Diplomacy in China, 1894–1900*.
55. Atwell, *British Mandarins and Chinese Reformers*, 215.
56. Young, *British Policy in China, 1895–1902*, 71.
57. *House of Lords Debates*, 56 (1898), 165–6.
58. Words of Foreign Office Under-Secretary George Curzon. Quoted by Schiffrin, *Sun Yat-sen and the Origins of the Chinese Revolution*, 132.
59. Wesley-Smith, *Unequal Treaty*, 28.
60. Young, *British Policy in China*, 85–7.
61. FO17/1340, MacDonald to Salisbury 122, 4 April 1898.
62. Anon (ed.), *Xianggang yu Zhongguo*, 181–2 (Tsungli Yamen to Emperor Guangxu, 14 April 1898).
63. Schrecker, *Imperialism and Chinese Nationalism*, 251.
64. Yu and Liu (eds), *Shijiu shiji de Xianggang*, 115.
65. Wesley-Smith, *Unequal Treaty*, 38.

66. Ibid. 41.
67. Ibid. 44 (Minutes of Bertie).
68. CO882/5, Chamberlain to Blake, confidential despatch, 6 January 1899.
69. CO537/34, Enclosure from Robinson to Ripon, secret despatch 24, 14 November 1894.
70. CO882/5, Report by Stewart Lockhart on the Extension of the Colony, 8 October 1898.
71. CO19/494, Convention of Peking.
72. Liang, *Chengzhai yu zhongying waijiao*, 4.
73. CO19/494, Convention of Peking.
74. CO882/5, Report by Stewart Lockhart on the Extension of the Colony, 8 October 1898.
75. FO17/1334, MacDonald to Salisbury, despatch 102, 27 May 1898.
76. Wesley-Smith, *Unequal Treaty*, 35.
77. CO19/494, Convention of Peking.
78. 882/5, Royal Order in Council 1898.
79. Ibid.
80. Wesley-Smith, *Unequal Treaty*, 33.

Chapter 4: Law and Justice

1. Ng, *New Peace County: A Chinese Gazetteer of the Hong Kong Region*, 1–2.
2. Ibid. 52–3; Ch'u, *Local Government in China Under the Ch'ing*, 1–2.
3. Hsiao, *Rural China, Imperial Control in the Nineteenth Century*, 316–7.
4. CO129/69, Note by Pauncefote, 3 August 1866.
5. Sayer, *Hong Kong, 1841–1862*, 201 (Elliot's proclamation of 2 February 1841).
6. CO129/2, Stanley to Pottinger 8, 3 June 1843.
7. Ibid.
8. Ibid.
9. Norton-Kyshe, *The History of the Laws and Courts of Hong Kong*, vol.1, 92–4.
10. See Munn, *Anglo-China*. This should be supplemented by Munn, 'The rule of law and criminal justice in the nineteenth century', 19–47.
11. Wesley-Smith, 'Anti-Chinese Legislation in Hong Kong', 91–105.
12. Godley, 'The End of the Queue: Hair as symbol in Chinese history', 55–7.
13. Endacott, *Government and People*, 36.
14. Norton-Kyshe, *History of Law and Courts*, vol.1, 92.
15. Munn, 'The rule of law and criminal justice', 40.
16. Wesley-Smith, 'Anti-Chinese Legislation', 97.
17. Munn, *Anglo-China*, 184–5.
18. Wesley-Smith, 'Anti-Chinese Legislation', 96–7.
19. Faure, *Documentary History*, vol.2, 47 (European District Reservation Ordinance, 1888).
20. Sayer, *Hong Kong, 1862–1919*, 129.
21. Lethbridge, *Hong Kong: Stability and Change*, 176.
22. For life in the Hotung family at the Peak, see Gittins, *Eastern Windows – Western Skies*.
23. Tsang, *Democracy Shelved*, 47.
24. Munn, 'The rule of law and criminal justice', 29.
25. Munn, *Anglo-China*, 173.
26. Endacott, *A Biographical Sketch-Book of Early Hong Kong*, 60–5.
27. Munn, *Anglo-China*, 173.
28. Quoted in Norton-Kyshe, *History of Laws and Courts*, vol.1, 378.
29. Munn, *Anglo-China*, 173.

30. Ibid. 207.
31. CO129/5, Woosnam to D'Aguilar, 14 March 1844.
32. CO129/5, Pottinger to Stanley 11, 30 January 1844.
33. Munn, *Anglo-China*, 208.
34. Eitel, *Europe in China*, 231–3.
35. Norton-Kyshe, *History of Laws and Courts*, vol.1, 327.
36. Munn, *Anglo-China*, 244.
37. CO129/55, Bowring to Labouchere 49, 26 March 1856. In the mid 1850s, there were only 113 names on the common jury list with 34 others on the special jury list.
38. Munn, *Anglo-China*, 261.
39. Ibid. 268.
40. Ibid.
41. CO129/5, Pottinger's minute of 24 January 1844.
42. CO129/86, Robinson to Newcastle 86, 6 May 1862.
43. Tsang, *A Documentary History of Hong Kong,*, vol.1, 163.
44. CO129/126, MacDonnell to Buckingham 416, 14 December 1867.
45. CO129/120, MacDonnell to Carnarvon 183, 7 January 1867.
46. Welsh, *History of Hong Kong*, 213.
47. Munn, *Anglo-China*, 439.
48. House of Commons, *British Parliamentary Papers: China 25*, 8 (Robinson to Newcastle, 16 December 1861).
49. Munn, *Anglo-China*, 450.
50. Hussey, *British History, 1815–1939*, 237.
51. The fullest account is in Norton-Kyshe, *History of Laws and Courts*, vol.1, 414–24.
52. Endacott, *History of Hong Kong*, 93.
53. Norton-Kyshe, *History of Laws and Courts*, vol.1, 417.
54. Munn, *Anglo-China*, 394.
55. Norton-Kyshe, *History of Laws and Courts*, vol.1, 418.
56. Munn, *Anglo-China*, 395.
57. Huang, *Civil Justice in China*, 225.
58. See Wakeman, *Strangers at the Gate*.
59. Wong, *Yeh Ming-ch'en*, 67.
60. Munn, *Anglo-China*, 330.
61. Yung Wing's account cited by Munn, ibid. 362 (note 172).
62. Wong, *Yeh Ming-ch'en*, 67–8.
63. CO129/149, Petition from the Chinese community of Hong Kong, February 1871.
64. Words of Governor Des Voeux cited in Munn, 'The rule of law and criminal justice', 20.

Chapter 5: Economy and Society

1. Chan, *The Making of Hong Kong Society*, 34–5.
2. Blake, *Jardine Matheson*, 108–14.
3. Wei, *Shanghai*, 32–45.
4. Graham, *The China Station*, 248–9.
5. Munn, 'The Hong Kong Opium Revenue, 1845–1885', 107.
6. Income from opium generally accounted for between 10 and 20 per cent of government revenue, though at its peak, during the course of the First World War, it rose from 34 per cent in 1914 to 46 per cent in 1918. Miners, *Hong Kong Under Imperial Rule, 1912–1941*, 212, 232.

7.   Myer, *Hong Kong as a Global Metropolis*, 59.
8.   Ibid.
9.   Ibid. 60.
10. Sinn, *Power and Charity*, 28.
11. See Hao, *The Comprador in Nineteenth Century China*.
12. Crisswell, *The Taipans*, 102.
13. Lin, *Xianggang Shihua*, 28–9.
14. Ibid. 30–31; Tsai, *Hong Kong in Chinese History*, 47.
15. Chien, *The European Diary of Hsieh Fucheng*, 41.
16. Mo Kai, 'Xiandai maoyi tixi de chengzhang licheng', 285.
17. 'South' originally meant southern China while 'north' referred to northern China. As trade expanded to Southeast Asia, the areas implied by 'south' and 'north' changed. Zhang, *Xianggang Huashang Shi*, 9–10.
18. Ibid. 12–3.
19. Endacott, *History of Hong Kong*, 65, 116.
20. Zhang, *Xianggang Huashang Shi*, 5.
21. Endacott, *History of Hong Kong*, 74–5.
22. Ibid. 125.
23. King, *The Hong Kong Bank in Late Imperial China*, 19. When it was originally founded, it was in the name of the Hong Kong and Shanghai Banking Company Limited and was then incorporated by a special ordinance in 1866.
24. Sinn, *Growing with Hong Kong*, 5.
25. Zhang, *Xianggang Huashang Shi*, 25.
26. Ibid. 39.
27. Coates, *Whampoa*, 11–17.
28. Drake, *Taikoo*, 19.
29. Zhang, *Xianggang Huashang Shi*, 42.
30. Lu, *Zhongguo zaoqi de lunchuan jingying*, 141.
31. Ibid. 84–8.
32. Zhang, *Xianggang Huashang Shi*, 53.
33. Faure, *Documentary History II*, 25–6 (Statement of Governor Hennessy on census returns of 1881). This is not an exhaustive list of workshops.
34. Tak-wing Ngo takes the view that British colonial rule imposed 'constraints on Hong Kong's industrial development' before the Second World War. Ngo, 'Industrial history and the artifice of *laissez-faire* colonialism', 119–40. This is as one-sided as the view he sets out to correct. Not protecting local industries or having a credible industrial policy should not be deemed as imposing constraints. The Hong Kong government did not have a credible policy towards trade either in its first century of rule.
35. Faure, *Documentary History II*, 24–5 (Statement of Governor Hennessy on census returns of 1881).
36. Though, as explained in Chapter 4, discrimination against the Chinese in fact occurred routinely, and discriminatory legislation did exist.
37. Kiernan, *European Empires from Conquest to Collapse, 1815–1960*, 156–8.
38. Tidrick, *Empire and the English Character*, 194–203.
39. Hoe, *The Private Life of Old Hong Kong*, 87.
40. Norman, *The People and Politics of the Far East*, 9; and Evans Thomas, *Vanished China*, 167.
41. Lethbridge, *Hong Kong: Stability and Change*, 185.
42. Ibid. 194.
43. Ibid. 208–9.
44. Halcombe, *The Mystic Flowery Land*, 185–91.

45. For the leadership situation in the Hong Kong region (i.e. including the New Territories, which only became part of Hong Kong in 1898), see Hayes, *The Hong Kong Region, 1850–1911*, 181–93.

46. CO129/312, Regulations for Hong Kong Cadets, 26 August 1902.

47. In the twentieth century, the prominence of Sir Man-kam Lo (son in law of Sir Robert Hotung) provides another illustrious example.

48. Lethbridge, *Stability and Change*, 177–9.

49. Ding, 'Lishi de chuanzhe: Zhimintixi de jianli he yanjin', 110.

50. Eitel, *Europe in China*, 172–3.

51. Ibid. 193–4.

52. Evans, 'Chinatown in Hong Kong: The Beginning of Taipingshan', 69–70.

53. Endacott, *A History of Hong Kong*, 175.

54. Ibid.

55. Faure, *A Documentary History II*, 22.

56. Miners, *Hong Kong Under Imperial Rule*, 61.

57. A notable exception was the refusal of the two Chinese members of the Legislative Council to support the reservation of part of Cheung Chau for the expatriates. However, this was never turned into a public campaign against segregation.

58. Tsang, *Democracy Shelved*, 26–7, 47.

59. Ting, 'Native Chinese Peace Officers in British Hong Kong, 1841–1861', 149–50.

60. CO129/6, Enclosure from Davis to Stanley 21, 18 June 1844 (Ordinance 13).

61. CO129/6, Davis to Stanley 10, 12 February 1844.

62. Ting, 'Native Chinese Peace Officers', 154–5; Endacott, *Government and People*, 37–8.

63. This was also helped by Loo's acquiring of an official rank from the Chinese government in the course of the Second Anglo-Chinese War in the late 1850s. Smith, *Chinese Christians: Elite, Middlemen, and the Church in Hong Kong*, 109.

64. Carroll, 'Chinese collaboration in the making of British Hong Kong', 23.

65. Eitel, *Europe in China*, 282.

66. Sinn, *Power and Charity*, 17.

67. Ibid. 33.

68. It was a 'Chinese hospital' as it was supposed to practise Chinese rather than Western medicine.

69. Chan, *Making of Hong Kong Society*, 79.

70. Lethbridge, *Stability and Change*, 56.

71. For the Kaifong Associations of the post-war period, see Wong, *The Kaifong Associations and the Society of Hong Kong*. She erroneously works on the premise that, as social organisations, kaifong did not exist in any meaningful form in Hong Kong until the latter part of the 1940s.

72. Report by the Social Welfare Officer for 1948–54, quoted in Hayes, *The Hong Kong Region*, 65.

73. Sinn, *Power and Charity*, 90.

74. Although Hong Kong's main hospital, the Civil Hospital, was available to the Chinese until the late 1880s or later, most Chinese would 'rather die like dogs than enter' it. Eitel, *Europe in China*, 462.

75. For the early history of the Po Leung Kuk, see Lethbridge, *Stability and Change*, 71–103.

76. Lethbridge, *Stability and Change*, 106–7.

77. Chan, *Making of Hong Kong Society*, 82.
78. For their identities and short bio-sketches, see Smith, *Chinese Christians*, 162–7.
79. Endacott, *Government and People*, 150–1.
80. *Hong Kong Telegraph*, 22 May, 1894.
81. Sinn, *Power and Charity*, 163–5.

Chapter 6: Agent for Change in China

1. To a lesser extent the International Settlement in Shanghai served a similar purpose. For an excellent exposition of how Shanghai was administered, see Elvin, *Another History*, 166–226.
2. For the Taiping Rebellion, see Spence, *God's Chinese Son*.
3. Hao and Wang, 'Changing Chinese views of Western relations, 1840–95', 156.
4. Wang, *Zhongkuo jindai zixiang shilun*, 14–28.
5. Li, *Xianggang Baoye Jitan*, 13.
6. De Bary, et al. (comp.), *Sources of Chinese Tradition*, 720.
7. Ibid. 720–1.
8. Li, *Zhongguo jindai sixiang shibian*, 54.
9. Tsai, *Hong Kong in Chinese History*, 156.
10. Ibid. 157–8.
11. Schiffrin, *Sun Yat-sen and the Origins of the Chinese Revolution*, 38–40.
12. De Bary, et al. (comp.), *Sources of Chinese Tradition*, 725.
13. Zhang, *Liang Qichao yu Qinggui gemin*, 32.
14. Levenson, *Liang Ch'I-ch'ao and the mind of modern China*, 30.
15. Li, *Xianggang baoye*, 25.
16. Huang, *Liang Ch'i-ch'ao and Modern Chinese Liberalism*, 91–9.
17. Zhongguo Guomindang Dangshihui (ed.), *Guofu zhuanji*, vol.2, 184.
18. Bergere, *Sun Yat-sen*, 153–72.
19. Schiffrin, *Sun Yat-sen*, 45–55.
20. Xie, *Huang Xing yu Zhongguo Gemin*, 28.
21. Rhodes, *China's Republican Revolution: The Case of Kwangtung, 1895–1913*, 204–5.
22. Cohen, *History in Three Keys: The Boxers as Event, Experience, and Myth*, 56.
23. On how this event was used to build up a heroic image, see Wong, *The Origins of an Heroic Image*.
24. Li, *Sun Zhongshan xiansheng geming yu Xianggang*, 70.
25. Bergere, *Sun Yat-sen*, 189. The legend mentions only 72 martyrs but the number executed was in fact higher.
26. Li, *Sun Zhongshan geming yu Xianggang*, 83.
27. Ibid. 70.
28. Chan, *China, Britain and Hong Kong, 1895–1945*, 79.
29. For the importance of the *Min Bao*, see Zhu, *Tongmenghui de geming lilun – Minbao gean yanjiu*.
30. Li, *Sun Zhongshan geming yu Xianggang*, 30–47.
31. Chan, *China, Britain and Hong Kong*, 71–2.
32. Yen, *The Overseas Chinese and the 1911 Revolution*, 308–9.
33. Beggere, *Sun Yat-sen*, 42–4.
34. Li, *Sun Zhongshan geming yu Xianggang*, 59–66.
35. Chung, *Chinese Business Groups in Hong Kong and Political Change in South China*, 44–5.
36. Chen, *Chen Shaobai xianshang aisilu nianpu*, 7.
37. Chan, *China, Britain and Hong Kong*, 60–2.

38. Rhodes, *China's Republican Revolution*, 215.
39. Tsai, *Hong Kong in Chinese History*, 243.
40. Ibid. 243–4.
41. CO129/381, Lugard to Harcourt, confidential despatch, 21 November 1911.
42. Chan, *China, Britain and Hong Kong*, 92.
43. CO537/2197, Galsworthy to Scott, letter, 8 August 1947.
44. CO129/283, Order by Governor in Council dated 4 March 1896.
45. CO129/283, Stewart Lockhart to Sun, letter 33, 4 October 1897.
46. CO129/286, Minutes addressed to Lucas, 15 July 1898.
47. Ibid.
48. CO129/285, Black to Chamberlain, confidential despatch, 8 October 1898.
49. Ibid.
50. CO129/322, May to Lyttelton, confidential despatch, 24 March 1904.
51. CO129/322, Minutes for Ommanney and Lyttelton, 29 April 1904.
52. CO129/317, Blake to Chamberlain, confidential despatch, 30 April 1903.

Chapter 7: The Great War and Chinese Nationalism

1. Young, *The Presidency of Yuan Shih-kai*, 116–7.
2. Liew, *Struggle for Decomcracy: Sung Chiao-jen and the 1911 Chinese Revolution*, 182–3.
3. Sheridan, *China in Disintegration*, 51.
4. Dreyer, *China at War, 1901–1949*, 47–8.
5. McCord, *The Power of the Gun: The Emergence of Modern Chinese Warlordism*, 245.
6. Chow, *The May Fourth Movement: Intellectual Revolution in Modern China*, 84–94.
7. Summerskill, *China on the Western Front*, 205.
8. Whiting, *Soviet Policies in China, 1917–1924*, 30.
9. Dirlik, *The Origins of Chinese Communism*, 41.
10. Wilbur, *Sun Yat-sen*, 114–5.
11. Galbiati, *P'eng P'ai and the Hai-lu-feng Soviet*, 173–202, 232–9.
12. Bruce, *Second to None*, 113.
13. Ibid. 114–5.
14. Sayer, *Hong Kong, 1862–1919*, 119.
15. Miners, *Hong Kong Under Imperial Rule*, 7.
16. Ibid. 7–8.
17. Bruce, *Second to None*, 114.
18. Sayer, *Hong Kong, 1862–1919*, 139.
19. Zhang, *Xianggang Huashang Shi*, 45–6.
20. Sinn, *Growing with Hong Kong*, 6.
21. Miners, *Hong Kong under Imperial Rule*, 9.
22. Ibid. 8; Faure, 'The Rice Trade in Hong Kong before the Second World War', 218.
23. Chesneaux, *The Chinese Labor Movement, 1919–1927*, 159.
24. England and Rear, *Chinese Labour under British Rule*, 76.
25. Chan, 'Hong Kong in Sino-British Conflict', 38.
26. England and Rear, *Chinese Labour under British Rule*, 76.
27. Chan, *Labour and Empire*, 46.
28. Kwan, *Marxist Intellectuals and the Chinese Labor Movement*, 83.
29. Chan, *The Making of Hong Kong Society*, 167; Chan, *China, Britain and Hong Kong*, 170.
30. Deng, *Zhongguo Zhigong Yundong Jianshi (1919–1926)*, 44–5.

31. Tung Wah Hospital Groups, *Tung Wah Archives*, Dongshiju huiyi lu, no.00942, Records of meetings of Board of Directors under the Chairmanship of Lu Gongzhu, minutes of meeting for the 19th date of the first moon of the Lunar calendar 1922.
32. CO129/474, Stubbs to Churchill, telegram of 11 March 1922.
33. Miners, *Hong Kong Under Imperial Rule*, 13.
34. Chan, 'Hong Kong in Sino-British Conflict', 40–1.
35. CO129/474, Stubbs to Devenshire, 18 March 1922.
36. Chan, *Making of Hong Kong Society*, 191.
37. Ma Chao-chun's words. Quoted in ibid. 191.
38. Hong Kong Government, *Government Gazette*, 28 February 1922, 82.
39. Deng, *Zhongguo zhigong yundong*, 66.
40. CO129/474, Stubbs to Churchill, telegram of 11 March 1922.
41. Chan, *From Nothing to Nothing*, 24.
42. Lu, *Gemin zhi zaiqi*, 373n.
43. Chang and Gordon, *All Under Heaven*, 99–107.
44. Esherick, *The Origins of the Boxer Uprising*, 311.
45. It should not be assumed that only the Chinese of Hong Kong did so. Other residents of some of the coastal provinces affected by the Sino-French War also demonstrated a very rudimentary form of proto-nationalism in the same period.
46. Tsai, 'From Anti-foreignism to Popular Nationalism', 14.
47. CO129/220, Bowen to Derby 89, 23 February 1885.
48. Tsai, *Hong Kong in Chinese History*, 141.
49. Ibid. 129.
50. Ibid. 127.
51. See ibid. 182–237 for the most detailed analysis of these two boycotts in Hong Kong.
52. Rhoads, *China's Republican Revolution*, 135–140.
53. Chan, 'Hong Kong in Sino-British Conflict', 33.
54. Ibid. 33–4.
55. Kwan, *Marxist Intellectuals and the Chinese Labor Movement*, 91.
56. Goto-Shibata, *Japan and Britain in Shanghai, 1925–31*, 15.
57. Shanghai shehui kexue lishi yanjiusho (ed.), *Wusa yundong shiliao*, vol.1, 709–13.
58. Goto-Shibata, *Japan and Britain in Shanghai*, 16–7.
59. Rigby, *The May 30 Movement*, 38–9.
60. Ibid. 42–3.
61. Ibid. 52.
62. Ibid. 59–62.
63. Boorman, *Biographical Dictionary of Republican China*, vol.2, 366–7.
64. Deng, *Zhongguo Zhigong Yundong Jianshi*, 239.
65. Chan, *China, Britain and Hong Kong*, 183.
66. Chan, *From Nothing to Nothing*, 59.
67. Wilson, *Britain and the Kuomintang, 1924–28*, 7.
68. Chan, *From Nothing to Nothing*, 64.
69. Ibid.
70. Deng, *Zhongguo Zhigong Yundong Jianshi*, 225.
71. Some of the strikers returned to Hong Kong later but a very large number remained in Guangdong until the boycott ended.
72. Liu and Wang, *Yijiuyijiu zhi yijiuerqi de Zhongguo gongren yundong*, 41.
73. Fung, *The Diplomacy of Imperial Retreat*, 41–2.
74. Ibid. 42.

75. Deng, *Zhongguo Zhigong Yundong Jianshi*, 230.
76. Bruce, *Second to None*, 131–2.
77. Gillingham, *At the Peak: Hong Kong Between the Wars*, 37.
78. Bruce, *Second to None*, 131.
79. Gillingham, *At the Peak*, 43–4.
80. Yu and Liu (eds), *Ershi shiji de Xianggang*, 107.
81. Deng, *Zhongguo Zhigong Yundong Jianshi*, 232.
82. Chan, 'Hong Kong in Sino-British Conflict', 45.
83. CO129/448, Stubbs to Amery, telegram, 17 July 1925.
84. Kwan, *Marxist Intellectuals and the Chinese Labor Movement*, 207.
85. Chan, *China, Britain and Hong Kong*, 198–201.
86. Miners, *Hong Kong Under Imperial Rule*, 17.
87. Fung, *The Diplomacy of Imperial Retreat*, 67–9.
88. Jordan, *The Northern Expedition*, 31–2.
89. Kwan, *Marxist Intellectuals and the Chinese Labor Movement*, 211.
90. Chan, *China, Britain and Hong Kong*, 202–8.
91. CO129/498, Clementi to Amery, secret despatch, 24 September 1926.
92. CO129/498, Beckett's minutes, 6 December 1926.
93. CO129/492, Clementi to Amery, 29 May 1926.
94. Tsang, *Documentary History of Hong Kong I*, 108–9.
95. CO129/493, Clementi to Amery, telegram, 24 June 1926.
96. Sinn, *Growing with Hong Kong*, 33.
97. Gillingham, *At the Peak*, 43.
98. Sinn, *Growing with Hong Kong*, 35.
99. Deng, *Zhongguo Zhigong Yundong Jianshi*, 237–9.
100. Tsang, *Documentary History of Hong Kong 1*, 208.
101. *Archives of the Tung Wah Hospitals*, Dongshiju huiyi lu, no.00942, Records of meetings of Board of Directors under the Chairmanship of Ma Zuichao, minutes of meeting for the 3rd date of the seventh moon of the Lunar calendar.
102. Chan, *China, Britain and Hong Kong*, 204–5.
103. Chen, *Chen Jieyu Huiyilu (xia)*, 258.
104. Qin (comp.), *Zhongtong Jianggong sixiang yanlun zhongji*, vol.9, 43–4.
105. Huang, *Zong da lishi de jiaodu du Jiang Jieshi Riji*, 41.
106. Chen, *Chengbai zhi jian*, 63.
107. Jordan, *The Northern Expedition*, 81–2.
108. Zhang, *Wode huiyi*, vol.2, 560.
109. Ibid. vol.1, 142.
110. Yang, *Zhonggong yu Mosike de guanxi (1920–1960)*, 112–3.
111. FO228/3156, Brenan to Macleay, 9 September 1926.
112. Kwan, *Marxist Intellectuals and the Chinese Labor Movement*, 219–20.
113. CO537/767, F3008/194/10, Memo by Newton, 25 June 1925.
114. Rosenberg and Young, *Transforming Russia and China*, 105.
115. Chan, *From Nothing to Nothing*, 78–94.
116. CO129/510/11, Clementi to Amery, 6 March 1928.
117. CO537/768, CC61(26), Cabinet conclusions of 1 December 1926.
118. FO371/11662, F5298/10/10, Statement of British Policy in China, approved by the Cabinet on 1 December 1926.

Chapter 8: Imperial Grandeur

1. Morris, *Farewell the Trumpets*, 209–10.
2. Judd, *Empire*, 310.
3. Coble, *Facing Japan*, 36–7.

4.   Miners, *Hong Kong Under Imperial Rule*, 20.
5.   Chan, *From Nothing to Nothing*, 174.
6.   Ibid. 165.
7.   Ibid. 187.
8.   Chan, *From Nothing to Nothing*, 78–125.
9.   Ibid. 154.
10.   Ibid. 179.
11.   CO129/588, 'Preliminary Report on the Hong Kong Police Force' by J.P.P. Evans, 11 July 1941.
12.   Chan, *From Nothing to Nothing*, 185.
13.   Ibid. 183–4.
14.   Ibid. 185.
15.   Madden and Darwin (eds), *The Dependent Empire*, 381, note 1.
16.   England and Rear, *Chinese Labour under British Rule*, 81.
17.   CO129/503/2, Draft telegram to Clementi, undated, January 1926.
18.   CO129/503, Clementi to Amery, paraphrase telegram of 19 January 1927.
19.   CO129/355, Lugard to Crewe, 26 May 1909.
20.   CO129/323, May to Lyttelton, 17 June 1914.
21.   Zhang, *China in the International System*, 104–5; Wesley-Smith, *Unequal Treaty*, 150–4.
22.   PRO CO129/503, Clementi to Amery, telegram of 19 January 1927.
23.   PRO CO129/503/2, Draft telegram to Clementi, undated, February 1927.
24.   Ibid.
25.   Wesley-Smith, *Unequal Treaty*, 158.
26.   CO129/503/2, Minutes by Gent, 3 July 1928.
27.   Cameron, *Power: The Story of China Light*, 44.
28.   Yu, *The Arches of the Years*, 37–45.
29.   Leeming, 'The earlier industrialisation of Hong Kong', 337–42.
30.   Rao, 'Xianggang gongye fazhan de guiji', 373.
31.   Liu, *Jianming Xianggang Shi*, 170–1.
32.   Zhang, *Xianggang Huashang Shi*, 178.
33.   Miners, 'Industrial Development in the Colonial Empire and the Imperial Economic Conference at Ottawa 1932', 53–72.
34.   For the former, see Coates, *A Mountain of Light*; for the latter, see Cameron, *Power*.
35.   Ngo, 'Industrial history and the artifice of *laissez-faire* colonialism', 124–5.
36.   Butters Report, 109.
37.   Ibid. 125.
38.   *Sessional Papers 1931*, Report of the Census, Table 39.
39.   Miners, *Hong Kong Under Imperial Rule*, 23.
40.   Banking Committee Report of 1931 quoted in King, *The Hong Kong Bank Between the Wars*, 243.
41.   Ooh, *Wartime Currency Stabilisation in China, 1937–1941*, 23. China had the added problem of having to cope with heavy military expenditure associated with civil wars and confronting Japanese aggression.
42.   Ibid. 24.
43.   King, *Hong Kong Bank Between the Wars*, 244.
44.   Miners, *Hong Kong Under Imperial Rule*, 24.
45.   Endacott, *History of Hong Kong*, 276, 289.
46.   Ibid. 289.
47.   Mills, *British Rule in Eastern Asia*, 383.
48.   Butters Report, 163.
49.   Yuying, 'Yingguo de fazhi jingshen', 423.

50. Butters Report, 120.
51. Ibid. 121.
52. Miners, 'The Attempts to Abolish the *Mui Tsai* System in Hong Kong, 1917–1941', in Sinn (ed.), *Between East and West*, 118.
53. Miners, *Hong Kong Under Imperial Rule*, 157–8.
54. Hoe, *The Private Life of Old Hong Kong*, 236–8.
55. CO129/478, Churchill's minutes, 21 February 1922.
56. Miners, *Hong Kong Under Imperial Rule*, 161–6.
57. Miners, 'The Attempts to Abolish the *Mui Tsai* System', 124.
58. Ibid. 127.
59. Miners, *Hong Kong Under Imperial Rule*, 190.
60. For the end of the opium monopoly and regulation of prostitution, see ibid.
61. Yu, *The Arches of the Years*, 28.
62. Butters Report, 155.
63. Ibid. 156.
64. Jennings and Logan, *A Report on the University of Hong Kong*, 11.
65. Ibid.
66. Jin, 'Chujian Gangda', 4–6.
67. Yu, *Arches of the Years*, 26.
68. Words of Acting Colonial Secretary, quoted in Endacott, *Government and People*, 169.
69. Tang, *Li Zhongren Huiyilu*, 451–2.
70. Wilson, *When Tigers Fight*, 36.
71. Sun, *China and the Origins of the Pacific War, 1931–1941*, 133.
72. Ch'i, *Nationalist China at War*, 56.
73. Shai, *Origins of the War in the East*, 162.
74. Zhang, *Xianggang Huashang shi*, 207.
75. Howard, 'British Military Preparations for the Second World War', 116.
76. Shai, *Origins of the War in the East*, 156–8.
77. Lowe, *Great Britain and the Origins of the Pacific War*, 98, 207.
78. Cameron, *Hong Kong: The Cultured Pearl*, 167–8.
79. Gillingham, *At the Peak*, 172–4.
80. Reynolds, *The Creation of the Anglo-American Alliance, 1937–41*, 264.
81. Thorne, *The Issue of War*, 18.
82. Ibid. 19.

Chapter 9: Japanese Invasion and Occupation

1. For a short but critical overview of Britain's defence, see Howard, 'British Military Preparations for the Second World War', 102–17.
2. Stokesbury, *Navy and Empire*, 355.
3. Dilks, *Retreat from Power I*, 16.
4. CAB23/89, CM36(37)5, 6 October 1937.
5. Lowe, *Great Britain and the Origins of the Pacific War*, 98.
6. Lee, *Britain and the Sino-Japanese War, 1937–1939*, 86–7.
7. Brice, *The Royal Navy and the Sino–Japanese Incident, 1937–41*, 148.
8. Kirby, *The War Against Japan*, vol.1, 56.
9. Endacott and Birch, *Hong Kong Eclipse*, 57–8.
10. Lindsay, *The Lasting Honour*, 2.
11. Elphick, *Far Eastern File*, 91. A long defence of the island alone was merely wishful thinking as nothing was done to ensure the supply of essentials like water for such a period.
12. Endacott and Birch, *Hong Kong Eclipse*, 60.

13. Ibid. 44–54.
14. Waijiaobu, *Zhanshi Waijiao*, vol.2, 171–2 (records of meeting on 6 August 1941, ROC Foreign Ministry, Taipei).
15. Ibid. 177 (report of discussions with the British over joint military actions submitted to Chiang Kai-shek, 18 August 1941).
16. Zeng, *Zheng Sheng Huiyilu*, 209.
17. Wang, *Jihjun Qinhua Zhanzheng 1931–1945*, vol.3, 1590–5.
18. A regular Japanese division was 22,000 strong. Hsu and Chang, *History of the Sino-Japanese War (1937–1945)*, 171.
19. Wang, *Jihjun Qinhua Zhanzeng*, vol.3, 1596–7. A Japanese source suggests the Japanese started preparing the invasion in July 1940 and thought it could take up to six months. Lu, 'Xianggang de hese xingdanri', 94–5.
20. Gillingham, *At the Peak*, 169.
21. Elphick, *Far Eastern File*, 86.
22. Alderson, *History of Royal Air Force Kai Tak*, 32–3.
23. Willmott, *Empires in the Balance*, 155.
24. Churchill, *The Second World War*, vol.3, 563.
25. Wang, *Jihjun Qinhua Zhanzheng*, vol.3, 1616.
26. Bruce, *Second to None*, 238.
27. Endacott and Birch, *Hong Kong Eclipse*, 88.
28. CO129/590, 'Operations by 2nd MTB Flotilla, RN', 3 March 1942.
29. CO129/590, Commanding Officer MTB 07 and 6th Subdivision to Commanding Officer, 2nd Flotilla, MTB, 12 January 1942.
30. CO129/590, Commanding Officer MTB 11 and 7th Subdivision to Commanding Officer, 2nd Flotilla, MTN, 19 December 1942.
31. CO129/590, 'Operations by 2nd MTB Flotilla, RN', 3 March 1942.
32. Carew, *The Fall of Hong Kong*, 143–5.
33. Wang, *Jihjun Qinhua Zhanzheng*, vol.3, 1617.
34. Ibid. 1621–2.
35. Endacott and Birch, *Hong Kong Eclipse*, 101–2.
36. CO129/590, Young to Secretary of State (Stanley), 28 December 1941.
37. Carew, *Fall of Hong Kong*, 216–7.
38. CO129/590, Young to Secretary of State (Stanley), 28 December 1941.
39. Gimson, *An Unpublished History of Hong Kong During the Japanese Occupation* (manuscript), 5–6.
40. Endacott and Birch, *Hong Kong Eclipse*, 103.
41. Willmott, *Empires in the Balance*, 218–9.
42. Ibid. 178.
43. Elsbree, *Japan's Role in Southeast Asian Nationalist Movements, 1940–1945*, 163.
44. Quoted in Thorne, *Allies of a Kind*, 157.
45. Waijiaobu, *Zhanshi Waijiao*, vol.3, agreement between Chiang Kai-shek and Mountbatten, October 1943.
46. Ibid. Roosevelt to Chiang, telegram of 31 December 1941.
47. For Chiang's thinking, see Tsang, *An Appointment with China*, 28–9.
48. Gu, *Gu Weijun Huiyilu*, vol.5, 14–15.
49. CO825/42/55104/2, Gent's minutes, 14 February 1942.
50. CO825/35/55104, Secret note by MacDougall, March 1942.
51. CO825/35/55104, Minutes of 35th meeting of the committee on post-war problems, 2 April 1942.
52. FO371/31804, Clarke to Eden, report of 11 June 1942.
53. CO825/35/55104, Minutes by Gent (on interdepartmental meeting of 30 June 1942) dated 1 July 1942.
54. CO825/35/55104, Gent's minutes of 17 June 1942.

55. FO371/31777, Cranborne to Eden, letter of 18 August 1942.
56. CO825/35/55104, Gater's minutes (for Cranborne), 31 July 1942.
57. CAB65/28, WM171(42) 21 December 1942.
58. For the negotiations, see Tsang, *Appointment with China*, 31–3.
59. *Wellington Koo Papers*, Box 55, Sino–British Treaty 1942–4, Soong to Seymour, 11 January 1943.
60. Ibid. Seymour to Soong, 21 January 1943.
61. Jones, *Japan's New Order in East Asia*, 333.
62. Elsbree, *Japan's Role in Southeast Asian Nationalist Movement*, 10.
63. Jones, *Japan's New Order*, 332–4.
64. Ibid. 332.
65. Ibid. 333.
66. Proclamation by Governor Isogai, quoted in Xie, *Sannian ling bageyue de kunan*, 40.
67. *China Mail*, 2 October 1945 ('Mr North lifts a veil').
68. CO129/594/6, MacDougall to Gent, 19 September 1945. The fourth member was Legislative Councillor Lee Tse-fong (Li Zifang).
69. Li escaped and wrote an account of occupied Hong Kong.
70. Xie, *Sannian ling bageyue*, 62–3.
71. Endacott and Birch, *Hong Kong Eclipse*, 142.
72. Sha, *Xianggang lunxian riji*, 92.
73. Liu, *Hu Die huyilu*, 190.
74. Endacott and Birch, *Hong Kong Eclipse*, 105.
75. Xie, *Zhanshi Rijun zai Xianggang baoxing*, 87.
76. Guan, *Qishinian lai jiaguo*, 40.
77. Xie, *Sannian ling bageyue*, 93.
78. Ye, 'Rizhi shiji de Xianggang', 121.
79. Endacott and Birch, *Hong Kong Eclipse*, 154–5.
80. Alderson, *History of RAF Kai Tak*, 40.
81. Gittins, *Stanley: Behind Barbed Wire*, 66.
82. Gimson, *Unpublished History*, 13.
83. Rhodes House Library, *Gimson Papers: Hong Kong 1942–1945*, diary entry for 5 January 1945.
84. Ibid., Diary entry for 14 June 1944.
85. Ride, *BAAG*, 53–6.
86. Cruickshank, *SOE in the Far East*, 157–8.
87. Ride, *BAAG*, 182.
88. Ibid. 328–30.
89. Ibid. 83.
90. Guangdongsheng Danganguan (ed.), *Dongjiang Congdui shiliao*, 11–2.
91. Dongjiang Congdui shi bianxiejuzu (ed.), *Dongjiang Congdui shi*, 57–8.
92. Xie, *Sannian ling bageyue*, 385. Chen Daming, Political Commissar of the guerrillas, claims the group had 600 guerrillas, though he has not specified whether this was the total number including casualties over the whole war or its maximum strength at a particular point of the occupation period. Chen, *Xianggang kangri youjidui*, 145.
93. Zeng, *Zheng Sheng Huiyilu*, 315–6.
94. Dongjiang Congdui shi bianxiejuzu (ed.), *Dongjiang Congdui shi*, 60–4.
95. Xu (ed.), *Huoyue cai Xianggang*, 34–7.
96. Zeng, *Zeng Shen Huiyilu*, 232–3.
97. For the parallel planning for Hong Kong by the Chinese government, see Tsang, *Appointment with China*, 34–9.
98. CO825/35/55104, Revised draft paper, 'British Far Eastern Policy', July 1942; Cranborne to Amery, letter of 20 August 1942.

99.   FO371/31777, Cranborne to Eden, letter of 18 August 1942.
100. CO825/42/55104/2, Gent's memo, 'Future Status of Hong Kong', 21 July 1943.
101. CO825/35/55104/7, Gent's memo, 19 June 1943.
102. CO825/42/55104/2, Gent's minutes, 29 December 1943.
103. For an in-depth analysis, see Tsang, *Democracy Shelved*, 13–24.
104. CO129/1650, Gent's minutes of 21 September 1945.
105. Tsang, *Democracy Shelved*, 18.
106. Ch'i, 'The Military Dimension, 1942–1945', 165.
107. CO537/4805, 'Summary of Assurances given by HMG since 1942 about the Future of Hong Kong'.
108. Quoted in Xiang, *Recasting the Imperial Far East*, 17.
109. FO371/46251, Sterndale-Bennett's minutes of 25 July 1945.
110. HS1/133, SOE cipher telegram to Melbourne 986, 16 May 1945.
111. FO371/46251, Sterndale-Bennett's minutes, 25 July 1945.
112. HS1/171, Notes of a meeting in the Colonial Office on 23 July 1945.
113. Ibid.
114. HS1/171, Britmis Chungking to War Office, 200900H, 20 July 1945.
115. Shai, *Britain and China, 1941–47*, 100.
116. CO129/591/16, Gent's minutes, 4 August 1945.
117. HS1/171, Foreign Office to Chungking 859, 11 August 1945.
118. HS1/171, Britmis Chungking to War Office, 200900H, 20 July 1945.
119. HS1/171, Rait's minute to DDMI (P/W), 19 August 1944.
120. FO371/46251, 'The Political Issues between Great Britain and China regarding Hong Kong', 7 July 1945.
121. Ibid.

Chapter 10: Return to Empire

1.   Bix, *Hirohito and the Making of Modern Japan*, 511.
2.   FO371/46251, Undated note, 'Arrangements for the Administration of Hong Kong in the Event of its Liberation by Regular Chinese Forces', c. late July 1945.
3.   Kirby, *The War Against Japan*, vol.5, 491.
4.   FO371/46252, Sterndale-Bennett's top secret minutes, 14 August 1945.
5.   Xie, *Xianggang Zhanhou Fengyunlu*, 30.
6.   Shih, *The Reminiscences of General Shih Chueh* (in Chinese), 197.
7.   The New First Corps liberated Canton on 7 September. Xie, *Yingyang Guowei*, 376.
8.   FO371/46252, Sterndale-Bennett's minutes, 14 August 1945.
9.   FO371/46252, Foreign Office to Chungking 916, 18 August 1945.
10. FO371/46252, Chungking to Foreign Office 857, 16 August 1945.
11. *Waijiaobu* 323, Foreign Ministry note on the handling of the Japanese surrender in Hong Kong, undated, c. early September 1945.
12. *Waijiaobu* 323, Foreign Minister to British Ambassador, 17 August 1945.
13. Mao, *Mao Zedong Xuanji*, vol.4, 1035–7.
14. Ibid. 1028.
15. Dongjiang Congdui shi bianxiejuzu (ed.), *Dongjiang Congdui shi*, 149–50.
16. CO129/591/18, MACHIN to AMSSO TW1688, 26 August 1945.
17. Dongjiang Congdui shi bianxiejuzu (ed.), *Dongjiang Congdui Shi*, 151.
18. Chiang's diary entry of 25 April 1945. Cited in Huang, *Jiang Jeshi Riji*, 429.
19. *Wellington Koo Papers*, Box 55, Folder 12b, London Embassy to Chiang, telegram of 13 August 1945.

20. Kirby, *The War Against Japan*, vol.5, 145.
21. FO371/46252, Chungking to Foreign Office 865, 17 August 1945.
22. CO129/591/18, MACHIN to AMSSO TW1688, 26 August 1945.
23. CO129/591/18, Gater to General Ismay, letter of 25 August 1945; PRO FO371/46253, Sterndale-Bennett's minutes of 1 September 1945.
24. FO371/46253, Sterndale-Bennett's minutes of 27 August 1945.
25. FO371/46253, Foreign Office to Chungking 1002, 28 August 1945.
26. FO371/46253, Sterndale-Bennett's minutes of 27 August 1945.
27. CO537/4805, 'Summary of Assurances Given by HMG since 1942 about the Future of Hong Kong'.
28. FRUS 1945, vol.7, 501–2 (Hurley to Secretary of State, telegram of 16 August 1945).
29. FO371/46252, Prime Minister to President Truman, 18 August 1945.
30. Truman, *Memoirs of Harry S Truman*, vol.2, 61–2.
31. *Waijiaobu* 323, Hurley to Chiang, 22 August 1945.
32. *Waijiaobu* 323, Foreign Ministry note on arrangements for the Japanese surrender in Hong Kong, undated, *c.* September 1945.
33. Waijioubu 312/72, Note on the handling of the Japanese surrender in Hong Kong, 9 October [1946].
34. *Wellington Koo Papers*, Box 55, Folder 12b, Foreign Ministry to London Embassy, telegram 273, 25–6 August 1945.
35. Xie, *Xianggang Zhanhou Fengyunlu*, 37.
36. FO371/46253, Chungking to Foreign Office 958, 27 August 1945.
37. FO371/46253, Sterndale-Bennett's minutes, 31 August 1945.
38. FO371/46253, Sterndale-Bennett's minutes, 27 August 1945.
39. FO371/46253, Chungking to Foreign Office 973, 29 August 1945.
40. FO371/46253, Chungking to Foreign Office 987, 30 August 1945.
41. Waijioubu 312/72, Note on the handling of the Japanese surrender in Hong Kong, 9 October [1946].
42. Hung On-to Memorial Library, *Franklin Gimson Papers*, 'Hong Kong Reclaimed', 169–76.
43. The order for Gimson is in CO129/591/16, Foreign Office to Chungking, telegram, 11 August 1945.
44. Endacott and Birch, *Hong Kong Eclipse*, 259.
45. CO129/591/18, 'War Diary: 29th August to 16th September 1945'.
46. CO129/591/12, Admiralty to Commander-in-Chief, Hong Kong telegram of 3 September 1945.
47. CO129/591/12, 'Civil Affairs Directive to the Senior Officer Commanding HBM's Forces in Hong Kong'.
48. CO129/592/6, Harcourt to Hall, personal and secret letter, 11 November 1945.
49. CO129/591/20, CCAO's general report on Hong Kong, 2 November 1945.
50. CO129/594/6, MacDougall to Garter, letter of 5 December 1945.
51. CO129/591/20, CCAO's general report on Hong Kong, 2 November 1945.
52. Record of Interview with David MacDougall on 17 February 1983.
53. CO129/591/18, 'War Diary: 29th August to 16th September' by Harcourt, 6 October 1945.
54. CO129/595/9, Report by the Chief Civil Affairs Officer – the New Territories, September to November 1945.
55. Donnison, *British Military Administration in the Far East*, 205.
56. Tsang, *Democracy Shelved*, 25.
57. CO129/591/20, Report on Fisheries Organization by G.A.C. Herklots to Brigadier MacDougall, 18 October 1945.

58. Record of Interview with Geoffrey Herklots on 19 January 1983.
59. *The British Military Administration Hong Kong*, 6.
60. CO129/594/6, MacDougall to Garter, letter of 5 December 1945.
61. CO537/1667, Lloyd to Cash, letter of 12 January 1946.
62. Hong Kong Public Records Office, HKRS211/D, S/2/11, Young to Hall 82, 10 May 1946; CO129/594/9, Ruston's minutes of 12 March 1946; and Hazlerigg to Gent, letter of 31 December 1945.
63. Harcourt, 'The Military Administration of Hong Kong', 15.
64. CO129/591/20, MacDougall to Gent, letter of 6 November 1945.
65. Tsang, *Democracy Shelved*, 26.
66. For an example, see *Wah Kiu Yat Pao*, editorial of 12 May 1946.
67. CO129/592/6, Weekly Intelligence Summary no.3 (to 10 October 1945).
68. FO371/53639, F16735/113/10, Young to Creech-Jones 165, 7 November 1946.
69. FO371/53634, F5435/113/10, Minutes of Kitson, 22 March 1946.
70. FO371/53638, F15424/113/g10, Sloss to Cripps, confidential letter of 11 October 1946.
71. CO129/594/6, Newspaper cuttings enclosed from MacDougall to Gater, letter of 5 December 1945.
72. CO129/594/6, MacDougall to Gater, letter of 5 December 1945.
73. FO371/46259, F11807/1147/10, Keswick's 'Note on Future of Hong Kong', 3 November 1945.
74. Ibid.
75. Ibid. Keswick's 'Secretary for Chinese Affairs', 24 September 1945.
76. FO371/53632, Foreign Secretary's minutes to Prime Minister dated 8 March 1946; and PRO FO371/53633, Prime Minister's minute to Foreign Secretary dated 9 March 1946.
77. CO129/594/4, Speech by Young, 1 May 1946.
78. Tsang, *Democracy Shelved*, 186.
79. CO537/1651, Young to Creech-Jones, confidential despatch, 22 October 1946.

Chapter 11: A Fine Balance
1. Thorne, *Allies of a Kind*, 704.
2. FO371/54052, F6208/2129/g6, 'British Foreign Policy in the Far East', 16 April 1946, 6.
3. FO371/54052, F6208/2129/g6, 'British Foreign Policy in the Far East', 16 April 1946, 1.
4. *Hong Kong Hansard: Session 1946*, 49 (record of 4th meeting, 20 June 1946).
5. Colonial Office, *Annual Report on Hong Kong 1946*, 26.
6. Census and Statistics Department, *Hong Kong Statistics 1947–1967*, 88.
7. *Hong Kong Hansard 1947*, 130–156 (record of 13th meeting, 1 May 1947).
8. CO129/595/3, Young to Creech-Jones, telegram 12 December 1946.
9. CO129/597/2, Creech-Jones to Grantham despatch 302, 24 September 1948.
10. For Young's reform attempt, see Tsang, *Democracy Shelved*, 32–62, 183–210.
11. CO129/594/9, Ruston's minute of 16 May 1946.
12. *Hong Kong Hansard 1946*, 63 (record of 5th meeting).
13. Ibid. 134 (record of 11th meeting, 12 September 1946). For an examination of Hong Kong's localisation policy, see Podmore, 'Localization in the Hong Kong Government Service', 36–51.
14. Colonial Office, *Annual Report on Hong Kong 1946*, 2.

15. CO129/611, Young to Creech-Jones, despatch of 15 November 1946.
16. Grantham, *Via Ports*, 105–6.
17. Louis, 'Hong Kong: The Critical Phase, 1945–1949', 1066.
18. *Xinsheng Wanbao*, 29 August 1946; CO537/1651, Young to Creech-Jones, despatch 145, 22 October 1946.
19. Louis, 'Hong Kong: The Critical Phase', 1066.
20. Tsang, *Democracy Shelved*, 60.
21. *Wah Kiu Yat Po*, 13 June 1946 (editorial).
22. CO882/31, Young to Creech-Jones, confidential despatch 70, 22 October 1946.
23. For a full analytical contrast between Young and Grantham's approach to political reform, see Tsang, *Democracy Shelved*, particularly 186–92.
24. Grantham, *Via Ports*, 111.
25. CO537/5400, Minutes of the 9th Smaller Territories Committee meeting on 12 July 1950 (item 4).
26. Grantham, 'Hong Kong', 121.
27. Huaqiao Ribao, *Xianggang Nianjian 1948*, 6–7.
28. This section is based substantially upon Tsang, *Appointment with China*, 56–77.
29. First draft in CO129/592/8, 'Status of Hong Kong', August 1945.
30. FO371/46257, GEN77/47, 23 October 1945.
31. FO371/46257, Kitson's minutes, undated, *c.* early November 1945.
32. FO371/53632, 'The Future of Hong Kong', 28 February 1946.
33. FO371/53632, 'The Future of Hong Kong', 28 February 1946.
34. FO371/53632, Sterndale-Bennett's minutes of 2 March 1946.
35. FO371/53632, Sargent's minutes of 19 March 1946.
36. Ibid.; and undated minutes by Bevin.
37. FO371/53635, 'The Future of Hong Kong', 18 July 1946.
38. FO371/53637, Lloyd to Dening, letter of 22 August 1946.
39. FO371/53637, Dening to Lloyd, letter of 9 September 1946.
40. CO537/3325, 'China: Annual Report for 1947' by Ambassador Stevenson.
41. FO371/63388, Dening's minutes of 10 May 1947.
42. *Waijiaobu 323*, Foreign Ministry to Executive Yuan 10479, 31 October 1945.
43. *Waijiaobu 312.72*, paper on questions relating to recovery of Hong Kong and Kowloon, undated *c.* October 1946.
44. *Guofengbu 062.23/5000.4*, vol.2, Xu Yongzhang to Chiang, submission of 18 December 1946.
45. A large number of them are filed in *Waijiaobu 312.72*.
46. *Wellington Koo Papers*, Box 55, folder 12b, Waijiaobu to London Embassy, telegram 273, 25–6 August 1945. English translation in PRO CO129/592/8, Extract from President Chiang's address, 25 August 1945.
47. *Waijiaobu 323*, Intelligence 243, 28 December 1945.
48. Tsang, *Hong Kong: An Appointment with China*, 64–5.
49. *Waijiaobu 317.72*, Foreign Ministry submission to Chiang, 15 November 1946.
50. CO537/2193, Governor of Hong Kong to Colonial Office, savingrams dated 5 February 1947 and 16 September 1947.
51. *Waijiaobu 313.72*, vol.4, Executive Yuan to Foreign Ministry, instruction of 17 February 1948.
52. For the military dimension of the Chinese Civil War, see Hooton, *The Greatest Tumult*; for the political dimension, see Pepper, *Civil War in China*.
53. Mao, *Mao Zedong Waijiao Wenxuan*, 55–62.

54. Chen, *China's Road to the Korean War*, 29.
55. Mao, *Mao Zedong Junshi Wenxuan*, 319.
56. Mao, *Jianguo Yilai Mao Zedong Wengao*, vol.1, 193.
57. *Renmin Ribao* (Beijing), 1 October 1982.
58. *Renmin Ribao*, 8 March 1963.
59. Guanggiaojing (ed.), *Xianggang yu Zhongguo*, 279 (Huang Hua's memo to the UN, 10 March 1972).
60. Mao, *Mao Zedong Wenji*, vol.4, 207.
61. FO371/63318, Boyce (Peking) to Chancery (Nanking), 30 December 1946. Xiang Lanxin has described Harmon as a 'British intelligence officer who had personal connections with the Communist leaders'. The original source describes him, a retired colonel, as 'the only British news correspondent stationed' in Beijing who went to Yenan for a visit for the first time. The available official PRC source also refers to him as a visiting British journalist. Xiang's citation and quotation are both partly inaccurate. See Xiang, *Recasting the Imperial Far East*, 101.
62. Xu, *Xu Jiatun Xianggang Huiyilu I*, 67.
63. Zeng, *Zeng Sheng Huiyilu*, 569.
64. CAB129/32, Appendix to CP(49)39, 4 March 1949 (translation of a Communist document captured in Hong Kong).
65. Catron, *China and Hong Kong, 1945–1967*, 70.
66. FO371/75779, Enclosure from Heathcote-Smith to Lamb, 2 December 1948. Qiao is identified as Chiao Mu.
67. Ibid.
68. Goncharov, Lewis and Xue Litai, *Uncertain Partners*, 40.
69. Zeng, *Zeng Sheng Huiyilu*, 570–1.
70. Xu, *Xu Jiatun Xianggang Huiyilu*, vol.2, 473–4.
71. Jin, *Zhonggong Xianggang zhengce biwen shilu*, 4–5.
72. CO537/6798, Colonial Political Intelligence Summary 1951, no.3, March 1951.
73. Zhou, *Zhou Enlai Waijiao Wenxuan*, 83.
74. Cheng, *Hong Kong: In Search of a Future*, 61.
75. Liang, *Zhonggong zai Xianggang*, 138. For the impact of the Cultural Revolution, see Chapter 13.
76. Rafferty, *City on the Rocks*, 411.
77. CAB129/31, CP(48)299, 9 December 1948.
78. A translation of one such document can be found in CAB129/32, Appendix to CP(49)39, 4 March 1949. See also Zhai, *The Dragon, the Lion, and the Eagle*, 30–1.
79. Feng, *The British Government's China Policy 1945–1950*, 105.
80. CAB129/31, CP(48)299, 9 December 1948.
81. FO371/75877, Draft paper for JIC Committee 'Communist Political Intentions towards Hong Kong', undated, July 1949.
82. CAB129/33, CP(49)52, 5 March 1949.
83. A detailed analysis of Britain's defence plan is in Zeng Ruisheng (Steve Tsang), 'Yingguo Fangwai Xianggang Zhengce de Yanbian', 68–80.
84. After the escape of HMS *Amethyst*, the incident came to be told as a story of British gallantry and valour. See Earl, *Yangtse Incident*. For a critical assessment, see Murfett, *Hostage on the Yangtze*.
85. CAB128/15, CM30(49)4, 28 April 1949.
86. DEFE6/10, JP(49)97(Final), 14 September 1949.
87. CAB128/16, CM54(49)2, 29 August 1949.

88. CAB128/15, CM33(49)2, 9 May 1949.

89. *Arthur Creech-Jones Papers*, Box 57, file 1, CP(49)177, RHL, 19 August 1949.

90. DEFE6/10, JP(49)118(Final), 16 December 1949.

91. *Creech-Jones Papers*, Box 57, file 1, CP(49)177, 19 August 1949.

92. CAB128/16, CM54(49)2, 29 August 1949.

93. See Martin, *Divided Counsel*.

94. *Truman Papers*, President's Secretary's Files Box 257, NSC, CIA Reports – ORE 1949, ORE78–49 of 4 October 1949, 2.

95. *Truman Papers*, President's Secretary's Files Box 206, [NSC] Meeting 47, 20 October 1949; 'NSC55/2 A Report to the National Security Council by the Secretary of Defence', 17 October 1949.

96. *Truman Papers*, President's Secretary's Files Box 206, NSC Meeting 47, Memorandum for the Secretary of Defense, 15 July 1949.

97. *Truman Papers*, President's Secretary's Files Box 206, NSC Meeting 47, Memorandum for the Executive Secretary NSC, 17 October 1949.

98. *Eisenhower Papers*, White House Office: Special Assistance to NSC: Policy Papers Box 28, NSC6007/1-HK, 'US Policy on Hong Kong (NSC6007/1)', 11 June 1960, 2.

99. Tucker, *Taiwan, Hong Kong and the United States, 1945–1992*, 214.

100. CO1030/1415, JP(58)164(A)(Preliminary Draft), 5 February 1959.

101. Tsang, 'Strategy for Survival', 297.

102. For China's military intervention, see Tsui, *Chinese Military Intervention in the Korean War*.

103. CO537/5310, Colonial Political Intelligence Summary no.11 (1950), 18–9. Both before and after the Chinese intervention, Chiang offered 30,000 of his best troops to join the UN operation in Korea.

104. Kau and Leung (eds), *The Writings of Mao Zedong, 1949–1976*, vol.1, 98.

105. Tsang, *Democracy Shelved*, 169–71.

106. See Chapter 12.

107. CO537/5628, Hong Kong to Colonial Office, 230, 5 March 1950.

108. CO537/4452, Annex to FE(0)(49)25, 16 May 1949.

109. For a critical analysis of how Hong Kong tried to maintain neutrality but in fact gave way occasionally, see Tsang, 'Strategy for Survival'.

110. CO1030/430, Hong Kong Governor to Colonial Office, 70, 24 January 1958.

111. Sung, *The China-Hong Kong Connection*, 5.

112. Jin, *Zhonggong Xianggang zhengce*, 23.

113. Yu, 'Economic Links among Hong Kong, PRC, and ROC', 114–5.

114. Bonavia, *Hong Kong 1997*, 78–80.

115. Yao, 'Hong Kong's Role in Financing China's Modernization', in Youngson (ed.), *China and Hong Kong: The Economic Nexus*, 58.

116. Yao, 'Banking and Currency in the Special Economic Zones: Problems and Prospects', 169.

117. CO1030/1300, Governor Black to Hilton Poynton, top secret and personal letter, 30 October 1962.

118. Ibid.

Chapter 12: Economic Take-off

1. Census and Statistics Department, *Hong Kong Statistics 1947–1967*, 48.

2. Ibid. 88.

3. Phelps Brown, 'The Hong Kong Economy: Achievements and Prospects', 3.

4. Myers, *Hong Kong as a Global Metropolis*, 159.

5.   Tak-wing Ngo argues that the government discouraged industrial developments in the pre-war period and obstructed industrial upgrading in the 1960s. This is as one-sided as to claim for the government a pivotal role in Hong Kong's industrialisation. Ngo, 'Colonialism in Hong Kong revisited', 8.
6.   CO537/7643, Acting Financial Secretary Arthur Clarke to H.P. Hall, letter of 18 April 1952.
7.   Ibid.
8.   *Hong Kong Hansard 1949*, 59–60 (Governor Grantham's speech, 16 March 1949).
9.   Wong, *Emigrant Entrepreneurs*, 17.
10. Wong, 'The Migration of Shanghaiese Entrepreneurs to Hong Kong', 217.
11. Chiu, *The Port of Hong Kong*, 95.
12. Espy, *The Strategies of Chinese Industrial Enterprises in Hong Kong*, 3.
13. King, *The History of the Hong Kong and Shanghai Banking Corporation*, vol.4, 344–5.
14. Census and Statistics Department, *Hong Kong Statistics 1947–67*, 49–50, 56.
15. Ibid. 56.
16. The Truman Library, *Dean Acheson Papers*, Box 70, January 1952, 'Memorandum of Dinner meeting on SS Williamsburg, 5 Jan. 1952 between President Truman and Prime Minister Churchill', 4–5.
17. Wilson, *Hong Kong Then*, 75.
18. Schenk, *Hong Kong as an International Financial Centre*, 41.
19. Ibid. 11.
20. Truman Library, *Truman Papers*, President's Secretary's Files Box 172, British, 'Memorandum for the President' from Dean Acheson, 25 September 1952.
21. Kelly, *Hong Kong: A Political-Geographic Analysis*, 57.
22. Grantham, *Via Ports*, 155–6.
23. CO1030/382, Governor Grantham to Secretary of State, savingram 395, 9 March 1955.
24. Phelps Brown, 'The Hong Kong Economy', 8.
25. Espy, 'Some Notes on Business and Industry in Hong Kong', 174.
26. Angus, 'Commerce and Industry Department', 25.
27. Phelps Brown, 'The Hong Kong Economy', 9.
28. CO1030/762, E.B. David (HK) to E. Melville (CO), confidential letter of 28 February 1957.
29. CO1030/763, S.A. Ogilvie's report 'Visit to Hong Kong', undated, *c.* August 1958, and her 'Comments for the Colonial Office on some points in the report', 27 August 1958, illustrate the zeal of a labour adviser who tried to persuade the colonial government to follow some of the British practices.
30. CO1030/763, Enclosure to Hong Kong, Savingram 1043, 26 June 1959.
31. Eisenhower Library, *Eisenhower Papers*, White House Office, NSC Policy Papers Sub-series Box 28, NSC6007/1, 'NSC6007/1 US Policy on Hong Kong', 11 June 1960, 13–4.
32. Wong, 'The Migration of Shanghaiese Entrepreneurs to Hong Kong', 225.
33. Y.K. Pao's building of his shipping empire with HSBC help provides a fine example. Hutcheon, *First Sea Lord*, 41–5.
34. King, *History of HSBC*, vol.4, 360–1.
35. Wong, 'The Migration of Shanghaiese Entrepreneurs to Hong Kong', 221.
36. Myers, *Hong Kong as a Global Metropolis*, 149–50.
37. Ibid. 150.
38. Census and Statistics, *Hong Kong Statistics, 1947–67*, 14.

39. Census Commissioner, *Report of the Census 1961*, vol.3, 20.
40. For the refugee situation, see Hambro, *The Problems of Chinese Refugees in Hong Kong*.
41. CO1030/763, 'Comments for the Colonial Office on some points in the report' by Ogilvie, 27 August 1958, 7.
42. Espy, 'Some notes on business and industry in Hong Kong', 174–5.
43. Myers, *Hong Kong as a Global Metropolis*, 166.
44. Espy, 'Some notes on business and industry in Hong Kong', 177.
45. Myers, *Hong Kong as a Global Metropolis*, 167.
46. CO1030/763, 'Extracts from the report to the government of Hong Kong on productivity', undated, 1958.
47. Turner, Fosh and Ng, *Between Two Societies*, 12–13.
48. Espy, 'Some notes on business and industry in Hong Kong', 172.
49. Owen, 'Economic Policy in Hong Kong', 141.
50. CO1030/763, report 'Visit to Hong Kong' by Ogilvie, August 1958.
51. Ibid.
52. Chaney, 'Job Satisfaction and Unionization: The Case of Shopworkers', 267–8.
53. England and Rear, *Industrial Relations and Law in Hong Kong*, 13.
54. Ibid. 167.
55. Catron, *China and Hong Kong, 1945–1967*, 140–4, 215–8.
56. CO1030/763, Minutes of Ogilvie, 26 August 1958.
57. CO1030/763, Enclosure to Hong Kong, Savingram 1043, 26 June 1959.
58. Hoadley, 'Hong Kong is the Lifeboat: Notes on Political Culture and Socialization', 211.
59. 'Take-off' of the economy in this book is used loosely as a general analogy to illustrate how the economy passed from one stage of development into another. It should not be taken to imply the author agrees fully with W.W. Rostow's definition of economic take-off in development economics.
60. For the confrontation, see Chapter 13.
61. See Chapter 14.
62. Scott, *Political Change and the Crisis of Legitimacy in Hong Kong*, 104–5.
63. Tsang, 'Government and Politics in Hong Kong: A Colonial Paradox', 73.
64. Hong Kong Government, *Hong Kong 1976*, 28.
65. Yu, *Entrepreneurship and Economic Development in Hong Kong*, 5.
66. An assessment confirmed by former Governor David Trench in private conversations.
67. Private conversations between the author and Cowperthwaite in St Andrews, Scotland, on 4 April 1983.
68. *Hong Kong Hansard 1969*, 211.
69. *Hong Kong Hansard 1962*, 51.
70. Youngson, *Hong Kong Economic Growth and Policy*, 58–9.
71. Ibid. 123–36.
72. Tsang (ed.), *Documentary History of Hong Kong I*, 145–8.
73. Youngson, *Hong Kong Economic Growth and Policy*, 64–5.
74. The dominant view of most older works describe Hong Kong government's policy in terms of *laissez faire*. Among the best known are works by Rabushka, such as *The Changing Face of Hong Kong* and *Hong Kong: A Study in Economic Freedom*; and Owen, 'Economic Policy'.
75. Youngson, *Hong Kong Economic Growth and Policy*, 16.
76. Rao, 'Xianggang gongye fazhan de guiji', 402.
77. Ibid.

78. Liu, *Jianming Xianggang Shi*, 299.

79. He, *Xianggang Fuhao Liezhuang*.

80. Chan, *Li Ka-shing*, 81–5.

81. England, *The Quest of Noel Croucher*, 241.

82. Youngson, *Hong Kong Economic Growth and Policy*, 8. The exchange rate for 1961 was $US1 to $HK5.71, and $US1 to $HK6.06 in 1969.

83. For problems of housing before the 1967 riots, see Goodstadt, 'Urban Housing in Hong Kong 1945–1963', 257–98.

84. There was little real improvement in living standards or rise in per capita income up to the early 1960s. Szczepanik, 'Problems of Macro-economic Programming in Hong Kong', 232.

85. Faure, *Documentary History II*, 308–9 (Dennis Bray's speech at Legco, 29 November 1973).

86. An important landmark development was the founding of the Christian Industrial Committee in 1967. See Li and Zhang, 'Xianggang jidujiao gongye weiyuanhui', 177–82.

87. Hong Kong Government, *Hong Kong 1979*, 36.

88. Schenk, *Hong Kong as an International Financial Centre*, 107–11.

89. England, *The Quest of Noel Croucher*, 237

90. Ibid. 238.

91. Hong Kong Government, *Hong Kong 1987*, 48.

92. Foot, *The Practice of Power*, 75.

93. Leung, 'Spatial Redevelopment and the Special Economic Zones in China: An Overview', 9.

94. Enright, Scott and Dodwell, *The Hong Kong Advantage*, 19.

95. Hong Kong Government, *Hong Kong – A New Era*, 49.

96. Sung, *The China-Hong Kong Connection*, 100–1.

97. Vogel, *One Step Ahead in China: Guangdong Under Reform*, 69.

98. Ibid. 62–3.

99. Hong Kong Government, *Hong Kong – A New Era*, 48.

100. Sung, *The China-Hong Kong Connection*, 173.

101. Lardy, *China's Unfinished Economic Revolution*, 19–20.

Chapter 13: The Rise of the Hong Kongers

1.   Tsang, 'Identity Crisis in Hong Kong', 11.

2.   CO129/604/6, Grantham to Creech-Jones, telegram of 19 December 1949.

3.   Hong Kong Government, *Hong Kong Annual Report, 1950* 2.

4.   CO1030/383, Annex to OAG, HK to Secretary of State, savingram 1744, 10 October 1956.

5.   For the scale of execution in the early Maoist years, see Domes, *The Internal Politics of China, 1949–1972*, 51; for the scale of death by starvation as a result of the Great Leap Forward, see Becker, *Hungry Ghosts*, 266–74, and Banister, *China's Changing Population*; for a single-volume treatment of the Cultural Revolution, see Barnouin and Yu, *Ten Years of Turbulence*.

6.   For a comparative study of the fate of the Chinese culture in the PRC, Hong Kong and Taiwan after 1949, see Tsang, 'The Confucian Tradition and Democratization', 30–45.

7.   *Ming Bao* (editorial), 31 August 1982.

8.   Wu, 'Xianggangren ying guanxin Xianggang zhengshi', 8.

9.   Ibid., translation from Tsang (ed.), *Government and Politics*, 249.

10. Lamb, *The Macmillan Years, 1957–1963*, 246.

11. Judd, *Empire*, 365–9.

12. CO1030/1300, Black to Poynton, top secret and personal letter, 30 October 1962.
13. Copper, *Colony in Conflict*, 2.
14. Yu, 'Zhou Enlai yaokong "fanying kangbao" neinmu', 6.
15. Hong Kong Government, *Hong Kong Disturbances 1967*, 5.
16. Jin, *Zhonggong Xianggang Zhengce*, 95.
17. Yen and Gao, *"Wenhua dagemin" Shinian Shi*, vol.1, 17–9.
18. White, *Policies of Chaos*, 4.
19. Jin, *Zhonggong Xianggang Zhengce*, 87–92.
20. Yu, 'Zaitan Xianggang liuqi baodong', 58–60. Yu is the penname of Yin Longbo, who worked in the Foreign Ministry at the time.
21. Yen and Gao, *Wenhua Dageming*, vol.1, 394.
22. Jin, *Zhonggong Xianggang Zhengce*, 94.
23. Jin, 'Xianggang "Fanying kangbao" fadong de neimu' in Yin and Ma (eds), *Zhou Enlai yu Xianggang*, 65.
24. Yu, 'Zhou Enlai yaokong "fanying kangbao" neinmu', 22–34.
25. Zhang, *Xianggang liuqi baodong neiqing*, 47–8.
26. Jin, *Zhonggong Xianggang zhengce*, 97–8.
27. Rhodes House Library, *Transcript of Interview with Sir David Trench*, 79–81.
28. Zhang, *Xianggang liuqi baodong*, 148–9 (Sir Jack Cater's account).
29. Luo, *Zhengzhibu Huiyilu*, 101–2; Tin, 'Xianggang "luiqi baodong" yu wenhua dagemin', 87.
30. Cradock, *Experiences of China*, 57; Liang, *Zhonggong zai Xianggang*, 138.
31. These company-strength units were called Police Training Units (PTUs) in 1967 but have since then been renamed Police Tactical Units. They are usually headed by a superintendent of police.
32. It is ironic that the Commissioner for Police when the disturbances started, Edward Tyrer, was a key figure in the forming of PTUs and thus made a significant contribution in giving Hong Kong the capability to deal with the disturbances but he was quietly replaced by his very able deputy, Edward Eates, as the Acting Governor lost confidence in him shortly after the Shatoukok incident.
33. Hong Kong Government, *Hong Kong 1966*, 153.
34. Hong Kong Government, *Hong Kong Disturbances 1967*, 57.
35. Hong Kong Government, *Hong Kong 1967*, 4–7.
36. See for example *Renmin Ribao*, front page news of 15 May 1967; editorials of 3 June and 5 July, 1967; and Zhou Enlai's statement on 24 June 1967.
37. Hong Kong Government, *Hong Kong 1967*, 12.
38. Hong Kong Government, *Hong Kong Disturbances*, 45.
39. Grey's ordeal is described graphically in Grey, *Hostage in Peking*; for a first-hand account of the sacking of the British Embassy compound, see Cradock, *Experiences of China*, 61–8.
40. FCO40/63, Commonwealth Office to Hong Kong 1801, 31 August 1967.
41. Barnouin and Yu, *Ten Years of Turbulence*, 150–1.
42. FCO40/63, Peking to Foreign Office 297, 298, 2 December 1967.
43. Jin, 'Xianggang "Fanying kangbao" fadong de neimu', 73–4.
44. Ibid. 74; Liang, *Zhonggong zai Xianggang*, 142.
45. Jin, *Zhonggong Xianggang Zhengce*, 141–5.
46. Hong Kong Government, *Hong Kong Disturbances 1967*, 45, 56–7.
47. Ibid.
48. Far Eastern Economic Review, *The Far Eastern Economic Review 1967 Yearbook*, 169.
49. Faure, *Documentary History II*, 287 (Report of the Commission of Inquiry).

50. Ibid. 290.
51. Zhang, *Xianggang Liuqi Baodong*, 14–5.
52. For the change in government policy from indifference to providing basic education for almost every child in the immediate post-war period, see Sweeting, *A Phoenix Transformed*, especially 92–119.
53. Hong Kong Government, *The Government and the People*, 10; Hong Kong Government, *Hong Kong 1966*, 17.
54. For a full list of civic organisations, see Hong Kong Government, *Hong Kong Disturbances*, 60–77.
55. Zhang, *Xianggang Liuqi Baodong*, 84.
56. Zhou, *Jianzheng Xianggang Wushi Nian*, 54.
57. Wang, *Lishi de Chenchong*, 82–3.
58. Young, 'The Building Years: Maintaining a China-Hong Kong-Britain Equilibrium, 1950–1971', 140.
59. Kong, 'Lunshuo Liuqi', 96–7.
60. Scott, *Political Change and the Crisis of Legitimacy*, 104–5.
61. Cater, 'The 1967 Riots', 111–2.
62. Hong Kong Government, *The City District Officer Scheme*, 2–3.
63. Rhodes House Library, *Transcript of Interview with Sir David Trench*, 74.
64. Scott, *Political Change and the Crisis of Legitimacy*, 105–6. Scott is not aware of Trench's intention to introduce the CDO scheme.
65. For the impact of the Nixon visit on US opinions, see Mosher, *China Misperceived*, 144–159.
66. Guo, 'Qishiniandai houqi de Xianggang xueyun', 65.
67. For the Lin Biao case, see Teiwes and Sun, *The Tragedy of Lin Biao*.
68. The 'Gang of Four' was formally headed by Jiang Qing, Mao's wife. The other members were all Maoists promoted to top positions as a result of the Cultural Revolution. They were Chang Chunqiao, Wang Hongwen and Yao Wenyuan, all close followers of Mao.
69. MacLehose, 'Social and Economic Challenges', 126–7.
70. For the corruption problem in Hong Kong, see Tsang, *Government and Politics*, 175–94; Lethbridge, *Hard Craft in Hong Kong*; and Lo, *Corruption and Politics in Hong Kong and China*.
71. Census and Statistics Department, *Estimates of Gross Domestic Product, 1961 to 1995*, 13.
72. For Pao's success story, see Hutcheon, *First Sea Lord*.
73. Siu, 'Remade in Hong Kong: Weaving Into the Chinese Cultural Tapestry', 184.
74. Yao, 'Xing Se Yi', 10–20.
75. Siu, 'Remade in Hong Kong', 184.
76. Ye, 'Bianyuan yu yunji de qiuling', 47.
77. Tsang, *Government and Politics*, 286.
78. *Hong Kong Hansard 1980*, Governor MacLehose's speech of 23 October 1980.
79. Far Eastern Economic Review, *The Far Eastern Economic Review Yearbook 1981*, 132.
80. Zhou, *Xianggang Ren Xianggang Shi*, 119.
81. Siu, 'Remade in Hong Kong', 187.
82. Cantonese rather than pinyin transliteration is used for these terms, as they were used in Hong Kong and gained common currency there.
83. Lau and Kuan, *The Ethos of the Hong Kong Chinese*, 178.
84. Burns and Scott, 'A Profile of the Civil Service', 30.
85. Jenkins, 'People – Hong Kong's Greatest Asset', 9–10.

86. Lau and Kuan, *The Ethos of the Hong Kong Chinese*, 189–95.

87. Tsang, 'Political Probems Facing the Hong Kong Civil Service in Transition', 138.

88. Baker, 'Life in the Cities: The Emergence of Hong Kong Man', 478.

89. Faure, 'Reflections on Being Chinese in Hong Kong', 105.

90. Concept borrowed from Hughes, *Borrowed Place Borrowed Time*.

Chapter 14: The Making of a Colonial Paradox

1. The main arguments for what constitutes the best possible government in the Chinese tradition are substantially based on Tsang, 'Government and Politics in Hong Kong: A Colonial Paradox', 62–83.

2. For Taiwan's democratisation, see Chao and Myers, *The First Chinese Democracy*.

3. Concept first used by Myers and Metzger, in Myers (ed.), *Two Societies in Opposition*, xviii.

4. Tsang, 'Strategy for Survival', 296.

5. Tsang, *A Documentary History of Hong Kong*, 152.

6. Sheridan, *China in Disintegration*, 204.

7. Ch'u, *Local Government in China Under the Ch'ing*, 1.

8. Grantham, *Via Ports*, 155–6.

9. Drakakis-Smith, 'Housing needs and planning policies for the Asian City – the lesson from Hong Kong', 115.

10. Sweeting, *A Phoenix Transformed*, 14–21.

11. The process did not really start after 1967, as various committees had been set up before the riots to inquire into, for example, local government. See, for example, Hong Kong Government, *Report of the Working Party on Local Administration*.

12. McKinsey and Company, *Strengthening the Machinery of Government Volume 1 – Report*.

13. Yuying, 'Yingguo de fazhi jingshen', 423.

14. Yu Sheng, 'Xianggang xiaoji', *Qiantu*, vol.2, no.5, 1 May 1934.

15. Tsang, *A Documentary History of Hong Kong*, 148.

16. Lethbridge, *Stability and Change*, 38.

17. Ibid.

18. CO129/80, 'Hong Kong Cadetship', 2 July 1861.

19. Tsang, *A Documentary History of Hong Kong*, 167.

20. CO882/6, 'Hong Kong, Straits Settlements, and Federated Malay States Police Probationers', February 1907.

21. CO129/120, Sir Richard MacDonnell to Lord Carnarvon, despatch 183, 7 January 1867.

22. CO131/116, Minutes of Executive Council meeting, 2 August 1946.

23. Hong Kong Government, *Second Report of the Commission of Inquiry under Sir Alastair Blair-Kerr*, 2.

24. CO1030/1386, Burgess to McLeod 354, 18 April 1960.

25. CO1030/1387, 'Sixth report of the Standing Committee on Corruption', 29 December 1961.

26. CO1030/1386, Black to McLeod 175, 26 February 1960.

27. Tsang, *A Documentary History of Hong Kong*, 171.

28. *Hong Kong Hansard 1969*, 67–8 (address by Governor Trench on 26 February 1969).

29. CO1030/1386, Solicitor General to Colonial Secretary, minute 20, 11 March 1961.

30. Lo, *Corruption and Politics in Hong Kong and China*, 89.

31.   *Second Report of the Commission of Inquiry under Sir Alastair Blair-Kerr*, 42–52.
32.   *Hong Kong Hansard 1973–74*, 15 (address by Governor Sir Murray MacLehose on 17 October 1973).
33.   Hong Kong Government, *Annual Report on the ICAC for 1983*, 17.
34.   Grantham, *Via Ports*, 156.
35.   Youngson, *Hong Kong Economic Growth and Policy*, 126.
36.   *Hong Kong Hansard 1972–3*, 4 (Governor's address, 18 October 1972).
37.   Tsang, 'China and Political Reform in Hong Kong', 69.
38.   FO371/63318, Boyce (Peking) to Chancery (Nanking), 30 December 1946.
39.   See Chapter 11, and Tsang, *Democracy Shelved*.
40.   FO371/99251, Oakeshott's minutes of 31 March 1952.
41.   There is, however, one businessman who reported a meeting with Zhou Enlai in which Zhou warned against the British allowing Hong Kong to attain 'dominion status'. This is not a reliable account of what Zhou actually said. For an analysis of this incident, see Tsang, *Appointment with China*, 117–8.
42.   CO1030/1300, Black to Poynton, top secret and personal letter, 30 October 1962.
43.   CO1030/1620, Trench to Wallace, confidential letter, 26 May 1965.
44.   CO1030/1620, Bollard (Foreign Office) to Carter (Colonial Office), secret letter, 20 August 1965.
45.   FCO40/42, Hong Kong to FCO 356, 18 March 1967.
46.   FCO40/42, Hong Kong to FCO 367, 20 March 1967.
47.   FCO40/42, Colonial Office paper 'Background Note', undated, late 1968.
48.   Hong Kong Government, *Hong Kong Annual Report 1952*, 11–4.
49.   Zhong, 'Xianggang de Daxuesheng kaici tan zhengzhi', 11.
50.   Hong Kong Government, *District Administration in Hong Kong*, 4.
51.   King, 'Administrative Absorption of Politics in Hong Kong, 422–39.
52.   Lau, 'Colonial Rule, Transfer of Sovereignty and the Problem of Political Leaders in Hong Kong', 225.
53.   Tsang, *A Documentary History of Hong Kong*, 53–6.
54.   Hayes, *Friends and Teachers*, 281.
55.   Xianggang Guangchashe, *Guangcha Xianggang*, 41–8.
56.   *Ming Bao*, editorials of 31 August 1982 and 9 September 1983.

Chapter 15: Fateful Decisions

1.   FCO40/55, 'Secretary of State's meeting with Sir David Trench', 2 May 1968.
2.   CO1030/1300, Black to Poynton, top secret and personal letter, 30 October 1962.
3.   The four were Mao's wife, Qiang Qing, and Zhang Chunqiao, Wang Hongwen and Yao Wenyuan.
4.   Far Eastern Economic Review, *Asia 1979 Yearbook*, 179.
5.   The rest of this chapter is a revised version of Tsang, *Appointment with China*, 83–110.
6.   Cottrell, *The End of Hong Kong*, 49.
7.   McLaren, *Britain's Record in Hong Kong*, 13–4.
8.   Cradock, *Experiences of China*, 165.
9.   Cradock claims in his memoirs that he doubted the Chinese would put nationalist considerations behind economic reform, though he did not explain why he nonetheless backed MacLehose's proposal. Cradock, *Experiences of China*, 166.

10. See Chapter 11.
11. Grantham, *Via Ports*, 107.
12. Hong Kong Government, *Draft Agreement on the Future of Hong Kong*, 2.
13. Freris, *The Financial Markets of Hong Kong*, 48.
14. King, *History of the Hong Kong Bank*, vol.4, 875.
15. Cradock, *Experiences of China*, 165.
16. Xu, *Xu Jiatun Xianggang Huiyilu*, vol.1, 82–3.
17. Ruan, *Deng Xiaoping: Chronicle of an Empire*, 56–9.
18. Han (ed.), *Diplomacy of Contemporary China*, 464.
19. Cottrell, *The End of Hong Kong*, 54–6; Roberti, *The Fall of Hong Kong*, 23.
20. McLaren, *Britain's Record in Hong Kong*, 14.
21. These include scholarly accounts like Tang and Ching, 'The MacLehose-Youde Years: Balancing the "Three-Legged Stool" 1971–86'; Scott, *Political Change and the Crisis of Legitimacy*, 167; and Yahuda, *Hong Kong: China's Challenge*, 64.
22. *Daily Information Bulletin*, Supplement, 6 April 1979.
23. See, for example, *South China Morning Post*, 7 April 1979.
24. The timing was confirmed by Foreign Minister Wu Xuejian in 1984. *Xianggang Wenti Wenjian Xuanji*, 17–8.
25. Li, *Huigui de Licheng*, 70.
26. Deng, *Deng Xiaoping Lun Tongyi Zhanxian*, 150.
27. Lee, *The Reunification of China*, 61.
28. Swaine, 'Chinese Decision-Making Regarding Taiwan, 1979–2000', 312.
29. Wu, *Bridging the Strait*, 74.
30. Guo (ed.), *Zhonggong du Tai Zhengze Zhiliao Xuanji: 1949–1991*, vol.1, 413.
31. Zhongguo Xinwen She (ed.), *Liaogong zai Renjian*, 184–5.
32. Xu, *Xu Jiatun Xianggang Huiyilu*, vol.1, 16.
33. Sima, *Ronyao Quangui Deng Xiaoping de Xianggang Qiantu Tanpan*, 2.
34. This section on the resistance within the Chinese leadership is based on Qian, 'One Country, Two Systems' – The Structure and Process of China's Policy Making towards Hong Kong (1979–1990).
35. *Xianggang Wenti Wenjian Xuanji*, 2–3.
36. Cradock, *Experiences of China*, 170.
37. Li, *Huigui de Licheng*, 77.
38. Cradock, *Experiences of China*, 172.
39. Li, *Bainian Quyushi de zhongjie*, 144–5.
40. Rafferty, *City on the Rocks*, 438–40.
41. For an analysis of the united front, see Van Slyke, *Enemies and Friends*.
42. Analysis of the drafting of the 12 points is based on Qian, 'One Country, Two Systems'.
43. Evans, *Deng Xiaoping and the Making of Modern China*, 267.
44. Thatcher, *The Downing Street Years*, 259.
45. Cradock, *Experiences of China*, 175.
46. Young, *One of Us*, 292.
47. Cradock, *Experiences of China*, 177–8.
48. Thatcher, *The Downing Street Years*, 259.
49. Deng, *Deng Xiaoping Wenxuan*, vol.3, 12.
50. Ibid. 14.
51. Ibid. 60.
52. Thatcher, *The Downing Street Years*, 260–2.
53. Han, *Diplomacy of Contemporary China*, 464–5.
54. Li, *Bainian Quyushi de Zhongjie*, 86.

55.   Cottrell, *The End of Hong Kong*, 86.
56.   Chung, *Hong Kong's Journey to Reunification*, 45–6.
57.   Hong Kong Government, *Hong Kong 1983*, 46.
58.   Hong Kong Government, *Draft Agreement on Hong Kong's Future*, 3.
59.   Chiu, *The People's Republic of China and the Law of Treaties*, 30.
60.   Cradock, *Experiences of China*, 184–5.
61.   The revised 12 points are reproduced in Li, *Huigui de Licheng*, 104–5.
62.   *Beijing Review*, no.52 (Beijing, 27 December 1982), 16.
63.   Cradock, *Experiences of China*, 185.
64.   Thatcher, *The Downing Street Years*, 489.
65.   *Xin Wan Bao*, 13 May 1982.
66.   Xu, *Xu Jiatun Xianggang Huiyilu*, vol.1, 86–7.
67.   *Pai Shing*, 16 July 1982, 4.
68.   Ibid. 7–8.
69.   See Chung, *Hong Kong's Journey*, 60–92.
70.   Thatcher, *The Downing Street Years*, 491.
71.   Xu, *Xu Jiatun Xianggang Huiyilu*, vol.1, 89–92.
72.   The two are Sir Quo-wei Lee and Lydia Dunn.
73.   Philip Mao argues Beijing's policy towards Hong Kong was essentially an
      application of the United Front approach. Mao, *The People's Republic of China
      in the Preparation for the Take-over of Hong Kong*.
74.   Wilson, *Hong Kong! Hong Kong!*, 207.
75.   *Pai Shing*, 1 July 1984, 3.
76.   Deng, *Deng Xiaoping Wenxuan*, vol.3, 60.
77.   Roberti, *The Fall of Hong Kong*, 79.
78.   Cheng, *Zhonggong Yuhe Tanpan*, 204.
79.   Kreisberg, 'China's Negotiating Behaviour', 454.
80.   Howe, *Conflict of Loyalty*, 366.
81.   *Financial Times*, 16 September 1983.
82.   Ibid.
83.   Thatcher, *The Downing Street Years*, 489–90.
84.   *Wen Hui Pao*, 21 September 1983.
85.   *Ming Bao*, 2 October 1983.
86.   Thatcher, *The Downing Street Years*, 490.
87.   Cradock, *Experiences of China*, 192.
88.   Ibid. 197.
89.   Ibid.
90.   Evans, *Deng Xiaoping and the Making of Modern China*, 268.
91.   Howe, *Conflict of Loyalty*, 374–5.
92.   Deng, *Deng Xiaoping Wenxuan*, vol.3, 67–8.
93.   Xu, *Xu Jiatun Xianggang Huiyilu*, 111–12.
94.   *Pai Shing*, 16 August 1984, 14.
95.   Cradock, *Experiences of China*, 198.
96.   Chung, *Hong Kong's Journey*, 109.
97.   Xu, *Xu Jiatun Xianggang Huiyilu*, vol.1, 112–14.
98.   *Ming Bao*, 26 May 1984.
99.   Hong Kong Government, *Draft Sino-British Agreement on Hong Kong*, 13.
100. Ibid. 11–13.
101. Hong Kong Government, *Hong Kong: Arrangements for Testing the Acceptability
      of the Draft Agreement on the Future of the Territory*, 18–25.

Chapter 16: The Beginning of the End

1. *Draft Agreement on Hong Kong's Future*, 15.
2. Ibid. 13.
3. Tsang, 'Maximum Flexibility, Rigid Framework', 421.
4. Xu, *Xu Jiatun Xianggang Huiyilu*, vol.1, 172–3.
5. Cheng (ed.), *Hong Kong: In Search of a Future*, 12–13.
6. Tsang, 'Realignment of Power: The Politics of Transition and Reform in Hong Kong', 33–6.
7. *Parliamentary Debates: Lords*, vol.458, no.17, 10–16 (Baroness Young's statement, 10 December 1984).
8. *Parliamentary Debates: Commons*, vol.69, no.22, 5 December 1984, 389–449.
9. Thatcher, *The Downing Street Years*, 493.
10. *Draft Agreement on Hong Kong's Future*, 7.
11. Lau and Kuan, *The Ethos of the Hong Kong Chinese*, 82–5.
12. Xu, *Xu Jiatun Xianggang Huiyilu I*, 177–80.
13. Tsang, 'Realignment of Power', 46–9.
14. See *Qishi Niandai*, no.152, September 1982, special issue on the 1997 question.
15. Lau, 'Colonial Rule, Transfer of Sovereignty and the Problem of Political Leaders', 225.
16. Li, *Huigui de Licheng*, 189.
17. Zhonggong Zhongyang Wenxian Yanjiushe (ed.), *Yiguo Liangjin Chongyao Wenxian Xuanbian*, 101–2.
18. Ibid. 191.
19. Lo, *The Politics of Democratization in Hong Kong*, 86–7. Prime Minister Thatcher had thought of initiating democratisation as a means to pressure the Chinese during the negotiations, but this met with no support. Thatcher, *Downing Street Years*, 488.
20. Walden, *Excellence, Your Gap is Growing*, 73. The number of British subjects was over 2 million in 1984 but well over 3 million by 1997.
21. *Qishi Niandai*, no.142, January 1981, 67–9.
22. The rest of this section and the following one are substantially reproduced from Tsang, *Appointment with China*, 122–131.
23. Hong Kong Government, *Green Paper: The Further Development of Representative Government in Hong Kong*, 4.
24. Ibid. 3.
25. Hong Kong Government, *White Paper: The Further Development of Representative Government in Hong Kong*, 14–55.
26. Xu, *Xu Jiatun Xianggang Huiyilu*, vol.1, 173.
27. Li, *Bainian Quyushi de Zhongjie*, 211–12.
28. Ibid. 172.
29. *Cheng Bao*, 22 November 1985.
30. Anon (ed.), *Jibenfa*, 117 (Record of Xu Jiatun's press interview on 21 November 1985).
31. Chang, 'How China Sees It', 138.
32. Xu, *Xu Jiatun Xianggang Huiyilu*, vol.1, 177.
33. This section is reproduced substantially from Tsang, *Appointment With China*, 125–31.
34. Youde, *The Chairman's Lecture: The Political and Commercial Prospects for Hong Kong*, 5.
35. Li, *Huigui de Licheng*, 190.
36. See So, *Hong Kong's Embattled Democracy*, 126–7.

37. Roberti, *The Fall of Hong Kong*, 161–4

38. Hong Kong Government, *Green Paper: The 1987 Review of Developments in Representative Government.*

39. *The Independent*, 11 February 1988.

40. Hong Kong Government, *Public Response to Green Paper: The 1987 Report of the Survey Office Part I*, 52.

41. Ibid. 57.

42. Hong Kong Government, *White Paper of 1984*, 8.

43. Hong Kong Government, *White Paper of 1988*, 8.

44. *The Independent*, 11 February 1988.

45. Even among the most vocal supporters of democratisation, the 'service professionals', only a few hundred marched against the manipulation. So, *Embattled Democracy*, 134.

46. Lau, 'Institutions Without Leaders', 191.

47. Tsang, *A Documentary History of Hong Kong*, 227.

48. Tsang, *Appointment With China*, 138–44.

49. Ye, 'Xianggang Xinhuashe fazhan shi', 189.

50. Tsang, 'Maximum Flexibility, Rigid Framework', 413–31.

51. The rest of this section is reproduced substantially from Tsang, *Appointment with China*, 134–8.

52. Vogel, *One Step Ahead in China*, 67.

53. Cheng, *Deng Xiaoping 'Yiguo Liangzhi' Sixiang Yanjiu*, 87–8.

54. Quoted in Zhao, *Interpreting Chinese Foreign Policy*, 238.

55. Deng, *Deng Xiaoping Lun Xianggang Wenti*, 6.

56. Deng, *Deng Xiaoping Lun Tongyi Zhanxian*, 278–9.

57. Deng, *Deng Xiaoping Lun Xianggang Wenti*, 14.

58. Deng, *Deng Xiaoping Wenxuan*, vol.3, 221.

59. Ibid.

60. Ibid. 154–5.

61. Ibid. 156.

62. Harding, *Organizing China*, 1

63. Zhou, *Zijing Kaichu Xing Zhaoxia*, 105.

64. Xu, *Xu Jiatun Xianggang Huiyilu*, vol.2, 432–3.

65. Miners, *The Government and Politics of Hong Kong*, 68–9.

66. Wu, *Renda Huiyilu*, 97, 152.

67. This section is reproduced substantially from Tsang, *Appointment with China*, 144–55.

68. Hong Kong Government, *Draft Agreement on Hong Kong's Future*, 13.

69. Basic Law Drafting Committee, *The Basic Law*, 5.

70. Xianggang Wenhuibao (ed.), *Jibenfa de Dansheng*, 205.

71. By the time the committee had completed its task in 1990, the number of its Hong Kong drafters had fallen to 18, since one had died, two had resigned and two had been expelled. Three mainland Chinese drafters had also died in the meantime.

72. Xu, *Xu Jiatun Xianggang Huiyilu*, vol.1, 156–8.

73. Xianggang Wenhuibao (ed.), *Jibenfa de Dansheng*, 22–3.

74. Whether they were card-carrying members of the Communist Party or not, they were subject to the party's control. In 1989, the Ta Kung Pao's status as a party organ was officially reaffirmed by senior leaders like Jiang Zemen and Li Peng. Jin, *Zhonggong Xianggang Zhengce*, 9.

75. Xu, *Xu Jiatun Xianggang Huiyilu*, vol.1, 161.

76. Ibid. 157.

77. Ibid. 160–1.
78. Anon. (ed.), *Jibenfa: Xianggang Weilai de Gouhua*, 91.
79. Ibid. 111.
80. *Pai Shing*, 16 December 1985, 6–8, 58.
81. Xu, *Xu Jiatun Xianggang Huiyilu*, vol.1, 164.
82. Chan, 'Democracy Derailed: Realpolitik in the Making of the Hong Kong Basic Law, 1985–90', 8.
83. Schram, *The Political Thought of Mao Tse-tung*, 316–17.
84. Li, *Bainian Quyushi de Zhongjie*, 169.
85. Based on Qian, *'One Country, Two Systems'*.
86. For commander-commissar relations, see Cheng, *Party-Military Relations in the PRC and Taiwan*.
87. Li, *Huigui de Licheng*, 146–71.
88. Xianggang Wenhuibao, *Jibenfa de Dansheng*, 231.
89. Li, *Bainian Quyushi de Zhongjie*, 184–5.
90. *Pai Shing*, 1 December 1988, 3–5; Xu, *Xu Jiatun Xianggang Huiyilu*, vol.2, 211–12. As it turned out Cha was wrong in his assessment of the PRC's bottom line.
91. Lo, *The Politics of Democratization in Hong Kong*, 121.
92. *Pai Shing*, 16 December 1988, 9–16.
93. So, *Hong Kong's Embattled Democracy*, 141–2, 161–2.
94. Lo, *The Politics of Democratization in Hong Kong*, 214–15.
95. *Beijing Review*, 27 December 1982, 16.
96. *Beijing Review*, 27 December 1982, 10.
97. Ibid.
98. Nathan, 'Political Rights in Chinese Constitutions', 121.
99. Xiao (ed.), *Yiguo Liangzhi yu Xianggang Tebie Xingzhengqu Jibenfa*, 8–13.

Chapter 17: The Final Chapter

1. Michael, 'China and the Crisis of Communism', 449.
2. Tsou, *The Cultural Revolution and Post Mao Reforms*, 250.
3. Han (ed.), *Cries for Democracy*, 5
4. Dittmer, *China Under Reform*, 98–9, 146.
5. Nathan, 'The Documents and Their Significance', xxxv–xxxvii.
6. Manion, 'Introduction: Reluctant Duelists: The Logic of the 1989 Protests and Massacre', xxvi–xxvii.
7. Zhang (ed.), *Zhongguo 'Lusi' Zhenxiang*, vol.1, 195–8.
8. Deng, *Deng Xiaoping Wenxuan*, vol.3, 303.
9. Chen, 'Report on Checking the Turmoil and Quelling the Counter-Revolutionary Rebellion', 1.
10. Brook, *Quelling the People*, 40–1.
11. Cheng, 'Prospect for Democracy in Hong Kong', 278.
12. Wong, *Red China Blues*, 235–6.
13. Cheng, *Behind the Tiananmen Massacre*, 204. Hong Kong's pro-democracy activists claimed a turnout of 1 million. The Hong Kong police's estimate was half a million.
14. Xu, *Xu Jiatun Xianggang Huiyilu*, vol.2, 368–9.
15. Best account in Brook, *Quelling the People*, 108–69.
16. Zhang, *Zhongguo 'Lusi' Zhenxiang*, vol.2, 993–8.
17. *Xin Bao*, 5 June 1989.
18. This section is based substantially on Tsang, *Appointment with China*, 164–80.
19. *Dongfang Ribao*, 5 June 1989; *Xin Bao*, 6 June 1989.

20. *Pai Shing*, 1 July 1989, 51; Lee, 'Community and Identity in Transition in Hong Kong', 312.
21. *South China Morning Post*, 12 June 1989.
22. Foreign Affairs Committee, *Second Report on Hong Kong (Session 1988–9)*, vii.
23. Miners, *The Government and Politics of Hong Kong*, 39.
24. Ibid.
25. Shawcross, *Kowtow!*, 37–8.
26. *Pai Shing*, 16 June 1989, 12–13. The remaining members of Hong Kong's population were not born there and therefore are not British subjects, except for those who have become naturalised.
27. *Far Eastern Economic Review*, 22 June 1989, 14.
28. *The Independent*, 5 April 1990.
29. *The Guardian*, 5 April 1990.
30. Thatcher, *The Downing Street Years*, 495.
31. *Far Eastern Economic Review*, 8 June 1989, 18.
32. Ibid.
33. Thatcher, *The Downing Street Years*, 495.
34. Ibid.
35. Tsang, *A Documentary History of Hong Kong*, 97 (British Foreign Secretary Hurd to Chinese Foreign Minister Qian, message of 12 February 1990).
36. Hong Kong Government, *The Draft Agreement on Hong Kong's Future*, 23.
37. Hong Kong Government, *An Introduction to Hong Kong Bill of Rights Ordinance*, 3.
38. 'China Sticks to HK, Macao Policy', *Beijing Review*, 3–9 July 1989, 6.
39. Ibid. 6.
40. Cradock, *Experiences of China*, 229.
41. Ibid. 230.
42. Xu, *Xu Jiatun Xianggang Huiyilu*, vol.2, 385.
43. Ibid. 384–5.
44. Cradock, *Experiences of China*, 232.
45. For the PRC's official position on the sacking of Xu, see Li, *Huigui de Licheng*, 211–2.
46. *Xin Bao*, 13 May 1990.
47. Xu, *Xu Jiatun Xianggang Huiyilu*, vol.2, 395–6.
48. *Renmin Ribao*, 21 July 1989.
49. For details, see Chan and Clark (eds), *The Hong Kong Basic Law*, 21–9.
50. Li, *Quyushi de Zhongjie*, 244–7.
51. Hong Kong Government, *Hong Kong 1990*, 5.
52. Leung, 'Summary Findings and Implications', 145.
53. Leung, 'The "China Factor" in the 1991 Legislative Council Election', 187–8.
54. Scott, 'An Overview of the Hong Kong Legislative Council Elections of 1991', 5.
55. Hong Kong Government, *Hong Kong 1991*, 21.
56. Cradock, *Experiences of China*, 237.
57. Deng, *Deng Xiaoping Wenxuan*, vol.3, 68.
58. Liao, *Xianggang Minzhuhua de Kunjing*, 91.
59. Ibid. 104.
60. Ian Scott, 'Political Transformation in Hong Kong', 216.
61. Cradock, *Experiences of China*, 239.
62. *South China Morning Post*, 9 February 1990.
63. *The Independent*, 5 July 1991.

64. Cradock, *Experiences of China*, 241.
65. Scott, 'Political Transformation in Hong Kong', 218.
66. *The Independent*, 3 January 1992.
67. Major, *Autobiography*, 505–6.
68. In his 790-page autobiography, Hong Kong, as such, takes up only four pages.
69. Major, *Autobiography*, 505. Major was in fact not the first leader of a major country to visit China after 1989.
70. Heald, *Beating Retreat*, 4–5.
71. Major, *Autobiography*, 309.
72. The rest of this section is reproduced substantially from Tsang, *Appointment with China*, 183–95.
73. Personal meeting with Patten in June 1992.
74. Ching, 'A Discredited Past? One Hong Kong View on Lord Wilson', 5.
75. Ching, 'Toward Colonial Sunset: The Wilson Regime, 1987–92', 192.
76. Major, *Autobiography*, 506.
77. Dimbleby, *The Last Governor*, 11.
78. Patten, *East and West*, 15.
79. Lau, '"Dear Governor": An Elected Lady Offers Some Advice', 7.
80. Liao, *Xianggang Minzhuhua de Kunjing*, 204.
81. Patten, *Our Next Five Years*, 32–3. Patten avoids mentioning that such an overlap is inherent in the British parliamentary system.
82. Ibid. 34–5.
83. Ibid. 35–6.
84. Ibid. 37.
85. Ibid. 38.
86. Basic Law Drafting Committee, *The Basic Law*, 66.
87. Ibid.
88. Patten, *Our Next Five Years*, 41.
89. Hurd, 'Governor Patten Unveils a Bold Blueprint for Hong Kong's Future', 2.
90. Dimbleby, *The Last Governor*, 135.
91. Ibid. 181. Ambassador McLaren in Beijing expressed a similar view to Dimbleby.
92. Patten, *Our Next Five Years*, 37.
93. Cradock, *Experiences of China*, 245.
94. Zhou, *Zijing Kaichu Xing Zhaoxia*, 173–4.
95. The real increase was from 15 to 18, for the draft Basic Law at that time sanctioned 15 directly elected seats before 1997.
96. *Wen Hui Pao*, 24 October 1992.
97. *Wen Hui Pao*, 3 December 1992.
98. *Renmin Ribao*, 22 October 1992.
99. *Wen Hui Pao*, 24 October 1992.
100. Wang, *Qishi Niandai Yilai de Zhongying Guanxi*, 243. Strictly speaking, by the Chinese calculation, the number concerned should be 39, not 40.
101. Ibid. 243.
102. Lai, *Peng Dingkang Zhenggai Fangan Mianmianguan*, Appendix.
103. Patten, *Hong Kong: Today's Success, Tomorrow's Challenges*, 37.
104. *Wen Hui Pao*, 27 December 1992.
105. Wang, *Qishi Niandai Yilai de Zhongying Guanxi*, 245; *Renmin Ribao*, 22 October 1992.
106. Deng, *Deng Xiaoping Wenxuan*, vol.3, 75.

107. Kristof and WuDunn, *China Wakes: The Struggle for the Soul of a Rising Power*, 405.
108. *Wen Hui Pao*, 28 January 1993.
109. *Renmin Ribao*, 24 October 1992.
110. Wang, *Qishi Niandai Yilai de Zhongying Guanxi*, 245.
111. Dimbleby, *The Last Governor*, 184. It provides the fullest account of Patten's visit from page 167 to 185.
112. Buckley, *Hong Kong: The Road to 1997*, 145.
113. This section is based substantially on Tsang, *Appointment with China*, 195–200.
114. Wang, *Qishi Niandai Yilai de Zhongying Guanxi*, 252–5.
115. Li, *Bainian Quyushi de Zhongjie*, 259–60.
116. *Wen Hui Pao*, 14 March 1992.
117. Patten, *Hong Kong: Today's Success, Tomorrow's Challenges*, 40.
118. Ibid.
119. UK Government, *Representative Government in Hong Kong*, 10.
120. Ibid. 39–40.
121. Ibid. 42.
122. Ibid. 16.
123. *Renmin Ribao*, 3 December 1993.
124. *Renmin Ribao*, 16 December 1993.
125. Cradock, 'Losing the Plot in Hong Kong', 23.
126. Dimbleby, *The Last Governor*, 281. This section is based substantially on Tsang, *Appointment with China*, 201–8.
127. Li, *Bainian Quyushi de Chongjie*, 266–8.
128. *Wen Hui Pao*, 24 October 1992.
129. Leung, 'The Basic Law and the Problem of Political Transition', 40.
130. Basic Law Drafting Committee, *The Basic Law*, 65.
131. Liao, *Xianggang Minzhuhua de Kunjing*, 228.
132. Xu, *Guoshi Gangshi Hua Sannian*, 30.
133. Wang, *Qishi Niandai Yilai de Zhongying Guanxi*, 264.
134. Ibid. 268.
135. Quoted in Li, *Xianggang Yijiujiuqi*, 67.
136. Zhong, *Xianggang Huigui Licheng*, 179.
137. Li, *Xianggang Yijiujiuqi*, 68.
138. Buckley, *Hong Kong: The Road to 1997*, 176.
139. See Dimbleby, *The Last Governor*, 326–43, for Patten's position and the reaching of a compromise with the Chinese.
140. BBC, *SWB* FE/2796/F/1, Xinhua report, 12 December 1996.
141. Zhongyang Wenxian Yanjiushi (ed.), *Yiguo Liangzhi Chongyao Wenxian Xuanbian*, 306 (Qian Quchen's speech, 31 January 1997).
142. Basic Law Drafting Committee, *The Basic Law*, 65.
143. BBC, *SWB*, FE/2802/F/1, Xinhua news agency report of 21 December 1996.
144. Ibid.
145. *Xianggang Shang Bao*, 22 December 1996.
146. BBC, *SWB*, FE/2796/F/1, Xinhua report, 12 December 1996.
147. *Far Eastern Economic Review*, 9 January 1997, 22.
148. BBC, *SWB*, FE/2801/F2, Zhongguo Tongxun She report, 19 December 1996.
149. BBC, *SWB*, FE/2798/F/1, Xinhua report, 16 December 1996. For Tung's business reliance on the PRC, see Leng and Wang, *Sheizhu Xiangjiang*, 23–6.

150. *Far Eastern Economic Review*, 13 March 1997, 25–6.
151. This information comes from a source close to the PRC establishment in Hong Kong. Prominent Hong Kong citizens' membership of the Communist Party is usually treated as a PRC state secret.
152. *Dateline Hong Kong*, 1997, issue 2, undated, March 1997.

Conclusion: Full Circle?

1. Knight, 'The Last Great Chapter of Imperial History', 129–30.
2. Ibid. 194–5 (Governor Patten's farewell speech, 30 June 1997).
3. *Renmin Ribao*, 30 June 1997 (editorial).
4. Jing, 'Jiang-Li gai cheng teda youting jingang?', 13.
5. *SCMP*, 1 July 1997 ('Dignity reigns as Britain lowers flag').
6. *The Basic Law* (Articles 2 and 158).
7. *SCMP*, 2 July 1997 ('Reunion assures better future for all').
8. *SCMP*, 1 July 1997 ('Tung and his team sworn in as Patten bids tearful farewell').
9. *SCMP*, 1 July 1997 ('Council meets in early hours to confirm bills').
10. Tsang, 'Changes in Continuity', 45.
11. Ibid. 54.
12. Ibid. 51–2.
13. *Renmin Ribao*, 2 July 1997 (Jiang's speech at founding ceremony of the SAR).
14. See Tsang (ed.), *Judicial Independence and the Rule of Law in Hong Kong*, chapters 1, 3 and 6. For a dissenting view, see Chen, *The Court of Final Appeal's Ruling in the 'Illegal Migrant' Children Case*.
15. Tsang, 'Political Developments in Hong Kong since 1997 and their Implications for Mainland China and Taiwan', 57–8.
16. For the institutional protection of judicial independence, see Wesley-Smith, 'Individual and Institutional Independence of the Judiciary', 99–131.
17. Goodstadt, 'Prospect for the Rule of Law: the Political Dimension', 180.
18. See Chapter 14.
19. Tsang, 'Political Developments in Hong Kong since 1997', 44.
20. Ibid. 45–6.
21. Ibid. 52.
22. Goodstadt, 'Hong Kong: An Attachment to Democracy', 499.
23. Tsang, 'Political Developments in Hong Kong since 1997', 54.

Bibliography

Primary sources

British Public Record Office, Kew
Cabinet Office (CAB) 23, 65, 128, 129
Colonial Office (CO) 19, 129, 131, 537, 825, 882, 1030
Foreign Office (FO) 17, 228, 371
Foreign and Commonwealth Office (FCO) 40
Ministry of Defence (DEFE) 6
Special Operations Executive (HS) 1

Butler Library, Columbia University (New York)
Wellington Koo Papers, Boxes 55 and 56

Eisenhower Library (Abilene, Kansas)
Dwight Eisenhower Papers

Foreign Ministry of the Republic of China (Taipei)
Waijiaobu, 312/72, 323

Ministry of National Defence of the ROC (Taipei)
Guofengbu 062.23/5000.4

Hong Kong Public Records Office (Hong Kong)
HKRS211

Hung On-to Memorial Library, Hong Kong University (Hong Kong)
Franklin Gimson Papers

Manuscripts in personal possession
F.C. Gimson, *An Unpublished History of Hong Kong During the Japanese Occupation*
Record of Interview with Geoffrey Herklots at 'Vanners', Chobham, 19 Jan. 1983
Record of Interview with David MacDougall in 'Mercers', Finchingfield, 17 Feb. 1983.

Rhodes House Library, Oxford University (Oxford)
Arthur Creech-Jones Papers
Papers of Sir Franklin Gimson
Transcript of Interview with Sir David Trench

Truman Library (Independence, Missouri)
Harry S Truman Papers
Dean Acheson Papers

Tung Wah Hospital Groups (Hong Kong)
Archives of the Tung Wah Hospitals: Dongshiju huiyi lu, no.00942

Printed documents

Chinese Documents

Basic Law Drafting Committee, *The Basic Law of the Hong Kong Special Administrative Region of the People's Republic of China* (Hong Kong: 1990)
Guangdongsheng Danganguan (ed.), *Dongjiang Congdui shiliao* (Canton: 1984)
Guanggiaojing (ed.), *Xianggang yu Zhongguo: Lishi Wenxian Ziliao Huibian*, vol. 1 (Hong Kong: 1984)
Gu Weijun, *Gu Weijun Huiyilu*, vol. 5 (Beijing: 1987)
Waijiaobu, *Zhonghua Minguo Zhongyao Shiliao Chubian: Duijih Gangzhan Shichi*, series III, *Zhanshi Waijiao*, vols 2 and 3 (Taipei: 1981)
Xianggang Wenti Wenjian Xuanji (Beijing: 1995)
Zhonggong Zhongyang Wenxian Yanjiushe (ed.), *Yiguo Liangjin Chongyao Wenxian Xuanbian* (Beijing: 1997)

Hong Kong Government

Annual Report on the Activities of the Independent Commission Against Corruption for 1983 (1983)
Arrangements for Testing the Acceptability in Hong Kong of the Draft Agreement on the Future of the Territory (1984)
The City District Officer Scheme: Report by the Secretary for Chinese Affairs (1969)
District Administration in Hong Kong (1981)
A Draft Agreement between the Government of the United Kingdom of Great Britain and Northern Ireland and the Government of the People's Republic of China on the Future of Hong Kong (1984)
Green Paper: The Further Development of Representative Government in Hong Kong (1984)
Green Paper: The 1987 Review of Developments in Representative Government (1987)
Hong Kong Disturbances 1967 (n.d., c.1968)
Hong Kong Government Gazette
Hong Kong Hansard: Reports of the meetings of the Legislative Council of Hong Kong
Hong Kong Yearbooks (various years)
An Introduction to Hong Kong Bill of Rights Ordinance (undated, 1991)
Public Response to Green Paper: The 1987 Review of Developments in Representative Government – Report of the Survey Office Part I (1987)
Report of the Working Party on Local Administration (1966)
Second Report of the Commission of Inquiry under Sir Alastair Blair-Kerr (1973)
Sessional Papers 1931, Report of the Census
Sessional Papers 1939, Report on Labour and Labour Conditions in Hong Kong by H.R. Butters (hereafter: *Butters Report*)
White Paper: The Further Development of Representative Government in Hong Kong (1984)
Census and Statistics Department, *Hong Kong Statistics 1947–1967* (1969)
_____, *Estimates of Gross Domestic Product 1961 to 1995* (1996)
Census Commissioner, *Report of the Census 1961*, vol.3 (1962)

UK Government

The British Military Administration of Hong Kong, August 1945 to April 1946 (A report to the Chief of Staff Committee) (Hong Kong: 1946)

Colonial Office, *Annual Report on Hong Kong*

Foreign Affairs Committee, *Second Report on Hong Kong (Session 1988–9)* (London: 1989)

House of Commons, *British Parliamentary Papers: China 25 (Hong Kong, 1862–1881)* (Shannon: 1971)

Parliamentary Debates: House of Commons (London: various years)

Parliamentary Debates: House of Lords (London: various years)

Representative Government in Hong Kong (Com 2432) (London: 1994)

Newspapers and Journals

Beijing Review (Beijing)
Cheng Bao (Hong Kong)
China Mail (Hong Kong)
Chinese Repository (Canton)
Daily Information Bulletin (Hong Kong)
Dateline Hong Kong (London)
Dongfang Ribao (Hong Kong)
Far Eastern Economic Review (Hong Kong)
Financial Times (London)
The Guardian (London)
Hong Kong Telegraph (Hong Kong)
The Independent (London)
Ming Bao (Hong Kong)
Pai Shing (Hong Kong)
Qishi Niandai (Hong Kong)
Renmin Ribao (Beijing)
South China Morning Post (SCMP) (Hong Kong)
Summary of World Broadcasts (SWB), BBC (Caversfield)
Wah Kiu Yat Pao (Huaqiao Ribao) (Hong Kong)
Wen Hui Pao (Hong Kong)
Xianggang Shang Bao (Hong Kong)
Xin Bao (Hong Kong Economic Journal) (Hong Kong)
Xinsheng Wanbao (Hong Kong)
Xin Wan Bao (Hong Kong)

Secondary sources

Books and Articles (in Chinese)

Anon. (ed.), *Jibenfa: Xianggang Weilai de Gouhua* (Hong Kong: 1986)

Anon. (ed.), *Xianggang yu Zhongguo: Lishi Wenxian Huibian* (Hong Kong: 1984)

Chen Daming, *Xianggang Kangri Youjidui* (Hong Kong: 2000)

Chen Deyun, *Chen Shaobai Xianshang Aisilu Nianpu* (No place: 1935)

Chen Jieyu, *Chen Jieyu Huiyilu (Xia)* (Taipei: 1992)

Chen Lifu, *Chengbai Zhi Jian: Chen Lifu Huiyilu* (Taipei: 1994)

Cheng Changzhi, *Zhonggong Yuhe Tanpan* (Taipei: 1999)

Cheng Lisheng, *Deng Xiaoping 'Yiguoliangzhi' Sixiang Yanjiu* (Shenyang: 1992)

Deng Xiaoping, *Deng Xiaoping Lun Tongyi Zhanxian* (Beijing: 1991)

———, *Deng Xiaoping Lun Xianggang Wenti* (Hong Kong: 1993)

———, *Deng Xiaoping Wenxuan*, vol.3 (Beijing: 1993)

Deng Zhongxia, *Zhongguo Zhigong Yundong Jianshi (1919–1926)* (Beijing: 1953)

Ding Xinbao, 'Lishi de chuanzhe: Zhimintixi de jianli he yanjin', in Wang Gungwu (ed.), *Xianggang Shi Xinbian*, vol.1 (Hong Kong: 1997)

Dongjiang Congdui shi bianxiejuzu (ed.), *Dongjiang Congdui Shi* (Canton: 1985)

Guan Shiguang, *Qishinian Lai Jiaguo* (Toronto: 1999)

Guo Limin (ed.), *Zhonggong du Tai Zhengze Zhiliao Xuanji: 1949–1991*, vol.1 (Taipei: 1992)

Guo Shaotang, 'Qishiniandai houqi de Xianggang xueyun', *Qishi niandai*, no.123, April 1980

He Wenxiang, *Xianggang Fuhao Liezhuang* (Hong Kong: 1995)

Huang Renyu, *Zong da Lishi de Jiaodu du Jiang Jieshi Riji* (Taipei: 1994)

Huang Yonghua, *Zhongguo Gudai Bingzhi* (Taipei: 1994)

Huaqiao Ribao, *Xianggang Nianjian 1948* (Hong Kong: 1948)

Jin Yauru, *Zhonggong Xianggang Zhengce Biwen Shilu* (Hong Kong: 1998)

Jin Yingxi, 'Chujian Gangda', in Liu Shurong (ed.), *Yizhi Yiye Zhongguanqing* (Hong Kong: 1993)

Jing Yu, 'Jiang-Li gai cheng teda youting jingang?', *Cheng Ming* (Hong Kong: July 1997), no.237

Kong Haofeng, 'Lunshuo Liuqi', in Luo Yongsheng (ed.), *Shei de Chengshi* (Hong Kong: 1997)

Lai Qizhi, *Peng Dingkang zhenggai fangan mianmianguan* (Hong Kong: 1993)

Leng Xia and Wang Tong, *Sheizhu Xiangjiang* (Hong Kong: 1996)

Li Hou, *Bainian Quyushi de Zhongjie* (Beijing: 1997)

———, *Huigui de Licheng* (Hong Kong: 1997)

Li Jiayuan, *Xianggang Baoye Jitan* (Hong Kong: 1989)

Li Jinjian, *Sun Zhongshan Xiansheng Geming yu Xianggang* (Taipei: 1989)

Li Yi, *Xianggang Yijiujiuqi* (Hong Kong: 1997; Taipei: 1996)

Li Yun and Zhang Cuirong, 'Xianggang jidujiao gongye weiyuanhui', in Chen Mingqiu (ed.), *Zhongguo yu Xianggang Gongyun Zonghuang* (Hong Kong: 1986)

Li Zehou, *Zhongguo Jindai Sixiang Shibian* (revised edition, Taipei: 1990)

Liang Binghua, *Chengzhai yu Zhongying Waijiao* (Hong Kong: 1995)

Liang Shangyuan, *Zhonggong Zai Xianggang* (Hong Kong: 1989)

Liao Guangsheng, *Xianggang Minzhuhua de Kunjing* (Taipei: 1996)

Lin Youlan, *Xianggang Shihua* (Hong Kong: 1984)

Liu Likai and Wang Zhen, *Yijiuyijiu Zhi Yijiuerqi de Zhongguo Gongren Yundong* (Beijing: 1953)

Liu Shurong, *Jianming Xianggang Shi* (Hong Kong: 1998)

Lu Fangshang, *Gemin Zhi Zaiqi* (Taipei: 1989)

Lu Shiqiang, *Zhongguo Zaoqi de Lunchuan Jingying* (Taipei: 1962)

Lu Yan, 'Xianggang de hese xingdanri', in Ye Dewei et al. (eds), *Xianggang Lunxian Shi* (Hong Kong: 1982)

Luo Ya, *Zhengzhibu Huiyilu* (Hong Kong: 1996)

Mao Zedong, *Mao Zedong Xuanji*, vol.4 (Beijing: 1960)

———, *Mao Zedong Junshi Wenxuan* (Beijing: 1981)

———, *Jianguo Yilai Mao Zedong Wengao*, vol.1 (Beijing: 1987)

———, *Mao Zedong Waijiao Wenxuan* (Beijing: 1995)

———, *Mao Zedong Wenji*, vol.4 (Beijing: 1996)

Mo Kai, 'Xiandai maoyi tixi de chengzhang licheng', in Wang Gungwu (ed.), *Xianggang Shi Xinbian*, vol.1 (Hong Kong: 1997)

Qin Xiaoyi (comp.), *Zhongtong Jianggong Sixiang Yanlun Zhongji*, vol.9 (Taipei: 1984)

Rao Meijiao, 'Xianggang gongye fazhan de guiji', in Wang Gungwu (ed.), *Xianggang Shi Xibian*, vol.1 (Hong Kong: 1997)

Shanghai shehui kexue lishi yanjiusho (ed.), *Wusa Yundong Shiliao*, vol.1 (Shanghai: 1981)

Shih Chueh, *The Reminiscences of General Shih Chueh* (Taipei: 1986)

Sima Yi, *Ronyao Quangui Deng Xiaoping de Xianggang Qiantu Tanpan* (Hong Kong: 1984)

Tang Degang, *Li Zhongren Huiyilu* (Hong Kong: 1986)

Tin Kuo, 'Xianggang "luiqi baodong" yu wenhua dagemin', in Yin Longbo and Ma Jisen (eds), *Zhou Enlai yu Xianggang 'Liuqi Baodong' Neimu* (Hong Kong: 2001)

Wang Ermin, *Zhongkuo Jindai Zixiang Shilun* (Taipei: 1977)

Wang Fu, *Jihjun Qinhua Zhanzheng, 1931–1945*, vol.3 (Shenyang: 1990)

Wang Hongxu, *Qishi Niandai Yilai de Zhongying Guanxi* (Harbin: 1996)

Wang Hongzhi, *Lishi de Chenchong* (Hong Kong: 2000)

Wu Gangsheng, 'Xianggangren ying guanxin Xianggang zhengshi', *Zhongguo Minchu Luntan*, vol.2, no.11 (1 June 1966)

Wu Kangmin, *Renda Huiyilu* (Hong Kong: 1990)

Xianggang Guangchashe, *Guangcha Xianggang: Xianggang Guangchashe Yanlunji* (Hong Kong: 1982)

Xianggang Wenhuibao (ed.), *Jibenfa de Dansheng* (Hong Kong: 1990)

Xiao Weiyun (ed.), *Yiguoliangzhi yu Xianggang Tebie Xingzhengqu Jibenfa* (Hong Kong: 1990)

Xie Hingyu, *Yingyang guowei* (Taipei: 1997)

Xie Jundu, *Huang Xing yu Zhongguo gemin* (Hong Kong: 1980)

Xie Yongguang, *Zhanshi Rijun zai Xianggang baoxing* (Hong Kong: 1991)

———, *Sannian ling Bageyue de Kunan* (Hong Kong: 1994)

———, *Xianggang Zhanhou Fengyunlu* (Hong Kong: 1996)

Xu Jiatun, *Xu Jiatun Xianggang huiyilu*, 2 vols (Taipei: 1993)

Xu Simin, *Guoshi Gangshi Hua Sannian* (Hong Kong: 1996)

Xu Yuqing (ed.), *Huoyue Cai Xianggang* (Hong Kong: 1993)

Yang Guisong, *Zhonggong yu Mosike de Guanxi (1920–1960)* (Taipei: 1997)

Yao Yao, 'Xing Se Yi', in Lu Dale (ed), *Puji Wenfa Zai Xianggang* (Hong Kong: 1983)

Ye Dewei, 'Rizhi shiji de Xianggang', in Ye Dewei, et. Al. (eds), *Xianggang Lunxian Shi* (Hong Kong: 1982)

Ye Lei, 'Xianggang Xinhuashe fazhan shi', in Liang Shangyuan, *Zhonggong Zai Xianggang* (Hong Kong: 1989)

Ye Yincong, 'Bianyuan yu yunji de qiuling', in Chen Qingqiao (ed.), *Wenhua Xiangxiang Yu Yishi Xingtai: Dangdai Xianggang Wenhua Zhengzhi Lunping* (Hong Kong: 1997)

Yen Jiaji and Gao Gao, *'Wenhua Dagemin' Shinian Shi*, vol.1 (enlarged and revised edition, Hong Kong: n.d., *c*.1989)

Yu Changgeng, 'Zhou Enlai yaokong "fanying kangbao" neinmu', in Yin Longbo and Ma Jisen (eds), *Zhou Enlai Yu Xianggang 'Liuqi Baodong' Neimu* (Hong Kong: 2001)

———, 'Zaitan Xianggang liuqi baodong', in Yin Longbo and Ma, Jisen (eds), *Zhou Enlai Yu Xianggang 'Liuqi Baodong' Neimu* (Hong Kong: 2001)

Yu Sheng, 'Xianggang xiaoji', *Qiantu*, vol.2, no.5, 1 May 1934

Yu Shengwu and Liu Cunkuan (eds), *Shijiu Shiji de Xianggang* (Beijing: 1994)

Yu Shengwu and Liu Shurong (eds), *Ershi Shiji de Xianggang* (Beijing: 1995)

Yuying, 'Yingguo de fazhi jingshen', *Dazhong Shenghuo*, 13 September 1941

Zeng Ruisheng (Steve Tsang), 'Yingguo Fangwai Xianggang Zhengce de Yanbian', *Guangjiaojing*, no.200, 1989

Zeng Sheng, *Zheng Sheng Huiyilu* (Beijing: 1991)

Zhang Guotao, *Wode Huiyi*, 3 volumes (Hong Kong: 1971–3)

Zhang Jiawei, *Xianggang Liuqi Baodong Neiqing* (Hong Kong: 2000)

Zhang Liang (ed.), *Zhongguo 'Lusi' Zhenxiang*, vols.1 and 2 (Hong Kong: 2001)

Zhang Pengyuan, *Liang Qichao Yu Qinggui Gemin* (Taipei: 1964)

Zhang Xiaohui, *Xianggang Huashang Shi* (Hong Kong: 1998)

Zhongguo Guomindang Dangshihui (ed.), *Guofu Zhuanji*, vol.2 (Taipei: 1973)

Zhong Min, 'Xianggang de Daxuesheng kaici tan zhengzhi', *Zhongguo Minchu Lundan* (Hong Kong), vol.2, no.8, 15 April 1966

Zhong, Shiyuan, *Xianggang Huigui Licheng* (Hong Kong: 2001)

Zhongguo Xinwen She (ed.), *Liaogong Zai Renjian* (Hong Kong: 1984)

Zhou Enlai, *Zhou Enlai Waijiao Wenxuan* (Beijing: 1994)

Zhou Nan, *Zijing Kaichu Xing Zhaoxia* (Hong Kong: 1997)

Zhou Yongxin, *Jianzheng Xianggang Wushi Nian* (Hong Kong: 1996)

Zhu Hongyuan, *Tongmenghui de Geming Lilun – Minbao Gean Yanjiu* (second edition, Taipei: 1995)

Books and Articles (in English)

Alderson, G.L.D., *History of Royal Air Force Kai Tak* (Hong Kong: 1972)

Angus, H.A., 'Commerce and Industry Department', in Hong Kong Government, *The Government and the People* (Hong Kong: 1962)

Atwell, Pamela, *British Mandarins and Chinese Reformers: The British Administration of Weihaiwei (1898–1930)* (Hong Kong: 1985)

Baker, Hugh, 'Life in the Cities: The Emergence of Hong Kong Man', *The China Quarterly*, no.95 (Sept. 1983)

Banister, Judith, *China's Changing Population* (Stanford: 1987)

Barnouin, Barbara and Changgen Yu, *Ten Years of Turbulence: The Chinese Cultural Revolution* (London and New York: 1993)

Becker, Jasper, *Hungry Ghosts: China's Secret Famine* (London: 1996)

Belcher, E., *Narrative of a Voyage Around the World*, vol.2 (London: 1843)

Bergere, Marie-Claire, *Sun Yat-sen* (Stanford: 1998)

Bernard, W.D., *The Nemesis in China* (New York: 1969) (reprint of 3rd edition, 1847)

Bix, Herbert P., *Hirohito and the Making of Modern Japan* (London: 2000)

Blake, Clagette, *Charles Elliot RN* (London: 1960)

Blake, Robert, *Jardine Matheson: Traders of the Far East* (London: 1999)

Blue, Gregory, 'Opium for China: The British Connection', in T. Brook and B.T. Wakabayashi (eds), *Opium Regime: China, Britain, and Japan, 1839–1952* (Berkeley: 2000)

Bonavia, David, *Hong Kong 1997* (Hong Kong: 1984)

Bonner-Smith, D. and E.W.R. Lumby (eds), *The Second China War 1856–1860* (Westport, Connecticut: 1981)

Boorman, Howard L., *Biographical Dictionary of Republican China*, vol.2 (New York: 1968)

Brice, Martin H., *The Royal Navy and the Sino-Japanese Incident, 1937–41* (London: 1973)

Brook, Timrthy, *Quelling the People* (Stanford: 1998)

Bruce, Philip, *Second to None: The Story of the Hong Kong Volunteers* (Hong Kong: 1991)

Buckley, Roger, *Hong Kong: The Road to 1997* (Cambridge: 1997)

Burns, John and Ian Scott, 'A Profile of the Civil Service', in John Burns and Ian Scott (eds), *The Hong Kong Civil Service* (Hong Kong: 1984)

Cameron, Nigel, *Hong Kong: The Cultured Pearl* (Hong Kong: 1978)

———, *Power: The Story of China Light* (Hong Kong: 1982)

Carew, Tim, *The Fall of Hong Kong* (London: 1960)

Carroll, John M., 'Chinese collaboration in the making of British Hong Kong', in T.W. Ngo (ed.), *Hong Kong's History* (London: 1999)

Cater, Sir Jack, 'The 1967 Riots', in Sally Blyth and Ian Wotherspoon (eds), *Hong Kong Remembers* (Hong Kong: 1996)

Catron, Gary Wayne, *China and Hong Kong, 1945–1967* (Harvard University: unpublished Ph.D. thesis, 1971)

Chan, Anthony B., *Li Ka-shing: Hong Kong's Elusive Billionaire* (Hong Kong: 1996)

Chan, Lau Kit-ching, *China, Britain and Hong Kong, 1895–1945* (Hong Kong: 1990)

———, *From Nothing to Nothing: The Chinese Communist Movement and Hong Kong, 1921–1936* (London: 1999)

Chan, Ming Kou, *Labour and Empire: The Chinese Labour Movement in Canton Delta, 1895–1927* (Stanford University: unpublished Ph.D. thesis, 1975)

———, 'Democracy Derailed: Realpolitik in the Making of the Hong Kong Basic Law, 1985–90', in Ming K.Chan and David Clark (eds), *The Hong Kong Basic Law* (Hong Kong: 1991)

———, 'Hong Kong in Sino-British Conflict: Mass Mobilization and the Crisis of Legitimacy, 1912–26', in Ming K. Chan (ed.), *Precarious Balance: Hong Kong between China and Britain, 1842–1992* (Armonk: 1994)

——— and Clark, David (eds), *The Hong Kong Basic Law* (Hong Kong: 1991)

Chan, Wai Kwan, *The Making of Hong Kong Society: Three Studies of Class Formation in Early Hong Kong* (Oxford: 1991)

Chaney, D.C., 'Job Satisfaction and Unionization: The Case of Shopworkers', in Keith Hopkins (ed.), *Hong Kong: The Industrial Colony* (Hong Kong: 1971)

Chang, Sidney and Leonard Gordon, *All Under Heaven... Sun Yat-sen and His Revolutionary Thought* (Stanford: 1991)

Chang, Dennis, 'How China Sees It', in William McGurn (ed.), *Basic Law, Basic Questions* (Hong Kong, 1988)

Chao, Linda and Ramon Myers, *The First Chinese Democracy* (Baltimore: 1998)

Chen, Albert H.Y., *The Court of Final Appeal's Ruling in the 'Illegal Migrant' Children Case: Congressional Supremacy and Judicial Review* (Hong Kong: 1999)

Chen, Jian, *China's Road to the Korean War: The Making of the Sino–American Confrontation* (New York: 1994)

Chen, Xitong, 'Report on Checking the Turmoil and Quelling the Counter-Revolutionary Rebellion', supplement in *Beijing Review*, 17–23 July 1989

Cheng, Chu-yuan, *Behind the Tiananmen Massacre: Social, Political, and Economic Ferment in China* (Boulder: 1990)

Cheng, Hsiao-shih, *Party-Military Relations in the PRC and Taiwan* (Boulder: 1990)

Cheng, Joseph Y.S. (ed.), *Hong Kong: In Search of a Future* (Hong Kong: 1984)

_____, 'Prospect for Democracy in Hong Kong', in George Hicks (ed.), *The Broken Mirror: China after Tiananmen* (Harlow: 1990)

Chesneaux, Jean, *The Chinese Labor Movement, 1919–1927* (Stanford: 1968)

Ch'i, Hsi-sheng, *Nationalist China at War: Military Defeats and Political Collapse, 1937–45* (Ann Arbor: 1982)

Chien, Helen Hsieh, *The European Diary of Hsieh Fucheng* (New York: 1993)

Ching, Frank, 'A Discredited Past? One Hong Kong View on Lord Wilson', *Hong Kong Monitor*, December 1992

_____, 'Toward Colonial Sunset: The Wilson Regime, 1987–92', in Ming K. Chan (ed.), *Precarious Balance* (New York: 1994)

Chiu, Hungdah, *The People's Republic of China and the Law of Treaties* (Cambridge, Massachusetts, 1972)

Chiu, T.N., *The Port of Hong Kong* (Hong Kong: 1973)

Chow, Tse-Tsung, *The May Fourth Movement: Intellectual Revolution in Modern China* (Stanford: 1960)

Ch'u, T'ung-tsu, *Local Government in China Under the Ch'ing* (Stanford: 1962)

Chung, Stephanie Po-yin, *Chinese Business Groups in Hong Kong and Political Change in South China, 1900–25* (Basingstoke: 1998)

Chung, Sze-yuen, *Hong Kong's Journey to Reunification* (Hong Kong: 2001)

Churchill, Winston S., *The Second World War Volume III: The Grand Alliance* (London: 1950)

Coates, Austin, *A Mountain of Light: The Story of Hong Kong Electric Company* (London: undated, c.1977)

_____, *Whampoa: Ships on the Shore* (Hong Kong: 1980)

Coble, Parks, *Facing Japan: Chinese Politics and Japanese Imperialism, 1931–1937* (Cambridge, Mass.: 1991)

Cohen, Paul, *History in Three Keys: The Boxers as Event, Experience, and Myth* (New York: 1997)

Copper, John, *Colony in Conflict: The Hong Kong Disturbances, May 1967–January 1968* (Hong Kong: 1970)

Costin, W.C., *Great Britain and China 1833–1860* (Oxford: 1937)

Cottrell, Robert, *The End of Hong Kong: The Secret Diplomacy of Imperial Retreat* (London: 1993)

Cradock, Percy, *Experiences of China* (London: 1994)

_____, 'Losing the Plot in Hong Kong', *Prospect*, April 1997

Crisswell, Colin N., *The Taipans: Hong Kong's Merchant Princes* (Hong Kong: 1981)

Cruickshank, Charles, *SOE in the Far East* (Oxford: 1986)

de Bary, Wm. Theodore, Wing-tsit Chan and Burton Watson (comp.), *Sources of Chinese Tradition* (New York: 1960)

Dilks, David (ed.), *Retreat from Power: Studies in Britain's Foreign Policy of the Twentieth Century, Volume One: 1906–1939* (London and Basingstoke: 1981)

Dimbleby, Jonathan, *The Last Governor* (London: 1997)

Dirlik, Arif, *The Origins of Chinese Communism* (New York: 1989)

Dittmer, Lowell, *China Under Reform* (Boulder: 1994)

Domes, Jurgen, *The Internal Politics of China, 1949–1972* (London: Hurst and Co, 1973)

Donnison, F.S.V., *British Military Administration in the Far East, 1943–1946* (London: 1956)

Drakakis-Smith, D.W., 'Housing needs and planning policies for the Asian City – the lesson from Hong Kong', *International Journal of Environmental Studies*, vol.1 (1971)

Drake, Charles *Taikoo* (London: 1970)

Dreyer, Edward, *China at War, 1901–1949* (Harlow, Essex: 1995)

Earl, Lawrence, *Yangtse Incident: The Story of HMS Amethyst* (London: 1950)

Eitel, E.J., *Europe in China* (Hong Kong: 1983)

Elphick, Peter, *Far Eastern File: The Intelligence War in the Far East, 1930–1945* (London: 1997)

Elsbree, Willard, *Japan's Role in Southeast Asian Nationalist Movements, 1940–1945* (Cambridge, Mass.: 1953)

Elvin, Mark, *The Pattern of the Chinese Past* (Stanford: 1973)

———, *Another History: Essays on China from a European Perspective* (Broadway, NSW: 1996)

Endacott, G.B., *A Biographical Sketch-Book of Early Hong Kong* (Singapore: 1962)

———, *A History of Hong Kong* (2nd edition, Hong Kong and Oxford: 1964)

———, *Government and People in Hong Kong, 1841–1962* (Hong Kong: 1964)

——— (ed.), *An Eastern Entrepot: A Collection of Documents Illustrating the History of Hong Kong* (London: 1964)

——— and Alan Birch, *Hong Kong Eclipse* (Hong Kong: 1978)

England, Joe and John Rear, *Chinese Labour under British Rule* (Hong Kong: 1975)

———, *Industrial Relations and Law in Hong Kong* (Hong Kong: 1981)

England, Vaudine, *The Quest of Noel Croucher* (Hong Kong: 1998)

Enright, Michael, Edith Scott and David Dodwell, *The Hong Kong Advantage* (Hong Kong: 1997)

Esherick, Joseph, *The Origins of the Boxer Uprising* (Berkeley: 1987)

Espy, John, *The Strategies of Chinese Industrial Enterprises in Hong Kong* (Harvard University: unpublished Doctor of Business Administration thesis, 1970)

———, 'Some Notes on Business and Industry in Hong Kong', *Chung Chi Journal*, vol.2, no.1 (April/May 1972)

Evans, D.E., 'Chinatown in Hong Kong: The Beginning of Taipingshan', *Journal of the Hong Kong Branch of the Royal Asiatic Society*, vol.10 (1970)

Evans, Richard, *Deng Xiaoping and the Making of Modern China* (London: 1993)

Evans Thomas, W.H., *Vanished China, Far Eastern Banking Memories* (London: 1952)

Fairbank, John King, *Trade and Diplomacy on the China Coast* (Cambridge: 1964)

Far Eastern Economic Review, *The Far Eastern Economic Review 1967 Yearbook* (Hong Kong: 1967)

———, *Asia 1979 Yearbook* (Hong Kong, 1979)

———, *The Far Eastern Economic Review Yearbook 1981* (Hong Kong: 1981)

Faure, David, 'The Rice Trade in Hong Kong before the Second World War', in Sinn E. (ed.), *Between East and West* (Hong Kong: 1990)

——— (ed.), *A Documentary History of Hong Kong, Volume 2: Society* (Hong Kong: 1997)

———, 'Reflections on Being Chinese in Hong Kong', in Rosemary Foot and Judith Brown (eds), *Hong Kong's Transition, 1842–1997* (Basingstoke: 1997)

Fay, Peter Ward, *The Opium War, 1840–1842* (Chapel Hill: 1997)

Feng, Zhong-ping, *The British Government's China Policy, 1945–1950* (Keele: 1994)

Foot, Rosemary, *The Practice of Power* (Oxford: 1995)

Freris, Andrew, *The Financial Markets of Hong Kong* (London and New York: 1991)

Fung, Edmund, *The Diplomacy of Imperial Retreat: Britain's South China Policy, 1924–1931* (Hong Kong: 1991)

Galbiati, Fernando, *P'eng P'ai and the Hai-lu-feng Soviet* (Stanford: 1985)

Gallagher, J. and R. Robinson, 'The Imperialism of Free Trade', *Economic History Review*, vol.6, no.1 (March 1953)

———, *Africa and the Victorians: The Official Mind of Imperialism* (2nd edition, London and Basingstoke: 1981)

Gillingham, Paul, *At The Peak: Hong Kong Between the Wars* (Hong Kong: 1983)

Gittins, Jean, *Eastern Windows – Western Skies* (Hong Kong: 1969)

———, *Stanley: Behind Barbed Wire* (Hong Kong: 1982)

Godley, Michael R., 'The End of the Queue: Hair as symbol in Chinese history', *East Asian History*, no.8 (1994)

Goncharov, S.N., J.W. Lewis and Litai Xue, *Uncertain Partners: Stalin, Mao, and the Korean War* (Stanford: 1993)

Goodstadt, L.F., 'Urban Housing in Hong Kong, 1945–1963', in I.C. Jarvis (ed.), *Hong Kong: A Society in Transition* (London: 1969)

———, 'Hong Kong: An Attachment to Democracy', *The Round Table*, no.348 (1998)

———, 'Prospect for the Rule of Law: the Political Dimension', in Steve Tsang (ed.), *Judicial Independence and the Rule of Law in Hong Kong* (Basingstoke: 2001)

Goto-Shibata, Harumi, *Japan and Britain in Shanghai, 1925–31* (Basingstoke: 1995)

Graham, G.S., *The China Station: War and Diplomacy, 1830–1860* (Oxford: 1978)

Grantham, Alexander, *Via Ports: From Hong Kong to Hong Kong* (Hong Kong: 1976)

———, 'Hong Kong', *Journal of the Royal Central Asian Society*, vol.46 (April 1959)

Gregory, J.S., *Great Britain and the Taipings* (London: 1969)

Grey, Anthony, *Hostage in Peking* (London: 1970)

Halcombe, C.H.J., *The Mystic Flowery Land* (London: 1896)

Hamashita, Takeshi, 'Foreign Trade Finance in China, 1810–50', in Linda Grove and Christian Daniels (eds), *State and Society in China: Japanese Perspectives on Ming-Qing Social and Economic History* (Tokyo: 1984)

Hambro, Edvard, *The Problems of Chinese Refugees in Hong Kong* (Leyden: 1955)

Hamilton, G.C., *Government Departments in Hong Kong, 1841–1969* (Hong Kong: 1969)

Han, Minzhu (ed.), *Cries for Democracy: Writings and Speeches from the 1989 Chinese Democracy Movement* (Princeton: 1990)

Han, Nianlong (ed.), *Diplomacy of Contemporary China* (Hong Kong: 1990)

Hao, Yen-p'ing, *The Comprador in Nineteenth Century China: Bridge between East and West* (Cambridge, Mass.: 1970)

Harcourt, Sir Cecil H.J., 'The Military Administration of Hong Kong', *Journal of the Royal Central Asian Society*, vol.34 (1947)

Harding, Harry, *Organizing China: The Problem of Bureaucracy, 1949–1976* (Stanford: 1981)

Hayes, James, *The Hong Kong Region, 1850–1911: Institutions and Leadership in Town and Countryside* (Hamden, Connecticut: 1977)

———, *Friends and Teachers: Hong Kong and its People, 1953–87* (Hong Kong: 1996)

Heald, Tim, *Beating Retreat: Hong Kong Under the Last Governor* (London: 1997)

Hoadley, J.S., 'Hong Kong is the Lifeboat: Notes on Political Culture and Socialization', *Journal of Oriental Studies*, vol.8 (1970)

Hobsbawn, E.J., *Industry and Empire* (Harmondsworth: 1969)

Hoe, Susanna, *The Private Life of Old Hong Kong* (Hong Kong: 1991)

——— and Roebuck, Derek, *The Taking of Hong Kong: Charles and Clara Elliot in China Waters* (Richmond: 1999)

Hong Kong Government, *The Government and the People* (Hong Kong: 1962)

Hooton, E.R., *The Greatest Tumult: The Chinese Civil War, 1936–49* (London and Oxford: 1991)

Howard, Michael, 'British Military Preparations for the Second World War', in David Dilks (ed.), *Retreat from Power: Studies in Britain's Foreign Policy of the Twentieth Century, Volume One: 1906–1939* (London and Basingstoke: 1981)

Howe, Geoffrey, *Conflict of Loyalty* (London: 1995)

Hsiao, Kung-chuan, *Rural China, Imperial Control in the Nineteenth Century* (Seattle: 1960)

Hsu, Immanuel C.Y., *China's Entrance into the Family of Nations* (Cambridge: 1960)

_____, *The Rise of Modern China* (4th edition, New York and Oxford: 1990)

Hsu, Long-hsuen and Ming-kai Chang, *History of the Sino-Japanese War (1937–1945)* (Taipei: 1971)

Huang, Philip, *Liang Ch'i-ch'ao and Modern Chinese Liberalism* (Seattle: 1972)

_____, *Civil Justice in China: Representation and Practice in the Qing* (Stanford, 1996)

Huang, Ray, *China: A Macro History* (Armonk, New York: 1988)

Hughes, Richard, *Borrowed Place Borrowed Time: Hong Kong and Its Many Faces* (London: 1968)

Hurd, Douglas, *The Arrow War: An Anglo-Chinese Confusion, 1856–60* (London: 1967)

_____, 'Governor Patten Unveils a Bold Blueprint for Hong Kong's Future', *Hong Kong Monitor*, December 1992

Hussey, W.D., *British History, 1815–1939* (Cambridge: 1971)

Hutcheon, Robin, *First Sea Lord: The Life and Work of Sir Y.K. Pao* (Hong Kong: 1990)

Jenkins, Graham, 'People – Hong Kong's Greatest Asset', in Hong Kong Government, *Hong Kong 1982* (Hong Kong: 1982)

Jennings, Sir Ivor and D.W. Logan, *A Report on the University of Hong Kong* (Hong Kong: 1953)

Jones, F.C., *Japan's New Order in East Asia: Its Rise and Fall* (London: 1954)

Jordan, Donald, *The Northern Expedition: China's National Revolution of 1926–1928* (Honolulu: 1976)

Joseph, Philip, *Foreign Diplomacy in China 1894–1900* (New York: 1971)

Judd, Dennis, *Empire: The British Imperial Experience from 1765 to the Present* (London: 1996)

Kau, Michael Y.M. and John K. Leung (eds), *The Writings of Mao Zedong, 1949–1976, Volume 1: September 1949–December 1955* (Armonk, NY: 1986)

Kelly, Ian, *Hong Kong: A Political-Geographic Analysis* (Houndsmill, Basingstoke: 1987)

Kiernan, V.G., *European Empires from Conquest to Collapse, 1815–1960* (Bungay, Suffolk: 1982)

King, Ambrose, 'Administrative Absorption of Politics in Hong Kong: Emphasis on the Grass Roots Level', *Asian Survey*, vol.15, no.5 (May 1975)

King, Frank H.H., *The Hong Kong Bank in Late Imperial China, 1864–1902: On an Even Keel* (Cambridge: 1987)

_____, *The Hong Kong Bank Between the Wars and the Bank Interned, 1919–1945* (Cambridge: 1988)

_____, *The History of the Hong Kong and Shanghai Banking Corporation Volume 4: The Hong Kong Bank in the Period of Development and Nationalism* (Cambridge: 1991)

Kirby, S. Woodburn, *The War Against Japan*, vols 1 and 5 (London, 1957)

Knight, Alan, 'The Last Great Chapter of Imperial History', in Alan Knight and Yoshiko Nakano (eds), *Reporting Hong Kong: Foreign Media and the Handover* (Richmond: 1999)

Knollys, Henry, *Incidents in the China War of 1860* (Edinburgh and London: 1875)

Kreisberg, Paul H., 'China's Negotiating Behaviour', in T.W. Robinson and D. Shambaugh (eds), *Chinese Foreign Policy: Theory and Practice* (Oxford, 1994)

Kristof, Nicholas and Sheryl WuDunn, *China Wakes: The Struggle for the Soul of a Rising Power* (London, 1994)

Kwan, Daniel, *Marxist Intellectuals and the Chinese Labor Movement* (Seattle: 1997)

Lamb, Richard, *The Macmillan Years, 1957–1963* (London: 1995)

Lardy, Nicholas, China's Unfinished Economic Revolution (Washington DC: 1998)

Lau, Emily, '"Dear Governor": An Elected Lady Offers Some Advice', *Hong Kong Monitor*, September 1992

Lau, Siu-kai, 'Institutions Without Leaders: The Hong Kong Chinese View of Political Leadership', *Pacific Affairs*, vol. 63, no. 2 (1990)

————, 'Colonial Rule, Transfer of Sovereignty and the Problem of Political Leaders in Hong Kong', *Journal of Commonwealth and Comparative Politics*, vol.30, no.2 (July 1992)

Lau, Siu-kai and Kuan, Hsin-chi, *The Ethos of the Hong Kong Chinese* (Hong Kong: 1988)

Lee, Bradford, *Britain and the Sino-Japanese War, 1937–1939* (Stanford: 1973)

Lee, Lai To, *The Reunification of China: PRC–Taiwan Relations in Flux* (New York, 1991)

Lee, Ming-kuan, 'Community and Identity in Transition in Hong Kong', in Reginald Kwok and Alvin So (eds), *The Hong Kong-Guangdong Link: Partnership in Flux* (Hong Kong: 1995)

Leeming, Frank, 'The earlier industrialisation of Hong Kong', *Modern Asia* (1975), vol.9, no.3

Lethbridge, H.J., 'Hong Kong Cadets, 1862–1941', *Journal of the Hong Kong Branch of the Royal Asiatic Society*, vol.10, 1970

————, *Hard Craft in Hong Kong* (Hong Kong: 1978)

————, *Hong Kong: Stability and Change* (Hong Kong: 1978)

Leung, C.K., 'Spatial Redevelopment and the Special Economic Zones in China: An Overview', in Y.C. Jao and C.K. Leung (eds), *China's Special Economic Zones: Policies, Problems and Prospects* (Hong Kong: 1986)

Leung, Joan, 'Summary Findings and Implications', in Rowena Kwok, Joan Leung and Ian Scott (eds), *Votes Without Power: The Hong Kong Legislative Council Elections, 1991* (Hong Kong: 1992)

Leung, K.K., 'The Basic Law and the Problem of Political Transition', in Stephen Cheung and Stephen Sze (eds), *The Other Hong Kong Report, 1995* (Hong Kong: 1995)

Leung, Sai-wing, 'The "China Factor" in the 1991 Legislative Council Election', in Siu-kai Lau and Kin-sheun Louie (eds), *Hong Kong Tried Democracy: The 1991 Elections in Hong Kong* (Hong Kong: 1993)

Levenson, Joseph, *Liang Ch'i-ch'ao and the Mind of Modern China* (London: 1953)

Liew, K.S., *Struggle for Democracy: Sung Chiao-jen and the 1911 Chinese Revolution* (Berkeley: 1971)

Lindsay, Oliver, *The Lasting Honour: The Fall of Hong Kong 1941* (London: 1978)

Liu, Shuyong, *An Outline History of Hong Kong* (Beijing: 1997)

Lo, Shiu-hing, *The Politics of Democratization in Hong Kong* (Basingstoke: 1997)

Lo, T. Wing, *Corruption and Politics in Hong Kong and China* (Buckingham: 1993)

Loewe, Michael, *The Pride That Is China* (London: 1990)

Louis, Wm. Roger, 'Hong Kong: The Critical Phase, 1945–1949', *The American Historical Review*, vol.102, no.4 (October 1997)

Lowe, Peter, *Great Britain and the Origins of the Pacific War: A Study of British Policy in East Asia, 1937–1941* (Oxford: 1977)

MacLehose, Lord, 'Social and Economic Challenges', in Sally Blyth and Ian Wotherspoon (eds), *Hong Kong Remembers* (Hong Kong: 1996)

Madden, Frederick and John Darwin (eds), *The Dependent Empire, 1900–1948* (Westport, Connecticut: 1994)

Major, John, *John Major: The Autobiography* (London: 2000)

Manion, Melanie, 'Introduction: Reluctant Duelists: The Logic of the 1989 Protests and Massacre', in Michael Oksenberg, Lawrence Sullivan and Marc Lambert (eds), *Beijing Spring, 1989: Confrontation and Conflict The Basic Documents* (New York: 1990)

Mann, Michael, *China 1860* (Salisbury: 1989)

Mao, Philip, *The People's Republic of China in the Preparation for the Take-over of Hong Kong: A Study of the Process of Implementing the Policy of 'One Country, Two Systems'* (University of Hull: unpublished Ph.D. thesis, 2000)

Martin, Edwin W., *Divided Counsel: The Anglo-American Response to Communist Victory in China* (Lexington, Kentucky: 1986)

McCord, Edward, *The Power of the Gun: The Emergence of Modern Chinese Warlordism* (Berkeley: 1993)

McKinsey and Company, *Strengthening the Machinery of Government Volume 1 – Report* (Hong Kong: 1972)

McLaren, Robin, *Britain's Record in Hong Kong* (London: 1997)

Michael, Franz, 'China and the Crisis of Communism', in George Hicks (ed.), *The Broken Mirror: China after Tiananmen* (Harlow: 1990)

Mills, L.A., *British Rule in Eastern Asia: Development in British Malaya and Hong Kong* (London: 1942)

Miners, Norman, *Hong Kong Under Imperial Rule, 1912–1941* (Hong Kong:1987)

———, *The Government and Politics of Hong Kong* (Hong Kong:1991)

———, 'Industrial Development in the Colonial Empire and the Imperial Economic Conference at Ottawa 1932', *The Journal of Imperial and Commonwealth History*, vol.30, no.2 (May 2002)

———, 'The Attempts to Abolish the *Mui Tsai* System in Hong Kong 1917–1941', in E. Sinn (ed.), *Between East and West* (Hong Kong: 1990)

Morris, James, *Farewell the Trumpets: An Imperial Retreat* (Harmondsworth: 1979)

Mosher, Stephen, *China Misperceived: American Illusions and Chinese Reality* (New York: 1990)

Morse, H.B., *The International Relations of the Chinese Empire* (Shanghai: 1910)

Munn, Christopher Charles, *Anglo-China: Chinese People and British Rule in Hong Kong, 1841–1870* (University of Toronto: unpublished PhD thesis, 1998)

———, 'The rule of law and criminal justice in the nineteenth century', in Steve Tsang (ed.), *Judicial Independence and the Rule of Law in Hong Kong* (Basingstoke: 2001)

———, 'The Hong Kong Opium Revenue, 1845–1885', in Timothy Brook and Bob Tadashi Wakabayashi (eds), *Opium Regimes: China, Britain, and Japan, 1839–1952* (Berkeley: 2000)

———, 'Colonialism "in a Chinese atmosphere": The Caldwell affair and the perils of collaboration in early colonial Hong Kong', in Robert Bickers and Christian Henriot (eds), *New Frontiers: Imperialism's new communities in East Asia, 1842–1953* (Manchester: 2000)

Murfett, Malcolm H., *Hostage on the Yangtze: Britain, China, and the Amethyst Crisis of 1949* (Annapolis, Maryland: 1991)

Myer, David R., *Hong Kong as a Global Metropolis* (Cambridge: 2000)

Myers, Ramon (ed.), *Two Societies in Opposition: The Republic of China and the People's Republic of China* (Stanford: 1991)

Nathan, Andrew, 'Political Rights in Chinese Constitutions', in Randle Edwards, Louis Henkin and Andrew Nathan (eds), *Human Rights in Contemporary China* (New York: 1986)

———, 'The Documents and Their Significance', in Nathan, Andrew and Perry Link (eds), *The Tiananmen Papers* (London: 2001)

Ng, Peter Y.L., *New Peace County: A Chinese Gazetteer of the Hong Kong Region* (Hong Kong: 1983)

Ngo, Tak-wing, 'Industrial History and the Artifice of *Laissez-faire* Colonialism', in T.W. Ngo (ed.), *Hong Kong's History* (London: 1999)

——— 'Colonialism in Hong Kong revisited', in T.W. Ngo (ed.), *Hong Kong's History* (London: 1999)

Norman, Henry, *The People and Politics of the Far East* (London: 1907)

Norton-Kyshe, J.W., *The History of the Laws and Courts of Hong Kong*, vol.1 (London: 1898)

Ooh, Che Chang, *Wartime Currency Stabilisation in China 1937–1941: Economic Expediency and Political Reality* (Oxford University: unpublished D.Phil. thesis, 1999)

Ouchterlony, John, *The Chinese War: An Account of All the Operations of the British Forces From the Commencement to the Treaty of Nanking* (New York: 1970)

Owen, Nicholas, 'Economic Policy in Hong Kong', in Keith Hopkins (ed.), *Hong Kong: The Industrial Colony* (Hong Kong: 1971)

Patten, Christopher, *Our Next Five Years: The Agenda for Hong Kong* (Hong Kong: 1992)
_____, *Hong Kong: Today's Success, Tomorrow's Challenges* (Hong Kong: 1993)
_____, *East and West* (London and Basingstoke: 1998)
Pepper, Suzanne, *Civil War in China: The Political Struggle, 1945–1949* (Berkeley: 1978)
Peyrefitte, Alain, *The Collision of Two Civilisations: The British Expedition to China in 1792–4* (London: 1993)
Phelps Brown, E.H., 'The Hong Kong Economy: Achievements and Prospects', in Keith Hopkins (ed.), *Hong Kong: The Industrial Colony* (Hong Kong: 1971)
Podmore, David, 'Localization in the Hong Kong Government Service, 1948–1968', *Journal of Commonwealth Political Studies*, vol.9 (1971)
Polachek, James, *The Inner Opium War* (Harvard: 1992)
Qian, Yujun, *"One Country, Two Systems" – The Structure and Process of China's Policy Making Towards Hong Kong (1979–1990)* (Oxford University: unpublished D.Phil. thesis, 1997)
Quested, R.K.I., *The Expansion of Russia in East Asia, 1857–1860* (Kuala Lumpur: 1968)
Rabushka, Alvin, *The Changing Face of Hong Kong* (Stanford: 1973)
_____, *Hong Kong: A Study in Economic Freedom* (Chicago: 1979)
Rafferty, Kevin, *City on the Rocks: Hong Kong's Uncertain Future* (London: 1989)
Reynolds, D., *The Creation of the Anglo-American Alliance, 1937–41* (London: 1981)
Rhodes, Edward, *China's Republican Revolution: The Case of Kwangtung, 1895–1913* (Cambridge, Massachusetts: 1975)
Richardson, S.S., *The Royal Marines and Hong Kong, 1840–1997* (Portsmouth: 1997)
Ride, Edwin, *BAAG: Hong Kong Resistance, 1942–1945* (Hong Kong: 1981)
Rigby, Richard, *The May 30 Movement: Events and Themes* (Canberra: 1980)
Roberti, Mark, *The Fall of Hong Kong: Britain's Betrayal and China's Triumph* (New York and London: 1994)
Rosenberg, William and Marilyn Young *Transforming Russia and China* (New York: 1982)
Ruan, Ming, *Deng Xiaoping: Chronicle of an Empire* (Boulder, 1994)
Sayer, G.R., *Hong Kong, 1862–1919* (Hong Kong: 1975)
_____, *Hong Kong, 1841–1862: Birth, Adolescence and Coming of Age* (Hong Kong: 1980)
Schenk, Catherine, *Hong Kong as an International Financial Centre* (London: 2001)
Schiffrin, H.Z., *Sun Yat-sen and the Origins of the Chinese Revolution* (Berkeley: 1970)
Schram, Stuart, *The Political Thought of Mao Tse-tung* (New York: 1969)
Schrecker, John E., *Imperialism and Chinese Nationalism: Germany in Shantung* (Cambridge, Massachusetts: 1971)
Schurmann, Franz and Orville Schell (eds), *Imperial China* (Harmondsworth: 1967)
Scott, Ian, *Political Change and the Crisis of Legitimacy in Hong Kong* (Hong Kong: 1989)
_____, 'An Overview of the Hong Kong Legislative Council Elections of 1991', in Rowena Kwok, Joan Leung and Ian Scott (eds), *Votes Without Power: The Hong Kong Legislative Council Elections, 1991* (Hong Kong: 1992)
_____, 'Political Transformation in Hong Kong: From Colony to Colony', in R.Y.W. Kwok and A.Y. So (eds), *The Hong Kong-Guangdong Link: Partnership in Flux* (New York: 1995)
Shai, Aron, *Origins of the War in the East: Britain, China and Japan, 1937–39* (London: 1976)
Shawcross, William, *Kowtow!* (London: 1989)
Sheridan, James, *China in Disintegration: The Republican Era in Chinese History, 1912–1949* (New York: 1975)
Sinn, Elizabeth, *Power and Charity: The Early History of the Tung Wah Hospital, Hong Kong* (Hong Kong: 1989)
_____, *Growing with Hong Kong: The Bank of East Asia, 1919–1994* (Hong Kong: 1994)
Siu, Helen, 'Remade in Hong Kong: Weaving Into the Chinese Cultural Tapestry', in Taotao Liu and David Faure (eds), *Unity and Diversity: Local Cultures and Identities in China* (Hong Kong: 1996)

Smith, Carl, *Chinese Christians: Elite, Middlemen, and the Church in Hong Kong* (Hong Kong: 1885)

Smith, Richard J., *China's Cultural Heritage: The Ch'ing Dynasty, 1644–1912* (Boulder, Colorado: 1983)

So, Alvin Y., *Hong Kong's Embattled Democracy* (Baltimore: 1999)

Spear, Percival, *A History of India*, vol.2 (Harmondsworth: 1970)

Spence, Jonathan, *The Search for Modern China* (London: 1990)

_____, *God's Chinese Son: The Taiping Heavenly Kingdom of Hong Xiuquan* (London: 1996)

Stokesbury, James, *Navy and Empire* (New York: 1983)

Summerskill, Michael, *China on the Western Front* (London: 1982)

Sun, Youli, *China and the Origins of the Pacific War, 1931–1941* (Basingstoke: 1993)

Sung, Yun-wing, *The China–Hong Kong Connection: The Key to China's Open Door Policy* (Cambridge: 1991)

Swaine, Michael D., 'Chinese Decision-Making Regarding Taiwan, 1979–2000', in David Lampton (ed.), *The Making of Chinese Foreign and Security Policy in the Era of Reform* (Stanford: 2001)

Swanson, Bruce, *Eight Voyage of the Dragon: A History of China's Quest for Seapower* (Annapolis: 1982)

Sweeting, Anthony, *A Phoenix Transformed: The Reconstruction of Education in Post-War Hong Kong* (Hong Kong: 1993)

Szczepanik, E.F., 'Problems of Macro-economic Programming in Hong Kong', in I.C. Jarvis (ed.), *Hong Kong: A Society in Transition* (London: 1969)

Tang, James and Frank Ching , 'The MacLehose-Youde Years: Balancing the "Three-Legged Stool", 1971–86', in M.K. Chan (ed.), *Precarious Balance: Hong Kong Between China and Britain, 1842–1922* (New York: 1994)

Teiwes, Frederick and Warren Sun , *The Tragedy of Lin Biao* (London: 1996)

Teng, Ssu-yu and J.K. Fairbank (eds), *China's Response to the West: A Documentary Survey, 1839–1923* (New York: 1969)

Thatcher, Margaret, *The Downing Street Years* (London: 1993)

Thorne, Christopher, *Allies of a Kind: The United States, Britain and the War against Japan, 1941–1945* (Oxford: 1978)

_____, *The Issue of War* (London: 1985)

Tidrick, Kathryn, *Empire and the English Character* (London: 1990)

Ting, Joseph S.P., 'Native Chinese Peace Officers in British Hong Kong, 1841–1861', in Elizabeth Sinn (ed.), *Between East and West* (Hong Kong: 1990)

Tong, Te-kong, *United States Diplomacy in China, 1844–60* (Seattle: 1964)

Truman, Harry S, *Memoirs of Harry S Truman Volume II: Years of Trial and Hope* (New York: 1956)

Trocki, Carl A., *Opium, Empire and the Global Political Economy: A Study of the Asian Opium Trade, 1750–1950* (London and New York: 1999)

Tsai, Jung-fang, *Hong Kong in Chinese History* (New York: 1993)

_____, 'From Anti-Foreignism to Popular Nationalism: Hong Kong between China and Britain, 1839–1911', in Ming K. Chan (ed.), *Precarious Balance: Hong Kong between China and Britain, 1842–1992* (Armonk: 1994)

Tsang, Steve, *Democracy Shelved: Great Britain, China, and Attempts at Constitutional Reform in Hong Kong, 1945–1952* (Hong Kong: 1988)

_____, 'China and Political Reform in Hong Kong', *The Pacific Review*, vol.2, no.1 (1989)

_____, 'Identity Crisis in Hong Kong', *Hong Kong Monitor*, September 1990

_____, 'Political Probems Facing the Hong Kong Civil Service in Transition', *Hong Kong Public Administration*, vol.3, no.1 (March 1994)

_____ (ed.), *A Documentary History of Hong Kong I: Government and Politics* (Hong Kong: 1995)

_____, 'Maximum Flexibility, Rigid Framework: China's Policy Towards Hong Kong and Its Implications', *Journal of International Affairs*, vol. 49, no. 2, Winter 1996

———, *Hong Kong: An Appointment with China* (London: 1997)

———, 'The Confucian Tradition and Democratization', in Yossi Shain and Aharon Kieman (eds), *Democracy: The Challenges Ahead* (Basingstoke: 1997)

———, 'Government and Politics in Hong Kong: A Colonial Paradox', in Rosemary Foot and Judith Brown (eds), *Hong Kong's Transition, 1842–1997* (Basingstoke: 1997)

———, 'Realignment of Power: The Politics of Transition and Reform in Hong Kong', in P.K. Li (ed.), *Political Order and Power Transition in Hong Kong* (Hong Kong: 1997)

———, 'Strategy for Survival: The Cold War and Hong Kong's Policy towards Kuomintang and Chinese Communist Activities in the 1950s', *The Journal of Imperial and Commonwealth History*, vol.25, no.2 (May 1997)

———, 'Changes in Continuity: Government and Politics in the Hong Kong Special Administrative Region', *American Asian Review*, vol.15, no.4 (Winter, 1997)

———, 'Political Developments in Hong Kong since 1997 and their Implications for Mainland China and Taiwan', *American Asian Review*, vol.18, no.1 (Spring, 2000)

——— (ed.), *Judicial Independence and the Rule of Law in Hong Kong* (Basingstoke: 2001)

Tsou, Tang, *The Cultural Revolution and Post Mao Reforms* (Chicago and London: 1988)

Tsui, David, *Chinese Military Intervention in the Korean War* (Oxford University: unpublished D.Phil. thesis, 1999)

Tucker, Nancy B., *Taiwan, Hong Kong and the United States, 1945–1992: Uncertain Friendships* (New York: 1994)

Turner, H.A., Patricia Fosh and Sek Hong Ng, *Between Two Societies: Hong Kong Labour in Transition* (Hong Kong: 1991)

United States Government, *Foreign Relations of the United States (FRUS) 1945 Vol.VII: The Far East: China* (Washington: 1969)

Van Slyke, Lyman P., *Enemies and Friends: The United Front in Chinese Communist History* (Stanford: 1967)

Vogel, E.F., *One Step Ahead in China: Guangdong Under Reform* (Cambridge: 1989)

Wakeman Jr., Frederic, *Strangers at the Gate: Social Disorder in South China 1839–1861* (Berkeley: 1974)

Walden, John, *Excellence, Your Gap is Growing* (Hong Kong: 1987)

Waley, Arthur, *The Opium War Through Chinese Eyes* (Stanford: 1968)

Wang, Erh-min, 'Changing Chinese Views of Western Relations, 1840–95', in Fairbank, John K. and Kwang-ching Liu (eds), *The Cambridge History of China, Volume II: Late Ch'ing, 1800–1911, Part 2* (Cambridge: 1980)

Wei, Betty Peh-t'i, *Shanghai: Crucible of Modern China* (Hong Kong: 1987)

Welsh, Frank, *A History of Hong Kong* (London: 1993)

Wesley-Smith, Peter, *Unequal Treaty, 1897–1997: China, Great Britain and Hong Kong's New Territories* (Hong Kong: 1983)

———, 'Anti-Chinese Legislation in Hong Kong', in Ming K. Chan (ed.), *Precarious Balance* (Hong Kong: 1994)

———, 'Individual and Institutional Independence of the Judiciary', in Steve Tsang (ed.), *Judicial Independence and the Rule of Law in Hong Kong* (Basingstoke: 2001)

White, Lynn T., *Policies of Chaos: The Organizational Causes of Violence in China's Cultural Revolution* (Princeton: 1989)

Whiting, Allen, *Soviet Policies in China 1917–1924* (Stanford: 1953)

Wilbur, Martin, *Sun Yat-sen: Frustrated Patriot* (New York: 1976)

Willmott, H.P., *Empires in the Balance: Japanese and Allied Pacific Strategies to April 1942* (London: 1982)

Wilson, Brian, *Hong Kong Then* (Durham: 2000)

Wilson, David Clive, *Britain and the Kuomintang, 1924–28: A study of the interaction of official policies and perceptions in Britain and China* (London: unpublished School of Oriental and African Studies Ph.D. thesis, 1973)

Wilson Dick, *When Tigers Fight: The Story of the Sino-Japanese War, 1937–1945* (New York: 1982)

_____, *Hong Kong! Hong Kong!* (London: 1990)

Wong, A.K., *The Kaifong Associations and the Society of Hong Kong* (Taipei: 1972)

Wong, Jan, *Red China Blues* (Toronto: 1997)

Wong, J.Y., *Yeh Ming-ch'en* (Cambridge: 1976),

_____, *The Origins of an Heroic Image: Sun Yatsen in London, 1896–1897* (Hong Kong: 1986)

_____, *Deadly Dreams: Opium and the Arrow War (1856–1860) in China* (Cambridge: 1998)

Wong, Owen H.H., *The First Chinese Minister to Great Britain* (Hong Kong: 1987)

Wong, Siu-lun, *Emigrant Entrepreneurs: Shanghai Industrialists in Hong Kong* (Hong Kong: 1988)

_____, 'The Migration of Shanghaiese Entrepreneurs to Hong Kong', in David Faure, James Hayes and Alan Birch (eds), *From Village to City: Studies in the Traditional Roots of Hong Kong Society* (Hong Kong: 1984)

Wu, Hsin-hsing, *Bridging the Strait: Taiwan, China, and the Prospect for Reunification* (Hong Kong: 1994)

Xiang Lanxin, *Recasting the Imperial Far East: Britain and America in China, 1945–1950* (New York: 1995)

Yahuda, Michael, *Hong Kong: China's Challenge* (London and New York: 1996)

Yao, Y.C., 'Banking and Currency in the Special Economic Zones: Problems and Prospects', in Y.C. Yao and C.K. Leung (eds), *China's Special Economic Zones* (Hong Kong, 1986)

Yen, Ching Hwang, *The Overseas Chinese and the 1911 Revolution* (Kuala Lumpur: 1976)

Youde, Edward, *The Chairman's Lecture: The Political and Commercial Prospects for Hong Kong* (London: 1985)

Young, Ernest, *The Presidency of Yuan Shih-kai: Liberalism and Dictatorship in Early Republican China* (Ann Arbor: 1977)

Young, Hugo, *One of Us* (London: 1990)

Young, J.D., 'The Building Years: Maintaining a China-Hong Kong-Britain Equilibrium, 1950–1971', in M.K. Chan (ed.), *Precarious Balance* (Armonk: 1994)

Young, L.K., *British Policy in China, 1895–1902* (Oxford: 1970)

Youngson, A.J., *Hong Kong Economic Growth and Policy* (Hong Kong: 1982)

Yu, A.F.L., *Entrepreneurship and Economic Development in Hong Kong* (London and New York: 1997)

Yu, Brian, *The Arches of the Years* (Toronto: 1999)

Yu, Teh-pei, 'Economic Links among Hong Kong, PRC, and ROC: With Special Reference to Trade', in Jurgen Domes and Yu-ming Shaw (eds), *Hong Kong: A Chinese and International Concern* (Boulder and London: 1988)

Zhai, Qiang, *The Dragon, the Lion, and the Eagle: Chinese-British-American Relations, 1949–1958* (Kent, Ohio: 1994)

Zhang, Yongjin, *China in the International System, 1918–20: The Middle Kingdom at the Periphery* (Basingstoke: 1991)

Zhao, Quansheng, *Interpreting Chinese Foreign Policy* (Hong Kong: 1996)

Index

Qi Ying, 12, 15
Qian Qichen, 264–5, 270
Qiao Guanhua, 153
Qiao Shi, 270
Qing dynasty, 4, 54, 77, 80, 84
Queen's Chinese, 45–7
Qianlong Emperor, 5

Racial prejudice (see also anti-Chinese legislation), 28, 47–55, 62, 65–6, 71–2, 128, 142, 146, 182, 194, 198, 200, 214
Red Guards, 184–5
Religion, 23, 62, 65
Refugees (see also Chinese immigrants), 180, 204, 207
Registrar General, 24–5, 52, 68–72
Republic of China, 76, 84–5, 157, 216
Resettlement Department (see also housing), 199
Revolution of 1911, 77
Riots (see also the Confrontation), 186, 188–9, 200, 275
Ride, Lindsay, 128–30
Rifkind, Malcolm, 267
Ripon (Lord), 27
Right of abode, 249, 252, 273, 275
Robinson, Sir Hercules, 25
Robinson, Sir William, 36, 81
Roosevelt, President Franklin D., 124, 136
Royal Instructions, 18–9
Royal Air Force, 139
Royal Marines, 16, 22, 139
Royal Navy, 6, 8, 10–11, 16, 21–2, 52, 57, 61, 99, 120, 122–4, 133–5, 138, 141
Rule of law, 8, 45, 52–5, 182, 195, 200, 274–5
Russell (Lord), 35

San Po Kong, 183, 185
Sanyuanli, myth of, 31
Sai Kung, 129
Seamen's strike (1922) 88–90
Second Anglo-Chinese War (1856–60), 20, 22, 29–36, 48, 53, 59, 74, 90
Second World War, 24, 26, 57, 119–20
Secretariat for Development, 146–7
Secretary for Chinese Affairs, 24, 105, 111, 127, 143, 190–1, 199
Secretary for Chinese and External Affairs, 143
Secretary for Home Affairs, 24, 191
Senggelinqin (General), 34
Seymour, Sir Horace, 136–7
Sha Tau Kok, 129, 187
Shang Bao, 75
Shamian Incident (1925), 94–5, 100

Shanghai, 57, 75, 92–4, 96, 101, 114, 152, 163, 167, 272–3
Shatin, 89
Shek Kip Mei fire (1953), 204
Shenzhen, 38, 177
Shing Mun Redoubt, 122
Shipping, 61, 95, 169
Shum Shui Po Camp, 128
Silk, 5
Silver, 6, 9, 108–9
Singapore, 122, 124
Sino-British Agreement (Joint Declaration of 1984), 177, 225–32, 235, 237, 246, 248, 250, 260–1, 263, 267
Sino-French War (1884–5), 90–1
Sino-Japanese War (1894–5), 77, 90
So Sau-chung, 188
Soviet Union, 85, 133, 152, 260
Special administrative region, 216, 221, 226, 233–4, 237–8, 242–4, 249–51, 253, 265–8, 270–8
Special economic zone, 176–7
Special Operations Executive (SOE), 129, 132
St Stephen's College massacre (1941), 127
Stalin, Joseph, 99
Standard Chartered Bank (See Chartered Bank of India, Australia and China)
Stanley (Lord), 20
Stanley Internment Camp, 128, 140
Star Ferry, 188–9
State Council, 183, 216
Stock market, 175–6, 220
Stubbs, Sir Reginald, 88–9, 95–7, 100, 112
Su Zhaozheng, 90, 92, 95
Sun Hung Kai group, 173
Sun Yat-sen, 74–6, 78–9, 81, 84–5, 88, 90, 98, 103, 237
Supreme Court, 50, 53–4
Survey Office, 234–5
Swire, 61, 162, 173
Szeto Wah, 243, 251–2, 255

Ta Kung Pao, 185, 239
Taipei, 196, 216
Taiping (rebellion/uprising), 22, 54, 58, 73, 269
Taipingshan, 65
Taipo, 129
Taiwan, 157, 182, 192, 197, 216–7, 221
Tea, 5–7
Tebbit, Norman, 249
Textile, 163–4
Thatcher, Margaret, 217–221, 226, 230, 249–50, 254, 274
Three Principles of the People, 76
Through train, 233, 259, 263, 266